Ricky Ponting's Underpants

Ricky Ponting's Underpants

Paul Lazenby

Copyright © 2010 Paul Lazenby

The moral right of the author has been asserted.

Apart from any fair dealing for the purposes of research or private study, or criticism or review, as permitted under the Copyright, Designs and Patents Act 1988, this publication may only be reproduced, stored or transmitted, in any form or by any means, with the prior permission in writing of the publishers, or in the case of reprographic reproduction in accordance with the terms of licences issued by the Copyright Licensing Agency. Enquiries concerning reproduction outside those terms should be sent to the publishers.

Matador
5 Weir Road
Kibworth Beauchamp
Leicester LE8 0LQ, UK
Tel: (+44) 116 279 2299
Fax: (+44) 116 279 2277
Email: books@troubador.co.uk
Web: www.troubador.co.uk/matador

ISBN 978 1848764 156

British Library Cataloguing in Publication Data.
A catalogue record for this book is available from the British Library.

Typeset in 11pt Bembo by Troubador Publishing Ltd, Leicester, UK

Matador is an imprint of Troubador Publishing Ltd

Printed in Great Britain by the MPG Books Group, Bodmin and King's Lynn

My dad, my mum, my girls.

ACKNOWLEDGEMENTS

Jeremy Malies, without whose tireless hard work, patience and always constructive criticism I would have been lost; this is as much your work as mine and I cannot thank you enough. Brian Halford, for reading the very first ramblings and being so generous and encouraging. Mark Jarvis, for fixing my computer, helping me get this published and for being my mate through it all. James Whittingham and Ed Hodson, for reading and editing when they had better things to do. Dave Gallagher, for the photos and for redefining pre-match preparation. All my friends at Stoneleigh Cricket Club for saving my sanity when I needed you to. Ruth Hayton, for giving me the push (the one that I needed).

PREFACE

In 1993, the literally one-time England captain, Chris Cowdrey, wrote an article in *The News of the World* in which he blamed the national cricket team's lack of success on the number of 'non-Englishmen' in the team. Cowdrey didn't define whom he meant by this. If he was talking about men born outside of this country he was including his own father. He wasn't the first, or last, man involved in English cricket to throw out a populist theory without thinking it through properly. Whoever he meant, he couldn't have been more wrong.

For a start, Cowdrey's reasoning was that such 'foreigners' lacked commitment, but two of those he focussed on were Robin Smith and Allan Lamb. At the point at which the article was written, Smith's Test average was 49.23 and he later played the bravest innings I've ever seen against Ambrose, Walsh and Bishop on the infamous Edgbaston terror track in 1995. As for Lamb, he is the joint record holder among English batsmen – ironically with Colin Cowdrey – for most Test centuries scored against the West Indies. However, Cowdrey junior's assessment is more fundamentally wide of the mark.

The problem with the England cricket team for most of the period from 1975 to 2005 wasn't that it included too many foreigners, but rather it was too English. Or, more precisely, the side's chances of success were adversely affected by the mentality and attitudes of a particular type of Englishman: the sort that thought that too much facial hair might explain an inability to play spin.

The England cricket team winning means a lot to me, which is why I want so badly to understand why it didn't for so long. How was I to know that it would take 30 years to work out that the answer lay in the Aussie captain's underpants?

ONE

'Body-line was not an incident, it was not an accident, it was not a temporary aberration. It was the violence and ferocity of our age expressing itself in cricket.'
C.L.R. James,
Beyond a Boundary

England weren't playing a Test match when I was born. I don't know if it was raining but the light might have been a bit dodgy at 4 am. Dickie Bird would probably have delayed my delivery until at least 11 o'clock. A week before 13th July 1964, England had been stuffed by an Australian side on their way to retaining the Ashes. A superstitious man might read all sorts into that. Most cricketers are superstitious and I'm no exception. In the game that finished at Headingley so shortly before my arrival, Australia had struggled to within 81 of England's first-innings total with only three wickets left. Then the home captain, Ted Dexter, took the second new ball. This disappeared for plenty and Australia ended up with a large lead that they converted into an easy win. Sound familiar?

Between my birth and the seminal date, in my life at least, of 1st August 1975, a lot happened: Martin Luther King and Bobby Kennedy were both assassinated; Concorde made its maiden flight; Neil Armstrong set foot on the moon; Jimi Hendrix died; France was 'widowed' by the death of de Gaulle and Lulu married one of the Bee Gees. It seems strange to me that I was alive when all these things happened, because I don't remember any of them.

My memories of that time are different: the black and red shirts Manchester City wore in the 1969 FA Cup final; two years later Charlie George, in yellow, smacking the ball past Ray Clemence and then lying down waiting for a mass cuddle; Tony Jacklin winning the US Open;

Peter Bonetti, in the phraseology of one famous Australian, dropping the 1970 World Cup and Red Rum winning his first Grand National. That last one sticks in the mind because my dad had a packet riding on Crisp, the poor, knackered individual who led all the way round until 'Rummy' smoothed past him at The Elbow. I would have had a lot less sympathy for him if I had realised he was Australian.

I lived in a household where sport was important. When my mum innocently recounted to the teenage me that she had been so overcome by tension during the 1966 World Cup final she had taken me to go and sit in the garage, I couldn't believe what I was hearing. 'What did you do that for, Mum? Why didn't you leave me with Dad? At least then I could say I saw England win the World Cup, even if I don't remember it!'

Football was the game that first caught my eye, but my reaction to that Charlie George goal gives a clue as to why I've never been a proper fan. After the 1971 FA Cup Final, I became a sort of 'demi-Gooner', supporting Arsenal in the same way as people all over the country pledge allegiance to Manchester United without ever considering attending a match.

Being young and innocent when I started watching football, I believed Brian Moore when he said the whole country would be willing Tommy Docherty's men to win some European match or other. I was unaware vast swathes of the population were actually thinking an 8-0 thrashing would be too good for them. Maybe it's because the first live game I attended was a 0-0 draw between Brighton and York City, but I never developed the same tribal feelings that consume so many of my contemporaries. There was always something missing and so I've only ever been friends with football.

What was missing, of course, was passion. This was a gap that politics couldn't yet fill. At the age of 11, my knowledge in this field extended no further than Mike Yarwood's impersonations of Heath, Wilson and Healey. As for girls, they were from another planet. I lived blissfully free of the head-over-heels foolishness of the hopelessly in love.

Then my father went and spoiled it all by saying something stupid like, 'Do you want to come to the cricket with me?'

My dad took me to the Lord's Test of 1975, part of the four-Test series that followed the inaugural World Cup. In those days a four-match rubber was not seen as a proper contest and so the Ashes were not at stake. Until recently, a short series was the only certain way of ensuring that whoever was captaining England at the time didn't 'do a Gower'. David Gower is the only England captain to have lost two series 5-0.

It's hard to know exactly why that day had the effect on me it did. Certainly Lord's on a glorious August morning is a very different proposition to the Goldstone Ground on a mucky November afternoon and, unlike the Seagulls' contest with York, when he spent most of his time talking to his mate, I had, for about the only time I can remember, my father's full attention. Whatever the reason, cricket turned my head.

It's extraordinary to me now that I lived eleven years of my life almost completely oblivious to cricket. Before this match, if you had said 'Ray Illingworth' to me I would have looked at you as if you were speaking French. By a series of pestering questions in the lead-up to the match I had established that the Australians had two very fast bowlers who had done quite a bit of damage to our batsmen in the winter and England were already 1-0 down in this series. Coming from Sussex, I also knew England had a new captain in Tony Greig. At the time, I didn't know he had got the job because Mike Denness had decided to bowl first at Edgbaston two weeks earlier. My father informed me that Australia were England's oldest enemies and 'Greigy' would sort things out. Even then, 'Greigy' didn't seem the most imaginative of nicknames, but I learned that if all else failed, cricketers searching for a nickname in the 1970s and 1980s were more than willing to make liberal use of the letter 'y'. Modern cricketers seem to prefer 'o', as in 'bowling Deano!' I am reasonably confident that, in addition to their captain, the 1975 England team contained a Woody, a Steeley, a Goochy, a Knotty and a Snowy. Even Derek Underwood's nickname was Deadly.

To begin with, it appeared Greigy had sorted it out. On the first day, England had, from 49-4, mustered a half decent 315, mainly on the back of the captain's own 96. Now, on the second, we were going to watch England in the field, something that to this day, and despite some of the canings I've witnessed, I prefer to watching them bat. At least when England bowl it's possible to relax slightly. The worst that can happen each ball is the opposition's score advancing by a number most likely in single figures. When they've batted, it's been like watching Ambrose bowl at Hick all day: tense with minimal hope of a favourable outcome.

At Lord's, my first day of live Test cricket began about as well as it possibly could. Australia subsided to 81-7, with only Ross Edwards of the batsmen left and my dad assuring me that none of Thomson, Lillee or Mallett could bat.

Unfortunately, my dad was more of a football man and all four remaining Aussies set about spoiling things.

I have two vivid memories of the cricket that day. The first is of being as gleeful as any 11-year-old could be at the misfortune of another when Edwards was dismissed one short of what, more than 30 years on, I am just willing to admit was a well-deserved hundred. The second is of Greigy insisting, in the face of mounting evidence, that he was the bowler to sort out Lillee. The Australian on the other hand was convinced that lamping Greig into the Tavern at frequent intervals indicated he was the one doing the sorting. I was so absorbed by what I was watching that I felt like I hated Lillee. Even the Polish goalkeeping 'clown' Tomaszewski hadn't inspired emotions like these. I was hooked.

Even though an Aussie fast bowler had taken the edge off my day, it was still love: the dangerous sort that can skew your perspectives. It took me nearly 20 years to realise how badly I had it.

At university I had an acquaintance called Nick. One summer day, just before our finals, I bumped into him: 'How are you mate?' 'Ooh not so good, England are 63-5'. Although this was at a time when Derek Pringle was batting at number seven for England and so 63-5 was even worse than it sounded, the devastation of England's middle order by Kapil Dev, Madan Lal and Roger Binny hardly compared to what Mrs Thatcher was doing to the miners. Yet here was a man, in the lead-up to potentially the most important exams of his life, measuring his mood by the fortunes of the England cricket team. In a moment of horrific self-awareness I realised I knew exactly what he meant.

On one level I know love for a sport is trivial and ridiculous, but I'm certainly not alone and am not, nor will I ever be, as obsessed as many others are about their football teams. But I do love cricket and I suppose in the same way as life is simultaneously totally pointless and unbearably precious, so sport is both utterly meaningless and earth-shatteringly important. Steve Waugh, captain of arguably the greatest side ever to play Test cricket, seems to have used this paradox of sport to good effect by taking his side to visit the ANZAC war graves at Gallipoli. Seeing something like that must put cricket into its proper perspective, allowing the game to be played with a clear and uninhibited mind. Inhibition isn't something you think of when you see Adam

Gilchrist bat. Keith Miller's 'Listen son. Once you've had a Messerschmitt up your arse it's all a bloody game' sums it up.

It may all be a bloody game but it matters. How else do you explain the emotional void felt by millions after England lost all those penalty shoot-outs? Sport isn't something that exists in isolation, it's an important escape from, and a reflection of, real life.

This brings me (sort of) to C.L.R. James. During most of my cricket-following life the England team have been something of a national in-joke, a byword for inefficiency and ineptitude. It's true that for a large proportion of the time they have been crap, but why? It can't just be they had crap cricketers. One of their worst runs of results came in the 1980s when Botham, Gower, Gooch, Lamb, Gatting and Willis all played. All of these and others were very good, arguably great, Test players, but the team was atrocious. So, in the same way as James suggests that Bodyline was a reflection of the way the world was in the 1930s, I've wondered whether the England cricket team, and the way that it has played for most of the last 30 years, is a reflection of the way life was going on around it or whether it basically wandered along in its own little world oblivious to the mores and social trends of the time. With the possible exception of short periods following Botham's exploits in 1981 or the Ashes triumph of 2005, cricket has never been fashionable in the same way as football became after Italia '90. But it was my obsession. How much of what was going on did I miss because I was so absorbed in a game?

What's certain is that Test Match in 1975 set something in motion, something in me which brought lots of disappointments but which also enabled me later to see England crush Australia and, more importantly, play for Stoneleigh Cricket Club.

More than anything else, despite the fact he didn't die for another 18 months, that match is the last thing I can really remember doing with my dad. Although, as I travelled home with him that day, I was disappointed England hadn't completely trampled on Australia, he had given me something. I hope I remembered to thank him.

TWO

One of the reasons why I probably remember my trip to Lord's so fondly is that the weather was beautiful. If 1976 had been cancelled my generation would have given their 'Now that was a summer' award to 1975. Unfortunately for my dad, Dennis Healey, and the England cricket team, 1976 went ahead as planned.

England went nowhere the previous winter. Although this could be said about numerous winters that followed, on this occasion it was simply because there wasn't a tour. The scheduled trip to South Africa had been shelved because of the Gleneagles Agreement. This document, in which the Commonwealth countries had agreed to 'discourage contact by their nationals with sporting organisations, teams or sportsmen from South Africa', was regarded by many in the cricketing establishment as an inconvenience forced upon them by the activities of troublemakers like the Young Liberals leader, Peter Hain. My dad was a gambling man; if he had put a few quid on Hain eventually becoming Secretary of State for Northern Ireland I could have paid off my mortgage by now.

Despite the fact they hadn't played together since the previous September, Greig was confident about his team's chances against that year's tourists, the West Indies. Unfortunately, Greig didn't say he thought his team would do well against a side fresh from a heavy defeat in Australia. He said they intended to make the West Indians 'grovel'. This was certainly not the most diplomatic choice of words for a six-foot-seven white South African Englishman to use about a West Indian team. As the tourists had two of the fastest bowlers in the world in Roberts and Holding and the best batsman in Viv Richards, it wasn't the cleverest thing to have said either. To be fair, we didn't know

Richards was the best batsman in the world when he arrived. We did when he left.

Some couldn't see what all the fuss was about and suggested Greig had been quoted 'out of context'. Bear in mind, the Race Relations Act didn't come into force until later that year, ITV still gave air-time to 'Love Thy Neighbour' and Ian Smith was still claiming to be head of a white Rhodesian government. Ironically, at around the same time as Greig was airing his views on Sportsnight, Dennis Howell, the Sports Minister, was banning a Rhodesian club side, Ridgebacks CC, from entering Britain on the basis that its proposed tour might 'further or encourage the unlawful actions of the illegal Rhodesian regime'. Nevertheless, the real context out of which the England captain was quoted was that of hundreds of years of slavery and oppression on the part of the English and apartheid on the part of the South Africans. The crassness of the comment was thrown into even sharper relief when the Soweto massacre took place the day before the Lord's Test. In any event it was a very effective rallying call, just for the wrong side.

Despite Greig's lack of discretion, the first two Tests were drawn. But England never threatened to win either of them and my two main memories, of Viv Richards scoring 232 at Trent Bridge (I thought only whole teams were allowed to score that many) and Mike Brearley groping uncertainly forward and having his off stump flattened by Andy Roberts, gave a clue of what was to come. I suppose the wonder of that latter memory is that I know it was Andy Roberts and not any one of a huge number of other cricketing greats, like Phil Carlson (Remember him? No, neither do I; found him in *Wisden*), who dismissed Brearley over the next few years.

It was 0-0 with all to play for. Then they went to Old Trafford. The Banana Splits Show, a favourite of mine, sometimes featured a cartoon series, The Arabian Knights, which had a character called Bez (not to be confused with the non-musical member of the Happy Mondays and Celebrity Big Brother winner) who could adopt the shape of any animal he chose. The England cricket team had a similar power involving fruit instead of animals. In the second half of this summer they chose a pear.

Brian Close was in the side at the age of 45. This was exactly the sort of selection my dad approved of. Close was older than him, came from Yorkshire and was hard as nails, or, as Pat Pocock put it, he 'took courage to the borders of insanity'. I'm sure dad thought Closey would have been able to sort out striking miners by challenging the lot of them to a head the cricket ball competition: last man standing decides whether they go back to work or not. In short, Close was just the sort to deal with someone from abroad who didn't like it up him.

In fact, Close's selection was typical of the way England went about things for much of the 70s, 80s and even 90s, picking the press's saviour of the month in an effort to turn the team into world-beaters overnight. To a 12-year-old boy who liked reading American comics about Batman, this seemed like a perfectly reasonable approach. The TCCB, on the other hand, should perhaps have come up with something slightly more sophisticated.

There is an old-fashioned, right-wing, view of history that it is shaped by the deeds of great individuals. Cricket in this country, for much of the time I have been watching it, could properly be described as both old-fashioned and right-wing. When, in the height of this sweltering summer, the MCC allowed its members not to wear jackets inside the pavilion for the first time in its 189 year history, *The Times*' cricket correspondent, John Woodcock, commented that had they extended the dispensation to ties this 'would have been like letting a man in with only a towel round his waist'. Perhaps the less than progressive attitudes of cricket's ruling classes go some way to explaining the apparent obsession with finding some inspirational individual to galvanise the team's performance. Or maybe it was just that examining the way they prepared and how the county system equipped players for Test cricket was a bit too complicated and time-consuming to be worth bothering with?

Even when there was some recognition that county cricket was failing to prepare players adequately, there still appeared to be a desire to find a panacea such as four-day matches. 'The England team will improve if they only pick X' was replaced by 'The England team will improve if they play longer championship games'. The result of this sort of thinking was England's gradual decline. Occasional blips, like the defeat of Packer-weakened Australian teams and Botham's feats of individual brilliance, only served to mask the true picture, of which Old Trafford 1976 was more representative.

Unfortunately, for Closey and John Edrich in particular, at Manchester the men from abroad, in the shape of Roberts and Holding, decided that what the batsmen wouldn't like up them was a cricket ball travelling at 90 miles an hour. England were blown away, scoring 197

(71 and 126) in the match. 'One banana, two banana, three banana, four. Four bananas bat for England, so do many more.' Gordon Greenidge totalled 235 on his own.

It's now acknowledged in modern Test cricket that teams target the opposition's captain in an effort to destabilise the whole side. This series, for obvious reasons, saw a ruthless demonstration of how to do it to dramatic effect. Of course, it's one thing to intend to unsettle someone, it's quite another to actually achieve it. With all due respect to England's opening bowlers at Old Trafford, I don't imagine Clive Lloyd was quaking in his boots at the prospect of being roughed up by the two Mikes, Selvey and Hendrick. Unfortunately for England's captain, Lloyd had both the will and the way. By the end of the third Test, Greig's series aggregate stood at 38.

Clive Lloyd had apparently already decided that the Australians, and in particular Lillee and Thomson, had pointed the way forward in Test cricket the previous winter. The Aussies had destroyed West Indies 5-1. Lloyd had discovered at first hand that pace was the way to demolish the opposition. But, he reasoned, why only have two very fast bowlers when you can have more?

In 1976, Holding and Roberts were sometimes supplemented by the relatively mundane Vanburn Holder and Bernard Julien, but the inclusion of Wayne Daniel provided us with a glimpse of cricket's future.

Despite having pace to burn, Daniel didn't really feature in the decade or more of dominance that followed for the West Indies. However, although the idea in its finished form actually involved the Four Fast Bowlers of the Apocalypse, Old Trafford 1976 was where the juggernaut first pulled out in front of the oncoming Mini. In the late 1970s, the future was red, round, hard and going very fast. And as quickly as the ball began approaching England's cricketers at that time, so their pretensions to being a power in the world game departed at similar velocity. Dennis Healey was in trouble at the time. Inflation was running at 25% and the Chancellor had humiliated the nation by borrowing money from the IMF. England could have done with borrowing Wayne Daniel because the West Indies didn't need him.

In an attempt to respond, at Headingley England assembled its fastest pace trio for many years in John Snow, Bob Willis and Alan Ward. It's safe to say that the last of these was something of a risk. Ward's temperament was such that it once caused him to refuse to bowl in a county game after John Hampshire smacked him all round Chesterfield.

His presence in the side alongside Snow and Willis is an example of another recurring theme in English Test selection: attempting to mimic the strengths of the opposition. West Indies ran up 437-9 in 83 overs on the first day and Ward was left nursing figures of 15-0-103-2. Despite the fact that England at least managed to come second in this game, he and Snow never played Test cricket again.

As always, the final Test was at the Oval and by the end of it Richards' 291 (just plain greedy) and Holding's 14-149 had turned England's avocado into guacamole. The match contained fantastic batting, lightning fast bowling on a dead pitch and one of the great pieces of television direction of cricket.

As Michael Holding was bowling to Chris Balderstone on the fifth afternoon, the BBC director, with fortuitous timing, decided to show his run-up from side-on. Holding reached the end of his enormously long approach, turned, dipped his head and caressed the accelerator. As if in winged sandals instead of bowling boots, he silently cruised in, coiled as he approached the stumps and began the sweep through of his right arm. It had just passed the vertical when the director switched to the main front-on view just in time to see the arm complete its arc, rendering the ball invisible until it reappeared three feet behind Balderstone's neatly buttoned sleeves, shattering his stumps. It was a moment of cricketing and televisual greatness, but I imagine most England fans watching were simply wincing and sucking in their breath like a mechanic just before he starts tutting.

As if to put a seal on the summer, Holding then did something very similar to Greig, except his stumps didn't shatter, they exploded to the accompaniment of Richie Benaud's 'Aw, well bowled!'. There is a now famous picture of Greig, horribly off balance with what was left of his wicket pointing in three different directions. If I had been trying to think of a 'great man of history' to best represent England's captain at that moment, Custer is the one who would have sprung to mind.

The summer had started with Greig being the one with the big mouth. By the end of it, Clive Lloyd and his men had gobbled him up.

Nevertheless, Greig retained the captaincy for the tour to India that winter. On 18th November 1976, Gavaskar, Amarnath and Viswanath all warmed up for England with half centuries against New Zealand in Kanpur.

I didn't register this at the time, but then my dad died that day.

THREE

He didn't have a pin through his nose and I never saw him gob on Dickie Bird, but in 1977 Tony Greig became the cricketing equivalent of Jonny Rotten. While I was trying to work out what life would be like without a father, the Sex Pistols were provoking apoplexy in anyone who professed an interest in what the world was coming to and Greig was doing the same to the cricketing establishment. Years later, when I was studying law, I found myself reading about Greig -v- Insole and others 1978. The 'others' in question were the TCCB and, in one of those strange moments when two apparently unconnected parts of your life suddenly overlap, I realised quite how significant everything the 13-year-old me had watched unfolding in the news had been. At the time though, I wasn't interested in improving the terms and conditions of England's cricketers. I just wanted them to beat Australia. It seemed to me they had a much better chance of doing that if Greig was playing and captain.

Our skipper had, by all accounts, done a pretty good job in India and England won 3-1. I didn't think much of this at the time, because the home side didn't have any fast bowlers, but I later came to realise what an achievement it was. Especially when I saw what happened to Keith Fletcher's team five years later.

After India, England had played in the Centenary Test in Melbourne. Staged to celebrate 100 years of Test cricket, incredibly this ended with the same result as the match it commemorated. Nowadays such an occurrence would have us all looking around to see if an Asian bookie called 'Joey' had wagered a substantial wad on a 45-run Australian win. However, this was still a world in which my gran was not alone in refusing to believe that the wrestling on *World of Sport* was rigged. This is why what followed the match came as such a shock.

On the face of it the Centenary Test, which ended on the fifth evening with its almost poetic result, seemed the perfect celebration of Anglo-Australian rivalry and the traditions of cricket. A 21-year-old David Hookes, batting in what looked like tennis shoes, in his own assessment 'made Tony Greig famous' by hitting him for five fours in a row, Rick McCosker batted swathed in bandages with a broken jaw and Derek Randall chattered, drove and hooked his way to an innings of 174, fit for the watching Queen. Even Rod Marsh, hardly a man with a reputation for sentimentality, kept wicket throughout the match with a picture of Australia's first Test keeper, Jack Blackham, in his pocket and called Randall back when he was on 161 for a catch that didn't carry, despite the fact that the umpire had already given him out.

However, in the same way as there were those blissfully unaware of any possibility of collusion between Mick McManus and Johnny Saint, so the cricket authorities had no idea what was going on behind the scenes at the Centenary Test. What was going on, of course, was Greig tapping up all of the world's best players on behalf of World Series Cricket (WSC), or 'Kerry Packer's circus', as the establishment insisting on calling it. Basically, Packer had been refused the television rights to Test cricket by the Australian Cricket Board, so he took the slightly unusual step of attempting to hire the Aussie team to come and play for him instead of them. When this worked quite nicely, he then had to hire someone for them to play against and picked up most of the West Indies' side, together with a raft of the best players from the other Test nations and South Africa to form a World XI, led by Greig.

The reaction of the cricketing establishment when the news broke was predictably puce and spluttering. John Woodcock went so far as to explain Greig's part in the affair as a product of him being an Englishman only 'by adoption', which was, of course, not the same as being 'an Englishman through and through'. It was ironic that in a sport where the Professional Cricketers Association has been described as the only union more right-wing than its bosses, the workers, or 'players' as they preferred to be known, were flexing their muscles at exactly the same time as their rather more left-wing counterparts. What was the country coming to if you couldn't even count on professional cricketers to know their place?

It didn't even seem to occur to those running English cricket that Packer might have been an accident waiting to happen. In 1976 an England player earned £210 per Test match. Even though this compared favourably with a miner at the coalface on a £61 a week basic wage, or a fireman on £71 for 48 hours, Packer was offering $A25,000 (about £12,500) for 12 weeks' work. The history of the relationship between masters and servants within English cricket is not the only context into which such an offer had to be put.

The economy was spiralling so far out of control that the Labour government had entered into the Social Contract with the Unions, under which wage demands were to be kept down in exchange for a commitment to protect investment in public services. English cricketers had to make a living in a Britain with an inflation rate of around 25 per cent, but could expect nothing in return from their employers if they turned down opportunities to maximize their income. County players were contracted for only six months of the year and were then cut loose to fend for themselves in the winter months. The idea that this might be balanced out by services such as pensions or health care wouldn't even have entered the head of a county chairman. If a player was lucky his employer might benignly grant him a benefit season after 15 years of loyal service. Greig may not have been the six-foot-seven stick of 'Englishman' rock that John Woodcock would have liked, but his actions have to be judged against this background.

As far as the cricketing establishment was concerned, the players were, it seems, supposed to turn Packer down for no other reason than it would be ungentlemanly to do otherwise. The fact that these men earned their living from cricket and could have their international careers ended by selectors not noted for their consistency was completely irrelevant. This wasn't the last time that English cricket suffered as a result of the game's rulers seeing nothing wrong in demanding loyalty from those to whom they showed none. The fact that England's cricketing 'Supremo', Ray Illingworth, could be found still demonstrating this attitude 20 years later gives a clue as to one reason why the England team didn't develop as well as it might have done.

Greig may have done a great deal to improve the financial lot of international cricketers in this country, but it's debatable whether the Packer 'revolution' did much to improve the wages of ordinary county cricketers. Test players may have seen their match fees quintupled, but I remember a leg-spinner called Andy Clarke playing for Sussex well into the 1980s only being paid about £4000 a year. In 1977, the firemen were earning £3,700 and on strike seeking a 30 per cent rise in defiance of the Social Contract's nominal ceiling of 10 per cent.

Certainly, although Greig and his associates won their case for restraint of trade in the High Court, the events of 1977 didn't have the seismic affect that, for example, Jimmy Hill's successful campaign against the maximum wage had in football. There are many possible reasons for this. Partly I think it's because cricket isn't the global game football is. At that time there were only six Test-playing countries. So even internationally, only a very few players had the clout to take away their bat and ball and have anyone notice. Primarily though, I think most professionals in this country didn't benefit to the extent they might have done because of the way cricket is regarded and followed in comparison to football. For most in this country, county cricket is an afterthought, something to do in the five days it isn't the football season. This must be to do with the game itself: the length of time it takes, the fact that it's played midweek and, more than anything, the small number of clubs and the disparate areas they represent. Someone from Wolverhampton and someone from Coventry may both support Warwickshire but it's hard to imagine them having the same tribal passion about the Bears as they do about Wanderers or City. This doesn't even take into account that large parts of the country don't even have a first-class team to support.

When rugby union went professional in the 1990s, clubs had to wake up very quickly to certain commercial realities, i.e. that, as Rob Andrew put it, 'bums on seats' would determine survival. A famous name and years of tradition were no protection, as Moseley found out. In cricket, the bums that mattered were on seats at the Test grounds and county clubs survived on handouts from the TCCB/ECB provided by the income generated from gate receipts and television money from international fixtures. Yet for years, many county chairmen remained resistant to changes aimed at promoting the better performance of the England side because they didn't suit their parochial interests. Ironically, given that Greig was their captain and the club defied a lot of pressure by originally keeping him as skipper and player for the 1978 season, Sussex remained in many ways a prime example of this. County cricket clubs had operated on much the same basis for more than 100 years. It was going to take more than an Australian media mogul and raging inflation to shake them out of their complacency. Despite Packer's intervention, it took more than 20 years for it to sink in that the money from international cricket might start to dry up if the England team remained consistent only in its ability to be embarrassingly inept.

In 1977, the England selectors managed simultaneously to demonstrate their disapproval of Greig, by sacking him as captain, and their pragmatism, some might say hypocrisy, by letting him carry on playing. The Australians, on the other hand, arrived without Dennis Lillee. They did have Len Pascoe, an equally frightening looking long-haired fast bowler of Yugoslav (we would now say Macedonian) extraction, whose real surname, being made up almost entirely of consonants, terrified scorers so much he changed it. It came as a bit of a surprise that this scary-looking man hurling himself at England's batsmen was a community arts officer, but the fact that he had to have this job helped explain why Packer's offer would have been so hard to turn down for the Aussies he approached. The touring side was supposedly divided between Packer and non-Packer players and one, in Jeff Thomson, who was sort of both, having first signed for WSC and then apparently changed his mind under pressure from the radio station where he worked as a public relations officer. Jeff Thomson in public relations, now there's an interesting concept: 'Welcome to Australia, you Pommie bastard!'

Greig's role as skipper went to Mike Brearley, someone who ended up with a reputation as one of the best captains and worst specialist batsmen England had ever had. Brearley was a brilliant man-manager and tactician. He was also highly intelligent and lucky. I'm not sure which of these latter attributes account for the fact that he never captained England in a Test against West Indies, but in 1977 his talents were enough to secure a 3-0 victory over an Australian side with Greg Chappell as their only batsman.

The year before, my dad had bought one of the new-fangled video recorders with hour-long tapes and, unlike my mum, I knew how to use it. Thanks to this, three pieces of cricket, all featuring Geoff Boycott, stick in my mind. The first of these, the comedy run-out of my hero Derek Randall on the Yorkshireman's comeback at Trent Bridge, was calamitous even by his high standards in this regard. As with Dennis Compton, Boycott's calling was never more than 'a basis for negotiation', but hitting it back to the bowler and setting off was a special effort. To this day I don't know why Randall didn't just stay in his crease and say 'Bye Geoff!'. He didn't even make it halfway before Rod Marsh demolished the stumps as if administering a bit of improvised bar-room dentistry.

The other two images from this year were rather happier for

Boycott: Rick McCosker dropping him when he had made 20 (in three hours) of the eventual 107 that made up for sawing-off Randall and the on-drive with which he brought up his 100th first-class century on his own home ground in the following Test. Even without the video, this image would probably have stayed with me, not just because it's one of the most often replayed moments in English cricketing history, but because Boycott's reaction to his achievement struck a chord.

One of the most memorable things about that shot is the non-striker Graham Roope's Eric Morecombe style comedy jump as the ball sped towards him. If Roope hadn't got out of the way, the ball might have deflected to mid-on and Boycott could have been out next ball for 96. However, Boycott was so absorbed in what he had achieved he ignored his partner when he went to congratulate him. I knew the feeling, it was like sitting in the stands at the Goldstone ground trying to talk to a man who wasn't really listening because he had a business deal to discuss.

At 36, Boycott was only six years younger than my father had been and seemed a little old to be making a comeback. Now I realise he was a mere slip of a lad. He was balding, he was from Yorkshire and I had mixed feelings about him. In short, he was an almost perfect fit for the big anti-hero shaped hole that had appeared in my life.

For me the tragedy is not that my father died when I was 12, it's that when my mother told me, my primary emotion was one of relief. I didn't know my father, or rather I never met the man whose loss devastated all the adults around me. To me he seemed driven and intolerant, and the pain he was in through five years of illness made him seem almost permanently on the edge of rage. I lived walking on eggshells and knowing that if I came second he would only want to know why it wasn't first. I never had the opportunity to know and enjoy him as an adult. The grief that everyone else obviously felt was, to borrow from Raymond Robertson-Glasgow, something I was 'old enough to feel but too young to take part in it'. When I grew up, I'm not sure I wanted to know how much better it could have been.

After 1977, Tony Greig never played for England again, Alan Knott never toured and England became a weak batting side in which Boycott was the key wicket and he knew it. After Headingley, the final match of the series at the Oval was almost literally a damp squib. Rain-ruined, it was memorable only for Mick Malone, a previously (and subsequently) unknown Australian swing bowler, sending down 43 overs in one day. I still remember the feeling of disappointment, almost of loss, as that final match petered out into a draw and my summer ended.

That long school holiday was the first since my dad had died and my mum was now going out to work. Without siblings, I had a lot of time on my hands. The cricket helped fill my day and Greg Chappell and his men were certainly preferable to the other crap Australians ITV had on offer. How terrible was *The Sullivans*? An Aussie soap opera from the days before they were contractually obliged to feature a member of the Minogue family, it was set in the 1930s and 1940s, obviously an age without unwanted pregnancy, recreational drugs and lesbians, and was probably the dullest soap ever broadcast. As for the programme that preceded it in the schedules, *Rainbow*, I was clearly the wrong age to be watching that. Either I was too old, though I confess I did sometimes find myself staring at it in the way that you might stand transfixed before a major accident, stunned and not quite believing what I was seeing. Alternatively, I was too young to be seeing fluffy pink hippos with any degree of regularity.

As is probably obvious, I spent quite a lot of time on my own that summer. I might have been lonely, but I wasn't. Derek and Geoff and Mike and Tony and Kerry had kept me company.

FOUR

The winter of 1977-78 was the first in which I was aware of England's tours and followed them as they were happening. In fact that's not quite true. I hadn't worked out yet that there was commentary on the radio and so only kept up with the matches through the newspapers. Judging by later years this was probably just as well from the point of view of my sleep pattern, particularly as the second half of the winter was in New Zealand. If I had been listening in the first half, sleeping wouldn't have been a problem. England and Pakistan played out three of the dullest draws imaginable. Probably the best thing you could say about the whole tour was that Andrew Flintoff was born during it.

The Test series in Pakistan was epitomized by the man who faced its first ball, Mudassar Nazar. In the opening Test he took nine hours and 17 minutes to get to 100. Then things calmed down a bit. Boycott took 20 minutes longer to reach 50 than Mudassar had and England took 135 eight-ball overs, or 1080 balls, to get 288. This was their best effort of the series. In the next two matches they scored 191 in 86 overs, 186 in 81, 266 in 123 and 222 in 89. The game's played slightly differently now. Maintaining the same scoring rate as they managed on the first day at Edgbaston in 2005 over 1080 balls, England would have scored 927.

It's fitting that a series slower than the donkey still pulling the mower at Karachi marked Boycott's debut as England captain. Mike Brearley had pioneered the use of a hard skull protector under his cap. Unfortunately, he didn't pioneer the arm guard and somehow succeeded in getting his arm broken by a fast-medium bowler called Sikander Bakht playing for a Sind XI on one of Pakistan's legendary flying greentops. It's probably just as well for his personal safety that Brearley never captained England in the Caribbean. As a result of this injury,

Boycott, who at the start of the year was still making himself unavailable for England, ended up in charge for the rest of the tour.

Before the final game, three Pakistani Packer players turned up at the nets and there was a threat from England to call off the game if they were selected. Unfortunately, they weren't and a match where the most interesting thing was how boring it was, went ahead. All 11 Pakistanis bowled and at one point Boycott went almost 18 overs with one scoring shot, a two. Mike Gatting, clearly a believer in starting as he meant to go on, made his debut and was out lbw playing no shot.

Once they had woken up, England moved straight to New Zealand. The opening Test was the first against Kiwis I had followed. It was also the first defeat by these opponents in England's history. The game was low-scoring and we were only set 137 to win. By the close on the fourth day our score stood at 53-8. At only 13, reading the morning paper that imparted this news I failed to appreciate two things. Firstly, given this was England, there was no way Phil Edmonds, Bob Willis and an injured Brian Rose were going to make a silk purse out of the pig's ear the rest of the batting had made of things and secondly, given the time difference, they already hadn't.

England bounced back and won the next Test. They were inspired by Ian Botham, who had made his Test debut in Boycott's comeback match at Nottingham the previous summer. Botham's performance included his first Test 100, but is now more famous for the deliberate running-out of his captain to help set up a declaration. It's said the Yorkshireman was so angry he was almost in tears and just buried his head in a towel when he returned to the dressing room. When Boycott was involved you had to make your own amusement and the rest of the team were probably crying too, but not for the same reason. I imagine them collectively making the sort of suppressed snorting and squealing noises you would normally associate with eight-year-old schoolboys when one of their number accidentally farts in assembly. As is usual, it can only have been made funnier by how unfunny Geoffrey found it. When, in response to a question about the timing of the declaration, the team received the slightly muffled and less than erudite reply of 'You can all fook off', the place must have dissolved.

Unfortunately, having had two positive results in a row, the teams then seemed to get a collective nosebleed and played out a six-day draw at Auckland. Clive Radley, in only his second game, seemed to have got the hang of how his captain felt things should be done and took over eight hours to reach his hundred. Botham's 53 off 114 balls was described by *Wisden* as 'exciting'. In the face of this sort of evidence it was hard to argue with some of my new schoolmates' assessment that 'cricket's boring'. Maybe the fact that I was forced to try and defend the indefensible at such a young age accounts for why I grew up to be a lawyer.

The winter had been a bit bland and the summer didn't get off to a good start either. Ipswich beat Arsenal at Wembley and England hadn't even made it to the World Cup Finals. Worse, Scotland were there. I had no particular desire to go 'off wi' Ally's army' to 'the Argentine' or anywhere else for that matter, but like every other Englishman I had no choice but to do what we always do in such circumstances and become 'British' for the duration of the tournament. Inevitably, with all of Britain cheering them on and despite Archie Gemmill putting them 'in dreamland' for a few minutes against Holland, they didn't shake us up and went out in the first round.

Things needed to liven up a bit. Fortunately, in 1978 *Grange Hill*, *Wonderwoman* and David Gower made their debuts. Linda Carter briefly acted as a bit of distraction to my devotion to the England cricket team and the previously unchallenged Debbie Harry. Then Gower arrived and, as far as England was concerned, everything went back to normal. It took until the following year, and the video for 'Heart of Glass', for me and Ms Harry to sort things out.

Most of us have images that stay with us through our lives. Debbie in that grey dress and Gower's entrance to Test cricket are two of mine. I don't know how the selectors came to pick him. The previous season he had played 21 games for Leicestershire and averaged 21.81. In 1978, he played nine County Championship matches and averaged 24.78. But if ever a man was born to play Test cricket it was Gower and his first ball is now legendary. His big mop of blond hair inspired the press to liken him to Shirley Temple and when the barely fast-medium Liaqat Ali bowled him a half-tracker first up, he was 'On The Good Ship Lollipop'. Most people getting a long-hop for their first ball in Test cricket might opt for a relieved defensive prod and survival. Not Gower; he did what came instinctively, swivelled and cracked it to the deep square-leg boundary. John Arlott got it right: 'Princely' he called it. Gower finished the summer having averaged 51.00 against Pakistan and 57.00 against New Zealand.

Just as the music charts of the time had The Boomtown Rats sitting uncomfortably alongside Olivia Newton-John and John Travolta, by the middle of the summer England had Gower and Boycott in the same side. The contrast between their approaches to the game crystallizes one of the major questions about professional sportspeople: how far should they consider themselves entertainers?

Boycott seems to have a different view about the answer to that question as a commentator than he did as a player. Certainly entertainment was in short supply while England were grinding their way across Pakistan the previous winter, yet as 'Hairgate' unfolded at the Oval in 2006, the Yorkshireman was among those in the broadcast media debating when 'they would get back out there for the sake of the paying public'. The implication was that this should be the most important consideration in the minds of those trying to sort the situation out. It's true that cricket survives because people pay to watch it, but what are they paying to watch? When one radio interviewer at the Oval collared Mark Butcher and asked him to comment, the Surrey left-hander put his finger on a vital distinction everyone else seemed to have missed. 'Do you think they could be playing again tonight Mark?' 'Well, no, I don't see how they can. The umpires have said the game's over. If you go back on that, you've got anarchy'.

When journalists talk about 'sporting theatre' they don't mean vaudeville, they mean something much closer in nature to the colosseum. The point that Butcher was making is that sport has to remain within certain parameters in order to be taken seriously. His use of the word 'anarchy' indicates that this essential seriousness is what makes it worth watching. The moment a sport steps outside credible boundaries is the moment it sets foot on the road to becoming a 'sportsertainment', like World Wildlife Fund wrestling. Barry Richards may have thought his cricket with Packer was the hardest he had ever played, but the establishment sought to diminish it by reference to that most frivolous of diversions, a 'circus'.

Therefore it's dangerous for any sportsman to have entertainment as his highest priority. When spectators turn up to pay professional athletes' wages, generally they want more than 90 minutes of amusement. They want to be able to believe in what they're watching. Just because something is entertaining doesn't mean it has the essential integrity of the genuine contest that makes sport worthwhile. At Lord's in 1978, Ian Botham's unprecedented feat of making a Test hundred and taking eight wickets in an innings of the same match was to some extent devalued by the absence of Packer players Imran Khan, Asif Iqbal, Majid Khan, Zaheer Abbas and my future team-mate Mushtaq Mohammed from Pakistan's touring party. Unfortunately, cricket ended up having to deal with more fundamental questions of integrity than those raised by a mere 'mis-match'. After the infamous Centurion Park Test match in 2000, Hansie Cronje said: 'As Test cricketers we have a duty to entertain and get full houses and this was far better than seeing spectators sitting there with long faces.' I'm sure every cricket lover present at Centurion would have gladly exchanged an afternoon watching a run chase for the knowledge that their sport wasn't fake.

All of this raises the interesting question of whether people watch sport because they enjoy it, and, if so, what is it they're enjoying? Can anyone really say, for example, they had fun watching the last 20 minutes of England-v-Argentina in the 2002 World Cup? I didn't, it was agony, but I was compelled to watch because I wanted to see us win. 'Us', you notice, not 'them'. What I enjoyed was being part of something that mattered: England beating Argentina at football. There were two key elements to that enjoyment: belonging and winning.

It's important not to underestimate either of these factors in making sport attractive to those who love it, or indeed unattractive to those it alienates. The education secretary of the day, Shirley Williams, one of the main architects of the newly introduced comprehensive education system, had made public her concerns about the negative effects of competitive games.

I could easily have been put off playing sport by my experiences at a school full of the sort of people even The Jam's David Watts would have wanted to be like. There were two brothers in particular, both equally talented at every game they turned their hand to, clever, handsome and, most sickeningly of all, good blokes. Fortunately, my self-esteem was bolstered by the cricket club I had started playing for.

Barcombe was, at the time, one of the best village clubs in the county. While I was playing for them they won the Sussex section of the national village competition twice. There were at least two first-team players who had recently been on county staffs. These were good cricketers and my experience of playing club cricket couldn't have been more different from what I had been used to. Whereas at school I was the hopeless understudy to the lad in my age group who played for the county, at my club I was a promising young wicket-keeper who had to be encouraged and groomed for the first team sooner rather than later.

More important, however, was the experience of just being part of a club. A new world opened up for me, populated by Oz, Pongo, Sparrow, Fred (whose name was Martin), Dick, Johnny and Daffy. Whereas before I had always been Paul, now I was 'Lazers'. I had a nickname! Not a very good nickname, it didn't even have a 'y' on the end, but a nickname nevertheless. I had never felt like I belonged so much in my whole life. I realised why I had got so cross with my mother for sitting in the garage with me during the 1966 World Cup final. I felt she had prevented me from being part of an exclusive club.

At this stage I was still only playing in the second team and certainly wasn't entertaining anybody on account of the minor cricketing problem of being unable to hit it off the square. I had watched too much of Boycott and failed to appreciate he had five days to bat and fully intended using all of them, whereas I had a maximum of 40 overs. I spent my time infuriating my team-mates by smacking the ball to all four corners of the popping crease. However, having no back-lift I was difficult to get out, so they let me open and my wicket-keeping kept me in the team. And being part of the team was what mattered.

However, the fact it was a winning team was, as Gower might have put it, 'not unimportant'. Obviously it's preferable if victory comes entertainingly. A good cricketing example would be an innings win on the back of a Gower hundred. However, football managers don't lose their jobs if they keep 'winning ugly'. They get the sack for losing on a regular basis. Even the most Corinthian of English cricket fans would eventually have become disillusioned if defeat had followed every time a Gower innings was nipped in the bud at 42 by an airy waft to second slip. Team sports may fulfil a basic need to belong which goes beyond the attractive qualities of the sport itself – which is why people who don't particularly like golf can nevertheless find themselves caught up in the Ryder Cup – but nobody wants to be part of consistent defeat, however prettily it's achieved. This is what explains Geoff Boycott. Every forward defensive he played seemed to be saying, 'Ah'm doin' summat important 'ere. If tha' wants entertainin' go and watch *Grease*.'

It's not just the good performances of your own team that can provide enjoyment. Demonstrating just the sort of attitude Shirley Williams was worried about, my favourite statistic from this summer was Brendon Bracewell's batting average. Bracewell's more famous brother, John, was an off-spinner who could bat well enough to score a

Test hundred. Brendon was a seamer. In six innings against England he scored 4 runs (an outside edge through the slips) and averaged 0.8.

Much later, one of my Stoneleigh team-mates, who to be fair had only taken up the game that year, went through an entire season with a highest score of 1 not out, an aggregate of 2 and an average of 0.857. He didn't enjoy himself very much. However, the following year he averaged exactly 9 and pushed hard for a most improved player award to be created on the basis that he couldn't believe anyone had ever increased their batting average by over 1000 per cent in such a short space of time. This man is a walking example of why Mrs Williams was right and why she was wrong.

The government's stance on competitive sport, which in a curious way was not a million miles from the more traditional emphasis on the overriding importance of not whether you won or lost but how you played the game, ran contrary to hardening attitudes at professional level. The furore that developed during and after the first Test of 1978 illustrates that this wasn't about winning as opposed to entertaining, but rather achieving victory while staying within acceptable moral boundaries.

The controversy centred on the fate of a Pakistani left-arm spinner called Iqbal Qasim. Coming in as night-watchman on the Saturday evening of the Edgbaston Test, the tailender did his job and survived until the close. In 1978, the shops still shut on a Sunday and Test cricketers were allowed a day of rest. When play resumed, Iqbal quickly found a reason to dislike Mondays every bit as much as Bob Geldof. He stuck around for more than half an hour before Bob Willis went round the wicket and immediately hit him in the mouth with a bouncer. He left the field bleeding freely and needing stitches.

The reaction to this incident reveals that these were gentler times. The Pakistan manager claimed that Willis' tactics were 'unfair' and a clear infringement of the playing conditions. It seems incredible now that these actually stated: 'Captains must instruct their players that the fast, short-pitched ball should at no time be directed at non-recognised batsmen'. Brearley defended the tactic by saying that Iqbal had come in at number three, was a competent player who was holding England up and the dividing line between recognised and non-recognised batsmen was sometimes a thin one. Nevertheless, after the match, the TCCB felt it necessary to say it 'bitterly regretted' the incident. Even *Wisden* referred to the performance as 'unnecessarily ruthless'. Admittedly this was at a time when helmets were not widely used but, nowadays, no-one bats an eyelid if a tailender gets hit. Obviously the fact we had only three television channels and Jim Callaghan was prime minister were not the only reasons why it was a different world, or perhaps more accurately another country. During the 1974-75 Ashes series, Jeff Thomson openly said he 'loved to see blood on the wicket'. The Australian Cricket Board didn't see the need to say that they 'bitterly regretted' his comments. The English clearly carried more baggage into their cricketing contests than some of their opponents.

The England cricket team were also weighed down by their own press. The papers and those in the broadcast media not directly associated with the game always seemed loathe to let go of their favourite joke. In 1978 England played six Tests, they won five and the other was a rain-ruined draw. However, hardly a match report went by without the absence of several of Pakistan's best players being mentioned. Simultaneously the same commentators were treating Tony Greig like the dodgy relative that nobody mentions while he is away 'on holiday' with Her Majesty. Much was made of Imran and co. not playing for Pakistan but little about England missing Greig, Knott, Underwood, Woolmer and Amiss. When comparisons started to be made between the game's new pin-up boy, Botham, and its former champion, Denis Compton, the great man was more than dismissive, 'Don't associate me with him! He was overrated. Botham only did well because all the best players joined Packer.' As for beating the New Zealanders 3-0, that wasn't much of an achievement as, to that stage at least, Packer hadn't even tried to poach any of them.

Perhaps this desire to diminish the deeds of our own team is to do with an English preference for the plucky underdog. Like Sussex in the 1978 Gillette Cup final for example.

My home county's opponents, Somerset, featured Viv Richards, Ian Botham and Joel Garner and vied with Essex for the title of strongest one-day team in the country. It was a bit like Brighton taking on Manchester United in the FA Cup final five years later. Except, fortunately, Gordon Smith didn't play cricket.

When Brian Rose hit Imran's first over for 14, prompting one wag in the press box to muse that Somerset were heading for a score of 840, I feared the worst. In fact, although Botham made 80, their 60 overs yielded only 207-7. In those days anything over 200 represented a challenge and they had a formidable one-day bowling attack, including

Botham, Garner, Graham Burgess and 'The Demon of Frome' Colin Dredge. Our overseas 'stars' Imran and Javed Miandad made 3 between them and it was left to Paul Parker to chip us home with 62 not out. I'm sure the neutrals would far rather have seen Botham and Richards in full sail but I didn't care, my team had won a cup.

In 30 years as an England cricket supporter I've learned to savour moments of triumph. Kipling's choice of opposite was never far away. However, this was a lesson I hadn't yet learned. As that summer came to a close I was no more aware that a winter of discontent and bread rationing lay ahead than I was that 26 years later the Dredge family would have their revenge.

FIVE

In the winter of 1978-79 lorry drivers, no doubt anticipating the coming rise in the price of milk to 15p a pint, put in a 25 per cent pay claim. Public sector workers went on strike demanding a £60 per week minimum wage for manual workers and a 35-hour working week. Rubbish lay uncollected in the streets and bodies weren't collected for burial. I didn't notice; I had a crush on a girl and England were stuffing Australia.

Bob Geldof could keep Mary of the fourth form. I had Caroline of the sixth form. Or perhaps more accurately I wished I had Caroline of the sixth form. In fact it was quite a knowing, 'Well I can dream can't I?' sort of a crush shared by every heterosexual boy in the school. And while I knew I was not exactly right at the back of the queue, it was a long queue and most of those behind me were still in the closet and covering their tracks by pretending to adore her. However, the fact I knew it was hopeless didn't stop me signing up as the soundman for the school play to be near her. She actually liked me in that 'You're quite nice', pat-me-on-the-head sort of a way that older teenage girls have with younger teenage boys. Obviously this wasn't exactly the reaction I was looking for and I attempted to impress her with my technical know-how. I illustrated this mainly by carrying a screwdriver everywhere with me.

Unfortunately my technical know-how was a) even if extensive, unlikely to impress an exceptionally pretty 17-year-old girl and b) didn't extend much further than knowing which end of the screwdriver I should be holding. This was amply demonstrated when I cued up the wrong sound effect during the dress rehearsal and the line 'Peace, count the clock' was greeted by an enormous clap of thunder. I can still feel the crushing, toe-curling humiliation of that moment. 'Thank you, God. Thank you so bloody much!'

Fortunately, thoughts of Caroline weren't the only thing keeping me awake at night. I had discovered Test match commentary on the radio for winter Tests. In this respect at least, things were going rather better than my imaginary love life.

The ACB, in an attempt to compete with what *Wisden* described as 'the jet-age razzmatazz' of Packer, tried to liven things up by having three skydivers drop in to deliver the coin for the toss at the start of the Ashes series. That worked really well on the radio. Thanks to World Series Cricket the game was developing and not just by the addition of the odd parachutist. This was the first series in which England were involved where most, if not all, of the batsmen wore helmets. All the radio commentators were beside themselves at this development. One or two people had worn them previously but this was the first series in which they became the norm. Packer had changed things and in this case not necessarily for the better.

The cricketing establishment had got a taste of the lengths a hard-nosed businessman would go to if he wanted something badly enough. This attitude was reflected in the way World Series Cricket was played. Greig was quoted as saying, 'The competition in WSC is so intense, teams can no longer afford to allow opposition tailenders to hang around. Consequently the pace bowlers are dishing out an unprecedented amount of bouncers to the "rabbits". So it is pleasing to see that cricketers like Dennis Lillee and Garth le Roux have got the message, swallowed their pride and are wearing helmets'.

Like parents not approving of what their child is growing up into, many of the old school didn't find this a 'pleasing' development. Sam Loxton, the Aussie batsman of the 1940s and 1950s, was particularly unimpressed: 'Mate, I didn't even wear a helmet at the battle of Tobruk.' However, with Packer providing competition, cricket had been dragged into a world of commercial reality and high stakes. Like so many things in life, once the initial shock of a particular line being crossed has subsided, things which were previously unthinkable quickly become accepted. Thus, barely six months after the Iqbal Qasim furore, everyone seemed to agree that anyone, including bowlers, who didn't wear a helmet could expect no sympathy if they got hit. As Kevin Costner's Eliot Ness put it in *The Untouchables*, establishment cricket had to 'become what it beheld' in order to try and compete.

In terms of whether they actually were competing, from the point at which Australia's official captain Graham Yallop won the toss at Brisbane there wasn't a lot of evidence of Mr Packer having too much to worry about. The Australians were 26-6 before the series was two hours old. It's not often that I've been able to say that so I'll say it again, the Australians were 26-6. It took a great deal of effort to stay silent while listening to this at 1 a.m. so as not to wake my mum. Thinking about it now it was similar to the effort I had to make years later watching Brighton from the Kop at Liverpool as they came back from 2-0 down to force a 2-2 draw in the FA Cup. Unfortunately I wasn't there when they beat Liverpool at Anfield in 1983 to knock them out, or at the Goldstone Ground a year later when they did it again and I could have screamed the stand down.

Apart from the need to remain silent, this business of listening to the cricket on the radio was great. In absolutely no time we were 2-0 up and this despite the fact that Boycott was having a complete nightmare. His tour was so bad that in the overall first-class statistics he was outscored and out averaged by Brearley. To be fair there were mitigating circumstances in that his mother had just died and Ray Illingworth had returned to Yorkshire, as team manager, like the Ayatollah Khomeni returning to Iran. This left Boycott cast as the Shah and ousted from the captaincy. These external distractions meant that he contributed just one half-century in the whole series, 77 at Perth, scored in seven and a half hours with one four (all run) including two overthrows. After this innings Boycott received a telegram from one irate Australian supporter telling him he had done for cricket what the Boston Strangler had done for door-to-door salesmen.

What this supporter thought of his countrymen's contribution to the game is not recorded. However, the establishment's team were hardly giving it the hard sell by having one of their openers run himself out in every match or, it seemed to me, by appointing someone called Kim to be their vice-captain. The rebels meanwhile were playing in canary yellow to the strains of the work of musical genius that was Packer's promotional song 'C'mon Aussie C'mon'. Amazingly, given that it appeared to be doing for cricket what the Smurfs were simultaneously doing for pop music, this is available today as a mobile ringtone.

Even though Packer's Australians held their own in the 'Super Tests', going down only 2-1 to the World side and winning 1-0 against the

West Indians, whom someone had managed to persuade to play in pink, these games lacked the crucial ingredient of legitimacy. The World XI's team sheet read like one of the imaginary sides you might have had contesting a game of Subbuteo cricket but despite the absence of any instances of six byes or any fielders standing bolt upright with their hands on their hips, they still couldn't possibly excite crowds in the same way as a proper Test match. Incidentally I did once play with someone who did field like that and also didn't bother walking in. Stationed at short fine-leg at one end and mid-off at the other he hardly moved all afternoon. At the end of the innings I went and looked at where he had been standing and found two foot prints in the grass.

In terms of trying to decide which team to support, the Australian cricketing public must have been like a child in a sweet shop constantly weighing up the competing pros and cons of a Curly Wurly and a Walnut Whip. Just as a Curly Wurly was chewy and would last longer but half the chocolate fell on the floor every time you bit it, so Packer's Aussies were quite good but not playing 'real' Tests. On the other hand in the same way as the Walnut Whip had thick chocolate and the creamy bit in the middle but was saddled with the glaring disadvantage of the walnut, so Yallop's men were playing for the Ashes but were rubbish.

Briefly, in Melbourne, things seemed to swing in favour of the official side as England were bowled out twice for under 200 by that cricketing rarity, an asthmatic fast bowler. Rodney Hogg took 10-66 in the match on his way to breaking Arthur Mailey's record number of wickets in an Ashes series. Mailey took 36 in 1920-21 while Hogg finished up with 41. Coincidentally Mailey's best innings figures in first class cricket were 10-66 against Gloucestershire in 1921, enabling him to title his autobiography *10 for 66 And All That*. He also once famously described dismissing his hero Victor Trumper in a Grade match as making him feel like he had 'just killed a dove', not the kind of analogy I can recall Hogg using when he bowled Boycott for one.

Suddenly, being awake at four o'clock in the morning wasn't as much fun as it had been. Jim Callaghan, returning from the Caribbean, might have thought there was 'no chaos here' (he never actually said: 'Crisis? What crisis?') but on the other side of the world there was. England followed up their defeat in Melbourne with two further first-innings balls-ups and had to be rescued by Randall's 150 at Sydney and Bob Taylor's 97 at Adelaide. I can still see Taylor, who never came close to a Test hundred before or after this, being caught down the leg side in the last over before lunch flicking at a leg stump half-volley. I didn't see it live, terrestrial television (the only sort there was in the 1970s) didn't cover overseas Tests, but I had recorded the highlights program with that martial trumpet music at the start. I watched it over and over again, each time willing Taylor to leave it or miss it and get his hundred after lunch.

It's said that smell is the sense most linked to memory but I can't hear that music without thinking of winter evenings not doing my homework, watching and recording those highlights. I don't know if, as in America, Australian television didn't use as many pixels to create the picture but it always looked like they were playing in a heat haze.

In fact it was England who were hot and the only time a 5-1 winning margin has given me more pleasure was when our footballers massacred Germany in the qualifiers for the 2002 World Cup. Sid Vicious clearly couldn't cope with this victory for the establishment and ended it all the day after we secured the Ashes by winning the fourth Test. Many professional cricketers have killed themselves after their careers were over but I doubt if any of them used heroin supplied to them by their own mother.

Perhaps, given that they shared 39 wickets in the series, England's spinners represented the difference between the sides? As if to back this up the *Wisden* report contains the now seemingly incredible comment: 'England are often chided for fragility facing leg-spin. They might not play it well, but it seldom gets them into the type of trouble Australia have in coping with off-spin.' Shane Warne or John Emburey and Geoff Miller? You choose.

Looking back on this series it feels like it was neither one thing nor the other. Obviously beating the Australians 5-1 is not bad, but then Packer cutting a swathe through their team hardly made it a stunning triumph either. My sense of that whole time is of being 'in between'. My albeit forlorn awakening to members of the opposite sex meant that I was no longer a child, while the terror that would have paralysed me if my yearnings had been reciprocated meant that I was some way short of being an adult. Parliament had prodded Jim Callaghan awake by delivering a vote of no confidence in his Government by a majority of one. The public then agreed that Labour wasn't working by electing Mrs Thatcher. Just think, if one MP had voted the other way or the MP for Batley hadn't been ill, it might never have happened. But happen it did and we entered a period of limbo between the union-dominated politics of the 1970s and the Thatcherite revolution.

Cricket, meanwhile, was in an even greater state of flux than my hormones, leaving behind a world of pimpled gloves, caps and leather boots but not yet fully embracing helmets, coloured clothes and bats that didn't need oiling.

In May, the Australian cricket authorities granted Packer what he had always wanted, the television rights to Test matches and other cricket in Australia. That decision changed the cricket world every bit as decisively as the one taken by the British electorate altered the course of our history.

Having said that, this being cricket, revolutionary changes certainly weren't going to happen overnight. For the second World Cup, played in England that year, the Australian Cricket Board didn't select any of Packer's men, everyone played in white and the captains could still put all their fielders on the boundary if they wanted to.

I was still at school when the tournament started and so couldn't see the matches live. Also the BBC had the highlights on in the prime 12.15 a.m. slot and so I had to rely on old faithful the video recorder to see any of it.

It's funny the things that stick in your mind. I remember Sunil Gavaskar hitting a ball from Andy Roberts almost completely vertically in the opening game and being caught by Michael Holding, England taking 60 overs to score 165-9 against Pakistan and winning, Viv Richards' diving one-handed caught-and-bowled to dismiss Imran Khan in the semi-final as Pakistan threatened to chase down 294 to win and Derek Randall running out John Wright to turn the other semi England's way. Oh yes and Mike Brearley getting nought against Canada, lbw to John Valentine, a French teacher from Montreal whose father was an Anglican bishop.

Although I vaguely recall that it was the game in which Boycott, still in his cap, was unveiled as England's bowling secret weapon, I don't remember much else about England thrashing Australia in their opening match. Given what had happened the winter before, I took this as read and so didn't commit it to memory as I would have done if I had known what the future held.

I do remember the final as I got to watch most of it. Boycott may have helped see off Australia and Pakistan, but going in against the West Indies with him as one of your front-line bowlers did seem, even at the time, a little optimistic. For a while we were on top and when Clive Lloyd was caught and bowled by Chris Old they were 99-4.

Unfortunately, unlike Sussex the year before, England couldn't get Richards out and he and Collis King, who never did anything so significant again, gobbled up our 'fifth bowler', Boycott, Gooch and Larkins, to the tune of combined figures of 12-0-86-0.

At the time staying at the YMCA might have been fun, but facing Holding, Roberts, Croft and Garner wasn't. Nowadays 286 in 50 overs would seem gettable target. Back then, even in 60, it looked far too many. The good news was that Brearley and Boycott put on 129 for the first wicket. The bad news was that they took 38 overs doing it. This left the rest to score 158 off 22 from four bowlers who had kept Malcolm Marshall out of the side. The last seven wickets fell for 11 and the West Indies won by 92 runs.

This didn't leave me with any kind of emotional void as I had fully expected us to get our arses kicked.

I then had about three weeks to wait until the subsequent Test series against India started on 12th July. On the previous day the perhaps not quite as aptly named as it might have been Sky-Lab proceeded vertically in a downward direction rather quicker and sooner than NASA had intended. Fortunately it missed Edgbaston. Unfortunately it also missed the army camp to which I knew I was heading for a whole week on the 14th, the prospect of which had dampened my enthusiasm for the start of the series.

You didn't have to go on the camp, unless you were an army cadet. Unfortunately, compulsory membership of a cadet force for two years was just the sort of character building behaviour my school believed would 'make a man of me'. Personally I would have much preferred it if Caroline had been given that particular task but sadly both she and the school authorities saw things differently. There was one alternative: a week's 'adventure training'. However, as the adventure in question was the *Poseidon Adventure* I chose the camp as the lesser of two big fat evils. To say I wasn't looking forward to going would be like saying the Shah didn't fancy Tehran for his holidays. I wasn't disappointed.

At least I had the pleasure of seeing David Gower score 200 not out on my birthday. However, when Randall was running out Gavaskar in India's first innings I was ankle-deep in mud being chased round a field and literally getting my arse kicked by a Regimental Sergeant Major who made Mossad look like the St John's Ambulance Brigade. While the teams were enjoying their rest day I was on an assault course hearing

'Follow me lads!' and an immediate loud splash as our platoon leader provided incontrovertible proof that even an idiot can fall off a log. This is particularly true when the log in question is four inches wide, 15 feet long, covered in moss and suspended above a pool of water that would have had Mother Teresa complaining about the stench.

Finally, as Botham and Hendrick were making the last six Indian wickets disappear for 26 runs in 10.1 overs, I was trying to do a vanishing act of my own to avoid the attentions of one character who appeared to be a direct descendant of Michael Palin's 'School Bully'. I can't remember many experiences I've resented having forced on me as much as that camp. I would have been even more annoyed if I had realised at the time that, while I was discovering at very close quarters just how green a Welsh valley could be, England were securing their only Test victory of the summer.

In contrast to the first Test, I saw the whole of the second, which ended up as a dull draw. Straight after this game the Indians were committed to a county match and so missed out on the unveiling, if that's the right word, of Brighton's new nudist beach. An enormous fuss was made about the opening of this facility at the time. As is usually the case in such circumstances, opinion was divided. Some felt that it demonstrated just what a shameless little hussy of a town I lived in and others felt it showed how grown up we all were. Then there were those who just went down there for an ogle. It was probably this last group who were most disappointed. I couldn't see what the attraction was. Having lived in Brighton all my life I knew what the beaches looked and more importantly, felt like. Some of those stones and shells were extremely sharp and anyone who chose to lie on a Brighton beach with no clothes on risked all sorts of intimate body piercings years before they became trendy. As for going down there and watching, not having confused naked with nubile I had better things to do.

Those better things included watching the third Test. Or so I thought. Unfortunately the nudist beach in December was busier than Headingley for the first three days of the match as it rained almost incessantly. The only thing that really happened was Botham smashing it all over the place on the fourth day. This innings earned him the man of the match award with Jim Laker describing it as 'one of the finest Test innings of the last 20 years'. So as far as Botham and Headingley were concerned, Laker didn't know that he hadn't seen anything yet.

The final Test was probably the best match I had watched to that point. If you were only ever going to play a single Test match this wouldn't have been a bad one to choose. Not that there was much choice about it for Mark Butcher's dad, Alan. I felt quite sorry for Butcher. After all he made 20 in the second innings, which I still thought was a reasonable score. Bo Derek only scored half that many and everyone was raving about her.

With wickets for Botham and Willis and a hundred from Boycott England set India 438 to win. As we had bowled them out for 202 in the first innings I was confident of sitting back and watching the inevitable easy victory. I was playing for my colts side on the fourth day and our manager, who later went on to coach at Sussex, said that Brearley had delayed his declaration far too long. Clearly there was a reason why he was a coach and Brearley was captain of England. India ended up nine runs short with two wickets left.

It was the first game I had seen where all four results were still possible going into the last over. I had read reports about 'the tied Test', a match that seemed to be spoken of in cricketing circles in much the same awestruck way as film buffs refer to *Citizen Kane*. I never thought I would have a chance of witnessing one.

On the final day, Gavaskar played an innings of 221 that was as near perfect as anything I have seen. For most of it I was cursing him but slowly it began to dawn on me that I was witnessing an effort that transcended my own partisan feelings. Here was a man playing at a level so high that he demanded your respect and, to some extent at least, your support, regardless of which team you followed. I can't say that I was willing him to get them home but I knew that, if he did, I wouldn't be wholly disappointed because in later years I would be able to say: 'I watched that you know'. This was a thought that would not have occurred to me even a year earlier.

Until 2005 it was never possible for me to make out a case that England were the best team in the world. However, at the end of 1979 you could at least have reasonably suggested they were the second best. They had beaten Pakistan and New Zealand the previous year, seen off Australia by a record margin in the winter and just beaten India. The West Indies were better but the only side in the world that could have given them a run for their money was banned from international competition. From a cricketing point of view I would have loved to have seen Lloyd's team play a South African side made up of Richards, Wessels, McEwan, Pollock, Barlow, P. Kirsten, Rice, Proctor, Jennings (the wicket-keeper and later batty national coach, rather than a moonlighting Northern Irish goalie), van der Bijl and Le Roux. Of course, the fact that this or a similar side would never have been allowed by their government to set foot onto the same pitch as the West Indies team, was why they were banned in the first place.

Before this year I had lived in a reassuringly simple world where the most difficult things I had to wrestle with were algebra and how to keep-wicket to my uncle's loopy leg breaks. Even the South African issue had seemed relatively simple to me: the regime was repressive so we didn't play with them. But then Caroline, Kerry Packer and the fall-out from the Soviet invasion of Afghanistan began to drag me to somewhere much more complicated. In short I was between the world of children and that of adults and, although there was only one way I could go, I was even more unenthusiastic about my destination than I was about Welsh army camps.

SIX

On 3rd October 1979, Devon played the South African Barbarians at rugby union. The match made the national news as a number of anti-apartheid demonstrators present were arrested. Devon's captain, John Lockyer, was quoted as saying: 'We're being criticised for playing against South Africa, yet nobody seems to condemn the staging of the Olympic Games in a repressive country like Russia.' At the time he didn't know what a good counter-point he had chosen. As part of the peace with Packer, England's cricketers, filling a gap in the schedules that might otherwise have been occupied by a tour to the Republic, were about embark on a hastily arranged three-Test visit to Australia. Before the second Test started in January, the Russians were in Afghanistan.

Despite the fact Devon's opponents were a multi-racial team, Peter Hain (yes, him again) was in no doubt that the sporting public were being 'hoodwinked' and that 'rugby in South Africa was still being organised on an openly racial basis with only a few black stooge players decorating international touring sides'. There were many in the international sporting community who agreed with him and the tour threatened Britain's participation in the Moscow Olympics the following summer. So much so that the Sports Council and the government called on the rugby Home Unions Committee to withdraw the 'Quaggas' invitation.

It's no great shock that the rugby union establishment's view of the Gleneagles Agreement was similar to that of their cricketing counterparts. What's more surprising is finding Mrs Thatcher effectively on Hain's side. This, after all, is a woman who said: 'The ANC is a typical terrorist organization...Anyone who thinks it is going to run the government in South Africa is living in cloud-cuckoo-land.' Throughout her premiership the 'leaderene', as Norman St John Stevas was to dub her, was obviously opposed to the sporting isolation of South Africa on the stated basis that it would have no effect.

However, just when it seemed British involvement in Moscow had survived the Home Unions Committee's refusal to back down, the Soviet invasion of Afghanistan prompted a new threat in the form of a Prime Minister who thought sporting boycotts did work on Russians.

Such a contradiction started to open the eyes of a 15-year-old whose understanding of the impact of politics on sport hadn't, until now, extended much further than 'we don't play South Africa at cricket because apartheid is bad'. It was this sporting controversy that made me realise you had to be careful not only about what you were being told, but also who was telling you. More than this, what wasn't said was sometimes more important than what was. In 1979, Geoff Boycott finished with a batting average of 102.53. This was the best for an English first-class season since 1953, when the Australian Bill Johnston managed 102.00. Leave it there and you might think Boycott and Johnston were equally remarkable batsmen. However, Boycott scored 1,538 runs and produced his average with the benefit of five not outs from 20 innings, while Johnston made 102 from 17 with 16 not outs.

Mrs Thatcher may have thought the British team should pull out of the Olympics, but maybe I didn't have to agree.

I wanted our team to go. I confess this was mainly because Steve Ovett used to run past my house every day and I wanted him to win a gold medal so I could have the pathetic vicarious fame that went with being able to say: 'That Steve Ovett, he runs past my house every day you know.'

On one occasion when I failed to apply the Green Cross man's advice on the pavement outside my house, Ovett nearly ran straight into me. That was the nearest I ever got to meeting him. I loathed his arch rival, Sebastian Coe, but he was the one I ended up sitting opposite at breakfast in a greasy spoon on the Ebury Road in London 21 years later.

The argument about the Olympics wasn't the only way in which politics began to invade my sporting world. Mike Brearley, either wanting to get into Australia incognito or believing more hair would give him Samson-like extra strength, had grown an improbably bushy beard. Alternatively, on what was to be his last tour, perhaps he was just moving into his version of John Lennon's hippy phase towards the end of his career. The Aussie press and public seized (metaphorically) on the beard and instantly nicknamed him 'the Ayatollah'. This was quite an insult as the real Ayatollah Khomeni was the West's major hate figure of the time. Today he would have been called 'Osama'.

As the real Iranian leader was being bombed by the West's ally, Iraq (led by their unknown President Saddam Hussein), so Brearley was subjected to a concerted campaign of abuse wherever he went. This included accusations of being gay because his short-sleeved jumper was long enough to cover his backside. In Melbourne the crowd were so abusive that the national team's manager, John Edwards, said their behaviour made him ashamed to be Australian. It must have been bad.

England had resisted a number of Packer innovations that the Australian authorities had proposed to introduce for this tour. These included coloured clothing, white balls during the day and fielding circles. England's refusal to accept the last of these led to Brearley becoming even more unpopular.

This Aussie winter featured a program of international cricket the like of which had never been seen before Down Under. For a start there were two teams touring at the same time. The Australians played alternate Tests against England and the West Indies rather than two three-match series one after the other. A triangular one-day international tournament featuring batsmen in white with coloured pads and gloves, was slotted in between the five-day games. In one of these England beat the West Indies by two runs. With his opponents needing three from the final ball and the last pair at the crease, Brearley ordered his wicket-keeper, David Bairstow, to take off his gloves and field on the boundary directly behind the stumps to avoid any chance of a fine edge for four. Although this was perfectly within the rules, the crowd reacted as if Brearley had just announced he was Douglas Jardine's long-lost illegitimate grandson. As far as they were concerned this was just another example, like employing six fielders on the leg side to an off-spinner on a turning pitch, of the unfair way the English played the game. As an underhand tactic, Brearley's actions hardly rated as highly as telling your brother to roll the ball along the ground to stop opposition's last man hitting a six, as Australia's captain Greg Chappell did 14 months later, but it still hastened the introduction of fielding circles in all one-day internationals and left the England captain third in the contest to be 'the man most often called a bastard Down Under'. At an Ashes reunion dinner in the 1950s, Australia's cricket-loving prime minister, Robert Menzies, speculated that he must be the man whose parentage had been questioned the most in the history of his country. A reporter at the back of the room put down his notebook and raised his hand: 'Surely Sir, I still hold that honour?' The journalist was Jardine.

Brearley may have triggered a change in the regulations governing one-day internationals, but it was an Australian whose actions caused a change in the laws of the game.

By now helmets seemed normal. However, on the first day of the Test series, a batsman being hit on the head wasn't the only thing going 'clang'. Dennis Lillee was involved in the manufacture of an aluminium bat. In another sign of increasing commercialisation, the fast bowler chose the opening day of a Test match to maximize the product's exposure in the pre-Christmas market. Put another way, he used a metal bat. Brearley quickly objected, claiming it was damaging the ball. The umpires asked Lillee to change his bat and he refused, causing a ten-minute delay that ended with Greg Chappell having to come out onto the field to persuade him to swap it for a wooden one. A furious Lillee relented but not before he had demonstrated clear dissent, both to the umpires and his captain, by hurling it several yards across the outfield. Shortly afterwards, Law Six was amended to add a requirement that the blade of the bat must be made of wood.

All of this was being reported by *The Times*, which, after a more than year-long dispute over manning levels and new technology, went back into circulation on the second day of England's opening tour match against Queensland. John Woodcock's reaction to Lillee's antics was as predictable as his opinion on Greig's involvement with Packer. He referred to a meeting between the umpires and 'Mr (if you please) Lillee' and called him a mixture of 'great bowler' and 'recalcitrant child'. Clearly David Frith's description of the fast bowler as a 'highly-strung gentleman' was an assessment Mr (no doubting his credentials) Woodcock would have only half agreed with.

Frith's comments on Lillee appeared not in *The Times,* but rather an editorial for *Wisden Cricket Monthly* on declining standards of player behaviour. His concern was that the Australian Board's decision to give their leading fast bowler what amounted to no more than a slap on the wrist for his outburst would lead young cricket fans to the conclusion that the 'Lillee spectacle… was all an acceptable part of the showbiz into which cricket is being transformed'. While the crack about 'showbiz' shows what Frith thinks about mere entertainment, it's the wider question about Australian attitudes to authority that's interesting here.

The Aussies were clearly more forgiving of their cricketing heroes than we were. The English touring party contained only one former Packer player, Derek Underwood. On the other hand, over half the Australian team for the first Test against England had spent the previous winter playing World Series Cricket. When Bob Woolmer and Alan Knott were selected at the start of the series with West Indies the following summer, *Wisden* couldn't resist describing them as returning to the team 'for the first time since they rejected their country in 1977'.

When David Hookes was asked why he hadn't gone into cricket administration after his playing career he replied: 'Because I haven't got a blue blazer and I don't have dandruff.' For the English, a lack of respect for authority was a crime difficult to forgive and forget. For the Australians, it was healthy.

Such an attitude allowed the Australians to more easily accommodate talented but what the English, with a traditional mistrust of passion, might have termed 'difficult' individuals into their team. Between his debut in 1952 and his final match in 1965, Fred Trueman featured in only 67 of the 120 Tests England played in that period. If you believed Trueman himself, he was hardly ever injured and he certainly wasn't left out of Hutton's touring party to Australia in 1954-55 or May's to South Africa in 1956-57 on fitness grounds. When he was finally picked to go to Australia in 1958-59, the manager Freddie Brown's first words to him at the gangplank were: 'Any trouble from you, Trueman, and you'll be on the next boat home.' If Freddie Trueman had maintained his strike rate over those 120 Tests he would have ended up with 550 wickets.

While it's true Dennis Lillee played in only 70 of a possible 117 Tests between his debut and retirement, almost all of those he missed (39 out of 47) were attributable to either the major back injury he suffered in the mid-70s or his association with Packer. If he had been English I doubt if he would have made it to 50 caps. Ray Illingworth's successful handling of Geoff Boycott and John Snow on the 1970-71 Ashes tour had demonstrated the benefits of accommodating talented, if temperamentally challenging, men into the team. But, as Gooch's treatment of Gower or Stewart's of Caddick illustrates, this was a lesson England failed to learn. As with knee-jerk responses to the selection suggestions of the press, this wasn't the only mistake the English repeated on a regular basis.

In the opening tour match of the 1979-80 winter, Derek Randall made 97 going in first and in so doing convinced the selectors he was an opener. As Boycott's partner for the first Test he made 0 and 1. The England selectors did the same thing to Mark Ramprakash 20 years later with almost identical results.

England went down 3-0 in the Tests. If we had won the third at Melbourne it might have been possible to argue we only lost because Greg Chappell won the toss at Sydney and put us in on a wet pitch. Instead, we lost a game that featured two of the recurring themes of the following 20 years; the inexplicable middle-order collapse after a good start on a blameless batting pitch and the inability to bowl the opposition out for a manageable score in the same conditions. On a surface on which Brearley made 60 not out, 170-1 became 306 all out and the Aussies made 477. Even Botham's first Ashes century couldn't save us from there. It was the only time England lost when Botham made a hundred.

As England struggled in Australia and then moved on to a one-off Test in India, the Olympic argument continued to rumble. The government sent what Sir Dennis Fellows, the Chairman of the British Olympic Committee, described as 'a rather heavy letter'. I don't think he meant it was very long. The letter made no difference, the government's wishes were ignored and Fellows confirmed Britain's participation in the Olympics because he believed 'sport should be a bridge not a destroyer'.

As a result, Steve Ovett and Sebastian Coe provided two of the enduring sporting images of the year. Ovett wrote 'I L Y' in the air to his girlfriend after his win in the 800 metres and Coe showed every vein in his neck as he breasted the tape with his arms outstretched in the 1500. Despite his defiance of Mrs Thatcher's wishes, Coe later became a Conservative MP. As for Steve Ovett, he used to run past my house every day you know.

Ironically, at almost the same time, black majority rule was coming to one part of southern Africa where sanctions had been imposed. Following his return home in January, Robert Mugabe had now been elected president of his newly-named country promising to 'bring about a government reassuring to all people of Zimbabwe'. As far as Mugabe was concerned, cricket was a vital part of this process. 'Cricket civilizes people and creates good gentlemen. I want everyone to play cricket in Zimbabwe; I want ours to be a nation of gentlemen.'

So, while one sporting boycott controversy was being resolved, the seeds of another were being sown.

I was glad we were going to the Olympics. The possibility of British success, increased by the absence of the United States, offered the chance of an enjoyable distraction from the prospect of my O levels. It didn't seem very likely the England cricket team would provide me with much to enjoy.

In 1980 the West Indies were touring and, like a Sloane Ranger flicking her hand dismissively at last year's jacket, they had decided Wayne Daniel was 'just too 1976'. This was bad news for Sussex.

Playing for Middlesex that year, Daniel featured in what I still think was one of the dimmest pieces of cricket I've ever seen. The fast bowler himself wasn't responsible, but rather a man who later captained his country to a famous World Cup victory, Imran Khan.

Sussex played Middlesex in the Gillette Cup semi-final at Hove. The game was rain-affected and went into the reserve day. Conditions were cloudy throughout and the pitch was obviously fast and juiced-up. Middlesex batted first and ended their innings on the second day. Just before this happened, Imran's brain departed for a short comfort break round the back of the deckchairs. When it came back all hell was about to break loose. I may never have captained Pakistan but I know hurling bouncers at one of the fastest bowlers in the world just before he's going to get use of a quick, seaming pitch might not be tactically astute. Bear in mind: Daniel had already broken Imran's team-mate Kepler Wessels' wrist in the Benson and Hedges Cup quarter-final earlier in the season and, in a championship match with Yorkshire, hit John Hampshire in the chest so hard that the seam and ball-maker's name were clearly visible on his shirt. Nevertheless, Imran gave the idea of bouncing Daniel a resounding thumbs up. At one point he even knocked his helmet off. In Wayne's world this was a bad thing and when Sussex came to bat it was neither 'party time' or 'excellent'.

John Barclay failed to survive the first over. John Spencer later told me his captain returned to the dressing room wondering mildly how one played a delivery that jagged back a foot going at 90 miles an hour. Daniel bowling down the slope that day was one of the most frightening things I've ever seen, and I was 100 yards away. He finished with figures of 10-2-15-6. The only man who seemed to be able to handle him was Colin Wells. Guess who ran him out? Went to Oxford did Imran Khan.

What Daniel produced that day was a great performance. Realising both he and the equally terrifying Sylvester Clarke were surplus to the West Indies' requirements made me realise that one measure of a great side was the quality of those it could afford to leave out.

Given that the four main fast bowlers picked for the tour were Roberts, Holding, Croft and Garner it was hard to argue with Daniel and Clarke's omissions. You could have made a case for one of them getting the fifth spot that actually went to the promising 22-year-old with only three wickets in as many Tests to his name. But then the young man in question was Malcolm Marshall.

Along with Bradman's 1948 'Invincibles' and the modern Australian side containing Shane Warne and Glenn McGrath, the team Marshall was about to enhance is generally regarded as one of the three greatest ever to have played the game. Apart from the bowling attack, the 1980s West Indians had one of the best ever opening pairs in Greenidge and Haynes and the man rated as the Bradman of his generation, Viv Richards.

Unlike, for example, Flintoff now, Richards didn't make a statement to the fielding side by marching out to bat practically before the last wicket had fallen, he swaggered in at his own pace with all the arrogance of the golfer Walter Hagan waggling his driver on the first tee and wondering, 'Ok, who's gonna come second.' Just as Alfred Hitchcock, who died in this year, deserves the term in his field so to me Richards is the only 'great' batsman of his time. Of the others I've seen, only Tendulkar and Lara come close. I have to discount Graeme Pollock and Barry Richards, as I never saw them bat in a Test match.

I've yet to hear a cricket follower deny Viv Richards was a great batsman. But why does he deserve such a title when others, like Ponting and Kallis, with significantly superior records, aren't regarded with quite the same awe? It can't just be to do with different eras, conditions and opponents. Tendulkar is generally seen as the 'great' of modern Indian cricket but his team-mate Rahul Dravid has for long periods had a better average.

As Steve Daley had proved the previous autumn, greatness is something that goes beyond mere figures. In September 1979, Wolverhampton Wanderers financed the £1.47m signing of Andy Gray from Manchester City by sending Daley in the opposite direction for the same fee. This may have made the midfielder the joint most expensive player in English football but it didn't qualify him for any superlatives. Unless that is, you mean the 'Biggest waste of money in footballing history'. Within 20 months of his arrival, City sold Daley on to Seattle Sounders for £300,000. It was this that led Nick Leeson, writing as a guest columnist for the Observer in 2001, to award him his unwanted title, prompting the succinct and wholly accurate reply from Daley of: 'At least I got away with it. Unlike that twat.'

Leeson, a 'twat' to whom we shall return, was of course responsible for what was until recently the biggest investment fraud in history. Proof, if it were needed, that being the biggest or the best at something doesn't make you great. Larry Hagman was, at the time, playing the biggest bastard on television, J R Ewing, and then there was the man (French from memory) who held the record for being able to get his pants on and off most times in a minute. The latter had appeared on *Record Breakers* in what looked like a pair of Speedos to have a crack at breaking his own record live on British television. 'Ah yes Monsieur Ewing, you may be the richest oilman in Texas but I can get my underwear on and off quicker than anyone else in the world.'

England's cricket team had two men vying for a similarly pointless record, that of 'world's best blocker'. Previously, Boycott had been unchallenged, but now he had almost literally stiff competition.

Chris Tavare was 25, but his impressively droopy moustache made him look older and gave him the sort of hangdog expression that suggested he was enjoying his cricket about as much as Marvin the paranoid android had enjoyed the last ten million years. He had an extraordinary grip, with his top hand right round the back of the handle. This enabled him to lift the bat above face height, useful against the West Indies, but restricted his stroke-play to the extent he quickly developed the reputation of being like Boycott but without the sense of danger. Tavare made his debut for England in this year and, in an incredibly accurate reflection of what was to come, managed to stretch his maiden one-day international innings over two days.

When Tavare batted he often appeared to be doing an impersonation of one of those 'street artists' who busk by standing completely still for hours on end. On the first morning of the Lord's Test he came in at number three after 26 minutes play. By tea he had made 27 and was in danger of being arrested for wasting bowlers' time. His final score of 42 came from 202 balls. On the second day, Viv Richards made 103 more from 43 fewer deliveries.

However, Richards' greatness obviously stretches far beyond the fact he could score quicker than Chris Tavare. Greg Chappell, Sunil Gavaskar and Javed Miandad, the other batting giants of the time, might have had better records on paper, but even in this company, and despite what the statistics said, Richards stood out. Perhaps this is in part because he was capable of playing, as Neville Cardus said of Archie Jackson, 'strokes that none but the elect can ever hope to perform'. Jim Cumbes, the former Worcestershire seamer, reckoned the best ball he ever bowled in first-class cricket was whipped over mid-wicket for six by Richards. However, this isn't enough on its own. Kevin Pietersen invites comparisons with Richards because of his similar ability to take good-length balls on or outside off-stump through the leg side, but he is not yet a 'great' player.

'Greatness' is, to some extent, an accident of birth or, in the case of the tragic Jackson, death. Leaving aside the massive potential for mismanagement of talent by this country's cricketing authorities, had Daniel and Clarke been born English they might have become one of the best new-ball partnerships we ever had. Similarly, England's 1980 candidate to 'fight fire with fire', Graham Dilley, had genuine pace and the ability to swing it away late from the right-hander, but his body never seemed to let him last a series. Had he played in the era of more sympathetic treatment and central contracts, he might have destroyed West Indies in the manner of Steve Harmison. However, just as Joe Corrigan was unfortunate enough to be born at around the same time as Peter Shilton and Ray Clemence, so it was Dilley's fate to be born in 1959 instead of 1978.

Archie Jackson was deprived of greatness for the opposite reason. A contemporary of Bradman and seen by many at the time as the better player, he made his debut against England in February 1929 at the age of 19. Opening, with Bradman down at number six, Jackson saw his first three partners disappear in no time to leave his side 19-3 in reply to England's 334. Completely unfazed by the situation, he glided to an apparently effortless 70 not out by the close, against an attack that included Harold Larwood and Maurice Tate. England's captain, Percy Chapman, felt his team hadn't been savaged; rather they had been picked apart by a master fencer. The next day, 97 not out when Chapman took the second new ball, Jackson made 67 runs in 70 minutes after lunch before finally falling for 164. The tragedy lies in the fact that this was his only Test hundred. By the time he played this innings he was probably already infected with tuberculosis and in fact it had been anything but effortless. When he came back to the dressing room at the end of the second day he was limp and his team-mate, 'Stork' Hendry, describes how 'they had to mop him with cold towels'. His strength was being taken from him and within two years his Test career was over. Archie Jackson died on 16th February 1933, the final day of the fourth Test of the 'Bodyline' tour; he was 23.

It's almost certain that Jackson wouldn't even have approached matching Bradman, who could? Chapman's description of his rapier-like stroke-play suggests more brilliance and less relentlessness. But, as with Duncan Edwards' in the Munich air crash, it's the death that makes the legend. Edwards was just 21 when he died and had played for England only 18 times. Yet Tommy Docherty thought: 'You could keep all your Bests, Peles and Maradonas, Duncan Edwards was the greatest of them all.' The likes of Archie Jackson and Duncan Edwards never lose form, never have the opportunity to do anything but promise greatness. Perhaps closer to the truth than Docherty was Frank Taylor, the only pressman to survive the Munich crash: 'So long Dunc! It was great while it lasted.'

Alongside Taylor on the plane was arguably the greatest football writer of his generation, the Guardian's Don Davies. By rights Davies shouldn't even have been there, only being called in to cover the game in Belgrade when his number two couldn't go at the last minute. Such an apparently insignificant switch cost football a great writer and spared cricket a great radio commentator. Don Davies' number two was John Arlott.

'That's the end of the over at 69 for 2 and after Trevor Bailey it'll be Christopher Martin-Jenkins.' Those are the last words of commentary spoken by John Arlott. They came on the final day of the sixth Test of that summer, England's Centenary match against Australia. To me Arlott was as great a commentator as Richards was a batsman. In the same way as nobody but Richards could even conceive, let alone execute, some of his shots, who else but Arlott could have seen 'Groucho Marx pursuing a pretty waitress' in Asif Masood's bent-kneed approach to the wicket or a 'not nearly so tolerant' Lord Longford in Vincent Van der Bijl.

John Arlott was the voice of the end my childhood, keeping me company not only through Tests but also innumerable Sunday afternoons watching John Player League games on BBC2. Perhaps the best way to sum up my feelings is: I missed him when he was gone.

But not everyone shared my high opinion. Don Davies' widow could never bring herself to talk to him and the death of his own son left him with none of the schoolboy light-heartedness that allowed his contemporary, Brian Johnston, to delight in a scorecard reading 'Lillee caught Willey bowled Dilley'. I may have preferred Arlott's wit to

Johnston's joke telling, but a friend confronted with my assessment of the 'Basingstoke Boy' as a great commentator offered: 'Yes, and then there are those of us who thought he was a pompous old windbag.'

The fact that my friend doesn't accept my opinion of Arlott means that 'greatness' is even more difficult to define than you might think. Certainly it goes beyond achieving records or even the manner of achieving them. In the previous winter's Jubilee Test in India, Bob Taylor broke the record for most wicket-keeping dismissals in a match by taking ten catches. If Taylor always seemed the epitome of dapper efficiency, the same could not be said of the man whose record he broke. Tubby, balding, not very agile and with a stance described by Ray Robinson as like 'a boy scout grilling a chop at a barbecue', Gil Langley, the Australian 'keeper who made nine dismissals at Lord's in 1956, was anything but dapper. However, it's results that count, not how smart you look. A point amply illustrated by the fact that the man who broke Taylor's record was Jack Russell. This is probably why Ricky Ponting isn't bracketed with Viv Richards.

Recently, Ponting has invited comparisons with Bradman. Certainly he executes conventional cricket shots brilliantly, possibly better and certainly at least as well as any batsman in the world. At his best he is the most complete coaching-book-pure batsman I've ever seen. Yet if you asked cricket followers outside Australia whether he deserves to be ranked alongside Richards I bet the majority would say 'No'. When he is out of form, Ponting is vulnerable to being lbw early in his innings because he falls over slightly to the off side. I don't ever remember Viv Richards being described as 'out of form'. The Australian captain's strength lies in the purity of his technique and his relentlessness. In these respects even he can't hope to compete with Bradman. What he lacks by comparison with Richards is the ability to play a shot beyond the conception of normal batsmen.

Not that Richards or his team lacked relentlessness. 'King Viv's' 291 at the Oval in 1976 was one of the best examples of grinding an opponent into the dust as you'll ever see. As for the rest of the team, the end of my exams and a cricket-loving biology teacher willing to make inappropriate use of the science department television gave me regular opportunities to see how remorseless they could be.

The television was meant to be used for showing childbirth videos which, judging by the fact that one lad in our class fainted, weren't for the squeamish. The same could be said for watching England bat. The top order usually disappeared quicker than you could say 'placenta' and the rest were hunted down with a persistence matched only by the Space Invaders on my mate's Atari.

These were the days before there was any minimum number of overs to be bowled in a day and the West Indies habitually sent down about 12 an hour. This allowed Clive Lloyd to rotate his four quick bowlers, keeping them fresh by using a pattern that meant any one of them didn't have to bowl many more than six overs in any two-hour period. From a batsman's point of view, an even share of the strike meant, on average, you would face 36 balls in an hour, a maximum 50 per cent of which would land in your half of the pitch.

Captaining, or not captaining, against such a side can have a dramatic effect on your reputation.

Mike Brearley had announced he didn't want to tour anymore. While this news was hardly as explosive as the ending of the Iranian embassy siege or even Trevor Brooking winning the FA Cup final for West Ham with a header, it made life difficult for the England selectors. Faced with playing the most daunting team in world cricket, they plumped for the 'great man of history' approach and gave their best player, Botham, the added responsibility of captaincy at the age of 24. Botham's tenure as captain is another example of how bare facts can perhaps conceal the true picture.

In purely statistical terms Botham's record as captain reads played 12, won 0, drawn 8 and lost 4. He only made one half-century, 57 in his first innings in charge. On the face of it this isn't very impressive. However, nine of those matches were against the West Indies (the other three against Australia), he managed six draws and one of the defeats was by only two wickets. This may be slightly misleading as the summer of 1980 was wetter than Bobby Ewing, but David Gower captained England against the men from the Caribbean ten times and lost the lot. Mike Brearley never led England in a Test against the West Indies.

On the final morning of the first Test at Nottingham, David Gower dropped a skyer from Andy Roberts. Had the catch been held the tourists would still have needed 13 for victory with only two wickets left. With Willis performing a passable trailer for his efforts at Headingley the following year, it's not too fanciful to suggest England would have been narrow favourites. The moment that Gower let the win slip, literally, through his fingers was the difference between victory and defeat in the series. The dampness of the summer ensured Lloyd's men won 1-0. The two-wicket defeat at Trent Bridge was the closest England got to winning a Test against West Indies for the whole of the 1980s.

England weren't alone in this respect. The West Indies steamrollered everyone. Yet even this team has its detractors. Their unsubtle method of wearing down the opposition and the fact that throughout their period of domination they never – with apologies to Roger Harper – fielded or, they would say, needed to field, a top-class spinner, means that some commentators believe Bradman's side and the modern Australians have better claims to greatness.

But if Lloyd's men weren't great how do you decide who is? Perhaps the answer lies with Bishen Bedi?

Commenting on modern spinners, the Indian left-armer offered this: 'The game's leading wicket-taker is one of the great masters in Shane Warne, and hard on his heels is a burglar, a thief.' It's not the scathing dismissal of Muttiah Muralitharan that's the point, but rather the mention of Warne. When *Wisden* came to choose its five cricketers of the twentieth century its 100-strong electorate of cricketing notables came up with Bradman, Sobers, Hobbs, Warne and Viv Richards. Nobody could seriously argue that any of them didn't deserve be called 'great'.

The answer then lies in the assumption that underpinned the question. No-one has ever denied to me that Richards was a great batsman because to do so would be as ridiculous as trying to deny that Coe, briefly the world record holder at four different distances – 800 metres, 1000 metres, 1500 metres and the mile since you ask – was a great middle-distance runner. That is the difference between greatness and mere high excellence. There is no room for debate. The truly great are those who don't divide opinion. Which is why Dickie Bird wasn't a great umpire.

The final match of the 1980 international summer was the Centenary Test between England and Australia. This was meant to be the high point of the season, a celebration of 100 years of Anglo-Australian cricketing rivalry in this country.

Unfortunately, appalling weather intervened again. Fifty minutes were lost to rain on the first day and all but an hour and a quarter on the second. When it rained again on Saturday morning, a soft area by the Tavern delayed the start. The umpires, rain-magnet Bird and David Constant, apparently oblivious to 20,000 increasingly angry spectators, the opinion of the ground staff and the fact this was a special occasion demanding some flexibility, carried out inspection after inspection to no apparent purpose. Finally, frustration boiled over as the umpires and captains returned to the pavilion after yet another look. MCC members involved themselves in an angry scuffle with Constant, who was grabbed by the tie on his way up the pavilion steps. *Wisden* noted with characteristic understatement that Botham and Chappell 'saw to it that matters got no worse'.

Despite the best efforts of God and Harold Bird there nevertheless seemed to be the prospect of an exciting finish. England were set 370 in 350 minutes. In the equivalent Australian fixture three years earlier, Greig's men had made a glorious stab at 463 for victory and ended up losing by only 45 runs. I was so convinced the present side would at least try to do something similar that I passed up the chance of spending the day with a teenage language student whose Swedish charms were obvious and not particularly well hidden. What I anticipated was Gooch, Gower, Botham and Gatting leading a charge at Greg Chappell's target. What I got was Geoff Boycott blocking the hell out of it for 316 minutes. Botham never even emerged from the pavilion.

'Yeah, thanks for that lads. That was…great.'

SEVEN

The end of the international cricket season of 1980 had left me feeling disillusioned and a bit depressed. Of course, being 16, that was exactly what I was supposed to be. I did my best to live up to what was expected and affected the obligatory 'everything's so pointless and boring' cool that went with listening to Joy Division/immediately post-Ian Curtis New Order. The fact Curtis had killed himself only made it cooler to listen to them. I imagined I would appear to be sensitive, deep and interesting and therefore a magnet for girls. In this respect, for 'disillusioned' you should read 'delusional'. In fact, what I appeared was pale, spotty and terminally dull. Can you imagine anything less attractive to a 16-year-old girl than a cricket-loving Joy Division fan? Taking this approach I had about as much chance with girls as *Blankety-Blank* contestants had of winning a worthwhile prize.

The irony is that, to a large extent, it was all an act. I was a depressive whose heart wasn't in it. I had a weakness for pappy pop music that I retain to this day. However, I wasn't any more likely to admit this openly than Elvis Costello was to go public with the fact he sang backing vocals on the R White's lemonade advert. Adam Ant may have thought ridicule was nothing to be scared of but he didn't go to my school.

Even if I was happier than I tried to appear, there wasn't a great deal that autumn and winter that would have forced me to show my true colours. Ronald Reagan was elected President of the US and if the *Not the Nine O'Clock News* team were to be believed we would all have been safer if the finger on the button had been that of his ape co-star in BBC2's alternative to the cricket on the Saturday of the 1981 Headingley Test, *Bedtime for Bonzo*. John Lennon was shot dead at the same time as Sheena Easton was embarking on a career that saw her win a Grammy

(Best Newcomer in 1981). On a personal level, I had again taken the 'sign up for the school play' approach to pursuing girls. The play itself, *The Cherry Orchard*, was hardly designed to make you look on the bright side of life. But my ham-fisted and blatantly transparent attempts to 'accidentally' bump into the new object of my affections, in a series of ludicrously improbable circumstances, resulted in crushing humiliation of a level I can still feel welling up at 25 years distance.

England's winter tour didn't promise anything better. A visit to the Caribbean meant that I had a long wait until after Christmas for things to get going. Even once they did, the prospect of the West Indian bowlers on their faster pitches meant the Test series promised to be the sort of X-rated affair I was going to have to watch from between my fingers.

Even before the tour started it promised to be controversial. The selectors had included Roland Butcher in the party. Butcher had made his England debut in the second one-day international against Australia the previous summer. He hit a sparkling 52 out of a total of 320-8, a score that will now almost certainly remain England's highest in a 55-over international for all eternity. Despite the fact that Bill Athey had then been preferred for the Centenary Test, the potential controversy wasn't in Butcher's selection for the tour ahead of the Yorkshireman. Rather, it was the fact we were visiting the West Indies and Roland Butcher was the first black African-Caribbean to represent England at cricket.

When the Cape Coloured Basil D'Oliveira toured the West Indies with Colin Cowdrey's side in 1967-68 he was subjected to taunts of 'traitor'. It was feared that England's newest middle-order recruit would receive a similarly hot reception.

Unlike Viv Anderson (Nottingham) and Laurie Cunningham (London) who had already turned out for the national football team, Butcher wasn't born in England. He spent the first 14 years of his life in the district of St Philip on the eastern tip of Barbados and his cousin Basil played 44 times for the West Indies. Although by 1980 he had been resident here for 13 years (considerably longer than Kevin Pietersen had before his debut), the decision to play for England was still 'not an easy one to make'. Butcher's reasons for opting to throw in his lot with England make interesting reading:

'What finally made up my mind was the thought of my son, whose future is in this country. You have got to face the fact that the prospects for many black youngsters here are not very bright. They feel it especially with the present unemployment situation. They feel they have not got much of a chance, very little to look forward to. A feeling that all is lost.

But for cricket, I suppose I might have been like that. I thought if I could show them that it is possible for a black person to make it, get to the top, it might give all those youngsters some encouragement, show them that they could make it as well, as long as they tried. If they could prove themselves good enough, they could get to the top. I wanted to show my son.'

Roland Butcher said that more than a quarter of a century ago. Has anything really changed? In the 30 years that have elapsed since Butcher was first selected, only 13 other black African-Caribbean cricketers have followed him into the England Test team. Of those, just four, Phil DeFreitas, Chris Lewis, Devon Malcolm and Mark Butcher, have more than 20 caps. Only the Surrey left-hander can boast more than 50.

One of the many criticisms that have been levelled at English county cricket over the years is that it's acted as a finishing school for overseas professionals. It's funny how no one ever seemed to make the same claims about our players. As far as English cricketers were concerned, the county game apparently left them hopelessly unprepared for what was needed at international level. In 1981, ten counties had at least one West Indian on their books and Hampshire, Lancashire and Somerset had two. Bear in mind that's ten out of a possible 16, as Durham did not yet have first-class status and Yorkshire still adopted a policy of only picking those born within the county's boundaries. Of the 13 Caribbean professionals on show that year only Clive Lloyd, Viv Richards and Gordon Greenidge weren't fast bowlers. The idea that African-Caribbeans had natural physical advantages when it came to bowling fast was generally accepted. No one could see an end to the West Indies' dominance of world cricket because it was assumed that simple genetics would ensure succeeding generations of immensely quick bowlers would emerge from the Caribbean. This was a trap that both the English and West Indian cricket authorities fell into.

From England's perspective such thinking was typical of a defeatist and excuse-making culture. 'Defeatist' because 'What chance have we got against this lot? You can't fight nature' and 'excuse-making' because 'the problem is all these foreigners coming over here nicking our jobs and improving themselves into the bargain'. The defeatism overlooks the pride and professionalism the West Indian team of the 1980s brought to their cricket. The dominance of Clive Lloyd and Viv Richards' sides wasn't an act of God. The excuse-making ignores the fact that facing Wayne Daniel and Sylvester Clarke on a regular basis made coming up against the West Indies a bit less of a culture shock than if the fastest bowler you had ever seen was Chris Old. Even if nature had given the men from the Caribbean a head start, surely it could have occurred to someone to try and tap into the 'physical advantages' present in England's own Caribbean community. That no one did is another reason for England's years of cricketing underachievement.

This failure to engage properly with Britain's African-Caribbean community isn't an exclusively cricketing one. The picture Roland Butcher painted was accurate and the Brixton riots and the murder of Stephen Lawrence still lay ahead. However, Butcher still saw the game's potential to challenge prevailing attitudes rather than reflect them. Sadly neither his own career nor those of the men who followed him had his desired effect.

Roland Butcher played three Tests, all of them on this tour. Once he returned to England he never even made the one-day side again. That didn't happen to him because he was black. England's selectors were crap to whole generations of young batsmen. Rob Bailey and Matthew Maynard, both jettisoned after unsuccessful tours to the Caribbean, spring instantly to mind. Glamorgan and Northamptonshire supporters would tell you that Maynard and Bailey simply played for the 'wrong' counties. However, the benefits that might have accrued to England had Butcher been given as many chances as his soon-to-be county captain, Mike Gatting, could have extended beyond the development of a single dashing middle-order batsman. Unfortunately, it took until 1997 for Mark Alleyne to be made the first home-grown black county captain, by which time the far greater financial rewards available to talented sportsmen from a resurgent football were all too obvious. As Warwickshire's 'keeper, Keith Piper, put it: 'To play cricket you've got to really love the game. With football you can think "I can make a million even if I don't love it".' Talented young black sportsmen, in the words of Mark Alleyne, 'work out the sums'.

In the 1980s, football had a serious problem with organised hooliganism, which was, in a lot of cases, not unconnected to extreme right-wing politics. Within the game many managers didn't want black players. Even where they were accepted, for example ironically under

Ron Atkinson at West Bromwich Albion, proud, professional sportsmen like Brendon Batson, Laurie Cunningham and Cyrille Regis, had to put up with being known collectively as the 'Three Degrees'. This may have been a harmless enough nickname in itself, but was illustrative of the fact that the black players were identified as a separate sub-set within the team. Rugby Union was an amateur game for public school boys and Rugby League's base was restricted to the north of England where hardly any of the black population lived. If ever there was a time for cricket to attract talented young black sportsmen this was it.

To steal a march on other major sports, cricket had to fight its own history. Perhaps it's little wonder that a game still run by an all-male private members club failed to even recognise, let alone deal with, how it was perceived by a potentially vital section of the community. Those running cricket at the time did nothing pro-active to break down the game's imperialist image to make it more appealing as a potential career for the talented sportsmen of the country's minorities. Athletics, admittedly unburdened with the same imperialist baggage, did a far better job, and a generation of talented black British athletes brought a period of unprecedented success in the late 1980s and early 1990s. Cricket did no better than football. At Middlesex, Roland Butcher, Wayne Daniel, Norman Cowans, Wilf Slack and Neil Williams were known as 'The Jackson Five'. Even as late as 2004, Brian Lara was still saying how much it meant to beat the 'colonial masters'. This is an important perception when you consider that, of the African-Caribbeans who have played Test cricket for England, two thirds were born in the West Indies.

It's in this last respect that the decline of the game in the Caribbean may be a bad thing for English cricket. As the West Indies handed out thumping after thumping throughout the 1980s, English cricket fans would have given a great deal to see something undermine their dominance. What neither English supporters nor those running West Indian cricket saw coming was the spreading influence of American culture brought about by the development of satellite television and the Internet. In the Caribbean this has seen a steady ebbing away of interest in cricket among young sportsmen in favour of basketball, a sport whose top-class professionals are 85 per cent black. When you consider that of black English Test cricketers only Mark Butcher, David Lawrence, Dean Headley, Alex Tudor and Michael Carberry were born here, a drop-off in interest in the sport in the West Indies is not just going to have a detrimental effect on the pool of talent available there.

Although American culture hardly lacks influence in this country, by far the greater problem in attracting young black British sportsmen to cricket is the money now available in football. In 1993, the Commission for Racial Equality launched the 'Kick Racism out of Football' campaign. The way this was received showed that, in general terms, the sport was serious about accepting both that it had a problem and about dealing with it. By 2004, the Daily Mirror was publishing figures that showed 27 per cent of Premiership footballers were black. In the spring of the same year, *The Cricketers' Who's Who* indicated there were 18 Caribbean-origin cricketers in the first-class game eligible to play for England. That's an average of only one per county. In 1994 the figure had been 33. There were 11 years between Alex Tudor's 1999 Test debut and Michael Carberry's. It's hard to escape the feeling that the recent 'Chance to Shine' initiative aimed at bringing cricket back into state schools where, let's face it, the majority of the country's black population are going to be, is too little, 25 years too late.

In the event, the issues surrounding Roland Butcher's selection proved by far the least controversial of the winter. Technically, based on ten years' residence, England could have picked Mike Proctor and the Zimbabwean (still then frequently referred to as 'Rhodesian') Brian Davison. If they had, the tour would almost certainly have been cancelled. An Indian-born, 35-year-old white medium-pacer who wasn't even in the original squad, nearly saw to it that it was anyway. But before that could happen, England had a Test match to lose.

On the final morning of the first Test, the incredible news came through that Mrs Thatcher, u-turning on an issue involving the miners, had announced increased subsidies for the Coal Board and scrapped plans to close 23 pits. Unfortunately, in terms of cricketing contests between England and the West Indies it was business as usual, even to the extent of England's captain having a 'why the hell did I go and say that?' moment.

When the home side's first innings ended on 426-9, an hour into the third day, Ian Botham said that if England, on a flat pitch, couldn't get a draw then 'heads would roll'. This was the cricketing equivalent of the bloke in the pub who says: 'Hit me in the stomach, hard as you like, go on!' It was followed by the cricketing equivalent of a smack, a groan and a thud as England went from 110-2 to 178 all out and followed on 248 behind. As the tourists tried to bat out time on the last afternoon, Botham saw off the fast bowlers in company with Boycott before dancing down the pitch to Viv Richards' part-time off-spin, aiming at Antigua and getting it as far as Michael Holding at mid-off. He stomped off presumably to seek out the local guillotine.

England had been blown away by the West Indian quicks and had next to nothing to fire back with. The tourists had included two what might be termed 'fast' bowlers, Bob Willis and Graham Dilley. When Willis broke down almost immediately and had to return home, they were never going to be able to 'fight fire with fire' and were forced to fall back on plan 'B': fighting fire with a fire extinguisher in the form of John Emburey. *Wisden* described Emburey as England's 'one world-class bowler'. In four Tests he took seven wickets at 59.85.

It was only four Tests because of what happened in Guyana. As the team arrived in South America it was announced that Prince Charles had got engaged to a 'delighted, thrilled and blissfully happy' Diana Spencer. Charles said he was amazed Diana was prepared to take him on. She wasn't the only one who caused surprise by going for an older man. When Willis' injury forced him home, England decided to replace him with Robin Jackman. At 35 he was four years older than Willis and hardly a pick for the future. Also, while he was a fine bowler, it was suggested that his naggingly accurate fast-medium style wasn't suited to West Indian conditions. Funny how no-one ever says that about Angus Fraser (12 Tests in the Caribbean, 54 wickets at 20.29). However, it wasn't Jackman's cricketing credentials that were the problem.

Jackman arrived in Guyana on 23rd February, five days before the second Test was due to start. It was no secret he had spent many winters playing and coaching in South Africa. Many English professionals, including several other members of this team, did the same thing. David Bairstow even captained a South African state side in the 1977-78 season, straight after the signing of the Gleneagles Agreement. However, two days after his arrival and despite the fact no one had objected to anyone else in the party, a radio commentator in Jamaica suggested the Guyanese government might be in breach of the Agreement by admitting Jackman to their country.

Much interpretation of the Gleneagles Agreement ensued, with the British government, through the minister for sport, Hector Munroe, offering the opinion that it didn't cover actions of one country against the nationals of another. Put another way, countries weren't allowed to send teams to South Africa, but they could neither prevent their nationals going there as individuals, nor could they stop South African professionals from plying their trade in any country they chose. Certainly the situation on the ground seemed to bear out this interpretation. English professionals clearly played in the Republic and many South Africans featured in county cricket. Two members of the West Indian side, Gordon Greenidge and Andy Roberts, played alongside Barry Richards for years at Hampshire.

However, the Guyanese government chose not to agree with this interpretation and on the day that England lost the one match they played in Guyana, the British High Commissioner was informed Jackman's visitors' permit had been withdrawn and he must leave. The England management, using words resonant of the MCC's refusal to tour South Africa in 1968–69 without Basil D'Oliviera, then announced they wouldn't play the second Test in circumstances where they weren't free to pick their team 'without restrictions being imposed'. The whole English contingent, including the press, left for Barbados the next day.

English professionals playing in South Africa had been raised in the planning stages of the tour and no government, including that of Guyana, gave any indication it would be a problem. Yet now, less than two years after international cricket had survived the Packer crisis, the issue threatened to split the game. John Arlott, writing in *The Guardian*, was in no doubt about the seriousness of the situation: 'This could be the last tour of West Indies made by an English, or conceivably, an Australian or New Zealand team…The administrators of all the cricketing countries must join with the will to save game from the destruction which is now imminent.'

The perceived wisdom in the Caribbean was that the Guyanese president, Forbes Burnham, had used Robin Jackman as a way of getting back at the British after an adverse report by Lord Avebury into alleged vote rigging. Representatives of the governments of Barbados, Montserrat, Antigua and Jamaica, the remaining venues for the tour, pulled the sport back from the brink by accepting Jackman as a legitimate member of the England team.

Nevertheless, it felt like no more than a stay of execution. The whole issue of South Africa seemed to hang over the sport for years, like the Cold War, constantly in the background threatening disaster.

The rest of the trip, a bit like the ball when England were batting, passed in a blur. The relief of the tour being saved and the movingly warm reception Roland Butcher received as he made his debut on the island of his birth, were almost immediately overtaken by the death of assistant manager, Ken Barrington, halfway through the Test match. 'Assistant manager' doesn't remotely cover what Barrington was to this side. Peter Roebuck once described his role as that of 'a coach, confessor, counsellor, cockney comedian and chum'. Barrington had been there and done it to the tune of 6806 Test runs at 58.67, walked out to bat with a metaphorical Union Jack fluttering behind him and now was, in the words of Frank Keating, 'always first with a great big consoling arm and some perky get stuck-in encouragement'. How could you not love a man who combined all that with such mastery of the malapropism that he was once able to announce proudly that he had 'slept like a lark'. Robin Jackman summed up the effect of Barrington's death on the side when he described being 'barely able to see the batsman' as he ran in to bowl his opening over the following morning.

As if that wasn't enough, the team had already suffered the psychological blow of seeing their best batsman taken apart in terrifying fashion. England began well enough, dismissing the West Indies for only 265. But Michael Holding's opening over to Geoff Boycott put that score into some kind of perspective. Gladstone Holder in the Barbados paper *The Nation* described it like this:

'Each succeeding ball was faster and I said: "This man Boycott had tremendous control." He had middled none but any lesser mortal would have been out.

Then came the last ball, delivered at such tremendous pace that it passed Boycott's still upraised bat at full pitch, struck the ground just short of the stumps, swung in and sent the off stump flying. Boycott appeared like a man who had seen the lithe, slim, athletic Holding turn into a monster before his eyes.'

The only other time I've seen a batsman look like that was Mike Gatting after Shane Warne bowled him the 'Ball from Hell' in 1993. England were routed for 122 in 47 overs. Satellite television, the Internet and the Barmy Army were more than a decade away and crowds in the Caribbean were still mostly made up of West Indies' supporters. Listening on the radio as wickets fell at regular intervals you had no chance of catching the detail of what had happened, you just knew someone was out and had to wait for the noise of celebration to die down before you could find out how. It must have been fantastic to be a West Indian supporter watching that innings. I longed to know what that felt like.

From such a pit of despair England somehow fashioned two draws to end the series. At Antigua the groundsman, Leonard 'Copperpot' Francis, a 'colourful' character who had lived on both sides of the adjoining prison walls, predicted before the game that 'the end of the world will come before this pitch breaks, and even then someone will have to dig it up'. Boycott made a hundred and if the game hadn't ended he would probably still be there now.

In Jamaica, Gower saved the game with 154 not out on the last day, but it was Gooch's brutal 153 on the first that changed my life.

Being right-handed I couldn't bat like Gower (that's my excuse and I'm sticking to it) and up until now the only similarity between Graham Gooch and I was that we both used Duncan Fearnley bats. However, if he was capable of taking apart the West Indies' bowlers, I thought there must be something in his method. As a result, when our season started almost immediately after the end of the tour, I stood with my bat raised at waist level as the bowler delivered. I know I wasn't alone. Batting like this was as 1980s as snoods and pixie boots. It was fashionable to combine this stance with an infeasibly heavy bat to produce what Glenn Turner, Worcestershire's New Zealand opener, called the 'pendulum effect'. This worked on the theory that once you got your railway sleeper in the air all you had to do to achieve a lot of power was let it drop in an arc onto the ball. It certainly worked for Turner. When he made his hundredth first-class century against Warwickshire the following year, he ended up with 311 not out in a day.

Whatever it did for anyone else, this approach revolutionised my batting and all of a sudden, with a built-in back lift, I started being able to hit the ball further than silly point. As a result, playing for the school third team, I made my first ever 50. The bowlers kept trying yorkers but ended up sending down a series of half-volleys that were battered to the boundary in an arc between point and mid-on by a batsman I didn't recognise. I was lucky all of this happened in front of the teacher in charge of the second team, whose away game had been rained off. The upshot was that when one of the second team batsmen got injured, I took his place.

My first ever second XI game was at Seaford. Having restricted the home side to about 120, we were making a bit of a mess of things when I came in. I reasoned I should trust the method that got me into the team in the first place and went for the drive at every opportunity. Even now I can remember hitting their captain over extra-cover for four more than once as I shared the decisive partnership with our team's most talented all-rounder. This lad was an incredibly gifted athlete, a fine rugby player and only not in the cricket first XI because of the embarrassment of talent available. He was just the sort of sportsman I looked up to and always wished I could be. I didn't know what I was doing on the same field as him. Gradually we edged closer to victory until he was out with about ten needed. I stayed to the end finishing 25 not out. On the way home on the coach we sat chatting like equals. When he said how disappointed he was at getting out because he had wanted us to see it through to the end, I nearly burst with pride. No one except me ever realised the effect of his words. In a tiny way, they were life-changing. It was a moment of acceptance, of sudden realisation that we're all more equal than we think, but most of all it was a moment of utter contentment.

In the short space of time this had happened to me, Bobby Sands had died, the Pope had been shot, the Queen had been shot at and the Australians had arrived. A combination of rain, political interference and some good batting had meant that we had only lost 2-0 in the West Indies. Even if, in subsequent years, a result like that would have seemed like a win, at the time it didn't promise much for our chances of retaining the Ashes.

This Australian side obviously meant business as they arrived for the first time ever with a coach, Peter Philpott. This took the number of back-up staff to a staggering four, including Philpott, the team manager Fred Bennett, a physiotherapist and a scorer described by *Wisden* as 'indefatigable'. Obviously the scorebox in those days was rather tougher environment than you might have expected.

One person who wasn't with them was Jeff Thomson. The Australian selectors had preferred Terry Alderman on the basis he would bowl better in English conditions. This was a setback Thomson greeted with his customary good-natured diplomacy. 'I've always said our selectors were a bunch of bloody idiots. All they've done now is confirm it.' As it turned out, Alderman picked up an Ashes record 42 Test wickets that summer, while Thomson picked up a hernia. Perhaps trying to prove a point, the scourge of David Lloyd signed to play for Middlesex. Injury ended his season in mid-June – quite a long county career for an overseas pro by modern standards – but not before he had become part of the first county side made up entirely of Test cricketers. Although this was a considerable feather in Middlesex's cap, it hints at another of England's failings. Of the nine Englishmen who played alongside

Thomson and Daniel that summer, only Brearley started the year with more than 20 caps. Gatting, Emburey and Edmonds went on past 50 and Downton made it to 30, but Radley, Barlow, Butcher and Selvey's international careers were behind them with a combined total of 14 appearances.

In the period from 1980 to 1995, England selected ten cricketers who only played one Test match and a further 25 who played five or fewer. In the same period, Australia picked three men who only played one match (one of whom was a wicket-keeper who got a game when Ian Healey was injured) and eight who played five or fewer. You can't possibly give your best if you think your next failure may be your last, but that's how our players were forced to play. It's little wonder so many of them failed.

The Australians may have lacked Thomson but included Lillee, Marsh and Chappell. Fortunately, the Chappell in question was the crap one, 'Ten-pin Trevor', the best underarm bowler in the world. Nevertheless, with Border and Hughes, the captain, to bolster the batting and a bearded left-arm spinner seemingly from the Aussie version of *The Joy of Sex* in Ray Bright, they looked strong. Dennis Lillee anticipated a close series: 'If I were a betting man I wouldn't know who to put my money on.'

This statement is inaccurate in at least two respects. Firstly, the words 'If I were' should be replaced with 'I am'. Secondly, it's not true, Lillee knew exactly where to put his money.

When Ladbrokes famously offered odds of 500-1 against England on the Saturday evening of the Headingley Test there was, as Richie Benaud might have put it, no point looking for Lillee and Marsh, let alone chasing them, they had gone straight into the betting tent and out again! To be more accurate, while this was the first time an Australian team had a coach on tour, it wasn't the first time they had been on one, and Marsh and Lillee got the driver to place bets on England to win. It seems incredible now that there were no rules against this and all they had to do was apologise and give the money back. But then everyone was certain these were just a couple of Aussie larrikins who couldn't resist ridiculous odds in a two-horse race. The very fact they did something as blatant as getting a bus driver to bung a tenner on at Ladbrokes shows that Lillee and Marsh weren't doing anything underhand and couldn't even conceive anyone would seriously think they threw a game for money. They, like the rest of us, knew the idea of anybody, let alone an Australian, doing that was just too ludicrous for words. How I wish I still had that certainty.

500-1 may have been stupidly generous, but long odds against England were still justified after the first two Test matches. Australia beat us 2-1 in the Prudential Trophy, a statistic I'm sure not unconnected to the fact the home side featured Jim Love and Geoff Humpage. By the time Ian Botham lost his job as captain, we were 1-0 down in the Tests as well. The first match, at Nottingham, was proof, if it were needed, that Botham was not a lucky captain.

The game was played on a pitch of the sort the Trent Bridge groundsman produced all season to offer generous seam movement to Richard Hadlee and Clive Rice. As a result of such surfaces, Nottinghamshire pipped Sussex to the county championship by two points that year. Not that I'm bitter or anything, you understand. In such conditions England made a respectable 185 and should have bowled Australia out for under 100. Unfortunately, they dropped six catches including a sitter to Downton when Border had made only ten of an eventual 63 (easily the highest individual score of the match). When the tourists were set 132 to win in the last innings (sound familiar?), Willis took 1-28 and they scrambled home by four wickets. If Downton had caught Border, England would almost certainly have won and cricket history would have been changed forever. It's funny how sometimes something that seems to be terrible at the time can turn out to be for the best if you wait a little while. Not that the glories of Headingley, Edgbaston and Old Trafford were the result of English cricket suddenly getting its act together.

Proving that it wasn't just the players they were indecisive about, the selectors couldn't make up their minds whether they wanted Botham as captain and appointed him on a match-by-match basis. This sent a clear message that he didn't have their complete confidence and dramatically increased the pressure on him to produce immediate results – hardly conducive to creating an atmosphere in which the captain and the team could play at their best. This mistake was another from which those running English cricket didn't learn. In the 1980s, England had nine official captains, ten if you include Derek Pringle who did the job on the final day at the Oval in 1988 when Graham Gooch was injured. In the same period, the most successful side in the world, the West Indies, had two.

After a draw at Lord's, Botham announced to plummy Peter West on the BBC that he had told the selectors he no longer wished to be considered for the captaincy on a match-by-match basis. Almost straight after this, the chairman of selectors, Alec Bedser, confirmed they would have changed the captain anyway. At first sight this seems a completely unnecessary thing to have done and just another example of crass man-management. In fact, to be fair to Bedser, West actually asked him a direct question about what the selectors would have done. A more politically-minded man might have diplomatically dodged the question but Bedser, being a fairly no-nonsense individual, gave a straight answer to a straight question and went on to express the selectors' concern for the pressures Botham and his family had been under and their desire to see him recapture his best form as a player.

Nevertheless, Botham still had a point when he said they could have just let him resign with dignity. Many would have forgiven him if he had just gone off to sulk in his tent for a few weeks. Fortunately, he didn't.

What can I say that hasn't already been said? It was incredible wasn't it? How on earth did 'Shaddap You Face' keep 'Vienna' off number one for so many weeks? He wasn't even a real Italian! Joe Dolce was Australian. After that, they deserved everything they had coming to them.

In deciding on Botham's replacement Bedser and his mates followed the teachings of the quick fix school of selection and gave Mike Brearley three matches in charge. This is the only time I can ever remember this approach working.

Certainly, if anyone's captaincy was going to make a difference it was Brearley's. However, at Leeds, the decisive thing turned out to be the return of a great all-rounder to the England team.

However, like everyone else, Chris Old, back after missing the first two Tests, saved his decisive contributions for the fourth and fifth days.

Ladbrokes' infamous odds were offered on the Saturday night and not when England were 135-7 on the Monday afternoon, still 92 behind. That was the point, before Old made his decisive contributions to the match, when you really wanted to get your money on England. At 4.15 that afternoon Thames television showed a Bugs Bunny cartoon called *Rabbit Rampage*. This is exactly what Australia were experiencing on BBC2.

Dilley (previous highest score 38 not out) made his flashing 56 as Botham went so famously, gloriously, brilliantly mad at the other end. Even so, when the Kent fast bowler was out England still only led by 25 and were heading for defeat. All Australia had to do was get Old out.

They couldn't. While Botham hit a few more fours at the other end and rearranged the Mars bars in the confectionary stall, Old accumulated steadily against the seamers, while Kim Hughes, obviously fearing the Yorkshireman's destructive power against spin, refused to bowl Ray Bright. Apart from one clump over wide mid-wicket off Geoff Lawson, Old allowed himself few liberties and the lead gradually grew to a point where it might challenge Australia. By the time Lawson clipped the Yorkshireman's leg stump, England led by 92. If Botham could gather a few more with Willis then we might have a match on our hands. Willis hung on despite nearly being run out off the last ball of the day and Headingley's short-lived electronic scoreboard with its ridiculous yellow display confirmed, for the few who could see it in the setting sun, that England were no longer 500-1.

If there is a single day of Test cricket from the whole of the last 30 years that I wish I had been at, the fifth day of Headingley 1981 is it. Sat at home, I started the morning hoping for another fifty runs. I got five, before Alderman removed Willis. England 356 all out (C.M.Old 29, I.T.Botham 149 not out), and the tourists' simple task spelt out in black and yellow: 'Australia require 130 to win'.

John Dyson, a school-teacher with next to no backlift, and 'Tenpin' got the tourists to within half-a-dozen overs of lunch at 56-1, before Willis' series of lifters removed Chappell, Kim Hughes' cap, the Aussie captain himself and Yallop in the blink of a widening English eye.

After lunch Brearley made the decisive decision of the match. Picking Willis down the hill wasn't difficult, he was bowling like a dervish and as Boycott might have put it, my mum could have made that decision. The important one was who to bowl from the Football Ground end. Brearley picked Old. Australia had edged up to 65-4 when the great man delivered the key wicket.

Through his career, Border foiled England more frequently than the Anthill Mob foiled Dick Dastardly, but this wasn't his day. Old kept bowling straight and as he sent down yet another good length ball on off stump, Border hesitated for a moment over whether to play back or forward; the result was that he did neither and succeeded only in edging it onto his wicket. The England team knew what a moment it was and Old (who incidentally looked as if he had nicked Brearley's beard) disappeared under his teammates.

I can't say this was the moment I knew we would win because, of course, I knew nothing of the kind. However, it was when I first genuinely thought we could. It would seem that it was also at this point that the same thought occurred to the Australians as they clearly panicked. Dyson, who had hardly hooked all day, went for Willis and nicked it to Taylor, Marsh slogged that huge catch up to Dilley at fine leg and Lawson ensured the match was obviously remembered for its wicket-keeping by providing Taylor with his 1,271st first-class catch to break John Murray's record.

All of a sudden they were 75-8 and Christopher Martin-Jenkins, in a rare outing on the telly, was clearly having as much trouble staying calm as I was, hurriedly adding: 'if it happens' to his excited comments about what a remarkable English victory this would be. However, not all of the Australians were panicking. Lillee had a lot of money riding on the result and he didn't want to collect.

As well as being a huge Bob Dylan fan, Bob Willis is also an acknowledged expert on the works of Jane Austen. Here he remembered that it is a truth universally acknowledged that an Australian fast bowler in possession of an independent batting style must be in want of a yorker. Abandoning, just in time, his previous policy of banging the ball in, Willis started pitching it up to Lillee. The Australian, set on the back foot, chipped the ball again but this time to mid-on where Gatting took his now famous diving catch.

There was still time for Old to take a final hand in proceedings. Botham had replaced him from the Football Ground end and Old had taken his place in the slips. Australia's number 11, Alderman, nicked Botham to Old's right, he dropped it, Alderman nicked him to Old's left, he dropped it again. I thought: 'I don't believe it, after all that they're going to lose by one bloody wicket!'

Willis bowled the next over, he pitched it up again, Bright aimed for the joy of six over wide long-on and...you know the rest.

At least I saw the heroics of Headingley. Botham's demolition of the Aussie tail at Edgbaston was, for me, a series of frequent cheers from my Barcombe team-mates as I ground out 50 against a touring side whose attack included an under 19 international opening bowler. If you asked me which country this cricketing colossus represented, I would be forced to mumble 'Denmark' quickly behind my hand. As for the blitzkrieg of Old Trafford, in the time it took Botham to go from 28 to his century ('What a magnificent way to go to a six!' - Jim Laker) I eked out seven in a damp field near Battle, before being caught and bowled off the inside edge courtesy of my extra-bouncy Sunil Gavaskar-style 'lightweight leg-guards'. These made me slightly quicker between the wickets – all things are relative – but susceptible to a series of unlikely bat-pad dismissals that had already taken in gulley and extra-cover. By the start of the following season they were, like Paul Parker's Test career, in the bin.

Unlike the only comparable Ashes series, in 2005, the final match was anticlimactic. It was as if the series had produced too much excitement for one summer and needed a quiet five days to recover. Set against all that had gone just before, the game was completely unmemorable. Which is harsh for the man for whom those five days represented an entire Test career.

After a successful season for Sussex, Paul Parker appeared certain to be selected as the promising young batsman to be taken on the winter tour. Then something disastrous happened: England picked him for the Oval. Surrey's ground was to become a graveyard for the fledgling international careers of many cricketers. Half of England's ten 'one-Test wonders' between 1980 and 1995 played their only match there. Paul Parker was the first.

The Sussex man was picked with Wayne Larkins to replace Gower and Gooch, both of whom were out of form. The way Parker and Larkins were treated sums up how England wasted innumerable talented players.

That winter England were due to go to India. It was expected that, as was usual, they would pick seven specialist batsmen. Of the six picked for the Oval, Brearley was certain to be missing. This left the remaining five, plus Gooch and Gower. Admittedly, when Keith Fletcher was made captain in preference to Willis, he took one of the batting places but logically the remaining slot should have gone to either Parker or Larkins. The latter certainly didn't disgrace himself in this match, making 34 and 24 and the former was making his debut and understandably nervous. Admittedly 0 and 13 hardly made out a compelling case for inclusion but Len Hutton made 0 and 1 on his debut. I'm not saying Paul Parker was as good as Len Hutton but on the other hand, how do we know how good he could have been, given that he didn't receive anywhere near the opportunities that others did? Mike Gatting for example, made his Test debut in January 1978 scoring 5 and 6. He didn't get his first Test hundred until December 1984 in his 54th innings.

Neither Larkins nor Parker went to India. The selectors went for Geoff Cook of Northants who clinched his selection, as so many did at this time, with an impressive innings in the Nat West Trophy final shortly before the team was picked. Cook made 111 but Larkins had got 52 himself. Faced with such capricious selection it's little wonder he decided a three-year Test ban was a price worth paying for the financial security provided by a 'rebel' tour to South Africa later that same winter. Crass inconsistency was just another of the cracks in English cricket, over which Botham's heroics only temporarily papered.

The memories of that summer were simple and glorious: Ray Bright's middle stump flying at Leeds; Rod Marsh's doing the same at Birmingham; Botham hooking Lillee off his eyebrows at Manchester and, for this Sussex fan at least, a young Oval debutant in an appropriately forlorn chase to the cover boundary to the accompaniment of Richie's 'Don't bother chasing that Paul Parker!' Thanks to the attitude of those running English cricket, a back row conversation in a bus on the coast road from Seaford to Brighton had a more lasting positive effect.

My school rugby team had a centre who combined rare pace with the elusiveness of a young Jeremy Guscott. One teacher darkly described our tactics as, 'Give it to Donaghy and wait for him to score.' Unfortunately, the events of 1981 led English cricket down a similar path. The lesson we seemed to have learned was, 'No matter how bad we are we've always got Botham to pull our nuts out the fire.' Because this was wrong, I'll always remember that year at least as much for the efforts of another all-rounder.

A long time later, ten maybe even 15 years, my mum rang me to tell me that she had read in the local paper that my batting partner that day at Seaford had killed himself. We hadn't become firm friends; he was no part of my life at all. But I hardly spoke for the rest of the evening, all I could think about was a coach ride home in the low evening sun. It took at least two weeks for my mood to lighten as it hit home how short our time is and how even more fleeting are our moments of true contentment. On the rare occasions these days when I manage to hit the ball over extra-cover, I still think of him.

EIGHT

Some things in life are inexcusable. Betraying a friend, Renee and Renato, wedge haircuts, that sort of thing. England's tour to India in 1981-82 was one of those things. I can't begin to defend it. With the exception of the first Test, which at least ended in a positive result, this series must go down as one of the dullest exercises in extended pointlessness in the history of the game. The only time I've seen a contest with more draws was when, years later, my daughters came up with their variation of 'rock, paper, scissors' called 'rock, rock, rock'.

The home side's captain was Sunil Gavaskar. I suppose I shouldn't have been surprised that a man who once famously made 36 not out in 60 overs during the first World Cup was quite happy to win a six-match series 1-0. Four years later, on Gower's tour, the same man, admittedly with a little help from the weather, extended the first innings of one match into the fourth afternoon. In 1981-82, Gavaskar was assisted, if that's the right word, by the presence in the England side of Geoff Boycott and Chris Tavare.

During the first Test, Boycott and Tavare indulged in an 'anything you can do I can do slower' partnership of 92 in 59 overs. Remember, the first Test is the one that finished in a positive result. In the fifth, Tavare took five-and-a-half hours to make 35. After this last innings the Kent man commented that he 'didn't actually enjoy Test cricket all that much'. Millions all over India knew the feeling.

As was usually the case when England visited the sub-continent during the 1980s, the only flicker of interest concerned the home umpires. Before the third Test, England objected to Mohammed Ghouse and succeeded only in getting him replaced by the extra-large Swaroop Kishen, one of the officials they had been unhappy with during their defeat in Bombay. The latter's enormous girth made him perhaps the most easily recognisable umpire in world cricket at the time and his career was certainly colourful. His first Test match, in Bangalore in December 1978, had to be abandoned because of civil unrest resulting from the expulsion from Parliament and detention of Indira Ghandi. The next year (again in Bangalore), Kishen, his fellow umpire and all the players had to throw themselves to the ground when swarms of bees invaded the stadium.

This was long before the international umpiring panel. Complaints about the home officials were a recurring theme in international cricket, and not just on the sub-continent. The last West Indies tour to New Zealand had been marred by umpiring controversies that had seen Colin Croft 'accidentally' barge into umpire Fred Goodall and Michael Holding famously kick the stumps out of the ground when a caught behind decision didn't go his way.

On the surface the arguments centred on competence. However, whenever the subject came up, players and commentators alike talked of the potential need for 'neutral' umpires. Certainly, beaten touring sides often seemed to imply they had the rough end of things. The nadir was Mike Gatting's infamous confrontation with Shakoor Rana on the 1987-88 tour of Pakistan. However legitimate some of the complaints were, this was another area in which the English demonstrated their sometimes self-deluding sense of superiority.

English commentators and officials seemed to think they had a God-given right to the moral high ground on the subject. 'English umpires are the best in the world' was chanted like a mantra, as if simply repeating it often enough made it true. The implication was that our house was in order but everyone else had to look at theirs. Jack Bannister, arguing against an independent panel on the grounds that it would amount to the authorities caving in to 'players' antics', even offered the opinion that, 'English umpires make mistakes but our players' acceptance of them – while perhaps not as stoical as in days gone by – causes much less offence than in other countries.' This complacent point of view was to be challenged only the following summer, when the English authorities turned down a Pakistani request to have David Constant replaced for the Headingley Test. Constant then made at least one howler that contributed to England's narrow win in the decisive match of the series.

There was also an element of childishness about the way the cricket authorities of all nations dealt with this issue. The Indians replaced Mohammed Ghouse at the tourists' request, so when they asked for Constant to be stood down from their Lord's Test the following summer the English agreed. The refusal to do the same thing for the Pakistanis was a large contributory factor to the Shakoor Rana debacle six years later. And things were only going to get more complicated. At the end of a dire tour, England brightened the mood slightly with a seven-wicket win in the first Test match to feature Sri Lanka, or 'Srilon' as consummate diplomat Keith Fletcher accidentally called it.

However, at the end of this tour, umpiring controversies were quickly shifted down the international cricketing agenda as a controversy that echoed the Jackman affair brought us back to Geoff Boycott.

Boycott and Geoff Cook had both played in South Africa in the recent past. Cook had even captained Eastern Province. Both men were on a United Nations blacklist of those with sporting associations with the Republic. As a result, Indira Ghandi's government announced that both were 'unacceptable' and would be denied entry into India. For about two weeks it looked as if the tour would be cancelled, which in turn could lead to the destruction of the international game John Arlott had feared. Just as cancellation seemed certain to be confirmed, the Indian government accepted both men's assertions that they abhorred apartheid and allowed them to tour. But that was very far from the end of the matter.

Boycott needed to go to India to get the runs required to beat Garry Sobers' record Test aggregate. He stayed on the tour long enough to pass Sobers' mark in the third Test, before going home shortly after playing golf on the last day of the fourth while John Lever was fielding as his substitute. It then emerged that 'Sir Geoffrey' had spent much of the year recruiting many of England's players to go and play on a rebel tour to South Africa. Boycott had been one of the first English players approached by Packer and had turned him down. But that was when he still had Sobers to aim at. Passing the record seemed, in the words of Mike Brearley, to 'remove the fragile structure of aspiration that held Boycott together'.

Several of those the Yorkshireman recruited, like Amiss, Woolmer and Knott had been Packer players and were either at or near the end of their Test careers. However, more damagingly for England's immediate future, Gooch and Emburey had also accepted offers and received the same three-year Test ban meted out to all of the 'rebels'.

Gooch expressed shock at the length of their exclusion from international cricket. I was surprised they hadn't been banned for life. The rebels' decision wasn't made in a sociological vacuum. The whole issue of race relations was high on the political agenda. In November 1981, Lord Scarman had published his report into the Brixton riots, noting in his conclusions 'the racial disadvantage that is a fact of British life'. Even in purely cricketing terms those who chose to sign up for the tour did so in the context of what had just gone before. The furore over Jackman had taken place only a year earlier, the Indian tour had been put in doubt over the same issue and in the autumn of 1981 the TCCB had written to all county cricketers warning about the possible repercussions of joining a tour to South Africa. In this letter the distinction was clearly drawn between accepting an individual coaching position and going as part of a team.

The rebels had their supporters, including the Prime Minister ('We do not have the power to prevent any sportsmen or women from visiting South Africa or anywhere else; if we did we would no longer be a free country') and Jayne Larkins ('There's nothing wrong with Wayne and his friends playing cricket where they like'). Nevertheless, it seemed clear that if you wanted to tour the Republic you had to be prepared to take the money (rumoured to be on a sliding scale between £10,000 and £40,000) and the consequences that went with it. You have to wonder whether the thought of having to share a dressing room with men who had taken money to play in apartheid South Africa wasn't just another reason why county cricket didn't seem an attractive career option for young black British sportsmen.

Before the tour, Gooch had been seen as a potential England captain. Instead he ended up in charge of the South African Breweries England XI when the players voted for him to lead the side ahead of Boycott. It was to be another six years before Gooch was made captain of the official England team towards the end of the summer of 1988. His confirmation as skipper for the winter tour due to follow, led directly to its cancellation. England's proposed destination in 1988-89 was India.

On the 27th February, those rebels not already in South Africa slipped secretly out of London. When the TCCB got wind of what was happening they cabled the tourists urging them to think again. But on the 3rd March, as the Queen opened the Barbican, the first match, against a South African under 25 XI, got under way.

English cricketers were almost as big news as *The Romans in Britain*.

That was saying something as Mary Whitehouse had brought a sensational private prosecution for public obscenity against the director, Michael Bogdanov. I followed this with interest as I had nearly been on the school trip to end all school trips to see the production in London. I was studying Roman history and our teacher was a kindly, ageing, old-school innocent who never did anything racier than umpiring for the third XI. Seeing only the title, he assumed he might be able to fire our interest by taking us to see a vivid portrayal of life in the period. When he approached the headteacher with the idea, it was suggested this portrayal might be just that little bit too vivid. The anal rape of a druid was perhaps not the ideal way to provoke discussion on the Emperor Augustus' foreign policy. The trip was hastily cancelled.

The English department didn't learn from this experience. Shortly afterwards we were taken to London to see what it turned out, after the tickets had been bought, was an all-male, gay, production of *Doctor Faustus* complete with Mephistopheles in nothing but the sort of jock strap that had no place on a cricket field. Mary Whitehouse might have turned her attention in that direction if the Attorney General's intervention hadn't ensured the halting of her case on the 18th March. Within a day, she and England's cricketers were old news.

On 19th March, as Gooch was winning the toss and deciding to bat in Cape Town, 50 Argentine scrap-metal workers landed on South Georgia.

Like most people, I had only the vaguest knowledge of the Falkland Islands. The whole conflict lasted only three months but through that time it seemed to dominate every waking moment like an intense but short-lived affair. All of a sudden everyone was talking about places like Port Stanley and Goose Green as if they actually knew where they were.

We were introduced to a set of characters: General Galtieri, Rex Hunt, John Nott and Ian McDonald, who swept swiftly into and out of our lives, briefly dominating television screens like the cast of a much-hyped, but quickly discontinued, new soap. It became almost a mortal sin to eat corned beef or to support Tottenham Hotspur while they continued to play Ricky Villa and Ossie Ardilles. The conflict made Brian Hanrahan the most celebrated plane spotter in history and after a period of respectful reflection, introduced a new word into sports commentary. Whereas before, Botham hit it 'like a kicking horse', now his shots went 'like an exocet'.

The Argentine writer J.L. Borges described the whole business as 'just like two bald men fighting over a comb'. Certainly it was a conflict that, when put alongside some of the cricketing issues of the day, helped to open my 17-year-old eyes to some of the absurdities of international politics in general and 'modern' Britain in particular.

On 1st May, as the MCC batted at Lord's against the champion county Nottinghamshire, the RAF bombed Port Stanley. Hanrahan counted them all out and counted them all back in again and for another day we rejoiced in a conflict with no known casualties. On the 2nd, MCC didn't play at Lord's because it was a Sunday. It seems ludicrous now that three days later the club had to have a vote on the principle of whether they should play cricket at Lord's on the Sabbath. There is something incredibly British about being concerned with social conventions when there's a war on, even one where the majority of the population are spectators. On the same day as cricket's headquarters stayed quiet for fear of what the other Lord would make of playing on his day, the Royal Navy sank the General Belgrano. When, on 4th May, *The Sun* printed a picture of the stricken battleship along with its infamous 'Gotcha' headline, for the first time in my life I felt uneasy about where I came from. This wasn't an emotion shared by most of my male schoolmates who seemed to have the same opinion of war as Jerome K Jerome had about work; they could watch it for hours.

The same day as that headline appeared, HMS Sheffield was destroyed by an Argentine exocet. The shock was palpable. Not only was this the first British warship to be lost for 37 years, but we could watch it on the news. It was all the more appalling because it wasn't supposed to happen. Just as with so many sporting occasions over the years (football versus Norway 1981, cricket versus Holland 1989) we arrogantly assumed all we had to do was turn up and some 'minor' country or another would take a beating without ever laying a finger on us. However, the shock didn't make my friends stop and consider what was happening. Quite the contrary, all they could think about was revenge and I saw up close how easily the original reason for conflict can become lost in a spiral of recrimination.

I, and just about everybody else, was oblivious to the Indian cricket team arriving in England. There had been a chance they wouldn't come when they and the other tourists that year, Pakistan, threatened to call off their visits if they were required to play against any of the rebels. The bans imposed by the TCCB placated both governments and the counties ensured none of those who had joined Boycott turned out against the tourists. In some people's eyes the TCCB succeeded in avoiding a conflict by backing down. John Woodcock in *Wisden* describes them as having 'bowed to political pressures' and a *Daily Telegraph* editorial of the time ran: 'Reasonable argument has nothing to do with most of the opposition to South Africa. It is this mistaken belief in the good faith of the critics that has led the English cricketing authorities, and even Mrs Thatcher's government, into their essentially impossible position. Hoping to save most of cricket (and perhaps in the politicians' case, worried about trade) they have paid their dues to the protection racket of the anti-apartheid lobby.' This notion of Mrs Thatcher as having somehow made herself the 'poodle' of the anti-apartheid movement is not only ludicrously inaccurate but also wildly in contrast to the 'hard' image she was trying to cultivate with the war in the South Atlantic.

The *Daily Telegraph* may not have been the last bastion of 'reasonable argument' itself, but it was true the South African issue prompted some fairly muddled thinking.

Argentina was shortly to have a change of leadership. England had already had one. The selectors had decided that one victory over 'Srilon' was not enough to save Keith Fletcher's job. The captaincy went to Bob Willis and his place in the batting order to Allan Lamb. Many found it absurd that someone born in Langebaanweg could be an acceptable opponent for the tourists while Leytonstone boy Gooch wasn't. Like Greig before him, Lamb qualified by virtue of a combination of his English parents and four years' residence. As he was less than a month from his 28th birthday when he made his debut, it seemed fairly clear he was using England as a back door to Test cricket and would have played for South Africa had they not been excluded. The previous winter, Lamb had played for Western Province. At the same time, the Indian government had been threatening to refuse entry to two Englishmen who had played cricket as individuals in South Africa. Now, the Indian team was prepared to play without a murmur against a man who was to all intents and purposes a South African. As such, Lamb wasn't 'an Englishman through and through' and with Greig's 'betrayal' still fresh in the memory, many doubted how committed he would be. By the end of his career, Lamb held the record – jointly with Colin Cowdrey – for the most Test hundreds for England against West Indies. Anyone who could do that against the Caribbean sides of the time isn't short on commitment.

By the time Lamb had made 35 and 99 in the one-day internationals, the Argentines had hit HMS Coventry, the Atlantic Conveyor, Sir Galahad and Sir Tristram. It was a strange experience watching these events unfolding on television. In one sense it was the ultimate in genuine 'reality TV', 20 years before the fake kind became fashionable. However, in another way the TV pictures created a false immediacy, as I could watch completely unthreatened in my front room. It must have been even stranger for those who had lived through the last World War. They may not have had the technology to watch what was going on in Europe but they didn't need it to feel the immediacy of the conflict when the room they were sitting in could be destroyed at any moment. The fact this war was covered live on TV meant the more gung-ho of my schoolmates felt that they were somehow involved in the 'glory' of the ultimate victory. This is exactly the same feeling you get when your team wins something important. The only difference was this time we had been watching war with the shooting.

Allan Lamb wasn't the only new member of the England team, he was joined by Derek Pringle. Being captain of Cambridge University, Pringle was hardly James Dean, but as far as some of the stuffier elements of the cricket-following public were concerned, he was a bit racy. For a start, he had an earring. What's more, he liked a very dangerous sounding band called Half Man Half Biscuit, whose back-catalogue included 'Fuckin'Ell It's Fred Titmus'. I would lay a very large sum of money on the new chairman of selectors, Peter May, not knowing all the words to 'Dickie Davies Eyes', 'The Trumpton Riots' and 'All I want for Christmas is a Dukla Prague away kit', but he still picked Pringle to supplant him as England's last undergraduate Test player.

We, and most of our opponents, quickly worked out there wasn't anything particularly dangerous about Derek Pringle. His reputation has suffered as a result of being the first in a long line of 'next Ian Bothams' (Phil DeFreitas, David Capel, Chris Lewis) who would have benefited greatly from being judged by ordinary mortal standards. This phenomenon illustrates not only the sporting public's desire for individual heroes but also the extent to which Botham's achievements the previous year had disguised the quality of the team. It was a tacit admission of how much the side relied on one man that even the flimsiest of evidence was seized upon as an indication there was someone waiting in the wings to replace him when the time came.

In the opening Test against India at Lord's, Lamb and Pringle helped ensure Willis got off to a winning start. He was the last England captain to do so until Nasser Hussain, 17 years and eight skippers later in 1999.

The day after that Test ended, the ICC Trophy started in the Midlands. The competition, between Associate (non-Test playing) members of the ICC, determined the final participant in the World Cup to be held in England the following year. Unsurprisingly, although an Associate member of the ICC, Argentina didn't participate. Despite the presence of D. Reeve in the Hong Kong side, the most important man in the tournament was the captain of the ICC's newest member.

The newly created Zimbabwe never lost a match. A five-wicket victory over Bermuda in the final ensured their involvement the following year and set up one of Australia's greatest cricketing humiliations. Their success was built on the first-class experience several of their players had gained with Rhodesia in the South African domestic competition. In David Houghton, Andy Pycroft and John Traicos they had men who were to play in Zimbabwe's inaugural Test ten years later. Traicos was an Egyptian-born off-spinner – how often can you say that? – who had already played for South Africa in their last series before isolation. However, the man who will go down in English cricket history was a right-arm medium-pace bowler and left handed batsman who never got near playing in a Test match. His name was Duncan Fletcher.

The previous ICC Trophy, in 1979, had also been played in central England and coincided with the wettest May in the region since 1722. In an attempt to avoid a repeat, the 1982 competition had been put back a month. It made little difference, as 22 out of a total of 60 matches were lost to the weather in what was, to that point, the Midlands' worst second half of June in the 20th century. CFCs might have been burning a hole in the ozone layer, but 'global warming' - what's that? 'Climate change? Chance would be a fine thing. It might cause a bit of extra skin cancer in Australia but it's never going to affect us is it?' If it was raining in the Midlands you could guarantee it was hammering down in Manchester.

The very first day of Test cricket scheduled to take place at Old Trafford in 1884 was washed out. Since then, the venue has lost 29 complete days to the weather. No other English Test ground gets close to that. However, only three of those 29 Manchester wash-outs have been in the last 25 years. This could partly be explained by improved covering and drainage, but neither of these are much help if it doesn't stop raining. Overall, Manchester has lost a whole day on average about every two and a half Test matches. Since 1982, it's every six and a third. We must all be in big trouble if even Lancashire's getting drier.

In between the end of the first Test and the start of the second, Yorkshire had given the captaincy back to a 50-year-old Ray Illingworth (can you imagine an Australian state side doing that?), the Queen had declared herself 'absolutely delighted' at the news Princess Diana was in labour and peace had been declared between Britain and Argentina. Anyone hoping for a sun-drenched carnival of cricket by way of celebration was to be disappointed. In 1982, Old Trafford was still reassuringly soggy. Not one day of the second Test was unaffected by bad weather and by the time it ended they hadn't finished the first innings. This gave me plenty of opportunities to watch re-runs of previous India tours as the second, almost totally drenched, day was officially my last at school.

I wasn't sorry to be going. I had been with the same people for the last five years, and with one or two exceptions, I was sick of them. Even the ones I wasn't close to knew the mistakes I made. The opportunity to start again in something I regarded as the 'real world' couldn't come soon enough. Whether the filing department at the headquarters of the Alliance Building Society counted as the real world was another matter.

As far as one of my new colleagues, 'Coughing Jeff', was concerned, our workplace was 'conveniently located' next to the dog track in Hove. Coughing Jeff was 22 but, having smoked 50 a day since the age of about 11, his skin had the appearance of an ailing 45-year-old. He wore a shiny silvery-grey suit – but not the fashionable kind favoured by the members of ABC who weren't Martin Fry – and, when outdoors in summer or winter, a John Motson-style sheepskin coat. Jeff 'liked a drink' in the manner of W C Fields, and loved a bet, especially on greyhounds.

Then there was Brian. He was the one who thought the office would cease to function without him. There's always been at least one of these everywhere I've worked. Brian was the self-proclaimed fastest filer in the office, a 'fact' he informed you of as if he was letting you know he was 'Billy the Kid'. Even if it hadn't been obvious from his accent, you would have been able to tell within three sentences he was from Northern Ireland. This was as long as it took him to inform anyone he was meeting for the first time that he knew George Best. Brian was one of those characters, like the trumpet player in 'The Commitments', who you thought was probably a complete bull-shitter but just maybe they weren't. Certainly, he appeared to use his 'connections' at Brighton and Hove Albion (who had a number of Irish players at the time) to engineer a trial for one of my two best mates, Kevin.

Kevin was the boy next door. He was smart, polite, good looking and he knew it. Being 16, his technique with girls hadn't progressed beyond inviting them to come and watch him play football. Surprisingly, this was a very successful tactic and he frequently had to execute stage two of his master plan, which involved hitching up his 1980s ultra-short football shorts as far as they would go to show his rippling thighs to their best advantage. This worked as well. He was two years younger and already did better with girls than I did.

Then there was Keith. He had the permanently half-closed eyes of Dylan from *The Magic Roundabout* which, combined with his pale skin, made him look constantly like he had the hangover from hell. Sartorially he took the fashions of the time to their limit in that he combined his white towelling socks with drainpipe jeans so narrow I swear his mum had to sew him into them every morning. As far as sport was concerned, I've never met anyone who let heart rule head to such an extent. I made the easiest £5 of my life when Keith bet me Tony Sibson would knock out Marvin Hagler (at that time the best pound-for-pound boxer in the world) to win the World Middleweight title. He won it all back at arm-wrestling at which, we found out too late, he was unbeatable owing to a Muttiah Muralitharan-style congenital deformity of the elbow. He employed 'rope-a-dope' tactics, delivering the *coup de grâce* only once his opponent got exhausted fruitlessly trying to break his arm. Keith was also incredibly sweet-natured with a wickedly dry sense of humour. When you added this to the fact he had even less success with women than I did, you had an almost perfect friend.

None of these people was particularly extraordinary. I know others will have had far more colourful colleagues. One of my friends worked at Hammersmith Job Centre where he reported to Dennis Nielsen. But these were the first mates of my adult life. We laughed, we drank, we talked endlessly about sport and we chased girls. As a sign of what Australians would call our 'mateship' we clubbed together to buy each other birthday presents which were chosen with a very un-male degree of attention to their appropriateness. When my turn came, I got a pair of pads that didn't send inside-edges flying out to long-on.

In the final match of the series, Ian Botham literally smashed the

Indians for 208. In the course of this innings, Botham drove Dilip Doshi straight back at catchable height with such force that when the bowler visibly pulled his hand away, Richie Benaud commented only 'Very wise Dilip! Very wise'. England's supreme all-rounder also broke the pavilion roof and Sunil Gavaskar's left leg. Silly-point is called that for a reason. By contrast, on the final afternoon at the Oval, our old friend Chris Tavare made 75 not out in 257 minutes. This was positively breakneck by his standards, but not quick enough to prevent one member of the crowd wandering into the middle to offer him a stool.

England's next opponents, Pakistan, didn't receive quite the same flag-waving reception that greeted HMS Hermes' return from the South Atlantic. Unlike 1978, they were at full strength. Imran Khan had been made captain after the first-choice side had effectively gone on strike the previous March, refusing to play if Javed Miandad remained in charge for this tour. Imran was joined in the tourists' bowling attack by the father of reverse swing, Sarfraz Nawaz. Nevertheless, the Pakistanis most fiendish weapon was the 1980s equivalent of Shane Warne, Abdul Qadir. Partly because I could only pick a leg-spinner if he shouted 'It's the googly!' at the point of release, I was convinced England were going to take a hiding.

In some cricketing circles it's seen as polite to provide 'one off the mark' to important members of the opposition. For the first Test, the England selectors seemed to have done something similar in the bowling line by providing Qadir with at least one certain wicket. They picked Ian Greig. As the next 20 years were to prove, my ineptitude against leg-spin hardly made me unique among English batsmen, but 'young Greigy' and I were special. Greig didn't last long enough to be touted as the next you know who. With Test career figures of four wickets (three of them tailenders) at 28.50 and 26 runs at 6.50 he only just scraped in as the next Ian Greig.

Leg-spinners didn't turn up much in Sussex club cricket, nor the county game for that matter. But, at the grand age of 18, I fancied myself a keen student of the game. Once I had watched Qadir for a couple of Tests, I wanted to show off. I longed for the opposition to turn up with a leg-spinner who liked bowling round the wicket. Be careful what you wish for; it might come true.

One bright Sunday, I had a flat pitch and, asked to go in first, a whole afternoon to bat. Our opponents pitched up with a leg-spinner who opened the bowling. When he marked out his run and indicated to the umpire he wanted to go round the wicket, I was delighted. How sad is that? Getting excited at the prospect of being able to pad someone away. Having already taken middle I pointedly changed this to middle-and-leg, opened out my stance to show everyone I knew how to handle this line of attack and waited for the first ball. Down it came, just as I wished, outside the line of leg stump. I shoved my left pad at it with the best look of calm distain I could manage. It dipped past me, pitched six inches from my heel, spun like a top and bowled me behind my legs. 'Crestfallen' is one way of describing how I looked, 'a twat' is another. In Test terms, the younger Greig was like me. As England's middle order did their best to lose the first Test at Edgbaston, one of my senior team-mates echoed my father in suggesting 'Greigy'll sort it out'. 'He won't,' I thought, 'they never do.' I. A. Greig bowled Qadir 7.

England did win at Birmingham, mainly thanks to an extraordinary hundred by Derek Randall. Described euphemistically by *Wisden* as 'improvised', Randall's innings demonstrated that 'uncertainty' against wrist spin wasn't limited to the all-rounders. Clearly unable to pick Qadir, he alternated between blocking and slogging into the leg side. A clue as to how Imran allowed this to go on for as long as it did is contained in his work as a television expert summarizer during the 1999 World Cup in England. During the group game between Australia and Pakistan, Imran expressed surprise at seeing a fielder standing in a position he had apparently never seen before. The man was patrolling the area between deep mid-wicket and deep long-on. Any village cricketer could have told him this is 'cow corner'. Most of Randall's scoring shots off Qadir went in that direction. Of course, Randall was a Test cricketer. He wasn't playing cow shots, he was 'employing the slog-sweep'.

Before the teams re-convened at Lord's, England Young Cricketers started a 'Test' series against their West Indian counterparts. This was the equivalent of what now would be called England Under 19. A look at the names on show is illustrative of how hard it is to become a full international. During the series England used 14 players and although many of them are familiar to anyone who followed the county game, only five became Test cricketers. The young men in question were David Capel, Richard Illingworth, Jack Russell, Paul Jarvis and Hugh Morris. Of these, only Russell's Test career extended beyond 15 matches. It also says something about how likely England were to blood young talent in this era that none of them played a Test before Capel made his debut five years later. Illingworth and Morris weren't selected for another nine years and in the latter's case managed only three matches before being jettisoned for good. By contrast, the West Indian captain, Roger Harper, played for the full side in not much more than a year. His opening bowler, Courtney Walsh, followed him 11 months later.

As with Wayne Daniel in 1976, England could have done with young Walsh at Lord's. Willis' absence with a neck injury lumbered his replacement as captain, Gower, with surely the most one-dimensional bowling attack to take the field for England.

Botham, Jackman, Pringle, I.Greig and Hemmings was hardly a combination to strike terror into the heart of any Test batting line up and Pakistan's opener, Mohsin Khan, helped himself to only the second Test double hundred at Lord's since the War. That's the Second World War not the Falklands. 'Only the second Test double hundred at Lord's in the last couple of months' wouldn't be much of a statistic. The first for 33 years is bit more impressive. Mohsin's predecessor was a New Zealander called Martin Donnelly who scored 206 for New Zealand in 1949. This remained the only Test double century scored by a New Zealander against England until Nathan Astle's amazing blitz at Christchurch in March 2002.

Although he was arguably the best batsman New Zealand ever produced – C.B. Fry said he'd never seen a better left-hander – I bet most cricket fans have never heard of Martin Donnelly. The reason that's true makes his career a window into another world. Donnelly only played seven Test matches. These were spread over two series, both against England, 12 years apart. Even though he was still only 31 in 1949, he never played Test cricket again after that summer. When he was named as one of *Wisden's* five cricketers of the year for 1947 it was on the basis of his exploits for Oxford University and a brilliant unbeaten 162 for the Gentlemen against the Players. The same year, he played at centre for England against Ireland at Lansdowne Road. In the modern world such a talented all-round sportsman would make a fortune. As a post-war amateur, Donnelly had to find a career outside of sport to provide for his family. When he sailed for Sydney in the autumn of 1950 to become the sales and marketing manager of Courtaulds Australia it was, as Frank Keating put it, 'as if cricket had been a student pastime, a youthful wheeze not worth mentioning anymore'. Martin Donnelly spent what should have been the best years of his career fighting in North Africa and Italy. He earned not a penny from sport. Graham

Gooch had just earned in the region of £40,000 for less than a month's work. My school mates watching war in their living room weren't the only ones who didn't know they were born.

Mohsin's double hundred and England's inability to cope with Mudassar Nazar, a medium-pacer who made Ian Greig look like Harold Larwood, ensured the teams came to Leeds all-square.

It was at this point that, at least as far as Imran Khan was concerned, David Constant took a decisive hand, or, more precisely, left index finger, in proceedings.

England scraped home by three wickets to take the series 2-1. As the tourists had been struggling to set a challenging target in their second innings, the Pakistani number ten, Sikander Bakht (the man who had broken Mike Brearley's arm four years earlier), stuck around with his captain. The stand for the ninth wicket had reached 30 when Sikander propped forward at Vic Marks and the ball flew from his pad to Mike Gatting at short-leg. Replays showed it had missed his bat by several inches but Constant fired him out. Imran identified it as the decisive moment of the series. Pakistan's captain had a point about English arrogance when it came to their umpires and he was right that Sikander wasn't out, but he may also have been deluding himself.

Over the years I've made many such excuses for my side when apparently close contests have gone against them. However, ill fortune alone doesn't explain defeat and I've increasingly seen the truth in the old sporting cliché about the connection between practice and luck.

It can sometimes appear that weaker opposition rarely gets the rub of the green. However, I now realise the reason why my team failed to win was simply because they weren't as good as opposition who, by their superiority, created more opportunities for themselves. The more chances to seize a game you create, the less it matters if some slip away because of sheer bad luck. In the 2001 Ashes series, Australia dropped more catches than England. They also took 58 to the home side's 34 and won 4-1. Sometimes sportsmen, either consciously or unconsciously, create controversies to disguise failure and to provide an explanation for it that doesn't require remedial action. It's much easier to deal with being beaten if a) it wasn't your fault and b) you don't have to work any harder to ensure it doesn't happen again. Just as England might have done better on the sub-continent if they could have played spin, so as an alternative to criticising the umpires, Imran might have looked at the fact that his opponents' leading run scorer in the series was Extras.

The idea of creating truth for ourselves isn't restricted to sportspeople. In his book *The Kingdom By The Sea*, Paul Theroux records his journey around the coast of Britain in 1982. He recounts a meeting with someone he identifies as Mr. Bratby who offers the opinion that: 'Our society is changing from one based on the concept of the individual and freedom... to one where the individual is non-existent – lost in a collectivist state.' In the same year Bob Willis was quoted as saying: 'As for the way everyone's been going into raptures about leg-spin bowling, it doesn't win Test matches.' When you know that Mrs Thatcher turned 1980s Britain into a monetarist's dreamland and that Shane Warne exists, both statements sound ridiculous. The fact they obviously weren't ridiculous at the time brings into focus how much of the past we re-write for ourselves with the benefit of hindsight.

If you had have asked me what life was like in 1982, even though I knew the Falklands conflict effectively saved Mrs Thatcher's premiership, I still would have said that we were already living in the most individualistic period in our in history. As for Abdul Qadir, I would have told you he ran rings round our batsmen that summer. In fact, Qadir took 10 Test wickets at 40.60. Sometimes this process happens because we genuinely remember things wrongly (as a lawyer I was taught that eye-witness evidence is notoriously unreliable) and sometimes because we deliberately recreate the truth to make us feel better about ourselves. It happens more and more as you get older and the mistakes that you've made but would rather not admit to, mount up.

Sometimes it's just the very process of getting older that alters the perception. When I told a 25-year-old friend I was reading Theroux's book, he said: 'Oh yes. Louis Theroux's father.' Bearing in mind I was talking to an English teacher, this struck me as an example of how far television has taken over as our cultural touchstone. To me Louis Theroux was the reasonably talented son of a famous father. To my friend, Paul Theroux was identified through the celebrity of his son.

Finally, perhaps like Mr Bratby and Bob Willis, you misperceive simply because things are slowly and imperceptibly changing around you while you are forming your opinion; a bit like ageing really. When you are in your teens, as I was then, ageing seems a good thing. I could drive, I could vote, I had a job and I fancied that I had picked up some life experience from having lived through a war. I thought I was an adult. In fact what I had done was lived during a war, which isn't the same thing at all. As far as life was concerned, I knew (and know) no more about it than poor old Ian Greig knew about the difference between Qadir's googly and his flipper.

NINE

In my experience it doesn't do to presume too much in life. If you get too confident you're bound to be heading for trouble. Perhaps this is just my superstitious nature seeking refuge in pessimism; everyone knows if a commentator says a batsman is playing well he's about to get out. Alternatively, it could be my English reserve showing itself. If you anticipate the worst happening and are proved right, at least no one can accuse you of having been too cocky, a serious social sin in this country. If you are wrong you can bask in that most English of feelings, pleasant surprise.

The cricket-loving drama critic, James Agate, once said that: 'The English instinctively admire any man who has no talent and is modest about it.' If we have a motto it's 'Pride comes before a fall'. From 1970s rock musician Terry Kath's unfortunately inaccurate last words 'Don't worry, it's not loaded', to Henry VIII watching his pride and joy, the *Mary Rose*, sink on its maiden voyage, not to see the light of day again until two days before England left for their tour to Australia in October 1982, history is littered with the disasters of the overconfident. This attitude is a big part of one of two apparently diametrically opposed English characteristics that go a long way to explaining our consistent failure to dominate the world of sport in general and cricket in particular: arrogance and reticence.

The arrogance is a product of having had an empire, an assumption that our status in the world extends beyond mere sporting achievement, something that we had just proved by booting the Argentines off the Falklands. It also comes from our assertion that we gave these games to the world and so we have a God-given right to beat everyone else forever. In other words: all we have to do is turn up to win. This sort of thinking ensures everyone hates us so much that our opponents at anything raise their game against England. In cricket this was allied to the fact that although the players were paid, 20 years on from the last Gentlemen-v-Players match they still prepared in a way that harked back to the time when amateurs walked the earth.

Bob Willis' training regime before he toured Australia in 1982-83 consisted of running for 20 minutes or so each day and spending three mornings a week at the gym. England's captain described this as 'the most strenuous preparation I have undergone for any tour'. At the time, Willis had a reputation among his fellow cricketers as something of a fitness fanatic and he states in his tour diary that if his determination to get his team fit 'means less time spent around the pool at lunchtime with a bottle of wine, then that is how it may have to be'. It certainly sounds as if you didn't have to be Daley Thompson to be better physically prepared than the England cricket team.

On the other side of the coin there is reticence. We live in a society where this is a virtue and we are taught more than anything to be 'good losers'. We want our national team to win but they aren't allowed to be so presumptuous as to expect to and they have to have the decency to be mildly embarrassed about it if they do. To some extent this comes from an inherent distrust of anyone who pushes themselves forward too much and explains the way in which sporting and other heroes are torn down almost as quickly as they are built up. More than anything else though, I think this is born of an absolute terror of looking foolish. If you get excited about something it becomes obvious it matters to you. Bear in mind, this is a country in which the biggest compliment you can pay the food is to describe it as 'moreish'. It's far safer to act like you expect to be beaten. Even if this makes defeat a lot more likely, at least you can't possibly look stupid if it happens.

In the end this culture of 'good losing' becomes self-perpetuating: you are no longer merely acting as if you expect to lose, you really do expect it. In the summer of 1982, England had beaten India and Pakistan but Willis states they had done so without 'looking particularly formidable' and describes the victories as: 'Better than I had a right to hope for.' As far as the coming tour to Australia was concerned England's captain, employing what he calls his 'native realism', describes his team as 'no world beaters' and expresses fear about the prospect of England's batting frailties being 'brutally exposed'. Even when he tries to sound a more positive note he still expresses praise faintly and uses cautious, negative language: 'We were not mugs.' Apart from himself, Willis had at his disposal Ian Botham, David Gower, Allan Lamb and the best wicket-keeper in the world, Bob Taylor. However, he wasn't focusing on them. Obviously a captain has to recognise the weaknesses of his team before he can hope to remedy them but all of this seems to go further than mere recognition. It seems more like an exercise in damping down; what would be known in 'corporate speak' as 'managing expectations'. It is, in effect, saying to the cricketing public: 'Don't expect too much of us because we're not very good.'

I wouldn't have been any different. In fact I'm certain I was thinking exactly the same things, but this innate caution is something the Australians have ruthlessly exploited for most of the last 30 years. Before the trip, Willis gave an interview to Australia's channel 10 just after the touring party had been announced. The first words out of the interviewer's mouth were, 'Well, Bob, this must be the worst English team ever to leave your shores.' The team hadn't even left England and the process of undermining them psychologically had begun. This is something that has been honed and developed to the point where Steve Waugh gave it a name, 'mental disintegration'. Although this is based very often on the twisting of half-truths, like describing Alec Stewart as 'England's most defeated cricketer', its effect became increasingly apparent in a period when the disparity in playing quality between the two sides was more and more painfully obvious. In addition, the Australians created for themselves a legend of invincibility. Any team playing them has to see through this illusion before they have any chance of winning. Do you know which specialist batsman in Test history has made the most ducks? Steve Waugh.

England paid for their inherent conservatism both in the short and the long term. They had the better of a draw in the first Test at Perth, but Bob Willis' reaction to the match's major incident was more significant for the future of the game in this country.

Early on the second day, Willis spotted a group of youths who had begun chanting 'in the style of soccer fans'. At a time when the reputation of English football 'supporters' could not have been worse, the connotations of his description are deliberately negative and he predicts that they will cause trouble later in the day.

After tea, when Willis nicked Terry Alderman for 4 to bring up 400, about 20 'supporters' waving Union Jacks lumbered into the middle.

Clearly the worse for drink, they made the usual harmless exhibition of themselves before starting to trundle off again. What followed illustrates how big a responsibility professional sports stars have to keep calm in public. As one of the intruders was leaving he passed Alderman and cuffed him on the back of the head. The sensible course would have been to let the idiot wander off into the arms of the stewards. Instead, Alderman set off after him and brought him down with an Aussie Rules tackle, dislocating his own right shoulder in the process. Border and Lillee then jumped on the youth and pinned him down until the police arrived. If Alderman had let the lad go this incident would have been less disruptive than, for example, the pitch invasion that followed Boycott's 100th century. However, the sight of one of Australia's finest being carried off on a stretcher triggered a mass brawl between English and Australian supporters which carried on even after the players had returned following a brief suspension.

The next day the Australian papers were full of words like 'shameful' and 'disgusting' and Willis expressed the opinion that 'the boot boys had spread to cricket'. In the days long before the Barmy Army, the majority of those who had invaded the pitch, while professing allegiance to England were, in fact, migrants who had lived in Australia for many years. As such they were, at worst, part of English footballing culture by proxy. On the day in question they had been drunk and, in one individual's case, provocative, but trouble wouldn't have flared without Alderman's injury. However, the reaction to the incident is indicative both of the paranoia that surrounded football at the time and also the desire of the cricket fraternity to see themselves as inhabiting a special world of their own, untainted by the social problems that blighted society in general and football in particular. In short, cricketers were terrified of the naughty boys coming over their side of the playground.

This fear and the attendant wish to keep out undesirables meant a golden opportunity to popularize cricket was lost. In the 1980s, because of the hooligan problem, football was as unpopular as it was ever going to get. In many ways this was because television highlighted the worst excesses of violence and created a monster which, while real enough, was not as big as it appeared through the lens of a camera. Nevertheless, the cricketing public were not the only ones to perceive football grounds as the dark side of town, where 'nice' people and particularly women and children didn't go. The chance was there for another sport to attract the tens of thousands who shared this perception. While cricket could never realistically hope to compete with football's mass appeal, Botham's performances in 1981 had shown that it could catch the public's attention. With a little imagination, some success for the national team and (heaven forbid) some marketing, cricket could have reinvented itself. Turning from the stuffy irrelevant province of the privileged into, if you like, the acceptable national game. Even if many of those attracted would still have found their way back to football, cricket could have significantly broadened its fan base and, by extension, the pool of sporting talent playing the game.

The chance passed by unseized. Throughout the whole of the decade, apart from the identity of the sponsors, the only change made to cricket's domestic competitions was the introduction of some four-day championship matches. This aside, little of meaning was altered in terms of how the game was structured to enable the national side to be more competitive and arguably, in terms of popularizing the county game, four-day cricket was a backward step. Admittedly the problems of the limited length of the season and the fact that much of the game is played mid-week would still have been there. However, the popularity of summer rugby league and the success of the Twenty-20 competition illustrate that these difficulties can, at least in part, be overcome. By 1990, the opportunity had gone and the dire fare on offer in the championship that year stands in stark contrast to the heroics of Gazza and the rest at the World Cup finals in Italy that set off football's Big Bang.

The tone of Willis' account of the incident at Perth isn't unique. Reading his tour diary, you start to suspect it might have been ghosted by Eeyore. Apart from his usual sunny assessment of the team's performances, England's captain spends an inordinate amount of time going into detail about the treatment of the blisters on his feet.

There are some people you come across who feel simply informing you that they suffer from a particular condition is insufficient. Years later, playing for Stoneleigh, I had a teammate, Paul Price, who, you won't be surprised to hear, had the nickname of 'Pricey'. Amongst many other things, Pricey had ingrown toenails. Every Saturday any member of the team who couldn't get out of the changing room quickly enough was treated to a vivid account of the various oozings and spurtings that had afflicted him during the previous week. As captain, I was treated to more of this than anyone else as his problems sometimes constituted a reason for unavailability. Perhaps because he was, at the time, the best batsman in the club, he felt the need to provide me with ample justification for his absence. Whatever the reason, Pricey was someone for whom the phrase 'too much information' might have been invented. I still shudder at the memory of the phone call about the week in which his piles had flared up at the same time as he caught a sickness and diarrhea bug.

England's conservatism was far more ingrained and difficult to shift than even the blisters on their captain's toes.

In the second Test at Brisbane, England trailed by 122 with just over two and a half days to go. Showing his usual positive thinking, Willis comments that he could see 'no route to victory'. This was based on his assessment that there was insufficient time left in the match for England to score enough to set Australia a testing second-innings target and illustrates a big difference in mentality between then and now. The tourists' final total of 309 spanned 127.3 overs at a scoring rate of 2.42. Even if they had scored at 0.75 of a run per over faster, giving an overall run rate of 3.17 (hardly lightning by modern standards), Australia would have been set 282 in 77 overs on the last day. As it was, the target was 188 and Australia won by 7 wickets with 16 overs left in the match.

At Adelaide, Willis put Australia in when all cricketing reason screamed 'Bat!'. It was only when Willis' book came out the following year that anyone realised it wasn't just the captain's personality that was the problem.

Willis recounts how he thought England should certainly bat first. However, every player he consulted came up with the opposite view. The batsmen feared collapsing against the Australian fast bowlers if there was any moisture left in the pitch on the first morning. This left the captain with an invidious choice between imposing his will on a reluctant batting line-up or going with the majority against his better judgment. By the end of the day he clearly had cause to regret doing the latter. Pilloried in the press and in the stands (one banner read: 'They call the Irish stupid! But Willis won the toss!!') he spent the rest of the match, like a minister bound by cabinet responsibility, publicly defending a decision he didn't agree with. England went down to their second successive defeat.

Supporting England at this time was like following one of those football clubs (Sunderland, Ipswich, Leicester) who perennially yo-yo between the Premiership and whatever the division below it is called this week. Most of the time it is a story of failure against the best but with just enough moments of inspiration and exhilaration to keep you interested. Norman Cowans' 6-77 to help win the Boxing Day Test in Melbourne was one of those moments.

Cowans was an example of a consistent English selection for Australian tours; the young fast bowler picked mainly on his reputation for pace. The West Indies, with their battery of fast bowlers, dominated world cricket and England's selectors kept trying to unearth someone to give us the firepower to dominate opponents in the same way. That they consistently failed to do so is, at least partially, explained by the reasons why England's captain had never even seen Cowans play before he helped pick him.

Willis had never seen Cowans as he hadn't turned out for Middlesex against Warwickshire. In those days county cricketers played seven days a week. Throughout the season Willis would either have been involved with England or playing for Warwickshire and so had no chance of seeing any young fast bowler unless he lined up against his county. Obviously this was a disadvantage for Willis in his role as an England selector but, more than that, his workload goes a long way to explaining why no one bowled consistently fast for England during this period. Quite simply, it was physically impossible to bowl at 90 miles an hour day in, day out. Fred Trueman may have said he bowled 1000 overs in a season but he played in an era when there was no county cricket on a Sunday and no one-day games with all the extra physical demands that the necessary fielding efforts place on the body. I'm also sure that not every one of those 1000 overs could possibly have been bowled flat out. In the 1980s, with frequent declarations towards the end of the first day of a three-day game, opening bowlers in county cricket did have to bowl pretty much every day and were expected to push themselves in the field on a Sunday. You had a choice between trying to bowl flat out every day and having a short, injury-ridden, career, or cutting your pace to 80-85 mph. Even then the sheer amount of cricket could still take its toll.

In 1982, Norman Cowans was only 21 and hadn't yet been ground down by years on the circuit. By the time he was 25, his Test career was over and he served out his days bowling fast-medium for Middlesex and Hampshire.

Even Cowans' brief moment in the sun and Geoff Miller doing the most exciting thing he ever did in his Test career (catching a rebound from Tavare six inches above the turf to win the Melbourne Test by three runs) weren't enough to save the Ashes.

Kim Hughes and Allan Border ensured a draw at Sydney before Willis' men rounded things off nicely with a disastrous one-day campaign. England lost nine out of 13 ODIs, New Zealand played in beige and, in Brisbane, the Australian crowd released a pig onto the outfield with 'Botham' painted on one side and 'Eddie' (Hemmings) on the other.

As Richard Ingrams commented in the *Spectator* at the time: 'There is no earthly reason why anyone of intelligence should want to watch it.' Actually he was talking about breakfast television, which had just started on BBC 1, presented by Frank Bough (in his cardigan rather than his gimp suit) and Selina Scott. Ms Scott had defected from ITV and was apparently there to attract male viewers. She seemed unlikely to do this with her intimate knowledge of sport, as she once memorably (to me at least) suggested to Bob Wilson, the former Arsenal goalkeeper and sports presenter on the show, that his side's double-securing 1-0 victory over Tottenham must have been an easy match for him, as he didn't have 'any goals to save'. However, to the British public, this level of sporting exchange mattered as little as Mr Ingrams' opinion and within a year *Breakfast Time* had viewing figures of 1.5 million, while its ITV competitor *TV-am* had 1.2 million. On the BBC we had Russell Grant and the Green Goddess (an aerobics teacher in shiny, tight, green lycra as opposed to an army fire engine). ITV replied with 'Mad' Lizzie (only mad in the 'I'm mad me', not really mad at all, sense) and, later, Roland Rat. The concept of the C list celebrity was born.

Given their performances Down Under our cricketers weren't even on the 'C' list. In the period that England were playing the pyjama game, Brighton knocked Newcastle, Manchester City and Liverpool (at Anfield) out of the FA Cup, seat belts became compulsory, Klaus Barbie was returned to Lyon to be put on trial and Shergar was kidnapped. It must be slightly deflating for a professional sportsman to realise your profile is so low that a horse is more likely to be kidnapped than you are.

Under normal circumstances the defeats in the one-day games wouldn't have bothered me, as the only one-day tournament that really mattered was the World Cup. Unfortunately this was the next competitive cricket England were going to play and it was only three months away.

In the interim there was plenty to keep me occupied. There was a General Election and Brighton found themselves in the uncharted territory of the sixth round of the Cup where, instead of 'monsters', it was a case of 'here be Norwich City'. Having disposed of them 1-0 they joined Manchester United, Arsenal, and Sheffield Wednesday in the semi-finals. When the draw was made I was huddled round my radio at work with my mates whispering 'please let them get Wednesday' over and over again. They got Wednesday and we got tickets for Highbury. Though we made hard work of it, a 2-1 win started off a bad couple of months for Roy Hattersley, left us in the final with United and triggered the great Jimmy Melia wig shortage of 1983.

For anyone who wasn't a Brighton fan at the time (i.e. anyone who had any sense), Jimmy Melia was the team's manager. He had a penchant for white disco shoes and a hairstyle like Max Wall.

There are moments in life you have to seize because they will never come again. Teams like Brighton only get to the FA Cup final once. Because Melia and his men came so agonizingly close to seizing their day, there are two sporting images from this year that I'm sure are going to flash past me just before I die.

The first is of Gordon Smith effectively passing the ball back to United's keeper, Gary Bailey, with the goal at his mercy in the last minute of extra time. I blame Michael Robinson; he should have just buried it himself. After that, a 4-0 thrashing in the replay was 'inevitable' wasn't it?

If Smith's miss is shared with anybody who was supporting Brighton that day, the second image I'll take to my grave is, I think, a much more individual memory of the World Cup final.

England's semi-final defeat to India was softened by Zimbabwe beating Australia (Man of the Match: D Fletcher 69 not out and 4-42) earlier in the tournament and the thought that our conquerors had as much chance of beating West Indies as Lech Walesa had of becoming President of Poland.

After India's innings it looked as if I was right and one shot from Kris Srikkanth would be an isolated moment of defiance.

'Adam Gilchrist on speed' gives you some idea about how Srikkanth approached opening the batting. In Kris' world it wasn't lunch that was for wimps, it was defensive shots. Like anyone who takes this approach, he was capable of breathtaking brilliance and mind-numbing ineptitude in almost equal measure. A Test average of under 30 testifies to his inconsistency but on this day he produced a single moment that has stayed with me for over twenty years.

Andy Roberts had already removed Gavaskar, and though nearing the end of his career, was still a fearsome prospect on his way to figures of 3-32 from ten overs. *Wisden* reports that 14 of those runs came from three balls bowled at Srikkanth but I only remember the third. Tearing in from the Nursery End, Roberts bowled a half-volley, possibly a fraction wide of off stump. Most openers would have left it but Srikkanth stretched forward and, down on one knee, played what I can only describe as a front-foot scythe of such power that the sounds of the shot itself and of the ball crashing into and through the boundary board seemed almost simultaneous.

This wasn't the defining moment of the match. India didn't win because of it, they won because the West Indies' top batsmen arrogantly tossed their wickets away and the medium pacers did what they had done to us three days earlier by strangling the middle order. But that shot was, to me at least, an instant as memorable as Warne's ball to Gatting in 1993. I wish I hadn't watched it alone.

Indian supporters probably remember Kapil Dev's running catch to get rid of Viv Richards or Jeff Dujon beating his right hand on the ground with frustration when he played on to Mohinder Amarnath. Those moments haven't stayed as vividly with me because as they were happening I was dealing with a West Indian giant of my own. The name of this literal colossus of cricket was, I swear to you, Tyrone Wildman.

On the afternoon of the World Cup final, Barcombe were facing Sidley, the runaway leaders of the first division of the East Sussex League. By reputation they were a very good side with a strong hand of quick bowlers. I had never played against them and my teammates spent most of the fortnight before the match winding me up with tales of the terrors I would face at their ground. About the only thing they didn't tell me was the tea lady was descended from Lucrezia Borgia but most of their efforts focused on Tyrone.

Some people have names that fit them perfectly. Dwayne Bravo, for example, couldn't be anything but a West Indian cricketer. Therefore it won't surprise you to learn that the answers to the questions: 'Is Tyrone West Indian by any chance?' and 'Is he enormous?' were 'yes' and 'yes'. However, after this point the responses became less straightforward: 'How quick is he then?' was met with 'You'll see' and 'Come on lads he can't be that quick' merited only a sharp intake of breath. On and on it went, I started to feel like a doomed teenager in a slasher movie: 'Come on guys, stop kidding around!… Guys?'

On the car journey there, despite my transparently feigned nonchalance, I still couldn't escape. 'You alright Paul?… Don't worry about Tyrone. You're young…you've got quick reactions.' We arrived and there he was, he was real, they hadn't made him up. At first sight he didn't seem particularly tall but then that was probably just an optical illusion created by the width of his shoulders. It was a good thing tight cricket shirts were fashionable then, because there wasn't one made that would have been baggy on him. He laughed a lot but this was little comfort. It seemed too maniacal for my liking. In short, he gave the expected appearance of someone for whom happiness was an opponent's empty bowel.

We lost the toss and were put in. 'Right Lazenby! The rest of us have got families. You're opening!' 'Bastard!'. Although helmets had been worn in Tests for about five years by now, anyone who sported one in club cricket at our level was seen as a bit of a wuss. Therefore the best wishes of my captain ('Good luck…you're going to need it') easily reached my unprotected ears.

At one end of the ground was a substantial slope and I had a vision of Tyrone charging down it. Kris Srikkanth's square drive off Andy Roberts popped into my head. My nemesis marked out his run; one, two, three, four, five. 'Five! Bloody hell this bloke doesn't even need a run up!' I took guard for the third time but then there was no delaying it any longer, I had to face the first ball. My mouth was dry, I gripped the bat tightly, every muscle in my body (i.e. about as many as there were in Tyrone's little finger) tensed. Down it came.

The gentlest bloody off-cutter you'll ever face. I played it back to him and turned to look at my teammates. They were pissing themselves. As Alfred Hitchcock put it: 'There is no terror in the bang, only in the anticipation of it.'

A few years later, when I became a little more self-aware, I realised the degree to which I had been a victim of my own prejudice. All I had found out about Tyrone was that he was big and black and from that just assumed he was going to bowl terrifyingly quickly. Roger Harper was big and black and he was an off-spinner. You could argue my assumptions were harmless enough because were based on stereotyping that, as is usual, had at least some basis in fact – lots of West Indian bowlers did bowl very quickly – and were confined to expectations of how a particular person was going to play a game of cricket. However, it came as a bit of a shock for me to realise later that the sort of assumptions I had made that day were not dissimilar to those informing why the police at this time had developed a reputation for stopping any black bloke driving anything more flash than a Mini Metro.

At Sidley all my preconceptions were blown away, just like our batting. The real cricketing laxative was a white left-arm seamer flying in from the other end.

After the World Cup, a Test series against New Zealand seemed like a bit of an anti-climax. England duly won the first match when, for the one and only time in Test history, Phil Edmonds and Vic Marks combined to spin a side to defeat. Then, at Headingley, England lost to the Kiwis for the first time on home soil courtesy of a first-innings collapse – to Lance Cairns of all people – that saw the last seven wickets disappear for 50.

My memory seems full of England collapses like that. The sports reporter at the end of the news would sigh his weary sigh and smile the inclusive smile that preceded another report of English batting disaster. But was it really like that? Did we really collapse anymore than anyone else or did it just seem that way because it mattered to me and I was focused on it, like everyone noticing a wicket falling at 111 because it's supposedly an unlucky number? Actually, yes we did.

Over the whole of the 1980s, in completed innings (i.e. when they were all out, as opposed to declaring or winning/drawing with a few wickets down), England lost their last seven wickets for fewer than 100 runs approximately 39 per cent of the time. Only one country, Sri Lanka, had a worse record and their figure of 43 per cent may be skewed by the fact they played fewer matches than everybody else. The rest vary between 21 per cent (West Indies) and 31 per cent (Australia). In other words, you could say that England were almost twice as likely to collapse as the West Indies. When England's batting imploded and we all tutted and thought 'typical', it really was.

At 1-1 against a side we had never lost to, England got some luck. Phil Edmonds ricked his back getting out of a car. His replacement, Nick Cook (remember him?), took 17 wickets in two matches and England won by impressively large margins.

As the series drew to a close, David Frith concluded that 'it was truly time for the football yobs to take over' and Bob Willis headed for a holiday in France where he avoided the beach because he had 'always associated sand and sunshine with Pakistani Test matches'.

I ended the season making the third highest score (3) in a total of 33 all out. It was the last time I played a league match for Barcombe. At the end of that summer I left home. I was off to be a student. Sex and drugs and rock and roll were on the horizon. On England's winter tour to New Zealand that is, not my university career.

TEN

England's visit to New Zealand in 1983-84 has become known as the 'sex and drugs and rock and roll' tour. Certainly, England were about as collectively appalling against the Kiwis as they have ever been in all the time I've been following them, but in essence the allegations about the team's extra-curricular activities amount to little more than Ian Botham's admission that he smoked pot.

Unless you count the team meeting Elton John, there was no rock and roll. Judging by how they performed on the field, if they had started chucking the hotel television about they would either have missed the window altogether or it would have gone for overthrows. As for sex, not even Botham was accused of breaking any beds with a former Miss Dunedin. The fact the tour has been labelled in this way illustrates quite a lot.

Most obviously, it's another example of the game's conservatism. Generally speaking, the most dangerous thing a cricketer ever does is sweep a leg-spinner bowling into the rough from round the wicket. Pringle's earring was bad enough, but the idea that the team's real all-rounder had indulged in a bit of blow, well the fellow needed stringing up didn't he? What Botham actually got was a 63-day ban from all first-class cricket when he admitted the allegations two years later.

The way this tour has been represented also shows how certain sections of the British media will never let the truth get in the way of a good bit of sensationalism. Given his high profile at the time, this is something probably not unconnected to why Botham might have felt the need to indulge in a bit of illegal relaxant in the first place.

Finally though, I think the whole 'sex and rugs and rock and roll' thing is just another excuse that avoids dealing with the real underlying reasons for poor performance. England didn't lose series to New Zealand and Pakistan for the first time because the players had a 'rock and roll' lifestyle. Those running the game and the team were just as culpable.

The Mail on Sunday alleged at the time that some members of the party had smoked pot in New Zealand. Yet a TCCB investigation cleared all the players of having done anything off the field that might have affected their performance on it. In other words, they failed to find something that the press later forced Botham to admit. This demonstration of super-efficiency was preceded by the imposition of a ridiculous itinerary – clearly designed to keep time spent in that dreadful Pakistan place to an absolute minimum – that resulted in nothing but international cricket from the start of the second Test in Christchurch until the end of the winter. England started the first Test against Pakistan within 60 hours of arriving from New Zealand. Their attitude to being there was summed up by Willis' assertion that they were better playing straight off the plane than going off 'up country' and risking illness and by Botham's infamous quip about mothers-in-law. Unsurprisingly, they were spun to defeat by Abdul Qadir and ended up losing the series 1-0.

Even that was an improvement on going down to the Kiwis, courtesy of one of the most inept performance England have ever produced. You don't watch England for more than 30 years without seeing some bad cricket, but Christchurch in February 1984 was really special.

Unfortunately, when Bob Willis said that it was 'some of the worst' he had seen, he was talking about England's bowling rather than Michael Jackson's Pepsi advert burns. The doctor treating Jackson, blissfully unaware of the irony of what he was saying, said that the singer might need 'surgery on his head'. He might just as easily have been referring to England's bowlers as, in conditions offering lavish seam and swing movement, they concluded that a series of long-hops were required. Tony Pigott came in for his one and only Test as cover for the injured Dilley and Foster and took 2-75 in about the most helpful conditions he could ever have wished for. How the tour selectors came to prefer Pigott, who was returning from injury, to Neil Mallender who had just taken match figures of 6-63 from 28 overs for Otago against the tourists, is another matter. Even when New Zealand were apparently in trouble at 87-4, that was probably 30 runs too many and two wickets too few.

Richard Hadlee smashed a 99 which he described as 'worth 300'. The New Zealanders' total of 307 was at least 150 runs bigger than it should have been and 131 more than they would need to win by an innings.

Pigott's wedding was arranged for the fourth day of the match and he postponed it to make his Test debut. He needn't have bothered, England were shot out for 82 and 93 and lost inside three. I've never been more embarrassed as a player or supporter of any team of 'mine'. Not even when I was in a side that was bowled out for 13 (at least we were all only nine at the time) or of the school football team that lost 11-2 when I was in goal. By now I was moving in politically more left-leaning circles where it's fair to say supporting the national cricket team was not fashionable. Performances like this one would have made it very easy for me to disown them altogether.

That was never going to happen of course. In the same way as football supporters are 'always a red', following England's cricket team was part of who I was. Admittedly 'always a white' didn't have quite the same meaning and sounded a bit too much like Eugene Terre'Blanche for my liking, but it was going to take more than a bit of political re-evaluation and some pathetic batting to change me that fundamentally. Anyway, as I told my new left-wing friends, C.L.R. James was a Marxist, so that was alright then.

Sometimes you're just in the wrong place at the wrong time: like being left-wing in the 1980s for example. On 12th March 1984, the second Test against Pakistan and the miners' strike started. In their own ways both focused on leaders who found themselves in charge at exactly the wrong moment.

The strike, presented in many parts of the media as a battle of wills between Mrs Thatcher and Arthur Scargill, was triggered when the chairman of the National Coal Board, Ian MacGregor, announced the closure of 20 'uneconomic' pits with the resultant threat to 20,000 jobs. Just as every news bulletin in March and April 1982 started with word from the Falklands, so for a year from March 1984, all else was played out in front of the back drop of the 'civil war' that was literally being fought out on the picket lines. Scargill openly admitted his desire to bring down the government and had behind him nearly all of the country's 187,000 mineworkers. Mrs Thatcher had stockpiles of foreign coal, a largely supportive media and, perhaps most crucially of all, the winter of discontent and the power cuts of the early seventies still fresh in the memories of most of the adult population.

In many ways the eighties were an easy time for me to become more politically aware. The edges were nowhere near as blurred as they are now; you either believed in the monetarist revolution or you didn't, hated Thatcher or loved her. It was as straightforward as being an Aussie or a Pom. As Billy Bragg put it: 'Which side are you on boys? Which side are you on?' In 1984 I chose my side. It was a good job I was used to losing.

In Faislabad, David Gower had inherited a demoralized England team when Willis was taken ill. The left-hander produced innings of 152 and 173 not out and, in company with Vic Marks (previous highest Test score 12), ensured two creditable draws. Marks' last three scores in this series were 83, 74 and 55. He never played Test cricket again. Gower's 152 was the first Test hundred by an England captain since Tony Greig at Calcutta in January 1977, but then for the majority of the period since then England had been led by either Mike Brearley or Bob Willis. Suddenly faced with the possibility of having a captain capable of scoring more than 28, the selectors gave Gower the job on a slightly more permanent basis for the following summer.

In March, Cambridge's Boat Race crew ran into a barge on the Thames with predictable results. Unfortunately for Gower, the tourists in 1984 were the West Indies. It may have been more than 60 years since the only time England had lost a series 5-0 (against Warwick Armstrong's Australians in 1920-21) and their worst result against the Windies may have been Greig's 3-0 defeat in 1976, but given a dry summer history was always going to be bunk. It stayed dry and Gower's England, deprived of Gooch, Boycott (still averaging over 60 for Yorkshire at the age of 43), Underwood and Lever (more than 100 wickets for Essex) ran aground in spectacular fashion. For stockpiles of foreign coal, read Malcolm Marshall; for a supportive media, read Michael Holding and for memories of the seventies, read Viv Richards. At least Gower, unlike Tony Greig, hadn't announced his intention to bring down Clive Lloyd.

If the new captain could have been forgiven for a slightly sarcastic 'cheers for that lads' in the direction of the selectors, he wasn't the only one who was going to end up with cause to regret the timing of his promotion. A 17-year-old called Graeme Hick might have saved Mashonaland U25s from humiliation with a heroic 134, but he was going to have to wait a while longer for his chance to be roughed up by the lads from the Caribbean.

In 1980, David Lloyd might, with hindsight, have wished he had started the season with a series of ducks rather than the run of good form that saw him recalled to England colours for the first time since Jeff Thomson had done him over in 1974-75. Having missed out in the intervening period on the likes of Liaquat Ali, Lloyd got back into the side just as Andy Roberts and co. were rolling into town. He made one in the first ODI of the summer and was dropped for good. Four years later, his namesake Andy made the mistake of starting the season in the form of his life. As a result, he was at Edgbaston on 14th June embarking on arguably the shortest Test career in history. At least he got more than double Andy Warhol's 15 minutes (33 to be exact) before a ball from Malcolm Marshall crashed into the side of his head, detached his retina and simultaneously finished his season and international career. At the point of impact I doubt whether he would have agreed with Alfred Hitchcock about the terror in the 'bang'. I had some idea how he felt.

A couple of months earlier I had, against my better judgment, agreed at the last minute to play in goal in a Sunday-league football match for 'The Gay Eleven' (manager: Roger Gay) against 'Red Star Belgrano'. Two thirds of the way through the first half I had run full tilt into my own central defender, caught my studs in the ground and forced my left knee into a manoeuvre it wasn't designed for. I should have known better than to play football for a 21-year-old man whose proudest possession was his beer gut.

If I had known then the extent of the injury, how poorly treated it would be and the fact that I would never be able to keep-wicket regularly again, I might not have so easily consoled myself with the thought that at least it was a good way of meeting young nurses.

By the time Andy Lloyd was being helped off at Edgbaston I had just about regained a similarly unsteady ability to walk in a straight line. As a result I was in a position to encounter my first love, Sarah. She was beautiful and, miraculously, when I asked her out she said 'yes'. I adored her. You know you're in trouble when you stay up talking until five in the morning, camp out under the stars and say you've missed someone when they've only been to the toilet. It lasted less than six weeks.

Perhaps we are all condemned to be taught the same lessons in life over and over again. In David Gower's case the lesson was 'don't flick at good length balls just outside off stump'. For me, saying that by the end of the summer Sarah had dumped me for a vicar her parents didn't approve of tells you all you need to know. It comes to something when the rebellious option by comparison with you is marrying a man of the cloth. I certainly didn't feel dangerous. And, like the second Test, it had all started so well.

At Birmingham, a 10-man side had taken a hiding by an innings and 180 runs. However, at Lord's, thanks to Lamb's 110 England had worked their way into a position where they could declare 20 minutes into the final day. The West Indies were set 342 to win in five and a half hours, i.e. at better than a run a minute. Gordon Greenidge smashed 214 not out and the tourists won with 11.5 overs to spare. Watching Greenidge that day was like visiting a gallery so full of great art that it's impossible to take it all in. In the end the brilliance before you becomes boring by virtue of how often it's repeated: 'Oh look! Another savage square cut to the point boundary'. Gower became the first England captain since 1948 to have declared in the second innings and lost, it wasn't the last unenviable captaincy record he would end up having by the end of the summer.

Any residual dreams I may have had of playing for England suddenly started to become less attractive but I still sought the more minor glories of playing club cricket. On the other hand, despite a growing interest in real politics, the Student Union variety didn't interest me. Like *It's a Knockout* it was amusing enough to watch but not something you would want to take part in yourself. This seemed to be the general attitude towards it and explained how the Sports Officer was an overweight Accountancy and Finance student who was elected on the strength of his one residual sporting talent: the ability to do a flick-flack. If real elections had worked like that Suzanne Dando would have been prime minister.

That's not to say student politics was completely unconnected to the real world. There was one particularly interesting member of the University Conservatives who, I think it's fair to say, had a reputation for having what might be termed 'strident' views. His summer job was rumoured to be fighting with the Contras in Nicaragua.

I worked as waiter at Butlins. Believe me, this had its own dangers. There had been an outbreak of legionnaires' disease among the guests and venereal disease among the staff just before I had started. One of the cooks, Bo, a bald bulldog of a man with permanent beads of sweat on his forehead, looked like he could warm the food up just by giving it one of his looks. The first head chef I met was there one morning and not the next. I never did establish whether his indiscretion was financial, sexual or a combination of the two, but it can't have helped that the environmental health inspector picked him up on the fact he kept the door from the kitchen to the bin areas permanently open so his dog could get in and out.

I was employed as a plate waiter – none of your fancy silver service rubbish here – working three shifts a day, six days a week for £64. Tips were vital and my 'mentor', Paul Kearns, legendary for going home at the end of the week with his pockets full of change, passed on his secrets to me in the style of Obi-Wan Kenobi. Fortunately these were not quite as time-consuming to master as the 'Force', consisting as they did of handing a punter a plate of salad and saying 'careful it's hot' or, if that didn't work hitting them with the real killer: 'What do you want for pudding? Sultana sponge or Spotted Dick?' The frightening thing is it worked. We had them eating out of our hands; literally in the case of the chef with his dog.

Having said that, some of my colleagues had been seduced by the dark side. One waitress in particular, Katie, waited-on like Darth Vader minus the charm but never seemed to make the connection between this and her slim pickings at the end of the week. 'How come you've got £40 in tips and I've only got £15?' 'Dunno, maybe it's because I didn't call table five "a bunch of wankers".'

I also had a colleague who claimed to be the brother of the former Hampshire batsman David Rock, but that's about as interesting as he got. Much more entertaining was his mate 'the Sniffer' and his efforts to ingratiate himself with any young woman who caught his eye (i.e. all of them). He seemed to work on the basis that any girl he fancied must fancy him because she was in the same room. Given that the hotel's dining hall was approximately 50 yards long by about 25 yards wide, in his mind he was spoilt for choice. The rest of us knew that Mavis from Coronation Street (proposed to by two different men in 1984) was doing better than he was.

Obviously desperate, his greatest humiliation came when he tried to impress a particularly pretty new waitress with how quickly he could serve his tables. Rushing to the front of the queue of waiters in the kitchen, he grabbed his rack of dinners in his left hand and the spare in his right, marched to the exit, flashed his best Magnum PI raise of the eyebrows and kicked open the door to the dining room with his right foot at the exact same moment as his left hit a slick of gravy on the floor. I had only ever seen cartoon characters parallel with the ground in mid-air before. He hit the deck half in the kitchen and half in the dining room. There was a fraction of a second of eerie silence before his plates landed on him, attracting the attention of 100 diners. If I had known I was about to be blown out for a man of the cloth I might not have laughed quite so hard, but it was a moment almost as humbling as what was being dealt out to England's cricket team.

If England's defeat at Lord's was every bit as psychologically damaging as the one handed out to Flintoff's men at Adelaide in 2006, at Headingley they were beaten by a one-armed man. On the first morning, Malcolm Marshall sustained a double fracture of the left thumb fielding in the gulley. Unfortunately it turned out that we weren't even very good at injuring them effectively.

In the West Indies' first innings, Marshall came out at number 11, saw Larry Gomes to his hundred and even hit a one handed four of his own. When the tourists bowled a second time, Marshall emerged with his left hand in plaster and took 7-53, including a caught and bowled from Graeme Fowler just as he and Gower were threatening to make a match of it. 104-2 became 159 all out, leaving West Indies only 128 to win. They strolled home by eight wickets.

From 3-0 down against a far superior side, even the A-Team armed with some sheet metal and a blowtorch couldn't have saved England now, and the morale of the team can't have been raised by the news announced on the opening day of the fourth Test that Botham wasn't going to tour the following winter. Although the fact the tour was to India might have had something to do with the timing of the decision, no one could really argue with the stated reasons that he had played eight years of continuous cricket and needed to spend some time with his family. It was unarguable that the amount of cricket Botham, Hadlee, Imran and Kapil Dev played couldn't be sustained without the risk of injury or burn-out. Imran had played in the last World Cup solely as a batsman because of a stress fracture in his shin. This perhaps gives a clue as to why the modern game lacks great all-rounders.

After 2000, arguably only Kallis and Flintoff had the ability to make it into their respective sides as a batsman or bowler alone and even Kallis seemed to prefer to see himself as a batsman who bowls. This could simply be explained by the 1980s being a fortunate blip in history. Alternatively it could be that with the amount of international cricket now played it's almost impossible to maintain the necessary level of performance in both disciplines to be worthy of your place for one alone. Botham played 102 Test matches over a 15-year Test career (with

116 one-day internationals in one year longer), Kapil Dev 131 Tests in 15 ½ years (225 ODIs), Hadlee 86 Tests in 17 years (115 ODIs) and Imran 88 Tests in 21 years (175 ODIs). To the end of the 2005 English season, Jacques Kallis had already played 93 Tests and 217 one-day internationals in his ten-year career. No wonder he didn't feel like bowling all the time. Flintoff's problems with injury were legendary. It could be that the Lancashire all-rounder's bowling action made him an injury waiting to happen, or it could be that he was just a product of his time: like Allan Lamb.

In the fourth Test at Old Trafford, England needed 301 to avoid the follow-on. In the course of reaching 278-7, Paul Terry had his left arm broken by Winston Davis and had, not unreasonably, retired hurt. When Joel Garner removed Pat Pocock and Norman Cowans in one over, everyone started to troop off, only to see Terry striding out with his arm in a sling under a big sweater. England needed 23 and with Lamb on 98, this was not impossible if Terry could match Marshall's effort from Headingley. Clive Lloyd pushed the field back to give the two-armed batsman a single and he resisted until the last ball of an over from Holding which he nudged to fine-leg. However, instead of trotting a single to retain the strike, Lamb sprinted two to take him to his century and made as if to leave the field, expecting a declaration. He had assumed that Terry had been sent out to get him to his personal landmark rather than to pursue the greater team target. To me, it was a moment that encapsulated not only the England cricket team but Britain as a whole in the 1980s: individual first, team second.

Gower's post match comment that, 'It was left to Lambie to get his hundred when Paul went back in and the avoidance of the follow-on would have been a bonus. But we weren't really going to save it,' also gives an insight into the defeatism that hung over England's efforts in the series. This wasn't an attitude that was restricted to the team. John Thicknesse, the Standard's cricket correspondent at the time, wrote that the sides for each of the Tests in the series had 'to be picked within a framework of defensive strategy for England to get out even love-three losers' and also that 'at Old Trafford, with blind optimism still setting out their stall to win, the selectors got it wrong again'. The implication was that Gower knew perfectly well he had no chance, but those picking the teams kept saddling him with overly positive selections. The view that England would have been lucky to lose 3-0 was generally held but if you think a draw is the best you can hope for and trying to win is a mistake, then defeat becomes almost inevitable. At least the miners were trying to win.

The problem wasn't attempting to win, it was how they were going about it. There didn't appear to be any coherent plan of how victory was to be achieved other than 'charge!'. Before England toured the West Indies under Graham Gooch in 1989-90, Ian Botham commented that whatever his heart felt about their chances, his head said 5-0. Just about everybody, including me, thought the same thing. If it hadn't rained on the last afternoon in Trinidad, England would almost certainly have won that series and at very least shared it. That didn't happen by accident, the West Indies' then manager Clive Lloyd commented after the first Test in Jamaica: 'He (Gooch) has done his homework on every single one of our batsmen and knew exactly what fields to set to them.' Under Gooch, England's bowlers stuck to a rigid off-stump line and the batsmen guts it out. It was as if no one in the England set up had ever thought of doing this before.

However, in 1984 Gooch was still banned from playing let alone captaining and at the Oval, Gower's first 5-0 defeat was completed. As with every game in the series except Edgbaston there was a moment when we were on top. Here we got the good stuff out of the way on the first day, bowling the West Indies out for 190. By now we all knew what was coming. Just before he went out to bat as nightwatchman, Pat Pocock told the England physio, Bernard Thomas: 'I've cleaned my teeth and gargled, just in case you have to give me the kiss of life!'

The BBC had to move one of their effects microphones when it was discovered that it was picking up conversation from one of the boxes, in which leading members of Britain's defence network were being entertained. They didn't need to take one from outside the tourists' dressing room. The West Indies plan of 'bowl very fast' was hardly a secret. We skittled them for less than 200 and still conceded a first-innings lead of 28. England were set 375 to win and, on the final afternoon, Holding recalled 1976 by suddenly coming off his long run and the 'blackwash' was sealed by 172 runs.

Even then the English cricketing establishment looked for excuses and seemed to try and make out a case that morally we had won because we hadn't 'stooped' to the West Indians' methods. Len Hutton referred to Lloyd's apparent lack of control over his 'Bouncing Billies', John Woodcock said that 'It was not, I believe, cricket as it was intended to be played' and Robin Marlar suggested the West Indians' tactics were 'deeply offensive to the essence of cricket'. Perhaps the 'essence of cricket' had changed 20 years later, but I don't remember too many remarks of this nature when Andrew Flintoff cut Pedro Collins' chin open at Old Trafford in 2004.

In any case, claims that England had only lost because, to paraphrase Bill Woodfull, they were the only team out there playing 'cricket', were about to be made to look as ridiculous as Morrissey and his gladioli on *Top of the Pops*.

The cricketing summer wasn't over. The Sri Lankans had patronizingly been thrown the scrap of one Test on the basis that they were the worst international side in the world. After five days at Lord's there was another team laying claim to that title. As with Bangladesh in 2005, the plan was simple: put them in, roll them over for next to nothing, smash their 'dibbly-dobblies' all over the place for a while and then roll them over again.

Gower executed part one of the plan to perfection by winning the toss and putting Sri Lanka in. Then things went slightly wrong; they made 491-7 declared. Their opener, Siddath Wettimuny, good but hardly Sunil Gavaskar, batted for nearly two days making 190 and then Botham decided their captain, Duleep Mendis, was a candidate for a bouncer barrage.

When teammates now question my timing when I bring myself on, I tell them there is a knack to bowling at 12 year-olds that not everybody has. Clearly there's also a knack to bouncing the hell out of somebody. The West Indians had it and Botham, at least on this occasion, didn't. Three times Mendis hooked him for six. For me there seemed to be a bit of a theme developing involving England all-rounders bowling from the Pavilion end and the ball landing in the Tavern.

Having cocked up part two of the plan, part three went a bit wobbly too. At Chester-le-Street in 2005, England scored 400 in two sessions. At Lord's in 1984, they took nearly two days to make 370.

From an England supporter's point of view the whole match was awful to watch but great to listen to, thanks to the Sri Lankan guest commentator on Test Match Special, Gammy Goonesena. Seemingly from the Peter West school of cricket commentary, he referred to batsmen playing 'orf-drives' (he had plenty of opportunity to do this when Sri Lanka were batting) and entered in to the Test Match Special spirit by offering the opinion, during Tavare's 138-minute innings of 14, that we could all do with a 'touch of Bollinger'. However, it's his gaffes that will live with me. Three in particular stand out. Firstly, when Wettimuny started limping towards the end of his epic innings, Gammy informed listeners that the batsman was 'prone to crabs' (I think he meant cramp). Then on the fourth day he apologised for being late back from lunch and assured listeners that he had 'just had the most fearful bollocking from Peter Baxter'. Finally though, my personal favourite is the big hello he said to John Arlott whom he was sure would be 'pleasuring himself' on Alderney.

If that last image is not one on which I care to dwell for too long, the same could be said for the whole of that summer. If, by the end of it, Geoff Boycott was celebrating a new one-year contract with Yorkshire and being made chairman of Melchester Rovers (as in Roy of the.), the unusual combination of Margaret Thatcher, the West Indies and the Church of England had made it a few months to forget for me.

The winter didn't look too promising either. England were going to India and Ian Botham's replacement as the team's all-rounder was Chris Cowdrey.

For Arthur Scargill however, the future was even bleaker. In March the miners' strike had started over a threat to 20,000 jobs. At the time, that figure represented just over 10% of the total mining workforce in this country, almost all of whom were members of the National Union of Mineworkers. By the time Sri Lanka were given their first Test series in this country in 2002, the NUM's total membership was only 5,000.

ELEVEN

On 15th September 1984, Prince Harry was born. His maternal grandfather, Earl Spencer, was quoted as saying: 'I hope one day the boy will play for Gloucestershire.' Given that Gloucestershire came bottom of the county championship in 1984 it's not totally clear whether or not he was putting a bizarre family curse on the poor lad. Alternatively, as the royal family hardly had an impressive cricketing pedigree – in 1751 the Prince of Wales, Frederick Louis, was killed, according to at least one account, by the delayed effects of a blow from a cricket ball and in 1971 Prince Charles went out to bat for the Lord's Taverners on a horse – I suppose he could have been cursing the county.

Despite the pounding his side had taken in the summer, England's princely left-hander had retained his own dubious blessing; the national team's captaincy. Some leaders, like Mike Brearley, make up for their own shortcomings with tactical brilliance. Others, like Graham Gooch, lead by example. Having secured the job on the back of being the first England captain in eight years to score a Test hundred, David Gower seemed to fall into the latter category. Generally, English cricket followers remember Gower as a sort of mirror image of Brearley: a wonderful, instinctive player whose insouciant brilliance simultaneously enabled him to produce the most effortlessly uplifting strokeplay of his generation and left him utterly unsuited to leadership. But then all the best heroes are flawed. That's why Batman is better than Superman. The latter is boring because he is perfect, literally not human in fact. On the other hand, it's safe to say the Caped Crusader has a few issues.

David Gower's issues usually resulted in the ball flying at catchable height in the direction of second slip. In the series with the West Indies,

Gower averaged 19.00. Against India he only managed 27.83 by virtue of making 78 and 32 not out in the last Test.

Such figures might suggest the tour was almost as disastrous as the home series that preceded it. However, despite being stripped of the armour of a significant personal contribution to the cause, David Gower was about to become the first, and so far only, England captain to win in India coming from behind. The following summer, he became only the fourth since the war to win back the Ashes. To put that into context, only Jardine and Greig had ever won a series in India at all, and the previous post-war Ashes-winning captains were Hutton, Illingworth and Brearley. And none of these others had to deal with the sort of circumstances in which Gower's tour started.

England trips to India in the 1980s seem to have been fated. Four years previously the 1981-82 tour had hung in the balance for weeks while Indira Gandhi decided whether to let Boycott and Cook into the country and Gooch's selected 1988-89 tourists didn't even make it onto Indian soil. This time everything was thrown into chaos when Mrs Gandhi was assassinated by two of her own Sikh bodyguards the day after the team arrived. The resultant anti-Sikh violence left the team grateful for the Sri Lankan president's offer of a place on his plane home after the state funeral. As a result, England started their tour of India in Colombo being taken for 105 by a 19-year-old called Aravinda de Silva. On the same day, Ronald Reagan ensured Walter Mondale would go down in history as the biggest loser in U.S. presidential election history. Slightly ironically, the Sandinistas, no doubt to the annoyance of at least one member of the Federation of Conservative Students, had won the Nicaraguan election only two days earlier.

Even when England returned to India things didn't look up. On the field it was bad enough as they lost by an innings to India U25s (M. Azharuddin 151) but worse was to follow off it. The First Test was due to start on 28th November and on the evening of the 26th the team were guests at a cocktail party hosted by Britain's Deputy High Commissioner in India, Percy Norris. The following morning, Mr Norris was murdered on his way to work by two gunmen. He had only been in India for six weeks and it was to have been his last posting before retirement.

Both the murders of Mrs Gandhi and that of Mr Norris had taken place within a mile or two of where the team was staying and they felt under personal threat. If it had been left to the players, or indeed the majority of the British press contingent, they would have come home.

However, the tour manager Tony Brown took advice from the Foreign Office and the TCCB and based on an educated guess that the killing of Mr Norris was unconnected to the team's presence, the decision was made that the safest thing was to get on and play. Even so, the tour itinerary was revised to keep the team away from the north of the country where there was still unrest owing to the large Sikh population and armed guards and escorts accompanied the team wherever they went. How much use they were was another matter. At least one member of the British press was shown into the England dressing room after assuring the guards: 'It's alright, I'm from the IRA.'

Perhaps encouraged by a letter of support from Mrs Norris who said: 'I cannot think of any group with whom he would rather have spent his last hours.' England went ahead with the first Test as scheduled. Almost immediately it became 'business as usual'.

The Indians had an 18-year-old leg-spinner called Sivaramakrishnan whose name combined those of three Hindu gods. The first of these, Siva, the god of destruction, seemed the most appropriate as he took 12 wickets in the match as the tourists lost by eight wickets. England's middle order, consisting as it did of a horribly out of form Gower at four, an equally scratchy Allan Lamb at five and Chris Cowdrey and Richard Ellison at six and seven, contributed a total of 53 runs. The tourists' leading spinner, Phil Edmonds, had lost his run up and was reduced to standing at the crease and bowling. Then, there was England's old friend Swaroop Kishen.

John Thicknesse in *The Standard* went so far as to suggest Kishen 'brazenly ran through England's middle order'. This was a significant disadvantage if it was true, given that Tim Robinson was 'caught' off his pad in the first innings and lbw off the inside edge in the second, and he was one of the openers. The only positive from the match for England was Mike Gatting's first Test hundred in his 54th innings.

The day after Gatting made his maiden century there was a huge chemical leak at Union Carbide's pesticide plant near Bhopal. Nearly 3,000 people died that day and 50,000 others were treated for side effects including blindness and liver and kidney failure. Campaigners say that about 20,000 have died since. On average one person a day continues to die from the effects of exposure. I put a picture of one of the child victims on my wall to remind me that the odd dodgy lbw decision doesn't matter very much. It stayed there for years until I realised it had become like the wallpaper, hanging there for so long its effect had diminished to almost nothing. I still knew what had happened but it had stopped shocking me. Mike Gatting had been retired from Test cricket for nearly ten years by the time, in October 2004, that the Indian Supreme Court approved a compensation package of roughly $350 million to be split between the estimated 570,000 people affected in some way by the disaster. That's a 20-year wait for roughly $614 each.

Before the disaster, Bhopal was most famous for being the birthplace of the greatest captain in Indian Test history, 'Tiger' Pataudi. The Pataudi was as in 'the Nawab of', a title he inherited at the age of only 11. He was a glamorous, Oxford-educated, boldly adventurous cricketer who captained Sussex as well as his country. If, in terms of charisma and national pride, if not bowling ability, you imagine a 1960s Indian version of Imran Khan you won't be far wide of the mark. Taking over the reins at 21, Pataudi captained his country in 40 of his 46 Tests, winning nine and drawing 12. If that doesn't sound too impressive on paper, bear in mind that no previous Indian captain had ever won more than two matches and Pataudi led his men to their first ever series victory on foreign soil, against New Zealand in 1968. More than that though, by the sheer force of his personality he convinced his men that they could win and do so with pride by playing to their natural strengths. Pataudi's sides habitually included three spinners and the victory in New Zealand was achieved with an attack based on an off-spinner in Prasanna and two left-arm slows in Bedi and Nadkarni. If his personal contribution of six Test hundreds and an average just short of 35 sounds a little mediocre, one more thing needs to be considered. Pataudi achieved everything, including an undefeated double century against England, effectively with one eye, having been pretty much deprived of the use of his right in a car accident months before he became captain.

India lost more games than they won under Pataudi but he was undoubtedly the first hero of modern Indian cricket. He started a line that was to run from him to Gavaskar, through Kapil Dev and on to Tendulkar. All of these men undoubtedly were and are heroes but the imperfections of the middle two in the list were about to let Gower's men back into the series.

Over the years England could have done with taking a leaf out of Pataudi's book and put some faith in playing to their natural strengths. Later in the series, in Madras, it was an accurate fast-medium bowler and not the spinners who helped deliver the decisive victory. The quality of English spin bowling is something we can come back to, but despite the fact that neither of them took five wickets in an innings at any point, in this series Edmonds and Pocock at least gave Gower some degree of control in the field. India started the final day of the second Test, in Delhi, 17 runs ahead with eight second-innings wickets in hand. By mid-afternoon the lead was around 100 and Kapil Dev announced to his captain that the match was safe and he was 'going out to have a slog'. When Gavaskar cautioned him simply to play his 'normal game', Kapil responded with: 'Slogging is my normal game.' The all-rounder's effort that day; six over long-on one ball, caught at deep extra cover the next, reminded me of one of Robin Marlar's performances as a nightwatchman; stumped second ball for six. Confronted by a lower order that now didn't know whether to stick or twist and ended up doing neither, Edmonds and Pocock picked up four wickets each as the home side slid from 207-4 to 235 all out. England were set 125 in two hours and cruised home by eight wickets.

As a result, Kapil Dev was dropped for the first time in his career. Back home in Humberside, England's heroic all-rounder had his own problems, having been arrested along with his wife after 'certain substances' were discovered in his home and taken away for analysis. He was later fined £100 after pleading guilty to possession of cannabis.

If the Indian selectors had acted like their English counterparts they would have sacked the nation's other hero of the time, the captain, Sunil Gavaskar. This might not have been a bad idea, as he seemed to have been at some of Botham's fags.

Keats once described Calcutta as a 'city of dust and yellow frightfulness', and this about sums up the third Test. Gavaskar won the toss and batted. India's first innings was still going after lunch on the fourth day and Phil Edmonds was moved to emulate Warwick Armstrong by taking out a newspaper to read in the outfield. Even allowing for the loss of most of the second day to rain, it was clear Gavaskar was trying to make a point. Unfortunately, it wasn't clear exactly what the point was or to whom he was trying to make it, but slow scoring was definitely the way he showed his annoyance. Here he let Ravi Shastri, who took four hours to go from 50 to 100, do his boring for him. Ironically, the following week, Shastri, playing for Bombay against Baroda, emulated Garry Sobers by hitting 6 sixes in one over on his way to 200 not out in 113 minutes. This is still the fastest ever first-class double century in terms of time. Even a glimmer of such initiative might have given India a win, as England were bowled out for only 276. As it was, tactics that might have been understandable if the home side had been ahead only served to keep the tourists in the series.

Fortunately, in the years before satellite broadcasting, none of this was being shown on television. Even the radio coverage only started after lunch. What was on telly though was the imported mini-series *Bodyline*. The subject matter is obvious and as an Australian production it was as wonderfully entertaining a piece of black propaganda as I've ever seen. Despite the fact that, as they always are, the action scenes were awful – Bill Voce appeared to have been a fat left-arm spinner and Les Ames apparently stood up to Harold Larwood – it became my appointment television.

It was fantastic. There was so much naked bias to enjoy it's impossible to convey all of it but three examples stand out. First, there was Percy Fender presented as Machiavelli in a stripy blazer, plotting to create bodyline in secret meetings in London. Then there was Hugo Weaving portraying Jardine so that the only things missing were horns under his Harlequin cap. If you've seen him play Agent Smith in the *Matrix* films you'll have a fair idea. Finally though, the best bit was the entrance of Bradman at Melbourne. Having missed the first-Test defeat at Sydney through illness, the Don is shown walking out to bat in the second to such a rapturous reception that he feels compelled to hold his back-lit bat aloft like Excalibur to all four corners of the ground. He was bowled first ball by Bill Bowes but for some reason the producers seemed to have concentrated more on his second-innings century.

All joking aside, the way *Bodyline* was written showed how seriously the incident was still taken in Australia even 50 years on. What really happened after the 1932-33 tour is just as interesting. On the team's return, the MCC cricket committee, just beginning to get some understanding of why the Australians were so upset, drafted a letter of apology for Harold Larwood's signature. As he had been bowling to orders and believed he had done nothing wrong, Larwood refused to sign it. He never played Test cricket again. Jardine, on the other hand, remained as captain and continued to use bodyline against the 1933 tourists, the West Indies, and in India the following winter. When Larwood moved to Australia after the Second World War he was warmly welcomed with the respect due to a worthy adversary. Jardine and his patrician contempt remained hated.

By the time David Gower arrived in India 'leg theory' was, of course, long since outlawed. But Gower didn't need it, he had Neil Foster.

Back home, the Sinclair C5 had provoked a few concerns in its first road safety test, with Dr Murray McKay, the head of accident research at Birmingham University, describing it as 'a sort of milk float' that was likely to 'cause conflicts' in the traffic stream. 'Milk float' is one way of describing how England's quicker bowlers had compared to the Ferraris from the West Indies the previous summer but in Madras, Foster produced a display of fast bowling on a slow pitch worthy of any of the Caribbean's best. Sir Clive Sinclair was a considerable inventor and entrepreneur but is still best remembered for the ridiculous C5. Neil Foster was one of the most talented English fast-medium bowlers of his generation but was sadly let down by two major weaknesses situated midway between his hips and his ankles.

Foster's knees were too fragile to let him have a sustained Test career but here he showed what might have been if he hadn't had to bowl for Essex every day. He took 6-104 as India were crucially bowled out inside the first day and then 5-59 from 28 second-innings overs to ensure a nine-wicket win. In between, England at one stage reached 563-2 on their way to 652-7, as Fowler and Gatting became the first Englishmen to score double centuries in the same Test innings. After that, Gavaskar was welcome to his high-scoring bore draw in Kanpur.

By the time Gower and his men returned to England, the miners' strike was over and Mrs Thatcher felt fireproof. This isn't a state of mind you would usually associate with international cricket captains but, by the end of the summer, England's skipper must have felt as close to it as anyone would ever get. In 1985, The Pet Shop Boys re-released *West End Girls* after it flopped the previous year. David Gower did something similar with the England cricket team.

At the start of the season Surrey granted honorary life membership to Boris Karloff's widow. Karloff had been a frequent visitor to the Oval and together with C. Aubrey Smith (the only England captain to star in a film with Elizabeth Taylor) had been a founder member of the Hollywood cricket club for whom he played against Bradman in 1932. Given his most famous role was the *Frankenstein* monster it's perhaps surprising that he was a wicket-keeper. Mind you, if I keep wicket now that's generally how I walk for the next three days. It's a shame Bela Lugosi was a Hungarian: Bradman caught Frankenstein bowled Dracula, now that would have been a scorebook entry worth seeing.

Looming menacingly behind England were the Australians. However, they had lost several players to a 'rebel' tour of South Africa. Ironically, at the same time, England's South African rebels all became eligible for Test selection again. The Aussies were weakened by the loss of Terry Alderman and Kim Hughes, who had tearfully relinquished the captaincy only a few months earlier. The new captain, Allan Border, said 'All I want is 17 goers'. This may sound like the demand of an excessively greedy man, but it turned out that he wasn't looking for some west end girls of his own but rather: 'Guys who are prepared to work hard to get Australian cricket back where it belongs – on top'.

Among Border's 'goers' was Jeff Thomson (promising in his usual erudite way to 'bowl his arse off'), Dave Gilbert (who later helped put Sussex on the road to their first county championship title) and a leg-spinner who, in January, had bowled West Indies to their first Test defeat since December 1981.

Shane Warne was 15 at the time and the leg-spinner in question was Bob Holland. More significant was the fact that Gilbert's inclusion opened the way for an unknown 19-year-old to be given an Esso scholarship to come and play in England. The young man given this opportunity to come and hone his skills in English conditions was called Steve Waugh.

On 11th May, as Worcestershire's captain Phil Neale was making the first hundred against the tourists, 56 people died and a further 265 were injured in the Bradford stadium fire. A public enquiry was announced headed by Mr. Justice Popplewell, a former Cambridge wicket-keeper and father of Somerset's opening batsman Nigel Popplewell. As a result of the tragedy, sports stadia all over the country were inspected and several major cricket grounds were found wanting. A GLC inspection discovered a number of fire and safety hazards at Lord's and at the Oval the wooden top section of the pavilion was assessed as having too few exits. The Vauxhall Stand also had the same problem as well as housing inflammable materials. At Taunton, where the Australians had played their opening first-class match, the old wooden pavilion was closed to spectators after advice from the local fire service.

Although I had felt intimidated by the close-packed crowds and the fencing at football matches, it had never even occurred to me I might be in any danger at the cricket.

Given the findings of the safety inspectors, this was probably a complacency shared by some of the ground authorities. It came as a bit of a shock that the Bradford tragedy was probably caused by something as simple as someone dropping a cigarette in a wooden stand. Then, less than a month later, Heysel happened and overshadowed everything else.

In the first Test at Leeds, England, set 123 to win, nearly made an extremely ironic hash of it before Allan Lamb saw them home with 31 not out. Unfortunately, the match ended in chaos as Lamb top-edged a hook off Simon O'Donnell and Geoff Lawson tried to make the catch. Hundreds of spectators, simultaneously anticipating and ensuring it was the winning hit, swarmed onto the field and prevented Lawson from getting anywhere near the ball. The reaction, particularly in a period of hypersensitivity after Heysel, reflected the paranoia felt by cricket followers about the possibility of 'football style' behaviour encroaching on their game. David Gower described the spectators as 'a pack of mad dogs' and David Frith, in a revealing choice of language, talked of the invasion being 'a symptom of the peril closing in on cricket, perhaps moving across from the "game" of football'. Christopher Martin-Jenkins in *The Cricketer*, fearing some 'really serious incident', even mooted the possibility of high barbed wire fences. At the time Martin-Jenkins said this, Hillsborough was just where Sheffield Wednesday played. Four years later, high fences of the kind he was talking about were at least partly responsible for making Wednesday's ground one of the most tragically evocative place names in English football.

At Lord's, the MCC took the less extreme step of employing more and better stewards. The staff at Lord's aren't renowned for taking any nonsense anyway. At the Bicentenary match in 1987, a gateman, even though he knew who the Indian was and that he was playing in the match, refused Sunil Gavaskar entry because he didn't have his pass with him. My favourite though, is still the one who wouldn't let Sebastian Coe in because his ticket only entitled him to entry via another gate on the other side of the ground. After several minutes of remonstrating, Coe fatally resorted to: 'Don't you know who am? I'm Sebastian Coe.' only to be met with: 'Well it won't take you long to run round the other side of the ground then will it Sir?'

I still thought that playing at Lord's would inspire England's cricketers. In fact it seemed to have that effect on the opposition. Australia hadn't lost there since 1934 and in 1985 it certainly had a galvanizing effect on Allan Border.

Before the match it was announced that the TCCB had invested £10,000 in research by two different companies into electronic means of establishing whether a batsman was out lbw or caught. The first of these seems to have been a 1980s clockwork version of 'Hawkeye', employing two whole cameras to plot the projected path of the ball. The second sounds just plain mad, based as it was on the idea that a microphone implanted in a batsman's pad would send a signal revealing whether he had hit it or not to a breast-pocket receiver in the umpire's coat. During the course of the game Gooch, triggered by umpire Evans, might have wished that the researchers had successfully completed their work, while Wessels and Gatting, reprieved by the same umpire, had reason to be glad they hadn't. However, it was a mistake by a fielder rather than an umpire that turned the match.

After England had made a reasonable 290, they had the Australians in trouble at 101-4. However, Border and Greg Ritchie, described by *Wisden* as 'rounded of profile' ('fat' to you and me), started to pull them round. They had reached 183-4 when England's own rounded of profile short-leg fielder, Mike Gatting, made his decisive contribution to the match. Border, on 87, flicked Phil Edmonds off his pads and the ball hit Gatting and appeared to lodge between his legs. The Australian captain started to walk off, only for Gatting to try and throw the ball up in celebration but succeed only in flicking it across the pitch. I still think if he had tried to brazen it out, pretended he had meant to flick it away and gone and high-fived with Gower opposite at silly-point, he would have probably got away with it. Instead he launched himself after the ball and dropped it. Short of saying 'I didn't have that under control you know, Dickie', he couldn't have made it any more obvious. Border went on to make 196 and Australia led by 135.

England closed the third day on 37-2 and inexplicably employed two nightwatchmen. This handed Australia two early wickets and the momentum on the fourth morning. Despite Botham making 85 and Gatting, desperately trying to make up for his error, 75 not out, the tourists were left only 127 to win. Just the sort of target they love chasing.

A collapse to 65-5 inspired hope of another Aussie choke. But Border, revealing just how vital Chris Old's contribution had been four years earlier, saw them home with 41 not out to finish with 43% of his teams runs in the match.

In between the second and third Tests, 13-year-old Ruth Lawrence obtained a first in Maths from Oxford and 17-year-old Boris Becker won Wimbledon. Australia's best bowler was the 20-year-old Craig

McDermott who had seemingly taken to heart some advice from the Aussies' assistant manger, Geoff Dymock. Dymock told the Daily Mail: 'I've had to get alongside Craig and tell him his aggression is gone. He had fallen in love and his girlfriend has been over here. I told them both it is no use waking up in the morning and thinking what a great place the world is. He should wake up irritable'. Obviously Mrs Dymock wasn't going to get too many red roses, but McDermott took 8-141 in a draw at Old Trafford. I wasn't that old myself, my 21st birthday coincided with the Saturday of the drawn third Test and 'Saint Bob' exhorting me to send him my 'focking money' at the Live Aid concert. Nevertheless, I was already getting the uncomfortable feeling I was being overtaken. It's incredible how quickly you can go from being the promising youngster to yesterday's man. In the 1980s there was a whole generation of young batsmen (James Whitaker, Paul Johnson, John Morris, Rob Bailey, Kim Barnett) who seemed destined for long careers in England's middle order one minute and were practically forgotten the next. This wasn't just true of batsmen.

The previous summer the promising 24-year-old fast bowler, Jonathan Agnew, had made his Test debut against the West Indies. As a 25-year-old he made his third and final Test appearance at Manchester. Despite 101 first-class wickets in 1987 and 93 in 1988, Agnew never got another look in. In other words he wasn't given the chance to go away and learn his trade for a couple of years and come back a better bowler. If modern selectors worked like that, Arnie Sidebottom, who made his one and only Test appearance in the draw at Trent Bridge, and his son Ryan would have carried on being the only father and son one-Test wonder combination.

Even though England kept faith with Paul Downton throughout this series, generally it was no better for wicket-keepers. Arguments, like that between Duncan Fletcher and Rod Marsh about the relative merits of the likes of Geraint Jones and Chris Read, were nothing new. In 1985, one correspondent to *The Cricketer* offered the opinion that, with an established batting-up, 'the time is past when it is necessary to accept less than the highest standards in a wicket-keeper'. On the other hand, another, writing to *Wisden Cricket Monthly*, put in a plea for Geoff Humpage on the basis of his 1891 runs at 48.48 the previous season. Since I started watching them, the only time when there was broad agreement about who should keep wicket for England was when Alan Knott was in his prime. Since then, there has always been a superior 'keeper with inferior batting set against a better batsman whose glove-work was seen as a potential liability. In the 1980s England chopped and changed between 'Jack' Richards' allegedly superior batting and Bruce French's 'keeping, with Downton as the compromise candidate between the two. Through the 1990s it was a straight argument between 'Jack' Russell and Alec Stewart. Even though a freakish player like Adam Gilchrist distorted the picture, it's clear that in the modern game no side now wants to go into a Test with a wicket-keeper who can't make a century.

The Adam Gilchrist of the 1980s was the West Indies' Jeff Dujon, a man who made his Test debut as a specialist batsman. At the start of the summer, David Frith described Australia's keeper, Wayne Phillips, as a left-handed Dujon. While this conveys the high quality of Phillips' batting, it ignores the fact that he was essentially a slip fielder with gloves on, while Dujon was a proper wicket-keeper. One of the reasons why the West Indies were so powerful in this period was they had a world class keeper catching flies off the fast bowlers who could also score a hundred at number seven. This is also a simple but vital point often overlooked about Adam Gilchrist; he was a brilliant wicket-keeper capable of taking just about everything Shane Warne sent down. This makes him a very dangerous player for other countries to try and use a template for their keepers. Quite simply, Adam Gilchrist was a one-off. Alan Knott and Jeff Dujon both made five Test hundreds. Any modern side would give a great deal to have either of them at their disposal. When he retired, Adam Gilchrist had made 17 Test centuries, the nearest among his contemporaries was Mark Boucher with five.

Wayne Phillips made only two Test hundreds but nearly saved the Ashes with a battling 50 before falling victim to the unluckiest vital dismissal I've ever seen. In the fifth Test, at Edgbaston, rain ensured Australia's first innings of 335 didn't end until the third morning. Then Tim Robinson and David Gower kept Richie Benaud, deputizing as BBC television's scorer in the absence of an ill Wendy Wimbush, very busy for the rest of the day. England closed the day with a 20-run lead and only one wicket down.

Even though Robinson was out early on Monday ending the stand at 331, Gower and Gatting carried on smashing it all over the place, before Botham popped the cherry on the top by belting his first ball back over Craig McDermott's head for six and then repeating the dose two balls later. The Australians were in such disarray that when Thomson caught the England all-rounder, his gesture to the Eric Hollies Stand seemed to confirm it was the one thing he had done right all day.

England were 260 in front but given how much time had been lost they still needed to make things happen quickly. By the close Australia were 36-5. Hilditch obligingly hooked Botham straight to Ellison, one of two men out for the shot, Wood top-edged one so high that the fielders had time to elect Robinson as the one they wanted to catch it, Holland was plumb lbw first ball, Wessels nicked a crabby slash to Downton and after the BBC had cut away to their scheduled evening broadcasting, Border was bowled by Richard Ellison to a roar that almost drowned out Brian Johnston.

The final day was agony. The covers came off, then they went back on again. Play was due to start at 2pm then it rained. Finally they got out there at 2.30, bowled two balls and trooped off. Eleven minutes later they were back but instead of capitulating, Phillips started smashing Ellison all over the place and Ritchie wouldn't budge. They were still there at tea and all of a sudden instead of a day to get five wickets we now had a session.

After tea they still didn't show any signs of getting out. Then Phil Edmonds bowled a long-hop outside off stump. 'Here's another four' I thought and so did Wayne Phillips who rocked back and smashed his now famous cut shot straight into Allan Lamb's boot and up into Gower's hands. If there had been the option of a referral to a third umpire he would probably have been given not out because the television pictures were inconclusive about whether it had bounced. Fortunately, there wasn't a third umpire and David Constant at square-leg, ensuring there was another whole country he could safely cross off his Christmas card list, confirmed to umpire Shepherd that he could send Phillips was on his distraught way. Couldn't happen to a nicer Test-playing nation. At least Phillips could console himself that he hadn't suffered the fate of Dorset's Ian Saunders, who was timed out in the match against Oxfordshire that month, when his side lost three wickets in four balls while he was on the toilet.

Still there was only just over an hour to get four wickets but the end came even quicker than necessary. Ritchie, to his credit, walked for a bat-pad off Embury and once Lawson had prodded Edmonds to Gower at silly-point, Botham finished them off by bowling O'Donnell and finding a rib ball for McDermott. Normally, 2-1 up after five Tests means you've won. But despite the fact Bob Willis felt sure enough of himself to patronize 'dear old Thommo' for his lack of pace, there was still another Test to go.

Before the Oval, Botham hit his 80th first-class six of the season. This was and is a record, smashing Arthur Wellard's previous mark of 66 in 1935. However, Botham's feat is even more remarkable when you take account of the fact he only batted 27 times in first-class cricket that season and was at the time labouring under what might charitably be described as the 'misguided' management of Tim Hudson. Hudson was the stripy-blazered hippy-looking bloke who had somehow convinced Botham he was destined to be the next James Bond. Botham even visited Hollywood. He clearly needed someone sensible (i.e. not Tim Hudson) to tell him that two things James Bond didn't have were a ridiculous striped jacket and a streaked-blond mullet. It's a sad accident of history that all the pictures of Botham's most magnificent season of sustained hitting feature the worst haircut of his career.

At the Oval, all England had to do was make a big score. I was worried that the fastest pitch of the series would help McDermott and Lawson and we might struggle. Instead we were basically safe by the end of the first day. I don't remember too many triple century stands by English batsmen against Australia let alone two in as many matches. But after his effort with Robinson at Edgbaston, Gower joined Gooch to put on 351. As the captain creamed another cover drive towards the end of the evening session, Jim Laker described these as 'golden days for English cricket'.

Even one of our special collapses from 379-1 to 464 all out couldn't save the Aussies. They were forced to follow on, something that didn't happen again in an Ashes Test until Trent Bridge 2005. Although this was the only way the tourists could possibly get back into the match, they didn't. While I was stuck in road-works on the A23 into Brighton, Murray Bennett, chipping it back to the bowler, ended his last Test innings by giving Les Taylor his last Test wicket.

David Frith suggested there 'were tinges of sadness for the vanquished'. Not in my house there weren't. If I had known what was coming I would have enjoyed this even more than I did, which was a lot. I got so carried away I even told one friend I thought we would beat the West Indies in the Caribbean.

With the introduction of an England B team, for the first time I had more than one side to follow in the winter. The selection of such a team to tour Bangladesh, Sri Lanka and Zimbabwe seemed to me to be another sign that English cricket was moving in the right direction. However, the touring party was picked on the basis of being a genuine England second team rather than a development side and the fate of its members illustrates where we were still going wrong. Of the 14 men selected, only two, the captain Mark Nicholas and Tim Tremlett (Maurice Tremlett's son and Chris Tremlett's father) never played Test cricket. However, of the other 12, only Randall, whose international career was over, Pringle (30) and Athey (23) played 20 or more Tests. The selectors, it seems, could find any number of men worthy of a chance but hardly any they were prepared to back for any length of time.

As far as the main tour was concerned I had allowed the euphoria of winning the Ashes to push me over the thin line between enthusiastic support and delusion. If I had watched the last tour to the Caribbean from between my fingers, for this one I had to be right behind the sofa.

TWELVE

Ian Botham once said that his worst sporting memory was driving the 10th at the Belfry and then three-putting. On Prince Harry's first birthday the Europeans beat the Americans at the Midland course and the Ryder Cup returned to this side of the Atlantic for the first time in 28 years. By the time they opened their 1985-86 tour England hadn't beaten West Indies in a Test match for almost 12 years and hadn't won a series against them since 1969. Victory for Europe's golfers was obviously a sign the old order was about to change.

When Paul Downton dropped Allan Border at Trent Bridge in 1981 it seemed disastrous at the time but, hastening as it did the return of Brearley and the resurgence of Botham, it turned out well. Unfortunately this principle also works the other way round. Mrs Thatcher may have been glad in January 1986 that she had forced Michael Heseltine and his more pro-European views out of her cabinet over the Westland Helicopters affair, but making an enemy of him didn't do her much good in the long run. Graham Gooch made a statement saying he opposed apartheid and Lester Bird found this acceptable. Therefore, despite the fact that Gooch still wasn't sure if he wanted to stay at home anyway, the tour could go ahead. This, as it turned out, was a bad thing.

By the time the side returned home in April they might have wished that their tour had gone the same way as the Bangladesh and Zimbabwe legs of the B team's. Mark Nicholas and his men were at Heathrow ready to fly out when the Bangladeshi government sent a last minute telex to Lord's to the effect that Bill Athey, Martin Moxon, Kim Barnett and Chris Smith wouldn't be allowed entry unless they signed declarations that they would never go to South Africa again. The TCCB, having already lost one restraint of trade case against Greig in 1977, refused to put the players under pressure to sign anything. As a result the Bangladesh leg of the tour was cancelled. The Zimbabwe leg soon went the same way when Robert Mugabe made similar demands of the same four players as well as Mark Nicholas, someone whom he had quite happily met and shaken hands with the previous winter when the Hampshire man had toured as captain of an English Counties XI.

The result of all this was an extended seven-week tour of Sri Lanka. The fact that the whole touring party was acceptable there but not in Bangladesh or Zimbabwe only serves to illustrate how far the Gleneagles Agreement was open to interpretation (or manipulation if you prefer). This also begs the question why such statements were required from B team cricketers whereas a simple statement of opposition to apartheid sufficed for a member of the first choice side. A cynical man might conclude that, in commercial terms, the cancellation of a full England tour might cost the West Indies Board rather more than the loss of a week of the itinerary of England's second team might cost the Bangladeshi one.

As it turned out the main commercial headache that the West Indian Board had was lost revenue from the matches not lasting long enough. I had convinced myself that our apparently settled and powerful batting line-up would make big enough scores to enable us to exploit a perceived West Indian vulnerability to spin. Had I had the benefit of Marty McFly's DeLorean my assessment would have been slightly different.

If the writing was on the wall when we were bowled out for 94 by the Windward Islands, shortly afterwards it was right in the middle of Mike Gatting's face. England's vice-captain went into the first one-day international as the team's form batsman and came out of it requiring a two-hour operation on his nose, courtesy of an attempted hook off Malcolm Marshall and the lack of a visor on his helmet. In an effort not to lose his edge by seeing the injury up close, Marshall wandered away to retrieve the ball only to drop it like a grenade when he found a piece of bone embedded in it.

There are many stories of magnificently dim questions being asked at press conferences. One Nottingham scribe's first enquiry to Brian Clough after one of Forest's two European Cup triumphs was: 'So Brian, any injuries?' and a Korean journalist, straight after Florence Griffith-Joyner's double gold-medal-winning performance in Seoul, opened with: 'How long does it take you to paint your finger nails?'

However, the question put to Mike Gatting before he flew home to recuperate is right up there with the best. Sitting there with a livid gash across the middle of his nose and looking like a panda that had gone ten rounds with Frank Bruno, he was asked: 'So Mike, where did it hit you?'

That one-day match had also seen the international debut of Patrick Patterson. I had thought Colin Croft was nasty but this bloke was terrifying. He was huge, snarling, very fast and rocked so far back in his delivery stride that the batsman had a full view of the studs on his left boot. In short, he was an international version of what I had thought Tyrone Wildman would be like. When you combined him with Marshall, Holding, Garner and a hard, uneven pitch with grassy patches in the middle (cf. Edgbaston 1995), you had a problem for the opposition.

By the time the Test started Mrs Thatcher had also lost Leon Brittan from her team and England had added 'Mad Axe-Man' David Smith (for his apparent ability against fast bowling) and poor old Peter Willey to theirs. Smith made 1 and Willey a duck as we were blown away for 159 in 45.3 overs. The picture of Phil Edmonds after the match, like Brian Close at Lord's in 1963, showing off the huge bruises on his side and chest, sums up what it was like.

The only remotely quick bowler England had was Greg Thomas. Thomas was the 1980s version of Simon Jones. Picked on pace rather than results (34 championship wickets at over 32 in 1985 had hardly demanded inclusion) he was Welsh, fast and promising. But, lacking a 1980s Harmison, Flintoff and Hoggard to bowl with, he was no match for the West Indies.

Even though Ellison's 5-78 restricted them to 307, a lead of 148 was more than enough. Despite Willey's improvised, off-side counter-attacking bringing him 71, it was all over, by 10 wickets, inside three days.

As Peter Smith put it in the Daily Mail: 'England were torn apart and the carcass stripped bare as batsmen ducked and dived for safety. The West Indies hit squad was at its most deadly.'

From a supporter's point of view the rest of this tour was a depressing, hopeless experience. 'Hopeless' because there were so many reasons why England didn't have a chance of beating the West Indies. However, what made me and I'm sure many other cricket supporters, really angry, was that a lack of ability wasn't one of those reasons. Admittedly Gatting's injury robbed the side of one of its best batsmen but England could still call upon Gooch, Gower, Lamb, Botham and

Willey. In the bowling department they had Botham, two good spinners in Emburey and Edmonds, a genuine swing bowler (a cricketing rarity) in Ellison and an out-and-out fast-man in Thomas. When Gooch beat an almost identical West Indies team at Sabina Park in February 1990 the only men he could call on who had played more than eleven Tests were himself and Lamb and his bowling attack consisted of Devon Malcolm, Angus Fraser, Gladstone Small and David Capel.

The loss of Gatting not only deprived the team of an important player but also of a crucial leader within the team. Gower's attitude that these were professional players who could work out their own best method for success was all very well and it had apparently worked in India the previous winter. However, here he seemed to take it to extremes. He set the tone from the outset when, on the second day of the opening first-class match against the Windward Islands, having chosen not to play and seen his side bowled out for 186 on the first, Gower chose to go sailing rather than practise or even watch. Much was made at the time of how much optional practice there was and Peter May, the chairman of selectors who was present at the Barbados Test, made public criticisms of the team's attitude and commitment. After England had lost that match by an innings and 30 runs, the team took two days off and then had a non-compulsory practice session that the captain himself didn't attend. In the one-day international that followed, Gower signalled his surrender near the end by coming on to bowl himself and immediately conceding five from his first ball (courtesy of a throw over Downton's head with no-one backing up) and a four from his second to finish the match.

Judging by some of the stories that came out of this tour, it wasn't even that the captain just gave his men a free hand in terms of how they prepared for their cricket. It appears that they could do pretty much as they pleased full stop. This after all is the tour on which Gooch, out on an early morning training run, allegedly met Botham and Lamb on their way back from a night out. Unfortunately, Willey injured his knee on a similar run and had to return home which probably only served to reinforce some senior players' faith in their own training methods. To me, it all seemed uncomfortably like the attitude of the large numbers of young men in stripy shirts and red braces who were making a lot of money very quickly without really having to work for it.

Gooch may have replaced Gatting as temporary vice-captain but he was hardly in the right frame of mind, seeking as he was to opt out of the Antigua leg of the trip altogether. He went so far as to give Peter May a letter to take back to the TCCB which, it was believed, formalized this request. Gower had to work hard to persuade him to stay with the tour to the end. In the light of this it has always struck me as more than a little ironic that when he was captain, Gooch saw fit to criticise Gower (who never toured South Africa) for his attitude.

It wasn't all the players' fault. At least they were brave enough to go out and face probably the most consistently hostile bowling attack in the history of the game. In this respect there was more than an element of lions led by donkeys. The TCCB lacked professional administration and had a secretary who was effectively a servant rather than a chief executive. Once the side was picked, the team manager (Tony Brown) and his assistant (Bob Willis) had full responsibility and the TCCB effectively left it to them to organize things until the squad got home. It's fine to delegate as long as you provide the facilities to allow those you've put in charge to do their job. This doesn't seem to have been the case here. For example, it's now taken as read that cricketers watch hours of footage to let them see and iron out technical flaws in their own game and pick up on possible weaknesses in those of their opponents. In 1986 no facilities were provided to the tour management by the TCCB to enable them to film a single ball bowled and the players had to rely on offers from Mark Austin of the BBC and Jeremy Thompson of ITN to view their tapes. It's not as if watching tapes is a new idea that hadn't been thought of back then, it was a shortcoming that was pointed out at the time.

The other major problem was that, as Gower put it: 'The concept is emerging of cricketers now becoming more like pop stars in terms of media treatment.' This was probably only true of the likes of Botham who with his charity walks, Hollywood ambitions and scrapes with the law, was famous for reasons unconnected with cricket and possibly Gower himself and one or two others. However, there were elements of the press who seemed more interested in whether or not a former Miss Barbados rather than Joel Garner had been bouncing Botham. As Gower, the king of the double negative, admitted, 'most can appreciate that when we are coming second like this, a certain amount of criticism is not just to be expected but it is not necessarily going to be invalid either' but it was quite another thing for him to be forced to field a lot of very personal and intrusive questions about his love life. I found myself wondering whether or not these people cared one bit whether we won or not. The obvious answer was 'no of course not', they had papers to sell and in another reflection of the times, that was all that mattered.

In such circumstances the distinction between this sort of press and proper cricket journalists became blurred and despite the fact that some players took money for ghosted columns in tabloids, a siege mentality started to develop. After his second innings dismissal in the second Test, Botham (never one it seemed to take criticism that well) made a hangman gesture and explained it afterwards by saying: 'The pressbox had already placed me on the gallows so I was just telling you people you might as well go the whole way now and pull the rope.'

When you put all this together it's hardly surprising that they got a complete trouncing. The West Indies never made fewer than 307 in their first innings, England never more than 310 and that only in the final Test on an Antiguan shirt-front when their previous best effort had been exactly 200. In ten innings in the series we were bowled out for less than 200 seven times and Gower's 90 at Antigua was the highest individual score. Although the bowlers generally did their job, at the end of the series even they suffered the ignominy of Richards making the fastest Test hundred in history from just 56 balls. Even though this innings bought the West Indies enough time to prevent us holding on for the draw that would have stopped another blackwash, it's still a shame that the only film I have ever seen of it appears to have been taken by some bloke with a video camera standing at long-on/third-man. All in all this tour doesn't amount to one of my all time great cricketing memories.

While all this had been going on, Mrs Thatcher had, temporarily at least, pulled the thorn that was Ken Livingstone from her side by scrapping the GLC, Clint Eastwood had been elected mayor of Carmel in California, Wallis Simpson had died and the Soviets admitted that they might have had a little mishap at Chernobyl. This last minor local difficulty necessitated the construction of an enormous concrete sarcophagus over the entire power station. This degraded a little more quickly than anticipated and was due for replacement when the Indians were here in 2007.

If London had lost its leader and Carmel had gained a new one, England, at least in the short term, stuck by theirs. On 13th May Gower would have been 'not displeased' to discover that despite the winter's failings he had been retained as captain for the two one-day internationals and the first Test against India. Hearing Gower talk always reminds me of the story of a particularly dull lecture by a professor of linguistics. Cursed with a monotonous voice and a teaching style drier than a Karachi dustbowl, he ground his students into a state of near stupor before concluding with the thought that in all his years of studying the subject he had come across many examples of two negatives being used to mean a positive but never two positives to denote a negative. Having asked if there were any questions he was met by silence until one student at the back offered simply: 'Yeah...yeah'.

Gower had retained his position on instructions from the TCCB that England should improve their performance and he should show a 'higher profile' on the field. He later jokingly told Channel 4 News that he was thinking of wearing a tee-shirt with 'I'm in charge' on it.

Then, five days after his appointment, Gower's job got harder. On 18th May *The Mail on Sunday*'s headline read: 'BOTHAM: I DID TAKE POT'. Ironically Botham had sued the same paper after it had made similar allegations about his activities on the 1983-1984 tour of New Zealand and only two months earlier had sacked Tim Hudson as his agent after the *Daily Star* had quoted him as saying that the all-rounder smoked marijuana. Given Botham's difficult relationship with the press the reaction to his revelations was predictable. Opinion on what should happen to him varied between Peter Smith in the *Daily Mail* initially calling for a life ban and Frank Keating suggesting on *Newsnight* that he should be paid 'for bringing the game into repute'. However, the majority, whilst not quite in favour of such extreme measures, were at Smith's end of the spectrum. At the same time as the obituary writers were celebrating the life and times of Bill Edrich, described by his former teammate Trevor Bailey as a 'truly vintage bon viveur', their colleagues in the sports and news pages were subjecting Botham to little better than a witch hunt, cataloguing his various disciplinary 'misdemeanors' and offering the opinion that 'this time something must be done'. It was certainly true that Botham was an extremely high profile figure with an example to set but the moralizing tone of some of the pieces must have seemed a little rich to him coming from a profession not noted for abstinence itself. The difference between Botham and Edrich, for example, was that what the Somerset man was admitting to was illegal. This raises questions about the inconsistent attitudes that our society has towards the dangers of drugs and those posed by alcohol and smoking, but that's a different debate.

Botham was suspended from the Texaco Trophy one-day matches although he was allowed to play in the Sport Aid charity match at Edgbaston. I went to that game but spent most of my time trying to wrest control of the binoculars from my friend Julie who was showing an excessive interest in Imran Khan's backside. England's all-rounder faced a TCCB disciplinary sub-committee on 29th May and was found guilty of bringing the game into disrepute by using and admitting to using cannabis and previously falsely denying having used it. As a result he was banned from first-class cricket until 31st July. An appeal on 12th June that he didn't attend, proved fruitless.

Gower now had to save his captaincy without his best player and failed. I had hoped that India's bowlers would seem so slow by comparison with the West Indian quicks they had just encountered that England's batsmen would slaughter them. Unfortunately when you've had your confidence shredded and don't know where your next captain, let alone your next run, is coming from it doesn't quite work like that.

For the first Test at Lord's England had Derek Pringle batting in Botham's place at number six. At least 'Both' wouldn't be missed then. Pringle was in a bit earlier than I would have liked at 98-4 on the first day but amazingly he made 63 and put on 147 with Graham Gooch to rescue us from complete humiliation. One Essex supporter writing to *The Cricketer* described how this would be the start of a realization of his talent. He played 19 more times for England and never made 50 again. As for this innings, the only ball I watched knocked Pringle's off stump out.

By the end of that day India had lost only Srikkanth in reaching 83 and even he had the excuse of having had his concentration broken by Ashley Sommers, the topless model who reached the middle wearing nothing but a pair of pants and waving a 'Bring back Botham' banner. The stewards were somewhat tardy in removing her and, although she was finally ejected from the ground, she wasn't charged. A man who stripped to his pants on the same day was later fined £20 by Marylebone magistrates.

Ashley couldn't stop Dilip Vengsarkar from making his third century in as many Lord's Tests and India led by 47 on first innings. Despite the fact that our football team had lost to Portugal and drawn with Morocco in the World Cup finals I still hadn't worked out that this was not destined to be a summer of English sporting triumph and assumed that if we knocked up a quick 350 we could still put India under pressure on the last day. Instead of this we knocked up (if that's the right phrase) 180 in 96.4 overs. So slowly did we go that their left-arm spinner Maninder Singh bowled 20.4 overs and took 3-9. Left only 134 to win and a day to get them in India cruised home by five wickets and David Gower lost his job and symbolically handed his 'I'm in charge' tee-shirt to Mike Gatting.

Gower wasn't alone in being sacked. The Labour Party had expelled Derek Hatton and unemployment was so high that the government was reduced to altering the way the statistics were counted almost on a monthly basis. If Mike Brearley had hit upon a similar idea when he was in charge (e.g. dismissals by left-arm bowlers counted as not outs) he might have ended up with a Test batting average in the mid-thirties. In fact, given that he carried on playing for England and Leicestershire, Gower's position was more like that of a Tory minister losing one of his non-executive directorships rather than of a real unemployed person. So widespread was the problem that 'the unemployed' became a class, like pensioners and children, offered concessions on travel and entertainment. It must have been bad because the cricket authorities noticed. Northants started offering 'the unemployed' half price admission for their championship matches at Northampton.

The day after the first Test ended the ICC Trophy began. Before this there seemed to have been some good news for English cricket as 20-year-old Graeme Hick announced that he was pulling out of the Zimbabwe squad in order not to jeopardize his qualification to play for England, which at that time was due to be in 1993. His withdrawal made no difference to the outcome of the tournament as his teammates remained unbeaten throughout. The victory by 25 runs over Holland in the final was their closest match. At that time you could have got very short odds on Zimbabwe being the next new Test-playing nation and very long ones on Bangladesh being the next one after that. The Bangladeshis warmed up for the tournament with a match against a Worcester pub called 'The Lamb and Flag'. Reassuringly for an international side they won by 124 runs, but when it came to the real thing they managed only two victories, against Kenya (by nine runs) and Argentina (who lost to everyone). Less than 20 years later Bangladesh beat Australia at Cardiff.

While the ICC Trophy had been in progress play in a village match between Dowdeswell & Foxcote and Marle Hill was held up when, following a domestic argument, the local publican's wife marched onto the pitch and presented him with his Sunday lunch on a silver salver. England's new captain would have killed for service like that.

Mike Gatting was made captain for the second and third Tests and had an immediate effect on our fortunes. They got worse. Before the second Test it emerged that *Crocodile Dundee* had had Greg Chappell, Dennis Lillee and Rod Marsh among its financial backers. Marsh and Lillee were obviously two men that you would be well advised to talk to if you were thinking of taking a punt. Paul Hogan might have been frightening New York hoodlums with his bush-knife but at Headingley the only thing that Gatting might have terrified the Indians with was the size of his lunch. 'That's not a cheese and pickle sandwich. *That's* a cheese and pickle sandwich!'

Faced with a crisis of confidence England, of course, changed the wicket-keeper and Bruce French came in for his debut. With Gower on the sidelines nursing a shoulder injury, Chris Smith returned for what turned out to be his last Test match, Wilf Slack replaced Tim Robinson as Gooch's opening partner and Bill Athey (proud possessor at that point of a Test average of 2.83) was picked for the first time in five years to bolster the middle order. In the bowling, John Lever at the age of 37 was selected on a 'horses for courses' basis.

This wasn't the last time wholesale changes were made to the team during this summer. During the course of six Tests in 1986 England used 24 different players, 10 of whom were selected for one game and a further four for only two. Five men made their debuts and seven played their final Test (the unfortunate Mark Benson falls into both categories). Graham Gooch had five different opening partners. In short it was chaos. You could understand why Botham (obviously not destined for a career in the Diplomatic Service), speaking at a cricket dinner in Manchester during his ban, described the selectors as 'drunks' who once they had picked a touring party were given some more pink gin and put back in the loft with a sheet over their heads. Even though he was forced to write letters of apology to all of them, the evidence indicated that he might have had a point. In six months England went from arguably the second best team in the world to total disarray and this was due in large part to the panic of the selectors. In those circumstances it is little wonder that, even though you would have thought that there wasn't a Test pitch in the land more suited to England and less suited to India, we lost by 279 runs. When England won seven Tests out of seven in 2004 they employed 16 players and only one change to the team wasn't forced on the selectors by injury or retirement. In the 1980s it was really interesting listening for the England team on a Sunday morning to see who they had gone for next; now it's really boring.

The selectors could have argued that the recall of Athey was a success in that he made easily his highest Test score and England's best of the match. When you realise that the score in question was 32 it doesn't sound quite so impressive. The fact that India made 272 in their first innings and England only had two wickets in hand when they saved the follow-on gives you some idea of how inept they were. England only managed a combined total of 230 from two innings, John Woodcock in *The Times* pointed out that they had only made more than 200 twice in their last 12 attempts and offered the opinion that 'professional golfers playing as unsuccessfully as that would be sleeping under the hedges by now'.

What was going on in the middle was obviously so unpalatable that the spectators took to cheering themselves up by copying the World Cup crowds with the new 'Mexican wave'. *Wisden* was not amused, apparently this performance 'left Headingley's reputation as a ground for cricket lovers as much in tatters as the reputation of the England team'.

On the last morning of the match and for ever afterwards it seemed, the whole country was talking about one dropped catch. On the rest day Maradona had spilled one over Peter Shilton's head and despite Lineker's late heroics (how did the second one not go in?), we were out of the World Cup. Years later the English proved how balanced and forgiving they can be by voting his second goal in that match (the one where he beat Terry Butcher twice in the same run) as the greatest World Cup goal ever. Either that or there was one of those 'Well it had to have been the greatest goal ever for it to have knocked us out' things going on. As usual, I voted for the one that came second, Carlos Alberto's for Brazil against Italy in the 1970 final.

I had managed to watch the Argentina game without a sense of guilt because my final exams were over. Despite the fact that my results were at least one notch higher than I deserved, I still had no more idea about what to do next than the England selectors did. If Botham was to be believed, the similarities didn't end there, as my immediate plan involved alcohol. Their efforts so far that summer might have seemed consistent with being slightly tipsy; if so then they appeared to have been off their faces when they picked the team for Edgbaston.

Smith, Slack and Lever, having been given one match, were discarded never to return and Dilley had toothache. Their replacements were Neil Foster, Mark Benson, Neil Radford (a Zambian with Paul Mariner's hair who had played for South Africa U25s against Gooch's rebel team in 1982) and Gower. Benson in fact replaced a replacement, the selectors' most bizarre choice, Wayne Larkins. Where they got the idea to pick Larkins from I still don't know. He didn't have a reputation as a particularly good player of spin (he had been omitted from the 1981-82 tour to India partly for this reason), he had scored 58 runs in eight first-class innings all season and, perhaps most crucially of all at this time, was not being touted by any of the tabloid newspapers. He was also having an injury-riddled time and so it didn't come as a huge surprise that he missed the match with a chipped thumb anyway. Once he was fit they didn't go near him again for almost four years.

England got off to another flier and were soon 0-2. But Benson, leaving the ball like Trescothick by playing deliberately inside the line, played solidly in making 21 and started the recovery with Gower. The Kent left-hander made 30 in the second innings and must have been reasonably pleased with his debut. Let's hope so because those two innings were the only ones he ever played in a Test match. Graham Gooch made a pair on his debut on the same ground and ended up as England's leading Test run scorer.

If England had lost they would have equalled their worst ever losing streak, of eight straight games, a record that went back to 1921. They probably would have done if Gatting hadn't been dropped on four. England's captain edged one between Gavaskar at first slip and wicket-keeper Kiran More. Even though it went through Gavaskar's hands, the general view was that it was probably More's catch. The miss cost 179 runs, a bit expensive but nowhere near as many as the same man ended up owing his team when he dropped Graham Gooch on 36 at Lord's four years later. More might have looked like he was on a one-man mission to prove that you should always pick your best keeper, but even these two mistakes combined weren't as expensive as Chris Scott of Durham missing Lara on 18 in 1994.

Gatting guided England to 390 and India made exactly the same. England tried to cock it up by being bowled out for 235 second time round (six men past 20, no one more than 40) with nearly the whole of the last day left. When India were 101-1 eight defeats in a row was looking favourite, but a combination of Phil Edmonds (4-31 from 28 overs) and the Birmingham weather helped us escape. In September the previous year I had thought I was finally supporting a top cricket team, now I was grateful for a scrambled draw. Having said that, we'll never know how the side that played at the Oval in August 1985 would have got on against the Indians because by the time we had reached Edgbaston less than a year on, there were only five of them left in the team.

Four days after the end of the India series Tony Nasser, playing for Bradford Gymkhana CC, scored 107 in 23 minutes. He was in a hurry to meet his sister at Manchester airport but was still half an hour late. Someone else who didn't turn up on time was Sarah Ferguson, although with all the cameras trained on her journey to Westminster Abbey at least Prince Andrew would have known she was still coming. They were married the day before the first Test against New Zealand. If the interview she gave on US television in 2001 is to be believed, before the series was over she knew the marriage was heading for the rocks because of Andrew's naval duties. You would have thought the uniforms might have given it away before she married him.

Two days before the royal wedding Dickie Bird went to Buckingham Palace to collect his MBE. There is a wonderful picture of him standing outside, happily smiling and displaying the award, totally oblivious of the horse and carriage heading straight for him from behind. Someone's left hand just coming into view at the side of the shot perhaps gives a clue as to how he survived to umpire the first Test at Lord's.

Dickie wasn't the only MBE on show in the match. After Martin Moxon had made an accomplished 74 on debut and Gower 62, Richard Hadlee hit Bruce French on the head. As a result Bill Athey kept wicket for two overs at the start of New Zealand's first innings before 45-year-old Bob Taylor MBE was hauled away from his hospitality duties for Cornhill to take over. Despite the fact that he had been retired from first-class cricket for two years he still had his old gloves in the car and, although the rest of his kit was borrowed, he kept wicket immaculately. Unsurprisingly he wasn't sure that he could do it again for a second day running and although they only just caught him on his way out for the day, Bobby Parks of Hampshire was called in to cover the Saturday. Although, in 1999, Parks was appointed as a national team coach (of France), this was the closest he ever came to joining his father and grandfather as an England player.

England had been almost single-handedly restricted to 307 by Hadlee. *Wisden* suggested there were two different games going on; one when Hadlee was bowling and one when he wasn't. In the second two thirds of his career he had to carry his team's bowling as there was no-one in the side even remotely in his class. This makes his figures even more impressive than they look on paper. A career record of 431 wickets at 22.29 sounds good enough itself but when you consider that in his first 20 Tests he took 76 wickets at 33.43 that means once he had stopped trying to be a tear-away quick bowler and reinvented himself as a 1980s Kiwi version of Glenn McGrath, he took 355 wickets in 66 Tests at 19.91. Dennis Lillee took 355 wickets at 23.92 in his 70-match career and he had Jeff Thomson at the other end.

In England's first innings Hadlee took 6-80 in nearly 38 overs. Not bad for a 35-year-old opening bowler but arguably not as impressive as 73-year-old Jack Cleaver's 9-45 for Glenfrith against Hallaton the same month. These weren't the best figures of Mr Cleaver's career as he clearly recalled taking 'all ten' 57 years earlier in 1929.

England had nobody capable of taking all ten against New Zealand, or anyone else for that matter, and Martin Crowe's 106 eased them to a 35-run lead. Half of the fourth day was lost to rain and England would need to do something really stupid for there to be a positive result. So New Zealand were in with a good chance. Athey (right-handed) and Gower (left-handed) both contrived to be bowled behind their legs by the left-arm spinner Evan Gray and when Gatting dumped the same bowler into Crowe's hands on the final morning we were four down and only 101 in front. Fortunately Gooch saw off the second new ball and ensured another draw. It says a lot that not losing to New Zealand seemed like a triumph.

'Triumph' is not a word you would use to describe England's performance in the second Test. 'Crap' is nearer the mark. The depth to which we had sunk is probably best illustrated by Gatting's comment after the match that we had 'missed out' by about half an hour. What he meant was if we had batted for another 30 minutes they might not have had quite enough time to knock off the required runs. In other words what we had 'missed out' on was scrambling a draw that neither we, nor they, deserved.

Saying John Emburey was our top scorer in the match gives you some idea of how good everyone else was. Emburey did make 75 but the manner in which he did it (in the second innings when defeat was almost certain anyway) put me in mind of an international version of John Hare, a teammate at Barcombe who was famous for trying to drive bouncers, sweep long-hops and cut half-volleys. It's also true the Kiwis' number eight John Bracewell was their top scorer with 110 (yet another batsman to make his only Test hundred against us) but whereas their numbers six and seven made 50 and 68, ours managed 4 and 9.

Hadlee, inevitably, was the destroyer taking 10-140, his seventh match haul of 10 or more. He performed this feat twice more and his total of nine is the best by a seamer in Test history. Only Muralitharan and Warne have bettered this and Hadlee's 36 five-fors. Despite having served out his ban and the fact the selectors made another four changes for this match, England's leading all-rounder was elsewhere. Wellingborough School to be exact, hitting 13 sixes (a new competition record) and 12 fours in an innings of 175 not out for Somerset against Northants in the John Player League. England had Derek Pringle batting at six and lost by eight wickets.

By the time Botham was selected for the final Test he had other things on his mind. Somerset had announced they were going to release Viv Richards and Joel Garner at the end of the season and replace them with Martin Crowe who had stood in when the West Indies were touring in 1984. In cricketing terms the decision made some sense. Richards was 34 and expected to be absent with the West Indies in 1988 and Garner was 33 (not young for a fast bowler) and had suffered injury problems that year. However, the reaction to this decision couldn't be described as dispassionate. Botham threatened to leave if the decision was not rescinded and Richards, in his usual measured way, summed up his reading of the situation with: 'When you have two workhorses and you shoot them in the back, I think it's evil. You do not treat animals this way. The word was out. Bang bang – Viv and Joel are dead... The present regime at Somerset is pretty deadly. These people sat around with sad faces. The executioner always wears a sad face...I am not bitter.'

The upshot of all this was that, despite months of petitions and emergency meetings of the type you would normally associate with Yorkshire, the original decision finally stood. Botham fulfilled his threat and joined Worcestershire, Richards swaggered out of county cricket for three seasons until he returned with Glamorgan in 1990, Garner went off to the Lancashire Leagues and later to terrorize club batsmen around the West Country and they all ended up hating Peter Roebuck. But then they're not alone there.

A few years later, Stoneleigh went on tour to Somerset and we played a side that had faced Garner the previous weekend. Their ground had a substantial slope and anybody bowling downhill would have picked up quite a bit of momentum. You could still see the imprints from Garner's run up at the top end. It looked like Big Foot had been bowling. I could just stretch to get a boot on each of his footmarks without tearing my groin. I asked one of our opponents what it had been like facing him: 'I don't know, I had my eyes shut'.

If all the problems at Somerset were playing on Botham's mind it didn't show when he finally got back into the England side. He had stayed stuck on 354 Test wickets (one behind Dennis Lillee's all-time record) all summer. Everyone knows he equalled the record by removing Bruce Edgar with his first ball back and then went past it by trapping Jeff Crowe lbw in his next over. I've never seen the catch that drew him level with Lillee because the BBC's director was so concerned with concentrating on Botham's triumphant celebration that he cut away from Gooch before he had finished nearly dropping it.

This was a bad summer for the BBC. At the start of the season they had lost Jim Laker who had died at the age of only 64 and at the end of it Peter West retired.

Despite the fact that he turned the ball the other way, Laker always reminded me of my uncle, the loopy leg-spinner. He looked a little like him and came from the same generation that seemed to place so much emphasis on courtesy and respect for others. I imagined him (again like my uncle) never to be without a collar and tie even if, on a particularly hot day, he might allow himself the luxury of taking his jacket off. As a broadcaster he didn't attract attention like Benaud or Arlott but perhaps because he seemed allergic to the letter 'g' (everyone was always battin', bowlin' or fieldin'), his voice was reassuring. I felt safe listening to him. Which is more than can be said for the batsmen who faced him in his prime. As a player he can probably best be described as undemonstratively brilliant. This is best summed up by the story of his journey home after the Old Trafford Test of 1956. Having taken his, surely never-to-be-equalled 19 wickets in the match, to defeat Australia, Laker stopped on his drive home at a pub near Lichfield. He ordered a bottle of beer and a sandwich, sat in a corner of the bar and listened while everyone talked of what he had just achieved. No-one recognized him. It's ludicrous that the best off-spinner England ever had only played 46 Tests. John Emburey played 64.

Richie Benaud described Peter West's professionalism as 'an object lesson to me when I took over a similar presentation job with Channel 9 in Australia'. Televised Test cricket started in 1952 and West was on the commentary team. By the time he retired at the end of 1986 he had covered 35 cricket seasons, 27 Wimbledons and spent 15 years fronting *Come Dancing*. You don't last that long unless you're very good at what you do and although West sometimes gave the impression of being a bit of an upper class twit he was clearly nothing of the kind. Indeed he's one of the few people I've seen best Benaud on television.

At Edgbaston with the rain belting down, West, under his umbrella, was interviewing Richie. Unfortunately for the Australian, the umbrella wasn't quite big enough and the angle at which West was holding it meant the rainwater was running off it straight down the great man's neck. A true professional himself, Benaud soldiered on until the end of the interview when he was asked if he had anything he would like to add: 'Only that I'd be delighted to move to get away from the water running down my neck.' 'Never mind,' said West turning to camera: 'They tell me there's a drought in Australia.'

Australia was where England were going that winter and despite Botham's wickets and his 36-ball 59 not out, things didn't look good. Rain ensured a draw in the final match of the summer and for the first time we lost a home series to New Zealand. It felt like it was going to be a long winter and the Aussies had already started taking the piss.

England were due to play a match against a South Australia Country XI on 29th October in a place called Wudinna and 12 of the Eyre Highway Motel's 14 rooms had been booked to accomodate the team, two journalists and the team manager. However, the TCCB, displaying a slight lack of understanding of the nature of accommodation in up-country Australia, had also requested 'one complimentary suite, i.e. a bedroom and separate sitting-room' for the manager. The local newspaper pointed out that: 'Separate sitting-rooms are not standard issue in one-night stops along the long drag to the Nullarbor.' But the motel manager was keen to be helpful. 'Don't worry, we'll set him up a table in the sun.'

THIRTEEN

By the end of the summer of 1986 Britain's oldest twins, May and Marjorie Chavasse, had turned 100, 88-year-old Frank Twitchen of Victoria Park CC in Bideford (a man who had played with W.G. Grace) had completed his 80th season and Geoff Boycott's first-class career had finally come to an end at the age of 46. Yorkshire's decision to dispense with his services was made despite the fact he had finished the season with an average of 52.21 and failed by only eight to score 1,000 first-class runs for the 24th consecutive year. During the previous winter's disasters in the Caribbean there were even some who had suggested he should be coaxed from the press box to add some much needed steel to England's top order. I doubt if he would have disgraced himself or, given he said in his autobiography he would 'exchange the rest of his life for five more years of playing for Yorkshire and England', that he would have taken much persuading.

If batting had been a person Boycott would have been its number one stalker. When I feel I'm too obsessed with cricket I remind myself of Geoff Boycott. I've never practised my forward defensive stark naked in front of a mirror. It may seem sad that the thing he loved most in the world was batting but at least he knew it and he also knew when his chance to do it at a level he found meaningful was gone, it was gone forever. Perhaps that's why he was so concerned with becoming the leading runscorer in Test cricket. He was building his own monument.

Boycott wasn't going to Australia and neither was another Yorkshire opener, Ashley Metcalfe. Metcalfe had scored over 1,800 first-class runs with six centuries and had been described by Ray Illingworth (admittedly his father-in-law) as the best attacker of the younger generation of batsmen. He was just 22 and the most exciting young batting prospect in the country. Many saw him as unlucky not to be picked for Australia and although he described himself as 'bloody upset' at his omission, he concluded: 'There's always tomorrow.' Boycott could have told him this wasn't true. Ashley Metcalfe never played for England.

By the end of the first month of the tour it was a toss-up between England and Jeffrey Archer (forced to resign as Deputy Tory Party Chairman over allegations of payments to a prostitute) as to who was in more trouble. We lost to Queensland, narrowly scrambled out with a draw against Western Australia because of bad light and generally gave the impression, as Stoneleigh once did to Frome's overseas professional, of being a rugby team on a cricket tour as a joke.

In fact, after Botham produced the last great Test innings of his career, smashing 138 on the second day at Brisbane, the tour turned into a triumphant procession. From the moment that Merv Hughes, armed with the second new ball, disappeared for 22 in one over you could, as the great all-rounder himself put it, 'see Australia sinking'. England could do nothing wrong. They secured the Ashes with a win at Brisbane and a three-day victory at Melbourne, and swept aside their hosts, the West Indies and Pakistan in the course of victories in two one-day tournaments. It was as if 15 years of winning was being condensed into one tour.

It seemed a small group of previously untried or unsuccessful cricketers had blended with an experienced core to form a team worthy of support. In reality we were watching what was, for many in the touring party, the cricketing equivalent of being on *Big Brother*: huge amounts of exposure for a short time followed by a swift return to total anonymity.

But, like a doomed infatuation, for three months it was glorious. Phil DeFreitas, unsurprisingly the first man born in Dominica to represent England, was truly the 'next Botham' but with the added advantage of playing in the same side with an original still at the peak of his powers. Similarly, Jack Richards, who played only three more Tests after this tour, appeared to be the new Alan Knott. Richards was only the second Cornishman to play for England after Jack Crapp, a man who once dismissed the idea that emotion had caused Don Bradman to be bowled by Hollies' googly in his final Test innings with: 'That bugger Bradman never had a tear in his eye in his whole life.' Later, the older 'Cornish Jack' became a first-class umpire and was still standing alongside the likes of toothless Tom Spencer when I first started watching the John Player League on telly on Sunday afternoons. In the 1970s if you said the umpire was Crapp there was a good chance you were stating a fact rather than expressing an opinion. At Perth, Jack the younger became only the third England wicket-keeper, after Ames and Knott, to score a Test hundred against Australia. However, it was another previously peripheral figure who made the greatest contribution to the team's success.

Seeing Jack Hobbs, Herbert Sutcliffe, Wally Hammond and Chris Broad listed together might normally make you think you were being confronted by a very easy odd-one-out competition. However, Broad scored three Test hundreds that winter and, in so doing, joined three of the greatest batsmen we have ever produced as the only Englishmen to have achieved the feat in an Ashes series. This earned him the ridiculously overblown title of International Cricketer of the Year. Roughly translated, this meant the man who had scored the most runs or taken the most wickets in that Australian season and was another idea for which we could all thank Kerry 'Hyperbole' Packer.

Standing in the way of the International Cricketer of the Year and his cohorts were seemingly only two men, a bad Swedish rock star and a little bald bloke. Bruce Reid was a left-arm seamer who, at six-foot-eight, is the tallest man to have played in an Ashes Test and even if his blond moustache and mullet made him look like a Harry Enfield character, he was consistently Australia's best bowler and ended up destroying England four years later. Alongside him was Greg Matthews.

In the days before Ian Healey, Matthews was the Australian nominated to score exasperatingly important runs at number seven. Ostensibly an off-spinner (although an overall Test bowling average of 48.22 spared us having to see him more than was absolutely necessary), he was shorter, much more annoying and crucially for a later source of income, less impressively coiffured than his colleague.

Cricketers must be particularly sensitive about losing their hair (either that or wearing a cap all day makes it fall out) as Shane Warne, Graham Gooch and Alamgir Sheriyar have joined Matthews in advertising hair replacement treatments. Having said that, the rugby international Austin Healey has starred in one of the naffest television adverts you will ever see for a similar product. If the stories are to be believed, this Healey is about as irritating to the rugby fraternity as the Australian one was to English cricket supporters. Allegedly, he once emerged from the bottom of a ruck complaining he had been punched, only for the referee to respond: 'I didn't see anything Austin and let's be honest, it could have been any one of 29 other people on the field… Actually make that 30 other people.'

Even the efforts of Reid and Matthews couldn't stop England. Like the British government with Guinness, the Australian cricketing public could have been forgiven for wondering what was going on. On the rest day of the Perth Test, having realised something fishy was afoot, the government announced an enquiry into Guinness's affairs. It was more than three-and-a-half years before, on the day Gower began the hundred that secured his selection for the next tour to Australia, Chief Executive Ernest Saunders was jailed for false accounting, conspiracy and theft. In the shorter term the Australians might have wanted an enquiry of their own into England's batsmen. Having made 456 in the first Test they contrived to be bowled out for 197 and 82 by New South Wales and lost by eight wickets. Then, at Perth, they made 592-8 declared and Rod Marsh suggested that 'if they were horses they'd be dope tested'.

Even more puzzling for the home supporters was the fact their side was being outplayed by a team whose captain didn't turn up for the start of the game against Victoria because he overslept and who explained England's failure to bowl Australia out in the second innings at Perth with: 'The wicket didn't really do too much and when it did it did too much.' Perhaps he didn't oversleep at all and was just in need of a lie down in a dark room to allow time for his brain to cool down after trying to work out what that meant?

However crap they were in between, in the internationals England swept all before them. They even won the Benson and Hedges Challenge (Oh! The glory!). This was one of a number of events set to coincide with the America's Cup taking place off Freemantle. It was a four-way tournament between Australia, England, West Indies and Pakistan and was scheduled to finish only three days before what might have been the deciding Test in Sydney a mere 2,500 miles away. Utterly meaningless, I mention it only because Richie Benaud gave me a lesson in lip reading.

During England's match with the West Indies, Gus Logie nicked Graham Dilley to third man for four. The television director zoomed in on the bowler's face just as he appeared to me to be making an obscure reference to coprophilia. Richie put me right: 'Those of you blessed with the gift of lip reading will know that Graham Dilley was telling Gus Logie what a "fortunate shot" that was.'

Victory in this tournament represented only a small cherry on top of the large cake that was the Melbourne Test. On what was due to be the rest day Harold Macmillan died. Coming from a different generation, I have to confess when I saw the headline: 'Super Mac is Dead', my first thought was that the former Newcastle and Arsenal striker Malcolm Macdonald had passed away. This was of great concern to me as he had been a hero in my demi-Gooner days. His five goals against Cyprus had convinced the eight-year-old me he should be an international regular. When I accidentally broke one of my Subbuteo England team off at the knees and my rough, Airfix-glue repair job left the figure looking decidedly bandy, I simply stuck a tiny number nine on his back and said it was Malcolm. However, his cricketing pedigree was limited to having Reg Hayter, who also acted for Botham in his time, as his agent and turning out in the Gaymer's Old English Cider Celebrity sixes competition in La Manga in 1984. Here, under the unlikely captaincy of Lenny Bennett, Macdonald played against Botham alongside such cricketing luminaries as Patrick Mower, Jim Watt and Peter Cook. Even in the 1980s the addition of the word 'celebrity' to the title of an event didn't necessarily mean the participants were significantly more famous than the local mad vagrant.

As far as Macmillan was concerned, obviously the most important thing about him was that his grandson, Mark Faber, played for Sussex in the 1970s. I say he died on what was 'due to be' the rest day because England wrapped up the fourth Test while the former prime minister was still with us. England had maintained a 1-0 lead with a draw at Adelaide which saw James Whittaker play his only Test as an unlikely replacement for the injured Botham. For Melbourne the champion all-rounder was back (albeit at only about 75 per cent fitness) and after Gatting put Australia in, produced what he called 'probably one of my worst bowling performances'. Fortunately the Australians produced an even worse batting display and he ended up with 5-41. Gladstone Small, came in as a late replacement for Dilley and took 5-48 as we rolled our hosts over for 141. I'm not sure what a Tory like Macmillan would have made of Gladstone claiming some of the glory.

With the possibility of the Ashes being secured, the BBC broadcast the third day live on television and I stayed up all night to watch it. At 153-3, with Marsh and Waugh apparently entrenched, I was starting to worry and almost went to bed when the opener was blatantly caught off his glove but given not out. However, two balls later he got into a terrible mix up with his partner and was run out by half the length of the pitch. Jack Richards and I saw him off with a happy smile and a cheery wave. Baldy Matthews made a duck and the rest fell in a wonderfully clueless heap to Emburey and Edmonds. Peter Roebuck said at the time that witnessing the Australians' efforts to play Emburey was like watching kids brought up on calculators trying to do long division.

Although they didn't realise it at the time, the members of this team, despite the fact they never played anywhere near as well again, would linger in the memories of English cricket supporters for almost 20 years.

The seeds of Australian dominance in the period that followed were sown at Sydney by a bloke no one had heard of.

Peter Taylor had never managed a football team with Brian Clough. He was a sandy-haired off-spinner so obscure that when he was selected at least one television station assumed he was a typing error and sent a crew off to interview his namesake Mark. Although the New South Wales opener was the one who ended up never losing an Ashes series, in the short term the other Taylor helped Australia remember how to beat England by contributing 6-78 in our first innings and 42 in their second.

The way the Australians celebrated the victory you would have thought they had won the series. They hadn't and in the years that followed it was some small comfort to me to know the likes of Allan Border, Steve Waugh, Geoff Marsh, David Boon, Greg Matthews, Dean Jones, Craig McDermott and Merv Hughes all know what it feels like to lose the Ashes.

While all of this had been going on the National Coal Board (not content with thousands of miners) had announced they were making all their canaries redundant, a not so innocent George Davis had been sent down for his part in an attempted train robbery and Cynthia Payne (later a recipient of the BBC's *Good Food Show*'s Ideal Dinner Guest award and author of the wonderfully entitled *Entertaining at Home*) was acquitted of keeping prostitutes, charges which had ironically arisen out of events at the end of film party for *Personal Services*. Once the verdict was announced she emerged from Inner London Crown Court to a hero's welcome.

This was exactly what was accorded England's cricketers. Gatting was so obviously the right man for the job that for once the summer didn't start with a question mark hanging over who would take charge of England. We never won another match under his leadership.

If there was no change in the England captaincy there were plenty of other new appointments either made or contemplated before the season began. The General Synod voted in favour of women priests (although the first one wasn't appointed for another eight years). In a similar move, Clare Connor (the only girl in the school) was made captain of Brighton College Junior School's under-10s. Warwickshire signed an unknown 20-year-old South African fast bowler called Allan Donald and Mickey Stewart was made England's first full-time cricket manager.

The concept of a full-time manager was one of the two 'big ideas' of the time to halt the decline of the England side. The other, four-day championship cricket, had been delayed and fudged by counties reluctant to see fewer matches played with a potential drop in revenue. The result was that four-day cricket wasn't introduced until 1988 and then only on the basis of six matches in the middle of the season sandwiched between periods of three-day games at the start and end. The counties' arguments might have held a bit more water if spectators had turned up to watch championship matches in sufficient numbers to make the county clubs financially independent. In 1979, Essex won their first ever county championship title with a win at Northampton. Only 650 people, fewer than 100 of whom were Essex supporters, turned up to see it. The reality was that in the period of Thatcherism county cricket clubs were an anachronism; largely loss-making businesses reliant on what were effectively state subsidies from the TCCB to survive.

International cricket, certainly against the major Test countries, was still played in front of large crowds who provided the money for the handouts. However, if the national side continued to fail then even this would eventually dry up with the result that many counties would face going to the wall. In short, in sharp contrast to football which is built on the popularity of the domestic game, the whole structure of first-class cricket in this country was dependent on the revenue generated by international matches to survive. For that revenue to be secure there needed to be a successful England team.

Traditionally you would have more likely used the word 'abject' to describe the national side. Which begs the question: how did the game survive? Certainly our home games were usually sold out on the first three days at least, but only for the series against Australia in 2005 can I remember claims being made that the grounds could have been filled three or four times over. In other words, even though Lord's and the

Oval might have been full, Melbourne and Sydney would have been half-empty. Nevertheless enough people did turn up to fill the seats available. How did that happen in a period when the perception was we lurched from one failure to the next? Perhaps it's because there was a marked difference in our records at home and abroad? During the 1990s England played 50 Tests overseas winning only nine and losing 23. At home in the same period they contested 57 matches with 17 victories and 20 defeats. There is nothing particularly surprising in the home record being better, it's exactly what you would expect, but the point is these games were the ones the public saw. In other words, England's worst performances were generally when they were out of sight. At home they did just enough to keep sufficient people coming through the turnstiles.

If four-day cricket hadn't even been implemented yet, England did nothing in 1987 to suggest a full-time manager was going to make a significant difference on his own. For only the second time, Pakistan were given five Tests and Imran became the first Pakistani captain to lead his side to a series victory in England.

For a brief period after England's Ashes triumph in 2005 cricket became cool. Why else would Tony Blair have invited the team to Downing Street? In 1987, the only time the word 'cool' came up in connection with the England cricket team was when they were playing at Headingley. Even though pictures of what we were all wearing at the time and records of the music we were listening to (Nick Berry, Rick Astley, T'Pau) indicate Mike Gatting and his men were not alone in this respect, the notion that cricket could in any way compete with football in the popularity stakes was as laughable as Astley's blazer.

This was particularly true in Coventry where I was now living. Four years earlier I had seen Brighton turn into a Seagulls' paradise for about two months and now in my adopted home, nothing but Sky Blues did I see. Brighton's Cup Final team had included Mike's brother Steve Gatting but Coventry could top that since their goalkeeper, Steve Ogrizovic, had once bowled Viv Richards with a no-ball in the Natwest Trophy. Obviously, having greater cricketing credentials tipped the balance in City's favour and, thanks to Gary Mabbutt's knee, they grabbed their moment in a way Brighton had failed to.

Having said that, there was no shortage of interest in the cricket where I was working. I had found a job as an advice worker in Small Heath, a predominantly Pakistani-Asian area of Birmingham. It was the first time I had come across a community where football hardly registered and the majority of sporting conversations revolved around cricket. If I ignored the poverty, the dilapidated housing, the occasional burnt-out car and the presence of Birmingham City's ground at the end of the Coventry Road, I could have been in heaven.

However, I doubt if that's how the people who lived there thought of it. The problem of the 'inner cities' was one of the major political and social issues of the time. So much so that even the Church of England, with the former national cricket captain and then Bishop of Liverpool David Sheppard to the fore, had been moved to commission its 'Faith in the City' report into the causes of, and possible solutions for, urban deprivation.

If you lived outside the West Midlands and had heard of any particular area of Birmingham, the chances are it would have been Handsworth because of the riots. The popular press took the names of places like Handsworth, St Paul's in Bristol and Toxteth in Liverpool and demonized them, creating a two-dimensional image of disaffection and lawlessness that made any right-thinking person afraid to go anywhere near them. Small Heath may not have been as famous as Handsworth but it was every bit as poor and I hadn't approached the prospect of starting a job there with total confidence. Very early on I had told a native Brummie where I worked. 'I suppose someone's got to,' he said. 'But rather you than me mate.'

My first day left me feeling I might be in for a bit of a culture shock. In an effort to bond with my new colleagues I made a round of tea. I was then more than a little concerned to see the boss tipping his away when he thought I wasn't looking. I asked one of the others what the problem was. 'Don't worry,' she said. 'It's just that you used Mr Khan's mug. We keep a separate one just for him. He has tubercular leprosy.'

Despite this unfortunate beginning I settled in easily and quickly realised that although the criminality was real enough, it was, as is usually the way with such things, only a small part of a much bigger picture. The only time I felt remotely uncomfortable was in the immediate aftermath of a cricket match.

The teams had won a game apiece in the three-match one-day international series and the decider was at Edgbaston on 25th May. England won with their last pair at the crease when Neil Foster nicked Wasim Akram for four in the final over. But nobody was talking about that after the game as crowd problems made the national news. Many cricket fans would have been disturbed enough at having their view blocked by waving flags and their ears assaulted by blaring horns but this went far further. Groups of Pakistani supporters invaded the ground during England's innings and clashed with National Front skinheads in a series of skirmishes throughout the day. Flagstakes were used as clubs, the police were pelted with cans and one Pakistani had his jugular severed by a glass. Much of the trouble was blamed on inadequate manpower in terms of police and stewards as large numbers of Pakistani supporters got in without tickets. Interestingly, with Mrs Thatcher less than three weeks away from her third election victory, David Frith offered the opinion that a further problem was that the police's powers of control were 'severely limited in this "liberal" society'. Even so, 50 people were ejected from the ground and a further 20 arrested.

Cricket had recently been banned from the streets of towns in Kashmir after a scooter rider was killed by a ball and Ahmedabad in India was placed under curfew following a riot caused by the disputed result of a local match. Fortunately, despite the hand wringing they caused, events at Edgbaston didn't lead to such draconian measures and the simple expedients of checking that people had tickets, confiscating flags and employing more police and stewards seemed to work wonders. Just as the tension at work in the few days after the one-dayer had quickly dissipated and life had gone back to normal, so the Test series went off without serious incident. England might have wished it hadn't.

From our perspective the only time the first part of the series wasn't dull was when it was depressing. The first two matches were rain-ruined draws. Then they went to Headingley. By the time the third Test started Mrs Thatcher had trounced Neil Kinnock in the election in which, ironically given that Enoch Powell lost his seat, Britain's first black MPs were elected and I had met Mrs K.

Shunned by many in the community because she was estranged from her husband and living as a single parent with her two daughters, Mrs K, as she insisted on being known, had chosen to confront disapproval with a lively lack of deference. It was an unusual and brave, some might say foolish, choice to have made. In many ways she was like a small child constantly demanding attention, as if to remain silent for even a minute was somehow to submit to those who condemned her for having the temerity to flee domestic violence. Loud and annoyingly persistent on occasions, she was there practically every day, getting away with a series of queue-jumping stunts through the sheer force of a mischievous personality you could see in her eyes when she smiled. She was an unlikely kindred spirit for a 23-year-old posh lad from Brighton but work was a lot more fun when she was there.

However, as well as informing me that 'Asian people think white people smell of sour milk', she also claimed her father had played first-class cricket with Fazal Mahmood. Whether this was true or not, her love and knowledge of the game was real and many of her enquiries took twice as long as they should have done because she never missed an opportunity to tell me what 'her boys' were going to do to mine that summer.

After Gatting had won the toss at Leeds, she bustled in at alarmingly regular intervals to keep me up to date with the score as we slipped to 31-5. In fact I only got rid of her while David Capel (53 on debut) and Botham were putting on 54 for the sixth wicket.

On the second day it was announced that Barbie had got 'life'. This wasn't the victory for feminism it may sound, merely confirmation of the fate of the former Nazi war criminal and post-war U.S. counter-intelligence agent, Klaus Barbie. The furore that had surrounded the disclosure of Barbie's cold-war employment had provided an embarrassing side-show for the American Government but had no material effect on the outcome of the trial. England were about to be caught up in a similarly idle controversy.

Over 200 behind on a pitch still seaming generously and against Imran Khan and Wasim Akram, we had no chance. However, it didn't help when Chris Broad was given out caught off the glove when a) his hand wasn't in contact with the bat and b) the ball bounced before it reached the keeper.

The second part of this incident increased calls for television umpires to adjudicate on low catches in the mistaken belief this would remove such errors. In fact, once replays were introduced they merely produced another type of controversy, with batsmen surviving after the taking of what were probably perfectly good catches because the camera couldn't provide a conclusive answer. Michael Vaughan's escape at Adelaide in November 2002 is perhaps the most famous example. Apparently this is a problem caused by the foreshortening of the picture by head-on cameras. Sky television have conducted experiments which show that balls which are, in reality, in the hands, appear to be on the ground just short of the fielder because of this effect.

If Pakistan's wicket-keeper, Salim Yousef, might have been given the benefit of the doubt over Broad's dismissal, the same certainly can't be said about what he did later the same day. Botham had come in with a runner and was just starting to threaten a repeat of his 1981 heroics when he edged the ball to Yousef, who dropped it, secured it again with his back to the umpire once it had bounced and claimed the catch. It wasn't even as if he had gathered the ball again on the half-volley; it had bounced up several inches. I thought Botham was going to lay him out and Imran openly lectured him on the field. Salim clearly favoured the Captain Jack Sparrow attitude to being memorable. 'You are without doubt the worst pirate I've ever heard of.' 'But you have heard of me.'

If going 1-0 down wasn't bad enough, David Gower announced he wasn't going to be representing England in the forthcoming World Cup as he intended to have a winter off. The competition, in India and Pakistan, was the first to be staged outside England and for several months there had been a question mark hanging over whether anybody would be participating. Earlier in the year the West Indies had proposed to the ICC that from an unspecified future date any cricketer having sporting contact with South Africa should be banned. Crucially this included anyone coaching or playing as an individual. The idea was obviously not going to meet with the approval of professionals in this country who were bound to put pressure on their own authorities to resist any such move. Not that many of them would have needed much persuading, there were plenty of apologists for closer sporting links with South Africa in the upper echelons of English cricket and the issue once more threatened to split the sport.

As far as the competition itself was concerned there was the possibility that the make-up of the England team would again cause problems. Although Graham Gooch had been in poor form and hadn't regained his place in the England side, Gower's withdrawal made it much more likely that he would be included in the World Cup squad alongside Emburey. The chairman of the organizing committee, N.K.P. Salve, was quoted as saying that: 'We will never interfere in the selection of players of any country,' but also commented that Indian and Pakistani immigration laws were 'sacrosanct'. An Indian Home Ministry official suggested that any player who had toured South Africa might be required to provide a written apology for having done so and a letter condemning apartheid before they would be allowed entry into the country.

The ICC held a special meeting at Lord's on 26th June. Anybody familiar with cricket politics might be able to guess what they did to avert the crisis. They set up a select committee to 'consider the particular problems associated with South Africa'. This committee would then report back to the ICC's 1988 meeting well after the commercially lucrative World Cup had finished. The meeting that decided this, full of representatives from all around the globe, lasted just over three hours.

How disastrous it would have been from the players' point of view if the competition hadn't gone ahead is unclear. Certainly it was not high on some people's list of priorities. Gower, explaining his reasons for taking a winter off, described it as 'a series of one-day matches purporting to be a World Cup' and by the end of the summer it was clear that Botham wouldn't be going either. From my point of view, given that Australia's victory set them on the road to their extended period of world domination, perhaps it would have been better if it had been called off.

For the first four days most people watching it must have wished the same thing about the Edgbaston Test. It looked as if the most memorable things to happen during the match would be Botham becoming the first bowler to concede 10,000 Test runs and Jeffrey Archer (another captain Jack if ever there was one) winning record libel damages of £500,000 against the *Daily Star*. Asked to comment at the end of the trial Archer suggested that 'the verdict speaks for itself', a phrase which perhaps might more accurately be applied to the result of his 2000 trial for perjury and perverting the course of justice or the MCC committee's subsequent suspension of his membership.

By the fourth evening at Birmingham the first innings had barely been completed and although England's 521 had given them a lead of 82, the tourists started the final day only 44 behind with 10 wickets left. A score at lunch of 74-1 left the journalists, who had to be there, praying for rain so they could go home early. Then, on a pitch which had produced 20 wickets and 998 runs in four days, Neil Foster and Ian Botham suddenly reduced Pakistan to 116-6 by mid-afternoon and one of those wonderful runs-against-time equations began to develop. Mrs K was nowhere to be seen.

I knocked off early from work and got home just in time to see Akram's dismissal leave the tourists 165-8, 83 in front with more than 30 overs left. Imran and Qadir then hung on for 10 overs putting on 39. I was just giving up hope when Foster removed Pakistan's captain and then brilliantly ran out their leg-spinner one run later. England needed

124 in 18 overs to win. In a modern Twenty20 game played on a decent pitch, that would be seen as a cakewalk. However, this being a Test, there was no limit on the bowlers, no fielding restrictions, no one-day wides for balls just down the leg-side, no limit on bouncers and first-class cricketers in the 1980s didn't play Twenty20. Nevertheless, Broad hit 30 off 23 balls and we had 32-0 from the first four and 73-3 off 11. Gower fell to Imran, Gatting was run out and only six runs came in the next three overs. Again I started to give up, then Emburey took Captain Handsome for 15 including an extraordinary drive for six over cover.

At the other end Bill 'for God's sake get out' Athey was in the process of making 14 in seven overs and it came down to 17 needed off the last. The previous winter, Allan Lamb had won England a one-day international by taking 18 off the last over from Bruce Reid. On this day he made a small contribution to his side's total of 127 to secure victory. Unfortunately, he was in Northampton at the time helping his county see off Sussex. At Edgbaston, Emburey and Edmonds succeeded only in running themselves out in the space of three balls and England were left needing 15 off two. In 2005, I saw Warwickshire nearly make the 19 they required off three balls at the end of a Twenty-20 match when Worcestershire's opening bowler contrived to bowl a bouncer that went for five wides before conceding two successive sixes and, fortunately for him, a single. Gatting concluded that Wasim Akram was unlikely to be that generous, and the match ended in a frustrating draw. I knew what to expect from Mrs K the next morning.

Actually I had no idea. I arrived at work and walked into the sort of atmosphere that can only mean something really bad had happened. One colleague wasn't there and two more were in tears. I had assumed the reason Mrs K had been absent the previous day was the possibility of a defeat for Pakistan at cricket. In fact where she had been was in her kitchen being murdered by her husband dousing her in petrol and setting her alight. When I saw her 17-year-old daughter, now left with the task of bringing up a six-year-old sister, I realised how lucky I was to have got to 23 still in possession of the luxury of some illusions to shatter.

At the Oval, Javed Miandad made 260 and ensured Pakistan won the series. Quietly I was pleased. Miandad's dismissal, caught and bowled by Graham Dilley, is one of a few images from that late summer and early autumn I have stored away. Most of them I actually saw: the video for Los Lobos' version of *La Bamba*, *Spycatcher* author Peter Wright's ridiculous hat and Roger Harper's uber-run-out of Graham Gooch in an otherwise forgettable rain-ruined MCC Bicentenary match at Lord's. But the most vivid is one of a burnt-out kitchen conjured up by my imagination.

The MCC's celebration was not the only thing that was washed up. Two days later, Robert MacLennan (who?) was elected the new leader of the SDP replacing David Owen. This was not a seismic political event, as the electorate consisted of the party's five remaining MPs, three of whom opposed MacLennan (presumably he was one of the other two) but conceded on the basis that he accepted he didn't have the backing of the majority of the party. Everyone knew they were heading for a merger with the Liberals. England had no such leadership issues; Gatting was still captain for the World Cup, but given the way the team had been playing a merger, preferably with the West Indies, didn't seem like a bad idea. By the end of the winter a Pakistani umpire would be more famous than Robert MacLennan.

Unsurprisingly Mrs K's daughters left Small Heath. The last thing the elder one said to me was: 'You won't forget my mother will you?' Because she was speaking through an interpreter I've never been sure if she was making a statement or pleading with me.

FOURTEEN

Do you remember Greg Dyer? I wouldn't blame you if you don't, he was just one of a number of anonymous wicket-keepers Australia employed between the end of Rod Marsh's career and the start of Ian Healey's. He played six Test matches making 131 runs at 21.83 and made 24 dismissals (22 catches and two stumpings). Nothing particularly remarkable there but Greg Dyer is something no English cricketer has ever been: a World Cup winner. More than that he's the man who took the catch that ensured Australia won the 1987 final. Some sporting moments are memorable for their sheer brilliance even if they don't decide a match – Pele's outrageous dummy of the Uruguan goalkeeper in the 1970 World Cup finals didn't lead to a goal – while other more mundane incidents never leave you because of their importance.

Dyer's effort wasn't spectacular, but I'll never forget it because when the ball landed in his gloves his team-mate Steve Waugh might have been moved to ask him what it felt like to catch the World Cup. Chasing 254 to win, England had moved to 135-2. Gatting (41 from 45 balls) had dealt so severely with Australia's fifth bowler, Tim May, that Border was forced to try himself. His first ball was full, outside leg-stump and delivered, as it was, in Border's non-turning left-arm style was ripe for an orthodox sweep. Gatting premeditated a reverse-sweep and having to reach a long way, succeeded only in top-edging it into his shoulder and up into Dyer's gloves. Earlier in the tournament Bill Athey had made an excellent 86 against Pakistan before being bowled playing the same shot, this precipitated a collapse from 187-2 to 206-7 and cost us the match. The chairman of selectors, Peter May, commented that he was glad Michael Fish's non-existent hurricane had deprived his home of electricity so he was unable to see 'that shot'. At the moment of

Gatting's departure I could only wish that the 'Great Storm' had hit a bit further north. I've only ever witnessed one sweep more awful and that was Dick Van Dyke.

England and Australia weren't even meant to be facing one another. Australian television didn't make any advance arrangements for live coverage of a final most had assumed would be between India and Pakistan. When the co-hosts both made it to the semis everything was going according to plan. But then Pakistan blew it against Australia and ironically, given what followed, England literally swept into the final thanks to Gooch and Gatting who combated a dreadful Bombay pitch by practically taking up their stances down on one knee.

After Pakistan's defeat, Sarfraz Nawaz alleged they had lost on purpose saying that: 'At least 50 people, both inside and outside the stadium, told me that day I should bet on Australia.' At the time these suggestions were dismissed as the ravings of an eccentric. But then Hansie Cronje was an 18-year-old shortly to come and play for Flavells cricket club in Leamington and probably assuming he would never play full international cricket.

At the time the notion of match-fixing was laughable, particularly in a sport capable of throwing up an act of sportsmanship of the kind demonstrated by Courtney Walsh in the West Indies' opening match against Pakistan. The game came down to the final over with the home side's last pair together and 14 required. Viv Richards threw the ball to Walsh. In similar circumstances a week before he had conceded 28 from nine balls at the death to hand us an unlikely victory. The pressure he must have felt as a result of this only serves to make what followed all the more laudable.

Abdul Qadir and Saleem Jaffer took 12 from the first five balls of the over and as Walsh ran in to deliver the final ball with two needed, he spotted the non-striker, Jaffer, backing up too far. If Walsh had run him out West Indies would have won and probably pipped us for a place in the semi-finals. Instead he warned him, went back to his mark, ran in again and conceded two. After the match a grateful Pakistani presented Walsh with a free carpet and Martin Johnson in *The Independent* suggested he was seen trying to fly home on it.

As part of his allegations about Pakistan's semi-final defeat, Sarfraz had suggested some of the umpiring decisions had been 'very strange'. That might be a polite way of describing what was about to hit England.

For their various tours that winter England had picked four different wicket-keepers: Paul Downton for the World Cup, Bruce French and Jack Russell for Pakistan and French and Jack Richards for New Zealand. On the West Indies tour in 1985-86 French had been bitten by a dog while jogging, in Australia the previous winter he had collapsed with a mystery infection and spent several days in hospital and here, only five days after arrival, he needed stitches when a wayward throw from a spectator at practice hit him over his left eye. When he got to the hospital a car bumped into his legs and after the stitches had been put in he stood up and hit his head on a light fitting. Maybe the selectors just knew they needed plenty of cover, but whatever their reasons it wasn't their choices that were to have the greatest influence on the destiny of the Pakistan series.

Indirectly the problems had started at the beginning of the previous summer when the TCCB ignored Pakistan's objections to David Constant and Ken Palmer as umpires for the forthcoming series. The tourists' manager, Haseeb Ahsan, had stirred up feeling by describing Constant as a 'disgraceful person'. When the umpire issued Qadir with two official warnings for running on the pitch at the Oval, Haseeb ominously asserted that the matter of the English umpires was closed but Pakistan would be reverting to their own in the winter.

It's impossible to know whether what followed amounted to 'revenge', but *Wisden* described the tour as, '…one of the more squalid in international cricket's history.' Everyone remembers Shakoor Rana and Mike Gatting standing toe-to-toe jabbing fingers at one another at Faisalabad, but England didn't lose that game. The trouble started with a bloke called Shakeel Khan at Lahore.

England had objected to Shakeel's appointment but, unsurprisingly, the Pakistani Board had given them short shrift. He started controversially and got worse. The lbw he gave against Gatting in the first innings was the first shove on a snowball at the top of a very big hill. Given it was so controversial it goes without saying that the decision was palpably wrong. Gatting, sweeping, was hit on the front pad between nine inches to a foot outside off-stump. Even allowing for the fact that Qadir allegedly on occasions shouted 'It was the top-spinner' at the umpire when appealing, it still couldn't have been out. However, the most remarkable thing was the speed with which the batsman was sent on his way. If you freeze-frame the dismissal you can see the umpire's finger is in the air before Qadir has even finished turning round to appeal.

However, two other decisions caused the greatest controversy. Ironically, Qadir, who finished the innings with 9-56 and the match with 13-101, was on the receiving end of one of them and wasn't the beneficiary of the other. Having skittled England for 175, Pakistan then made 392 before Qadir was given out stumped to end the innings, despite the fact French had quite clearly missed the wicket with his first attempt. That was one dodgy decision that went England's way. However, a cynical man might point out the home side were already 217 in front, on a turning pitch, with the then most deadly spinner in the world in their ranks.

Despite this, Qadir exploded, telling anyone within range, including the umpire and Gatting, in no uncertain terms what he thought about it. It took him two minutes to leave the crease, an unacceptable delay quickly forgotten when Chris Broad, just over half-an-hour into England's second innings, refused to go at all when Shakeel gave him out caught behind off Iqbal Qasim.

The television pictures famously confirm Broad missed the ball by several inches and then stood there with his arms outstretched as if appealing to the fielders' better nature. He must have known it was pretty unlikely that the captain, Javed Miandad, was going to say: 'Don't worry old sport, I'll soon sort this out by withdrawing our appeal.' In 2005, it was announced Miandad's son was to marry the daughter of Dawood Ibrahim, a man wanted in India for allegedly masterminding serial bombings that killed 300 and injured 1000 in March 1993.

Having, unsurprisingly, got no change from the close fielders, Broad simply crossed his feet, lent on his bat and refused to go. Gooch had to wander down and persuade him that he should, a little ironic as the Essex man himself got a similar shocker not long afterwards. Broad received no more than a 'severe reprimand' from the tour manager Peter Lush, who then openly criticised the umpires himself and called for neutral officials in future. Chris Broad is now an ICC match referee with a particularly hard-line attitude to player conduct.

If England were glad that Shakeel wasn't going to be officiating in Faisalabad, they weren't happy to see his replacement was Shakoor Rana. Three years earlier, while England were on the wrong end of Swaroop Kishen in India, Jeremy Coney had led his New Zealand team from the field in Hyderabad after Rana had turned down an appeal for a catch off Miandad. It's fair to say he was already a controversial figure.

When he, in Gatting's opinion, triggered Graham Gooch on the first morning of the second Test, England's captain played a furious innings of 79 from only 81 balls to help the tourists to 292.

Three balls from the close of the second evening Pakistan were 106-5 when Gatting moved Capel up to save one at square-leg. The all-rounder came in too far and the captain waved for him to stop where he was just as Hemmings began to run in to bowl. Gatting later claimed he had told the striker, Salim Malik, about the field change and there appeared to be no advantage gained. However, Rana called 'dead ball' and accused Gatting of sharp practice. Or, put another way, called him a 'fucking cheating c**t'.

Everyone has seen what happened next. At least Gatting stopped short of killing Rana with a stump, which is what one wicket-keeper in Nagpur did to an umpire three weeks later. At first it looked as if both parties would say sorry and the game would proceed but then Rana, some say encouraged by Miandad, demanded a unilateral apology from Gatting – something he knew the captain was unwilling to give – before he would continue to officiate. The whole thing was then horribly mishandled by the TCCB. Why am I not surprised?

Concerned that the third day of the Test had been lost, but without apparently first having appraised themselves of exactly what had happened, the Board instructed Gatting to apologise. As a result he took a very small piece of paper and scrawled: 'Dear Shakoor Rana, I apologise for the bad language used during the 2nd day of the Test match at Fisalabad (sic). Mike Gatting 11th Dec 1987.' As apologies go it's up there with B.C. Pires' – 'I am sorry that Andy Caddick has big ears' – after the Somerset man objected to the journalist likening him to an aircraft.

The players then issued their own strongly-worded statement openly criticising their own governing body for forcing Gatting to apologise and the BCCP for not exerting similar pressure on Rana. Faced with such blatant dissent the TCCB's chief executive A.C. Smith and its chairman Raman Subba Row flew out to Karachi and, having met the players and obtained their version of events, secretly awarded them a £1000 'hardship bonus'. This was a response straight out of the 'Who's shouting at me at the moment?' school of management. When the payment inevitably became public knowledge they had masterfully succeeded in offending parties on both sides of the argument.

As a result of all this England lost their opportunity to square the series and didn't tour Pakistan for another 13 years. Independent umpires became a certainty. Now, one of the best umpires in the world is the Pakistani Aleem Dar.

In my work I've seen many examples of people getting the sack when an opportunity presented itself to an employer months after the real reason for dismissal. However, after this tour Gatting wouldn't have needed an employment lawyer to tell him he should watch his back.

The whole tour came to a dismal end with a bore draw in Karachi when the captains were so keen to bring matters to a conclusion they agreed to call it quits at tea on the final day and the umpires let them, even though there was no provision in the rules for them to do so.

For once England couldn't get to Australia quickly enough. Before they could end the winter in New Zealand, England had to stop off to play the Bicentennial Test match in Sydney. The previous summer there had been a match to celebrate 200 years of an English cricket club. By contrast we now had a game ostensibly to commemorate the existence of an entire country for the same length of time. What the Aboriginal population made of the suggestion that Australia had only existed for 200 years wasn't given a great deal of publicity. Neither, frankly, was the cricket.

Australia, with Mike Veletta (Test batting average 18.81) batting at five and Steve Waugh as their third seamer, were rightly described by *Wisden* as 'some way short of being a powerful five-day side'. When you add to this the fact that England were 'a team of no great flair' it's little wonder this draw will mainly be remembered for Chris Broad flattening his leg stump with his bat after Waugh bowled him for 139 and Bill 'Tiger' O'Reilly ending his Test match reporting career with the *Sydney Morning Herald*.

Before Shane Warne, O'Reilly was the best spinner who ever lived. When the man himself was asked whether, unlike Courtney Walsh, he had ever run out a batsman backing up, he laughed and said he had never seen anyone that keen to get down his end. Bradman called him, 'The greatest bowler I ever faced and the greatest I ever saw.' Despite the fact it would be probably be an understatement to say they didn't like one another, the respect was mutual and when O'Reilly describes being unexpectedly hauled off a train at Bowral station to play for his home team of Wingello in 1925, he recalls that he 'was about to cross swords with the greatest cricketer that ever set foot on a cricket field'. Bradman was 17 at the time and 'didn't have it all his own way, let me tell you. Well, not for the first couple of overs anyway'. By the end of the day the Bowral boy was 234 not out. 'Tiger' always claimed he had him dropped twice by an overweight slip fielder who was too busy lighting his pipe when the ball arrived.

A leg-spinner like Warne, O'Reilly was described by Jack Fingleton as a 'flurry of limbs, fire and steel-edged temper'. Although the last of these qualities was allegedly a product of deep frustration at not being able to bowl fast enough to fell batsmen, the bounce he extracted from hard 1930s pitches knocked a few wicket-keepers off their feet. All but one of his Tests were played in this decade, a period in which the likes of Bradman, Hammond, Headley and Sutcliffe dominated other bowlers. O'Reilly was never dominated. Even in England's total of 903-7 at the Oval in 1938, he bowled 85 overs and took 3-178 on a pitch so dead he described it as 'dosed up to the eyeballs'.

Watching him, Robertson-Glasgow said that, 'It didn't take long to see the greatness; the control of leg-break, the top-spinner and googly; the change of pace and trajectory without apparent change in action; the scrupulous length; the vitality; and, informing and rounding all, the brain to diagnose what patient required what treatment.' The brain was what equipped him for his second, brilliant, career as a journalist writing for the same paper for 40 years. In a time when you couldn't make a living from cricket, playing opportunities had been restricted by his job as a schoolmaster but the skills that he had learned enabled him to write with wit and imagination and to deal with stroppy players. When Geoff Lawson wrote O'Reilly a letter complaining about what he regarded as some over-harsh criticism in one of his pieces, the fast bowler received it back covered in corrections of his grammar. I can't imagine Warne doing that or being able to match O'Reilly's description of the second day of his first match against Bradman: 'The sun shone, the birds sang sweetly and the flowers bloomed as never before. I bowled him first ball with a leg-break which came from the leg stump to hit the off bail. Suddenly cricket was the best game in the whole wide world.'

If bowling Bradman first ball of the day might reasonably have made anyone feel cricket was the best game in the world, watching England play New Zealand in 1987-88 would probably have led to a different conclusion. *Wisden* describes the series as one that didn't capture the imagination. They got that right, I had completely forgotten it. Basically Richard Hadlee pulled his calf muscle on the first afternoon of the opening Test and England failed to capitalise. The match was a boring draw but Hadlee's replacement in the field by the Kiwis' 12th man did at least allow one New Zealand radio commentator to describe Gatting's dismissal as the result of a 'great catch by Greatbatch'. The second Test was memorable only for Martin Moxon having a perfectly good sweep for three signalled as leg byes before he was dismissed for 99. The same batsman then sat for two days on 81 not out as rain washed out the end of the series. Martin Moxon never made a Test hundred.

Botham's absence had hardly helped boost the excitement level in New Zealand. Supposedly having a winter off to recharge the batteries before the challenges of the touring West Indians the following summer, he was having a mixed time of it. On the positive side he had been voted 'Pipe smoker of the Year' for 1988 and could look forward to being presented with a specially made pipe by the previous winner Barry Norman. On the negative side he had been fined $A500 for using offensive language while playing for Queensland. Australians fining an Englishman for swearing might seem a bit rich, but worse was to follow when on a flight to the Sheffield Shield final in Perth Botham was asked to tone down his language by a passenger, Allan Winter. The all-rounder responded by forcibly turning Mr Winter's head to the front and shaking him by the hair. As a result he ended up in court charged with assault and offensive behaviour, to which he pleaded guilty. When he was arrested by Perth police, the duty officer asked Botham to sign a bat before formally charging him. He was bailed by Dennis Lillee, who turned up with a six-pack of beer and his 12-year-old son who begged to come along so he 'could tell his mates he had seen Botham behind bars'. This and another incident involving the England all-rounder, Lillee and damage to a dressing room in Tasmania, led to the early termination of Botham's contract with Queensland.

If that wasn't enough, England's finest was also facing the wrath of Brigitte Bardot, who was threatening to disrupt his Hannibal-style walk across the Alps with demonstrations against what she perceived to be his 'cruelty to elephants'. In fact the elephants were very carefully treated and, as always, Botham was trying to turn the incredible amount of publicity he attracted to good use. Even so, given his public persona, some might have felt this particular venture was more likely to be conducted in the style of Oliver Reed's Hannibal Smith than that of the Carthaginian general.

The England touring party's return home was delayed by 24 hours owing to a strike by Auckland airport's emergency firemen. While the team had been away, nurses had taken similar action here, the SAS had shot dead an IRA gang in Gibraltar, Saddam Hussein had undertaken the mass murder of thousands of Kurds at Halabja and an avalanche had hit Prince Charles' royal ski party. Something similar was about to hit England.

After the problems in Pakistan, Gatting must have come into the season knowing he was under pressure. Like Gower before him he was deprived of Botham's services just when he could have done with them most. In fact, although Botham played for England until 1992, Gatting was the last Test captain to have had the benefit of the great all-rounder.

Botham had suffered intermittent problems with his back for some time. On 19th May, playing for Worcestershire (ironically against Somerset) he dived to stop a ball in the slips and fell awkwardly aggravating the injury so badly he required an operation to fuse two vertebrae. Sidelined for the whole season, his bowling was never the same again. Losing both his pace and the late swing that had made him so dangerous he was forced to try and reinvent himself as slow-medium bowler in the style of his former mentor Tom Cartwright. It didn't work. In his remaining eight Tests Botham took 10 wickets at an average of 48.6 and scored 143 runs at 14.3 with a top score of 46. In cricketing terms those figures are as sad as the sight of an ageing Mohammed Ali getting beaten up by fighters who wouldn't have laid a glove on him in his youth. Perhaps it was some comfort to him that the real Botham's last wicket before the injury was Peter Roebuck.

Despite the absence of Botham and the presence of Monte Lynch, England won all three of the one-day internationals at the start of the summer. Picking Lynch was another top effort by the selectors. Firstly, given he was of Caribbean descent and had only just served out a three-year ban for taking part in a rebel West Indian tour of South Africa, it was a choice straight out of the Ian Paisley book of political sensitivity. Secondly, he wasn't very good and made a grand total of eight runs from three innings. However, Peter May and his men were only just warming up.

They must have wished they could have gone for Graeme Hick who had established a new English first-class record of 410 runs in April and followed this up by making nearly as many (405 not out) in his first innings in May. He wasn't alone in scoring heavily as two Indian schoolboys amassed the highest partnership in any form of cricket, 664 in a Bombay school match. One was 17 and the other only 14. The 17-

year-old was Vinod Kambli who later made 224 for India in the match in which Hick scored his first Test century. The 14-year-old was called Sachin Tendulkar.

However, Hick was still three years from being qualified. England went into the first Test against the West Indies with Derek Pringle batting at number six and didn't lose. This was despite their first innings subsiding from 125-0 to 245 all out and the tourists gaining a lead of over 200. A combination of rain, bad light and Graham Gooch and David Gower batting through most of the final day secured us our first draw against these opponents for 11 matches. For the first time in many years there was some cautious optimism that we might have a team capable of at least being competitive with the unofficial world champions.

However, as was usual at this time, the England selectors had a loaded revolver pointed straight downwards and chose this moment to pull the trigger. Gower recalls being called in to see them at the end of the match and imagined he was going to be congratulated for his excellent 88 not out. Instead he was torn off a strip for wearing blue socks. This triumph of morale building man-management was then followed by perhaps the period's definitive demonstration of blundering self-destruction from those in charge of the England team.

The Sun and *Today* printed allegations that Mike Gatting had been up to no good with a barmaid in his hotel room during the match. The selectors questioned Gatting about the alleged incident, confirmed they believed his assertion that nothing 'improper' had gone on and then sacked him for 'improper behaviour'. The behaviour in question was apparently 'inviting female company to his room for a drink in the late evening'. Never having attended a public school or an all-male Oxbridge college, Gatting clearly didn't realise this was just the sort of thing that could get you expelled or sent down and was therefore obviously the wrong man for the England captaincy.

It was complete nonsense of course. As Mike Brearley said at the time: 'Perhaps the Board does not believe Gatting's denial of the more lurid versions of the story but in that case it not only condemns a man on suspicion, it also covers up its reasons.' Even if they didn't believe him, given he wasn't a Tory cabinet minister preaching Victorian values, there was a case for saying 'What has this got to do with his ability to lead the England cricket team?' The argument that asking her to his room showed a lack of judgement on Gatting's part doesn't stand up because a) it's no reflection whatsoever on his ability to judge who should be bowling at the pavilion end and b) surely having a very public knock-down-drag-out row with an umpire showed a more relevant lack of judgment, and for that he and his team-mates had been rewarded with a £1000 bonus.

It's obvious Gatting was really sacked because of what happened with Shakoor Rana, and for effectively daring the TCCB to discipline him over the incident when he knew they couldn't risk a walk out by the players and the cancellation of the whole tour by being seen to back a 'bent' foreign umpire over the England captain. In certain quarters this would have been enough to have his card marked as a dangerous Trotskyite who was the 'wrong sort' to be leading England. This perception seemed to be confirmed the following year when the newly-appointed chairman of selectors, Ted Dexter, had his decision to appoint Gatting as captain for the Ashes series vetoed by the chairman of the TCCB's cricket committee Ossie Wheatley. It seems a little unlikely that one very minor indiscretion in a Nottingham hotel was enough on its own to prevent any possibility of rehabilitation.

Whatever the rights and wrongs, Gatting's dismissal illustrates more than anything that just as the Government of the day and millions in the north had very different ideas about the best way to run a country, so those in charge of England's cricket team and those playing in it were not part of a coherent whole but rather mistrustful acquaintances on opposite sides of an 'us and them' divide. It would have helped if there had been a plan for them all to buy into but there wasn't. When the much-maligned Lord MacLaurin announced that the ECB's aim was to make England the best Test playing nation in the world by 2007, everybody laughed. In fact, setting a clear and achievable goal was the first step to creating an England side capable of winning back the Ashes. The only people laughing in 2005 were the chief executives of sold-out Test grounds.

In 1988, Peter May and co.'s immediate plan was to appoint John Emburey as the next captain. This was a decision that worked on a number of levels; as an example of muddled thinking and insensitivity, that is. Firstly, if there was an appointment designed to maximize the possibility of losing Gatting's services as a player this was it. Not because he and Emburey didn't get on but rather because, having already overseen his public humiliation, they then chose to appoint someone who played under him at Middlesex to do his job. Unsurprisingly,

Gatting asked to be left out of the side for Lord's as he was not in the right frame of mind. Secondly, Emburey's recent contributions had moved Martin Johnson the previous year to offer the opinion that 'only his bowling is currently in the way of elevation to all-rounder status'. He had followed this up in the winter with 11 wickets in seven matches at an average of 53.18 and 2-95 from 16 overs at Trent Bridge. These figures suggested less the 'Follow me lads!' and more the 'I'm right behind you boys' school of captaincy. Finally, having decided he was the right man for the job, they gave him two matches rather than the remainder of the series to prove himself.

Like Gatting with the cricket team, I hadn't been in the right frame of mind to stay in Small Heath and was now working as a community worker in the area round my home in Coventry. My job involved visiting the large number of elderly people who lived on their own. One of these was Eugene, a cricket-loving Irishman. This isn't as rare as you might think. Even Martin McGuiness is a cricket fan on the quiet. Eugene was an amazing man who had fought in the Spanish civil war and now tragically, after the death of his wife, found himself living in the back room and kitchen of a three-up-two-down terraced house, unable to get up the stairs to make use of the other rooms. Judging by the huge number of empty boxes in his kitchen, he might have been up to fighting for land and freedom but his culinary skill extended no further than boiling eggs. I feared he would come to an end every bit as sticky as Elvis'. The only thing that stopped the tales he had to tell about his time in Spain from being fascinating as opposed to merely interesting, was that a combination of an incredibly broad accent and his penchant for an early morning touch of the tonic made it seem like I was talking to an Irish version of Paul Whitehouse's Rowley Birkin. He was frequently 'vey, vey drunk' when I arrived and I only understood about a third of anything he ever said. As a result when I asked him to tell me how he came to like cricket so much, I caught 'father', 'Hobbs', 'Sutcliffe', 'Oval' and '1926' but that was about it. Anyway, liking cricket was good enough for me and it was no coincidence I had him inked in my diary for a visit on the morning of the Lord's Test.

For about an hour-and-three-quarters Eugene and I had a great time. England were still level in the series and Graham Dilley came charging in from the Nursery End to reduce West Indies to 54-5. 'Finally,' I thought, 'at least we're going to give them a contest.' Then Derek Pringle dropped Gus Logie on ten, which would have left them

61-6. I didn't have to understand any of the actual words that came out of Eugene's mouth in order to be quite clear of the sentiments he was expressing. We were both still shaking our heads over it when I left him to his lunch (boiled eggs, as I recall). By the time I got home from my other visits Logie had made 81 not out and the West Indies 209. Even when we scrambled to 112-2 I knew they had got too many and the instant before Gower's attempted pull shot landed in Keith Artherton's hands at square-leg was the last in which we were competitive in the series. The last eight wickets fell for 53 and when they made 397 second time around Emburey was all but doomed.

No one has ever made 442 to win in the final innings of a Test and we hadn't made that many against the West Indies since March 1974 when Clive Lloyd was their third seamer. We lost by 134 runs and Mickey Stewart kidded himself that a total of 307 meant the West Indies bowlers could be tamed in the right conditions.

Seemingly the conditions were not ideal at Old Trafford. We were bowled out for 135 and 93. At least this was a small improvement on the 71 and 123 we had managed on the same ground in 1976. From my point of view the most encouraging thing about the match was England's selection of John Childs just over a month short of his 37th birthday. There was hope for me yet.

Childs was England's oldest debutant since another left-arm spinner, Dick Howorth in 1947. Howorth was one of those unfortunate sportsmen (like Bob Taylor before Alan Knott defected to Packer) who was very good but whose career overlapped with someone even better. Before the war he had little or no chance of being selected ahead of Hedley Verity and owed his place after it to the Yorkshireman's death at Caserta. It is a measure of Verity's stature that a post-war England touring side made a detour to Italy to lay flowers on his grave. Most laid orchids, the Yorkshiremen: white roses.

Unlike Childs, Howorth was a good enough all-round cricketer to achieve the double of 1000 runs and 100 wickets in a season three times. In 1988, Franklyn Stephenson performed this feat for what is, to date, the last time. Central contracts for England's finest and short term deals for overseas professionals committed to ever increasing amounts of international cricket, mean it may never happen again. Having finally made it into the side, Howorth took a wicket with his first ball in Test cricket and was the last Englishman to do this until yet another left-arm spinner, Richard Illingworth, managed it at Nottingham in 1991. Childs made no such impact taking 1-91 as we lost by an innings and 156 runs.

July 1988 was a time for changing leaders. The then Social and Liberal Democrat party elected Paddy Ashdown and he immediately announced that Labour would 'never again' form a Government. Fortunately for him he was wrong. Tony Blair made him a peer in 2001. At the time Ashdown could have been forgiven for his opinion, as could any England cricket follower who thought we would never beat the West Indies in a Test match again.

In 1966 Colin Cowdrey replaced M.J.K. Smith as England captain after the first Test against the touring West Indians and was then himself supplanted by Brian Close for the fifth. It was the last time England had used three captains in one series. Now Cowdrey's son Chris was appointed to replace Emburey for the final two matches of this series. Cowdrey junior had led a limited Kent side, devoid of star names, to the top of the county championship. However, many felt he wasn't worth his place in the side as a player and, as Graham Taylor's tenure as England manager was later to prove, the ability to work wonders with slim resources was no indicator of being able to engineer international success. At least his godfather thought his 'style of leadership is what is now required'. Normally this wouldn't be very relevant but when your godfather is Peter May it has some bearing on your appointment.

Cowdrey was to prove to be the Lady Jane Grey of England captains. Things started badly and went rapidly downhill from there. On the Wednesday before the match the Headingley gatemen (not noted for their encyclopedic knowledge of Kent cricketers) didn't recognize our new leader and wouldn't let him into the car park. With only four survivors from the squad from the previous Test, his team could have been forgiven for having to introduce themselves to one another. Tim Curtis and Robin Smith (largely on the strength of a few fours off a 34-year-old Michael Holding in the B and H final) were called up for their first Tests and Bill Athey for his last.

After the first couple of overs the game was held up for two hours because the drains were leaking onto Ambrose's run up. At the time Dustin Hoffman was receiving widespread critical acclaim (and ultimately the best actor Oscar) for his performance in *Rain Man*. For some reason (the title perhaps), while I was watching the film it struck me that, if ever the need arose, Hoffman would be the ideal man to play Dickie Bird. When I saw the umpire's reaction to this latest calamity I half expected to see Tom Cruise pop up to guide him, gently rocking, into the pavilion.

In the afternoon, from 80-4, Lamb and Smith counter-attacked with a series of woodchopper cut shots and the following day's papers presented the resulting overnight total of 137-4 as evidence of Smith being the latest quick fix for England's ills. Then the next morning Allan Lamb tore his calf and we went from 183-4 to 201 all out (C.S. Cowdrey lbw Marshall 0).

England's captain then took 0-8 from two overs as the tourists ground out a lead of 74. At least his figures were better than those of Graham Calway playing for Dorset against Cheshire at around the same time. With 11 overs left in the match, Cheshire, needing 201, were 92-6 and had shut up shop for what seemed an inevitable draw. However, Dorset's captain, the Rev. Andrew Wingfield-Digby (later the England team chaplain) instructed Calway to give away some runs in order to encourage the batsmen to open up and go for victory. Obviously a good Christian lad, Calway did as he was bade and apart from conceding four proper runs, sent down 14 wides all of which travelled unhindered to the boundary. Fortunately for him these were the days when such deliveries were only worth four each, otherwise he would have had even worse figures than the 1-0-60-0 he ended up with. Give and you shall receive. Suddenly finding themselves 156-6 Cheshire went for it and Dorset won by 18 runs.

Conceding any kind of lead to the West Indies usually opened up the possibility of an innings defeat. However, we avoided this and when we went ahead with only one wicket down I fell into the same trap as I had in the first innings of imagining that having Graham Dilley at number 11 meant that we batted all the way down and thus were assured of a reasonable total. We went for 80-1 to 138 all out with the captain ('Are you Brearley in disguise?') comprehensively castled by Courtney Walsh for 5. The photographs of this dismissal are uncannily reminiscent of Greig's at the Oval in 1976.

At the end of the series one wag writing to *The Times* suggested that were four innings in a Test match and it might be a better contest if England got three of them. At least we had more captains than them and we rubbed in that advantage by going for number four at the Oval.

Playing for Kent between the Tests, Cowdrey was hit on the foot by Somerset's former Sussex, fast bowling, eye-bulging axeman Adrian Jones. The resulting injury threatened his place in the Test team and he informed the selectors accordingly. Then it started to improve and it seemed he might make it after all. However, the selectors seemed to be experiencing similar emotions to those of waking up next to someone who appeared immensely attractive after 12 pints, but who in the cold light of day had proved to be one of the Ninja Turtles. From afar the communications seemed to run along the lines of :'I think it's getting better lads....Lads?... Are you listening? I said I THINK IT'S GETTING BETTER...'

Ostensibly the captain of England and only ruled out of one match by injury, Cowdrey commented at the time that 'Stewart promised to keep me in touch when I had to pull out of the fifth Test...he never did. I wanted to be involved because I felt it was my team, but though I was told I could come along if I wanted to, I got the impression I wasn't really wanted.' Poor lad was obviously more successful with women than I was. He clearly didn't have the first idea what 'I'll call you' meant.

The selectors gave Cowdrey's job to Graham Gooch. He may have been worth his place in the side – he was the only English cricketer to play in every match in the series – but the selectors completely overlooked the serious implications Gooch's appointment was bound to have for the forthcoming winter tour to India.

In addition to the captain, the England XI showed five changes from the team that had taken the field less than two weeks earlier. There were debuts for Matthew Maynard, originally selected as cover for Lamb, but who came into the side when Kim Barnett (touted as a possible England captain) was injured and Rob Bailey who was drafted in when his Northants team-mate failed a fitness test. By the end of this Test England's winless streak stretched back 18 matches and over 19 months to December 1986. It's no coincidence that during this time they had used 31 players (i.e. almost three different teams). It was starting to feel like I was supporting Charlie Brown's baseball team and the only way we would ever win was by default if the opposition got lost on the way to the ground.

Unfortunately, the West Indians' coach driver knew the way to the Oval. England collapsed in their first innings from 160-4 to 205 all out. The only light moment came when Derek Pringle, walking dejectedly away after his dismissal with his head down, failed to realise, despite the increasingly loud catcalls from the crowd, that he was nowhere near the gate to the pavilion. There is wonderful footage of him heading straight towards the TV camera on the boundary and only looking up suddenly at the last minute, before, to enormous cheers, finally detecting the exit fully 20 yards to his left. By Saturday evening he was in charge of the team.

On the Friday afternoon, Eugene and I became increasingly excited at a West Indian collapse which left England with a first-innings lead of 22. Gooch then batted throughout our second innings and helped set West Indies a target in excess of 200 to win. Unfortunately, this was 1988 and not 1991, so Gooch only made 84 rather than 154 not out and the target was 225 and not 278. Also, this was the Oval and not Headingley and we lost by eight wickets. At least we could all blame Pringle who had been left in charge when Gooch dislocated a finger attempting a catch off a no-ball from DeFreitas. Somehow, our captain putting himself out of the match dropping one that wouldn't have counted anyway seemed to sum us up.

We did win one Test that summer, against Sri Lanka. While this wasn't quite the equivalent of arresting a run of bad form by lining yourself up a quick series against the Banglas, it was the closest you could get in the 1980s. England picked four more debutants, Jack Russell (who hadn't played before because he couldn't bat and promptly made 94), Kim Barnett, Phil Newport and David Lawrence. Four years earlier, we had lost 5-0 to West Indies and then had the worst of a draw against Sri Lanka. In 1988, we only lost 4-0 and beat Madugalle's men by seven wickets. Obviously we were getting better. In fact this victory was England's only home Test win between September 1985 and July 1990. I was inter-railing round Europe and missed it. That means for almost five years I didn't see my team win at home. If I had been a football fan the season ticket would have been in the bin. It's a good thing for my theory about limited success at home just maintaining public interest that matters improved in the 1990s.

At least by the end of the match it was clear we would most likely be spared a winter of ignominy. On August 29th it was announced Gooch would be captain of the tour to India. Later the same day he revealed he had pulled out of a contract to play for Western Province in South Africa in order to take up the appointment. Asked whether he would have gone to India just as a player Gooch responded: 'That is a different kettle of fish.' On September 9th, the Indian Foreign Ministry confirmed that no player 'having, or likely to have, sporting contacts with South Africa' would be granted a visa to enter the country. As half the proposed touring party, including the captain and Emburey the vice-captain, fell into this category, the tour was doomed. It's a moot point whether the Indian government would have taken the same attitude if Gooch hadn't had such obvious and immediate links to the

Republic. But the selectors knew about those links and ignored them. In an interview with *The Cricketer*, Peter May was challenged about whether the selectors had given any thought to the political repercussions of the appointment and his reply was to the effect that their brief was to select the best team from a cricketing perspective regardless of outside influences. The inescapable logic of this response was that cricketing links with South Africa should have no bearing on one's suitability to captain England but having a barmaid in your room for a drink on your birthday was unacceptable.

Who they could have picked instead of Gooch is another matter. Gatting had by now made himself unavailable to England until further notice, Cowdrey wasn't good enough as a player and Emburey and the outside bet, Barnett, were also among the England players to whom the Indians had political objections. Unless, like me, you felt they could have gone for a Tony Lewis-like appointment of Sussex captain Paul Parker, Gower was the only realistic candidate who was politically acceptable and they would have to be mad to give the job back to him wouldn't they? So Gooch it was and on October 7th the tour was officially called off.

I was going to have to find something better to do with my winter. Like meeting my wife.

FIFTEEN

It is not strictly true that I met Fiona that winter, but I prefer to think of it that way. Although we had known one another vaguely at university, I later found out her assessment of me at the time was 'idiot'. I must have made a better impression second time round. She was gentle, kind and thoughtful. She had only one major fault, she was completely lacking in any strong feelings about cricket, but given time I knew I could change that. In the short term the lack of an England winter tour meant we could start to get to know each other without her suspecting the depth of my sad obsession with the national cricket team. We lived through the passing of the fatwa on Salman Rushdie, the Soviet withdrawal from Afghanistan and the Exxon Valdez oil disaster before the poor woman had any idea what was going to hit her.

As each generation ages it bemoans the standards of the one succeeding it, criticising new assumptions of what's acceptable in life, harking back to what it sees as its own more innocent, purer and, therefore better, past. E.W. Swanton, in a review of Jonathan Agnew's account of the 1988 county cricket season, *Eight Days a Week,* remarks that, 'One worrying note running through the book is the apparent acceptance of fast bowling at the man as an integral and persistent part of the modern first-class game. Even the old convention of a non-aggression pact among fast bowlers apparently no longer applies.' In the autumn of 1988 Ben Johnson was stripped of his 100 metres gold medal at the Seoul Olympics. The television commentators, who had either covered athletics for years or were athletes from a previous generation, expressed shock and righteous indignation in equal measure. What was there left to believe in if the Olympic champion was caught doing drugs?

The coming generation saw things differently. Agnew talks of Wayne Daniel trying 'to rip my head off, I try to do the same to him and then we go to the pub and buy each other a drink'. Even the sight of Florence Griffith-Joyner running away from the field in the women's sprints convinced me and most of my sport-loving friends things weren't that bad. Johnson, after all, had been caught and although Griffith-Joyner's triumphs smelt like a fishmongers, if a previously unremarkable athlete suddenly started burning off exceptional ones, surely that meant if there was performance enhancement going on, the best weren't indulging in it. In other words we wanted to believe and, by and large, still did believe in the integrity of what we were playing and watching. Few of us wanted to consider the alternative explanation that almost everyone in sprinting was on drugs. And, in the wider context, even if atrocities like Lockerbie acted as an acute reminder that the world was a far from perfect place, events in Eastern Europe later in the year made it clear people still had faith it could be made significantly better.

Fiona and I were together because we shared that faith. But I also wanted her to share my love of cricket, so I took her to a match. It was a beautiful ground and a stunning day and as we set up our picnic near the deep mid-wicket boundary I thought I was on to a winner. We fielded first and for much of the afternoon I was stationed about 30 yards from her in the outfield. I spent half my time smiling and waving like a loon when I should have been concentrating and spilled a catch pretty much right in front of her. Given the surroundings and the weather the reaction I was hoping for when I trotted across at tea-time was something along the lines of 'I could get used to this'. Instead the first thing she said was 'Were you batting or bowling?' This was followed shortly by 'I nearly moved because some prat kept waving at me and he was making me feel uncomfortable.' The realisation that she hadn't spotted it was me who had dropped the catch only partially eased my concerns about a drive home in the dark with a woman who clearly needed glasses. Converting her to cricket was going to be harder than I thought.

In 2005, cricket caught the public imagination as never before. As Angus Fraser put it on the radio, 'the tolerators' of cricket suddenly became genuinely interested. One afternoon during the final Test, I found myself standing in my daughters' school playground having a discussion about reverse swing. The point about this is not that I managed to bullshit my way through the conversation as if I actually knew what I was talking about, but rather that a) in two years of previous acquaintance the person I was speaking to had shown not a jot of interest in cricket, b) he had prompted the discussion and c) seemed genuinely interested in my incoherent ramblings on the subject. If I hoped England's performance against the 1989 Australians would prompt a similar reaction from Fiona, I was sadly disappointed.

When reverse swing was first used in England, to dramatic effect by Pakistan in 1992, most English commentators regarded it as cheating. By 2005, many of the same people were glorying in it as the foundation of our fast bowlers' dominance over the Australian batsmen and the resulting Ashes triumph. In 1989, 'reverse' was nothing more than a sinister twinkle in Sarfraz Nawaz's eye and in terms of swing, the nearest thing England had to a secret weapon was Phil Newport.

Even so no one could have predicted what happened that year. Neither England nor Australia were particularly powerful. The previous winter the West Indies, despite somehow allowing themselves to be bowled to defeat by Allan Border's 11-96 at Sydney, had delivered the Australians of a drubbing almost as sound as the one they had inflicted on England a few months earlier. The Ashes series was anticipated in much the same way as a Cup final between two lesser Premiership teams; with the prospect of sufficient skill on show to keep the purists happy but the promise of enough mistakes to keep it entertaining. There seemed little chance of two overly well organised sides cancelling each other out in a series of bore draws. In that respect we weren't disappointed.

Two decisions made before the season even started greatly affected how the summer went. The first was made by the ICC and the second by Ossie Wheatley.

In January, the ICC met and finally thrashed out a resolution on the issue of South Africa. The positions taken up by the member countries represented an almost exact mirror image of their later attitudes to the issue of Zimbabwe. England and Australia in particular were reluctant to go down a route of an outright ban on all sporting contacts, while the West Indies, India, Pakistan and Sri Lanka were proposing exactly that. When it was finally resolved that from 1st April 1989 any cricketer over 19 who visited South Africa in a playing, coaching or administrative capacity would receive a four-year Test ban (three years for under 19s) and anyone going on an organised cricket tour would be banned for five years, opinion was divided along the usual lines. Norris McWhirter, the chairman of the Freedom Association, seeing the TCCB delegates' agreement with this as a cave-in, offered the opinion that 'the price of blackmail is eternal ransom', while Peter Roebuck commented, 'If Malcolm Marshall had been born in South Africa he'd be inferior and not allowed a significant vote. This is the freedom that matters.' Ever the pragmatist, Mike Gatting showed unusual prescience by predicting, 'This will mean there is even more money knocking around to play in South Africa.'

As for Ossie Wheatley, I had to look up who he was. It turned out he was the chairman of the TCCB's cricket committee and as such apparently had a brief to look after the 'broader interests of the board'. This meant he could consider issues wider than just cricketing ones and to this end, although nobody outside the TCCB knew it at the time, he was given a veto over the decisions of the selectors. The upshot of this was that when the newly-appointed first paid chairman of selectors, Ted Dexter, and the coach, Mickey Stewart, put forward Mike Gatting to lead England in the Ashes series, Wheatley blocked the appointment. In other words, the man who, on the basis of 62 Tests with 30 as captain, had been entrusted with overseeing the selection of the best possible team to defend the Ashes had his first major decision overruled by someone who had never played a Test match in his life. As a result, with Gooch apparently not Dexter's cup of tea, David Gower regained the captaincy. None of this came out until Dexter's end-of-season report to the board somehow found its way into the public domain. How it got there isn't clear but, following a 4-0 drubbing, the new chairman wouldn't have minded the public getting at least some hint that Gower wasn't his first choice.

Having already established himself as the only leader in Test history to preside over two 5-0 defeats, Gower only avoided being the first man to see his side lose 6-0 because it rained at Edgbaston and the Oval. By the end of the summer Gooch was back in charge for the tour to the West Indies, Gatting had taken a share of the extra money 'knocking around' for playing in South Africa and Gower was contemplating an unscheduled winter off.

That summer was a nightmare for me. As the tourists were warming up for the first Test with a match at Derby, students younger than I was were being massacred in Tianenman Square. This made me realise I couldn't keep messing about forever and watching cricket with an unintelligible, octogenarian Irishman didn't really amount to a career choice. I was 25 and perhaps it was about time I decided what I was going to 'do' with my life. Unfortunately, just like almost everyone associated with the English cricket team that year, I didn't have a clue.

In 2005, Ricky Ponting ignored the groundsman's advice, put England in at Edgbaston and saw the series start to slip away from him from that moment. At least he had an easy first-Test victory and an attack with over 1,000 Test wickets behind him when he made his decision. At Headingley in 1989, David Gower didn't listen to Keith Boyce and inserted Australia with Pringle, DeFreitas, Newport and Foster at his disposal. The Ashes were on their way south from the first morning.

Australia made 601-7. Steve Waugh began what was to turn out to be 14 years of frustrating English cricket fans by making 177 not out. By the end of the third Test Waugh's average was 393. Even so, by the autumn I wasn't as sick of the sight of him as I was of Mark Taylor. Run out in both innings of his last Test before this tour, Taylor, as most people seemed to at this time, had a considerable upturn in fortune against us and ended up with a series aggregate of 839 runs, an achievement bettered in Test history only by Bradman and Hammond.

Despite England managing 430 in their first innings, the Australians still had time to leave them 83 overs to bat out on the last day. They lasted 56 and lost by 210 runs.

In April of that year Ralph Fenton of Sheffield had taken the life and career of W.G. Grace as his specialist subject on *Mastermind*. Mr Fenton came third in his heat, which was one place better than England managed in the Test series. Throughout the summer the home side faced the same question over and over again. The question was 'How do you play Terry Alderman?' and, despite plenty of opportunities to mug up, the answer we gave was always a resounding 'Pass'. The joke going around at the time was that scorers had taken to pencilling in 'lbw Alderman' next to Graham Gooch's name to save time.

At Headingley Alderman had added ten wickets to Steve Waugh's century. At Lord's the same two combined to end the series as a contest after only two matches. On the Friday evening Australia trailed on first innings by 21 with only four wickets left and Paul Jarvis swung the second new ball past the outside of Waugh's bat on several occasions without finding the edge. On the Saturday, he made 152 not out and led Australia to 528. Geoff Lawson made 74 at number ten and Fiona offered the slightly ill-timed opinion that it was 'only a game'.

Unfortunately, England's captain seemed to share her view, cutting short the evening press conference in order to make the start of Tim Rice's production of Cole Porter's *Anything Goes* at the Prince Edward theatre. This was simultaneously appalling PR and a bad omen. The show had opened on Broadway in 1934, the year Australia had last regained the Ashes in England.

On the Monday, Gower made a battling hundred and might have pointed to 1934 as the last year in which England beat Australia in a Lord's Test. However, Alderman ended England's slim hopes by producing a swing bowler's equivalent of the Warne wonder ball, with one that swung into Robin Smith before seaming away past an apparently perfect forward defensive to hit off stump. Unlike Gatting four years later, Smith had 96 at the time. Australia were set 118 to win and everyone inevitably went 'Headingley 1981 blah, blah'. There was time for Allan Border to be caught on the long-leg boundary by an 18-year-old substitute called Robert Sims but Australia's captain managed to get off the ground without screaming abuse at the England balcony and Boon and the inevitable Waugh saw them home.

The day before the third Test Oliver North escaped jail for his part in the Iran-Contra affair because, according to Judge Gerhard Gessell, he was 'a low-ranking subordinate who was carrying out the instructions of a few cynical superiors' and 'jail would only harden your misconceptions'. The only low-ranking subordinates on show at Edgbaston were the England cricket team and after their superiors had bossed them about to the tune of 424 (Australia's worst first-innings effort in the series) they got out of jail only because of appalling weather.

After England had just managed to save themselves in that match by scrambling past the follow-on on the final morning, Ian Wooldridge wrote in the *Daily Mail* that there seemed to be a 'palpable lack of passion or any sense of pride' and that, 'Our men in this series have reminded me of a team who regarded playing for England as much the same as an index-linked pensionable job with British Rail.' Judging by what happened next he wasn't far wrong.

By the time the teams got to Manchester for the fourth Test, Gower was the subject of the sort of tabloid campaign that usually involved England football managers and root vegetables. Despite maiden hundreds by Robin Smith and Jack Russell, two players who throughout their careers you could never have accused of not being proud of playing for

England, we lost heavily by nine wickets. Russell's effort was described by *Wisden* as a 'five hours 51 minutes representation of English cricketing pride'. Sadly it was a demonstration of exactly the opposite that kept Gower his job.

On the final morning at Old Trafford a party of 16 players contracted to undertake two tours of South Africa was announced. Of these, three, Robinson, Emburey and Foster were playing in the match and a further six had been involved earlier in the series. Only David Graveney, the designated player-manager, had never played Test cricket. Given that Graveney was later the chairman of England's selectors when the Ashes were regained in 2005, perhaps English cricket owes more to Nelson Mandela's spirit of reconciliation than you might imagine. The tours were scheduled to take place in the winters of 1989/1990 and 1990/1991 and as a result, with bans running from the date of the last sporting contact with the Republic, the players were effectively ruling themselves out of Test cricket for the next seven years.

At the time, as someone who had spent practically his whole life wishing he had been good enough to play for England, I was dumbfounded. With the previous 'rebel' tour the players could at least have made out a case that it wasn't clear what consequences would flow from their actions. Indeed, in 1981 Gooch had expressed genuine shock at the three-year ban he had received. However, now, any player signing up to go to South Africa knew exactly what would happen and yet it was even rumoured that some of those involved hadn't waited to be approached but had actively sought out Ali Bacher to indicate their willingness to go. Even leaving aside my personal feelings about the morality of such a tour, I knew I would have cried with pride if I had ever been selected to play for England. How could these players knowingly throw that away for the sake of two winters in South Africa? The simple answer, of course, is 'money' and it's tempting to hold this affair up as an example of the Thatcherite mentality working itself out in cricket. I do think there was an element of that, but a closer examination of the touring party revealed other reasons that were much more to do with the way cricket in this country and in particular the Test team, was run.

As we have already seen, even post-Packer, a career just as a county cricketer didn't make sound financial sense. Players were employed for the duration of the county season only and left pretty much to fend for themselves for the other half of the year. There were few employers, particularly in a time of spiralling unemployment, who would be willing to take on someone who was only available for six months at a time. Only a very lucky few could rely on the generosity of a cricket-mad headmaster of an independent school to provide a job with regular unpaid leave of absence in the summer. It is little wonder winter coaching jobs in South Africa were so attractive. When you add to this the fact that the nearest county clubs came to providing a pension scheme was the feudal notion of the benefit system and only the most limited of insurance was available for players who had their careers ended by injury, you begin to realise that life as a county cricketer was precarious at best. If county cricket was the limit of your ambitions then you had to be playing for love of the game. On the other hand if you wanted to make a 'proper living' in an increasingly consumerist society where being 'content with your lot' was not in the spirit of the times, you had to get into the England team.

The Packer revolution had meant playing international cricket was a potentially viable route to genuine financial security. However, what financial security meant before the period of Packer's intervention and what it meant by 1989 were very different things. In the 70s it meant having enough to keep a roof over your head, food on the table and, if you were lucky, an Austin Maxi in the garage. By 1989 it meant all of those things except the roof probably had an exorbitant mortgage on it, the food was most likely fresh pasta rather than roast beef and the Maxi was a Golf GTI. In addition you also had to be able to afford any number of 'essential' electrical goods without which no self-respecting home was complete. In other words expectations of life were considerably higher and more expensive. However, although getting into the England team at this time wasn't that much of a problem for many county cricketers, staying there was.

It says something that England could lose 15 players and still be able to select a side for the fifth Test containing only two debutants. Over the course of the 1989 series, England used 29 players by comparison with the 12 who appeared in 2005. Also, although they quickly dropped out after receiving scathing public criticism from other black sportsmen and threatening letters and phone calls, Phil DeFreitas and Roland Butcher were in the original party. For a black cricketer to even contemplate touring South Africa at that time he must have felt pretty strongly about the way he had been treated in the past and/or what level of financial security could be achieved playing for England.

Nine years earlier Butcher had been the much-trumpeted first black cricketer to play for England, had gone on the hardest tour imaginable to the West Indies and never been given another chance. In my work as a lawyer I have seen many employers defend claims of race discrimination on the basis that 'I treat everyone this way' (i.e. equally badly). Indeed, the validity of this seemingly bizarre defence was confirmed by the Employment Appeal Tribunal (the equivalent of the High Court) when, in their decision in former President Kamlesh Bahl's high profile race and sex discrimination claim against the Law Society, they stated that, 'All discriminatory conduct is unreasonable but not all unreasonable conduct is discriminatory.' On this basis the England selectors would have had plenty of evidence with which they could have refuted any allegations that they had discriminated against Butcher in any way. However, that didn't mean he had any less reason to think he had been shabbily treated. In DeFreitas's case it is probably enough to point out he ended his international career as the most dropped and re-selected man in English Test history.

Perhaps the most telling thing though about the touring party is that it contained three men, Gatting, Emburey and Chris Cowdrey, who had captained England only the year before. Something had to be badly wrong with the way the Test team was managed if within 12 months of holding the most prestigious job in English cricket all three of them had reached a point where they would rather take the money. The very fact there were three of them goes some way to explaining how they had got there. The only mild surprise was that Gooch wasn't joining them.

Once I realised county cricket wasn't going to give anyone a 'yuppie' lifestyle and that even if a player made it into the national team his future was in the hands of a bunch of men who had turned capriciousness into an art form, I began to at least have some better understanding of why Gatting and his men made the choice they did. Nevertheless none of this takes account of the issue of pride in playing for your country or of the more obvious moral one of playing in South Africa. Therefore working out some of the case for the defence may have left me less dumbfounded, but as someone who loved the England cricket team and wanted to see it succeed, it didn't leave me any less sad. Paul Weaver in *Today* summed up what I thought: 'Good riddance to the rebels. If only we could persuade the SACU to take our cricket officials as well.'

Unfortunately, if anyone had imagined the South African authorities had done us a favour by rooting out the cynical old hacks from the England side, Mike Atherton's account of his welcome to the England dressing room at Trent Bridge indicates otherwise. Atherton tells the tale of being taken aside by a 'senior member' of the England team and being told you play your first Test for pride 'and the rest for money'.

Little wonder then that the first day of the Trent Bridge Test was one of the most depressing I have ever endured. By the end of it Australia were 301-0 and Geoff Marsh and Mark Taylor had become the first pair to bat through an entire day of Test cricket in England. In the end it took us 744 balls to separate them. It took Australia four to break our opening partnership and a further two to take our second wicket. Robin Smith, for whom 'getting into the Test Team was an unbelievable experience', made a brilliant hundred. However, when the opposition have made 602, you are 37-4 and your team includes four players (Hemmings, Fraser, Cook and Malcolm) who, in batting terms at least, are less 'multi-dimensional' and more cardboard-cut-out, the writing is not so much on the wall as all the way down the street in ten-foot high letters. The letters said: an innings and 180 runs.

Even though bad weather earned us our second draw, events at the Oval still summed us up. And that was before the match even started. Malcolm was forced to withdraw with a back spasm and was replaced by DeFreitas who pulled a hamstring. Fraser succumbed to a knee injury and his proposed replacement, Greg Thomas, informed the selectors that he was off to South Africa with Gatting as a replacement for DeFreitas. Dexter and co. got a glimpse of what Friday night is like for a village club captain when two of his players decide they would rather go to a barbeque and another suddenly remembers Saturday is his wedding anniversary. As a result Alan Igglesden made his Test debut. On the batting front, the selectors, in a remarkable assessment of latent talent, picked John Stephenson (Test career – one match) ahead of Nasser Hussain (Test career – 96 matches).

In 2005, bad light at the Oval signalled the return of the Ashes and triggered the most high profile celebrations of an English cricketing victory I can remember. In 1989, it was more like it allowed England's players to sneak away under the cover of semi-darkness hopefully attracting as little attention as possible.

October 1989 saw a massive earthquake hit San Francisco. The relatively light death toll was put down to thousands leaving work early to watch the third match in the baseball World Series. It's a good thing we don't have natural disasters on that scale in this country; if a quake had hit during one of the Tests that summer everyone would have still been at the office.

SIXTEEN

At the end of the Ashes series Ted Dexter said: 'I'm not aware of any mistakes I've made.' That autumn I was saying something similar to my land law lecturer. In both cases the assertion needed to be qualified with: 'But then I don't have the first idea what I'm talking about.'

I had decided that what the world needed was more leftie lawyers and had signed up for two years of intensive study designed to turn a slightly flaky history graduate into, so I thought, a cross between Nelson Mandela and Rumpole of the Bailey. I studied law at what is now known as the University of Central England at Birmingham. When I was there it was Birmingham Poly. I had gone back to student life but not as I knew it. For a start there was a lot of hard work involved, particularly in land law which was similar to being an England cricket selector in that you could come up with lots of different answers without any of them being right. Grasping some of the concepts was like trying to get hold of that furry thing that used to zip round the walls during *Vision On*.

Things weren't helped by a lecturer who had clearly been roped in at the last minute to teach a subject about which he knew nothing and survived by staying one chapter ahead of us in the text book. He also favoured the double and even on occasions triple negative more often than David Gower. He once used the phrase 'not uninconsequential'; by the time we had unravelled it, he was four pages further on in his lecture notes.

There were lighter moments like Greig-v-Insole and others and the 1951 negligence case Bolton-v-Stone, which hinged on whether cricket clubs should have to erect fences to protect people who aren't even in the ground. The House of Lords, MCC members to man no doubt, decided that they don't. It was also an interesting time for lawyers with the cases of the Guildford Four and Birmingham Six raising serious questions about our criminal justice system. I was a long way from being involved in anything so significant and two years of almost constant tests and exams stretched interminably ahead of me. After that I had another two of proper nine-to-five lawyering to do before I was qualified. Life would never be the same again.

This wasn't the only way in which the world I had known was changing. In the last two months of 1989 the Berlin Wall was breached, Czechoslovakia's 'Velvet Revolution' saw the election of a non-communist government, the Ceausescus were executed in Romania and the Malta Summit heralded the official ending of the Cold War. At home Mrs Thatcher, by now depicted on *Spitting Image* as a suit-wearing, eye-rolling lunatic, was challenged for the Tory leadership by Sir Anthony Meyer. One in six of the Parliamentary Tory party failed to vote for her and despite Kenneth Baker (portrayed by Fluck and Law as a slug) asserting that the Conservatives had decided 'they want to be led into the 1990s and the next election by Margaret Thatcher', she was in fact on the very edge of the political bin.

Even the England selectors caught the spirit of the time and left the two most talented cricketers of my generation, Ian Botham and David Gower, out of the winter touring party to the West Indies. Ironically, as a result of Gatting's choice of winter destination, the England captaincy had passed back to Graham Gooch. It was less than a year since Gooch's own South African connections had led to the cancellation of England's proposed trip to India, but now he was an acceptable leader for a touring party in the West Indies.

Gooch, it should be remembered, had moped his way through England's last disastrous effort in the Caribbean under Gower's leadership. Apparently, he hadn't forgotten taking an early morning training run and passing Lamb and Botham on their way home or what the score in the Test series had been. The Essex man had no intention of joining Gower in the wrong section of the Test captaincy record books and seemed to make a conscious effort to lead in a way that was the complete opposite of his predecessor. Where Gower had been laid back, putting his faith in talent and individual expression, Gooch was a disciplinarian who favoured hard work and a strong team ethic. This approach fitted with the attitudes of the roundhead coach Mickey Stewart but could be easily undermined by strong willed individuals who refused to buy into the philosophy. Gooch wanted a team in his own image and if he was to impose his authority Gower and Botham had to go. Lamb survived on the basis of his record against West Indies and the belief that giving him the vice-captaincy would turn him into a game-keeper.

The original touring party reveals the selectors again had at least half an eye on 'fighting fire with fire'. Indeed Dexter said as much, but when Ricky Ellcock was ruled out of the tour with a back injury the remaining personnel dictated a more prosaic policy of bowling tight off-stump lines and waiting for the West Indians to get themselves out. It so nearly worked.

Much as I would have liked to believe we could have given the West Indies a taste of their own medicine, Devon Malcolm and Ricky Ellcock were hardly Garner and Ambrose in the accuracy stakes and we were better off playing to our own strengths rather than, as we have so often done, trying to copy the opposition's. I wasn't that sorry when Ellcock dropped out, particularly as it opened the way for the most exciting young cricketer in England to join the team.

Of all those I've seen represent England over 30 years Chris Lewis is the one who wins my 'If only I'd have had your ability' award. Whether it was Lewis himself who frittered away his talent or the system that failed to harness it effectively, is a moot point. Lewis made everything look so easy and was still around showing flashes of brilliance for Lashings in 2005. Certainly Andrew Flintoff had the good fortune to be nurtured within a system that prevented him from being ground down by endless county cricket and while both he and Lewis were let down by their bodies, it's also true that after a disappointing start to his career, Flintoff's manager Neil Fairbrother sat him down in the Old Trafford dressing room and delivered a verbal kick up the arse that laid before him the stark choice between hard work and failure. Flintoff achieved some great things. Chris Lewis gave the impression that if anyone had given him a kick up the arse he would have missed the next Test complaining of 'heavy buttocks'.

Lewis' contribution to this expedition was a wicket and a catch in the first one-day international. England's previous experiences in the West Indies might have led him to believe that he was bound to get a chance in the Tests at some point. That he didn't is indicative of how close we came to one of the biggest upsets in Test history.

By the time the first Test started on 24th February, Mike Gatting's decision to go to South Africa was, with hindsight, looking less than astute. On 2nd February, President F.W. de Klerk announced the lifting of the ban on the ANC and nine days later millions watched as Nelson Mandela walked out of Victor Verster Prison. Demonstrating both the depth of his incarceration and a fine set of priorities, Mandela's second question on his release was 'Is Don Bradman still alive?'

South Africa had been banished from international cricket for 20 years. After 19 of those years the ICC had finally laid down a clear policy on the consequences of cricketing links with the Republic. Now, no more than a year on, that policy was being rendered irrelevant before our eyes.

Gatting's men were trying to play while all of this was going on and it came as no surprise when their visit was cut short and the second tour, planned for the following winter, ultimately cancelled. Gatting's unfortunate timing couldn't but remind me of my neighbour Al. The author of many doomed business ventures, Al's crowning glory was to set up a door-to-door egg delivery service the day before Edwina Currie made her pronouncements about salmonella.

Sometimes though it isn't just a matter of luck. Gower might claim he has a poor record as captain because he had the misfortune to lead England in two series against the West Indies and had two 5-0s on his CV as a result. Graham Gooch also led England in two series against the West Indies and his record is an unlucky 2-1 defeat and a 2–2 draw.

Some things seem like they will never end. The world I knew had an Iron Curtain, an Iron Lady and a West Indian cricket team with an iron grip round England's throat. In nearly 15 years I had never seen us beat them in a Test match. I thought I never would. When Australia kept trouncing us for all those years I clung onto the memory of March 1st 1990 at Sabina Park. The day after we won, I bought four newspapers so I could read about it over and over again. And to think it might not have happened if Devon Malcolm hadn't been short-sighted.

On the morning of the first Test, Viv Richards went out for the toss without knowing what he was going to do if he won it. When the coin came down his way he had to go off to consult with Clive Lloyd before deciding to bat. With a flat pitch and one of the greatest opening pairs in Test history at his disposal the decision didn't seem like it should have been that difficult. Greenidge and Haynes started in a way that seemed to be asking what all the fuss was about and they cruised to 61-0. Then Greenidge tucked Fraser to fine-leg where the myopic Malcolm failed to gather and the ball cannoned into his knee. Evidently assuming that 'never run on a misfield' doesn't apply when the fielder usually requires the assistance of a labrador, Gordon set off for a second and an instant later was experiencing that sick feeling you get at the sight of a perfect throw flying straight at a stationary wicket-keeper while you're still yards from safety. After that I couldn't believe what I was hearing. David Capel bounced out Richie Richardson, Fraser bowled a spell of 6-3-6-5 after tea and 62-0 the instant before Russell broke Greenidge's wicket had become 164 all out an hour before the close. Sky's text service once reported that Sussex had scored well over 200 in a Twenty20 game against Surrey. In fact they had got it the wrong way round and listening on that first day I half expected Christopher Martin-Jenkins to say: 'Sorry, our mistake, England were batting'.

Even though it really was the West Indies who had been rolled over, Clive Lloyd had once said that if his side was dismissed for ten he was confident his bowlers could clean up the opposition for nine. I fully expected us to get even fewer than 164. What I didn't expect was a 200-run lead courtesy of Lamb's fifth hundred against the West Indies and a laborious 50 from Smith so dull that even he couldn't remember 'a single shot (he had) played'.

Sky couldn't have picked a better match with which to begin their coverage of England overseas and my abiding memory is being able to sit in a pub watching a West Indian supporter dropping his head into his hands as Malcolm bowled Richards in the second innings. It was to be another four years before Atherton's team collapsed so disastrously in the second innings at Trinidad, so I was confident we could make 41 to win.

Fittingly, the day after the death of Colin Milburn, it was a Northamptonshire opener, Wayne Larkins, who saw us home with 29 not out. Milburn always struck me as a cricketing equivalent of Paul Gascoigne; a prodigiously talented Geordie who seemed slightly lost once he was deprived of the ability to perform at the highest level. In Milburn's case the loss was sudden and the timing cruel, with a car accident depriving him of his left eye in his destructive prime at the age of only 27.

Gooch had played a strong hunch in practically demanding the inclusion of the similarly naturally-blessed-but-unpredictable Larkins in his team. I doubt Milburn would have received similar backing given that his Bunteresque physique was not suggestive of many early morning runs and he wasn't known for taking things too seriously. On occasions Milburn even bemoaned the fact he didn't have a bloodshot glass eye to put in when he was drunk. As Geoff Boycott said of England's tour to the Caribbean in 1968: 'It's the only tour I did where team meetings ended in total chaos. They'd be serious for a while but then the cabaret would start. Ollie, a mad keen Tom Jones fan, took centre stage. Can you imagine it, the England team supposedly assembled to discuss tactics and technicalities and there was this roly-poly man belting out *The Green Green Grass of Home?*'

The grass must have been pretty green in Guyana by the time England left. Torrential rain saw the Bourda ground under water and the second Test was abandoned without a ball being bowled. Things were getting better and better. I had thought that we would be looking at 5-0, now it couldn't be any worse than 3-1.

I ought to have known better than to pray for rain, but then that's how negatively I tended to think after years of underachievement. Unfortunately these things have a way of coming back and biting you and the shower that turned into a downpour when we were 73-1 at lunch on the final day at Trinidad chasing 151 to win, cost us at the very least a share of the series. Ok, so it wasn't just the rain, it was also the ability of the West Indies to get away with bowling 17 overs in two hours after the resumption and Graham Gooch having his hand broken by Ezra Moseley. The latter did at least leave us with a fantastic 'Does it hurt if I do *this*?' photograph of Laurie Brown holding Gooch's hand while he reacts as if he has just been picked off by a sniper on a grassy knoll between the stands.

What followed seemed to have the inevitability of Brighton's 4-0 defeat to Manchester United in the FA Cup final replay. Wins in Barbados and Antigua allowed Richards to boast that his team had emerged 'victorious'. In fact, as with most such things, the West Indies' comeback was merely likely and only became 'inevitable' after it had happened.

Despite England's ultimate defeat, the early part of the tour revealed the first cracks in the West Indian edifice. The poll tax riot that took place in London three days after the rain in Trinidad meant you didn't need the soon-to-be launched Hubble telescope to see similar signs for Mrs Thatcher. Interviewed at the time, the then Chancellor of the Exchequer, John Major, was asked if he would rather be prime minister or captain of England's Test team. Concluding an article about his 'consuming passion' for cricket, he answered: 'There's no choice is there?' By the end of the year he was in the wrong job.

Being in the wrong job is certainly something that could apply to any number of those who have, at one time or another, been responsible for the administration of English cricket. For example, in 1990 at least one bright spark or, come to think of it, more likely, a whole committee of them, came up with the idea of taking a sledgehammer to a peanut. It was widely felt that mediocre bowlers in county cricket were using an abnormally helpful ball to produce misleadingly good figures. To address this the TCCB changed the ball to one with apparently next to no seam. They combined this with the introduction of stricter penalties for poor pitches, thus depriving themselves of any way of judging whether it was the playing surfaces or the ball that were the main problem. All this led to was a series of mediocre batsmen making inflated scores, which hardly made for entertaining viewing designed to bring the crowds flocking. A season in which the eventual champions, Middlesex, drew more games than they won, was epitomized by Surrey's match with Lancashire which, in early May, saw the visitors reply to the home side's 707 (Ian Greig 291, yes that Ian Greig) with 863 (Neil Fairbrother 366). Anybody watching that match must have thought it was going to go on forever.

The international scene was no better. A dull, rain-affected start to the series against New Zealand (hardly a big draw anyway) seemed to catch the mood produced by my contract law lecturer. A blind East German, he had managed to overcome his disability to the extent that he had qualified as a lawyer on both sides of the Berlin Wall and in the English legal system. Unfortunately, as with Graham Gooch, inspirational didn't equal interesting. To be fair he was using his second language, but was nevertheless cursed with the lecturing style of a speak-your-weight machine. I felt like I was being taught by a member of Kraftwerk.

From a commercial point of view it was doubly unfortunate that the men in white chose this moment to produce entertainment levels equivalent of listening to *Autobahn* over and over again. They had just come within touching distance of defeating the unofficial world champions in their own back yard, but let that iron cool off without even striking it. Worse, and more importantly, this all coincided with Italia '90.

All of a sudden, the England football manager who once legendarily called Bryan Robson 'Bobby' ('No! You're Bobby!'), stumbled across a system that worked and took us to within the width of a post of a World Cup final in which we would 'inevitably' have beaten one of the worst Argentinean teams I've ever seen. For my generation Italia '90 is probably the definitive World Cup tournament: Roger Milla (not King of the Road); Nessun Dorma; Platt's 120th-minute winner against Belgium; Gascoigne's tears; 'Have a word with him' and the penalties, oh Lord the penalties! I may love cricket more than football but every one of those images is logged in the same memory file as Kris Srikkanth at Lord's. On the other hand, I have no recollection whatsoever of Graham Gooch making 154 on the first day of the Edgbaston Test. Maybe that's because he started his innings less than 24 hours after Chris Waddle blasted his kick over the bar? Gooch could have batted naked and most of the country's population wouldn't have noticed.

For reasons that still remain a mystery to me, I went to that match. My life might have been very different if my first Test had been like this. I spent an overcast day sitting among the drunks of the Eric Hollies Stand watching Eddie Hemmings work his way through New Zealand's batting. In terms of thrills it was hardly up there with a Flintoff century. The 6-58 Hemmings took that day may have represented his best Test figures, but I still think the closest he came to cricketing greatness was having his name daubed on the side of a pig whose other flank read 'Botham'.

Eddie might object to being dismissed so rudely by a cricketing non-entity like me. However, surely one of the major functions of professional sportspeople is to enable us to feel better about ourselves by shouting at someone ten times more talented than we are that they resemble a wheelie-bin or alternatively are simply a useless waste of space? Chris Lewis made his Test debut at Edgbaston. He made a promising 32 in England's first innings and took 3-76 in New Zealand's second. A career in microcosm if ever there was one.

With the exception of a win over whipping boys Sri Lanka in 1988, England hadn't come out on top in a home Test since September 1985. So it was a bit of a shock when they won this one. But probably not as much of a shock as Fred Trueman got when his daughter married Raquel Welch's son. Can you imagine Granddad in the back garden coaching the product of that union? "Ow many times 'av ah got to tell thee lad? If you're going to land a role throwing spears at dinosaurs tha's got to get *sideways on*!'

Despite the fact he never seemed to have the first idea 'what was going off out there', dear old Fred was still in his pomp as an expert summariser on Test Match Special. The existence of a great open-chested fast bowler like Malcolm Marshall hadn't prevented an apparent insertion into his contract of a clause demanding him to repeat 'cricket is a sideways-on game' at least ten times a day. The embodiment of John McEnroe's quip that 'the older I get the better I used to be', he wasn't noted for self-deprecation and unintentionally invited jokes at his expense. The best of these has to be the fax he read out on air which, starting in grovellingly admiring tones, informed Fred what a great man he was and how the correspondent had taken to heart his advice about the nature of the game. He only realised he had been had when he reached the final sentence about the record number of byes the writer had apparently conceded as a result. David Lloyd was allegedly responsible for that one.

I had spent much of the day on which England won that Test discussing with one of the partners of the law firm where I was going to do my training, the recent arrest of the Assistant Director of Public Prosecutions for alleged kerb-crawling. More accurately, we were discussing the press coverage and in particular the tabloid headline that had gloriously summed up the story with: 'POLICE NAB BIG NOB'. However, it was wandering out into the clients' waiting room to catch glimpses of the cricket on the TV that was to change my life.

An astute man, the partner worked out that I might like cricket and asked if I played for anyone. When I told him I didn't, he put me in contact with Larry Connor.

Larry is one of the nicest men in the world and has only one discernable fault: he supports Kent. Mainly a bowler, he had an 'individual' approach to the wicket, which has been described variously as resembling dressage or the 'funky chicken'. From this run-up he produced viciously ripped deliveries, all of which proved to be top-spinners. More importantly, he played for Stoneleigh Cricket Club and invited me along to nets.

At the start of his *A History of Cricket*, Benny Green describes the vale of Hambledon as having, 'The aspect less of reality than of an English idyll plucked from the pages of some illustrated guide-book… like James Hilton's happy valley in *Lost Horizon*, (the ground) seems protected by providence from most of the curses of modern life.' When I arrived at Stoneleigh for my first evening practice I knew what he meant. What I had before me was, to borrow from Neville Cardus, 'the richness of the open air of England and the murmur of summer on the most beautiful of playing fields which spread and mingled with the pastoral land of Warwickshire'. In 2003, *The Wisden Cricketer* gave the ground its award for the most beautiful in Britain. In short, it's a place fit for heaven's first team. Within a year of starting to play there I knew where I wanted my ashes scattered.

I had felt almost instantly at home. Part of that feeling might have come from somehow having convinced my prospective team-mates that I knew what I was doing and part from how fantastic they were to play with. Given the series of long hops and full tosses I served up in my first match, it was just as well it wasn't only my appearance of competence that made me feel comfortable.

My batting was no better than my bowling. Opening with Martin Webster – not the former leader of the National Front – I made seven. In any social group everybody has their own characteristics and quirks. The key thing at Stoneleigh seemed to be that, unlike Fred, everyone was aware of their own and managed to have a sense of humour about them. Martin's were that he could moan for England (not in an erotic sense, you understand) and would be late for a game staged in his own back garden. Legend has it he paid his tardiness fines by direct debit and on one occasion, down to bat at number three, he famously came whistling over the fence and across the outfield, bag jauntily over his shoulder, as I was facing the first ball of the ninth over.

More than anything else, my new-found teammates had cricket in its proper perspective in a way I know I didn't. Therefore it was no surprise to me that, almost to a man, they were on the same side of the major cricketing debate raging through the summer.

On England's return from the West Indies, Gower was picked for the one-day internationals against New Zealand but, asked to open, failed and was dropped again for the Tests. Gooch, it seemed, didn't want him and as the captain was embarking on a period in which he transformed himself from a very good player into a great one, the silky left-hander could never feel secure in the side again.

Ironically, Gower did return for the start of the series against India in which the Gooch legend began to be forged. At Lord's, the captain produced the only triple and single century combination in the history of first-class cricket. I saw him interviewed about the triple once and he revealed that, 190 not out on the first evening, he 'went out to dinner with Doug Insole and …' At this point he paused and I expected him to come out with something like, 'He told me I could put English cricket back on the map if I went on and broke Sobers' record.' What he actually said was…. 'Norma'. Frankly Graham, knowing Insole's wife was there doesn't really add anything. Maybe this accounts for why many remember the match more for Kapil Dev making the 24 required to save the follow-on with four successive sixes off Hemmings?

The captain made another hundred at Old Trafford but ended up indebted to Gower's 157 not out at the Oval for the series victory. In between these two efforts came Tendulkar's maiden Test century, made at the age of 17 years and 112 days. What scares me is that the boy is now well into his 30s and on the verge of retirement.

On 1st November that year Geoffrey Howe resigned as deputy prime minister. Within a fortnight the 'dead sheep' had savaged the Iron Lady in a Commons speech in which he likened her hampering of ministers' efforts at negotiation in Europe to sending her openers out with broken bats. By the end of the month she was gone.

Major had to be an improvement. After all, Thatcher had never won the *Evening Standard's* 'Best Young Cricketer of the Year' award. However, after years longing for the day when we would see the back of her, when she finally dissolved under Geoffrey's bucket of cold water I couldn't understand why I felt slightly uneasy.

That summer, Graham Gooch, at the age of 37, made more than 1,000 Test runs at an average of just over 96. He ended up scoring more after his 35th birthday than he did before it. At the time these were just two of the millions of statistics that cricket throws up. Now they are facts to which I cling with increasing desperation.

SEVENTEEN

My mother was delighted when I decided to become a lawyer. It wasn't that she had any cynical desire for easy access to free legal advice, any job that involved shaving every day would have done. The fact I would be joining the suit-wearing classes was a fantastic bonus. More than anything I think she felt it was a sign I wasn't going to 'waste my life'. Of course there are innumerable ways you can do that, including choosing a way of life that squeezes every ounce of joy from all you do, leaving you a 'success' in one sense and a catastrophic failure in another.

Squeezing the joy out of everything is certainly something Graham Gooch was accused of doing on England's tour to Australia that winter. Like many driven men who have found a formula for their own personal success, Gooch seemed not to appreciate that his way wasn't a universal answer and not everyone could be moulded into his image. Michael Vaughan's England team may have had a strong work ethic but managed to accommodate within that a degree of freedom of expression and, perhaps more importantly, enjoyment. Gooch's England had only the first of these qualities and the punishment of Gower and Morris after the Tiger Moth incident at Queensland is only the most extreme example of the management's attitude to fun on the cricket field. Queensland was the only first-class match we won on the whole tour.

Also, to a large extent, this team relied too heavily on the captain's contribution as a player. England only lost to the West Indies after Gooch had been ruled out by his hand injury and the victories over New Zealand and India had been built on his own phenomenal batting form. Leading by example is all very well as long as you don't set the standards so high that others become convinced of their own inability to attain them and start to see themselves as the supporting cast. In short,

Gooch's puritanical mentality may have brought the best out in himself but it didn't always have the same effect on his team.

Sometimes when England were batting the game resembled one of those involving mixed teams of fathers and sons, where the result depended on whose dad got out for the fewest. I had always hated those sorts of games. This was partly because as a child you were basically a spectator, but more especially in my case because my own father was, like the unfortunate Abdul Aziz, 'absent dead'.

Abdul was a very unlucky young man. At the age of 19 he had the misfortune to be batting at the other end when Hanif Mohammed ran himself out for 499. However, two weeks later this paled into insignificance when a viciously turning offspinner hit him over the heart, causing him to collapse. He was taken to hospital and never regained consciousness, leaving the scorers to record their forlorn second-innings entry accompanied by a rather superfluous 0. Eddie Paynter once famously left his hospital bed to make 83 in Brisbane but 'Absent dead…83', now that really would have been worth seeing.

Graham Gooch wasn't dead, but he did have a dangerously poisoned hand and when this caused him to miss the first Test it was a disaster. Whereas four years earlier England had swept all before them, now they were swept aside. They lost the Ashes series 3-0 and failed to beat Australia in a single one-day international. It wasn't just Gooch's Calvinist tendencies that were to blame. For a start, the captain himself thought it was all David Gower's fault, particularly after Adelaide where the left-hander chose the last over before lunch to clip a ball off his legs to one of no fewer than three men placed on the boundary for the shot. In Gower's defence, he top-scored in both innings of the first Test at Brisbane, made centuries at Melbourne and Sydney and his series aggregate (407 runs at 45.22) was second only to Gooch's own. The real problem lay in the almost total inability of several other members of the team to bat, bowl or field. At the end of Gatting's tour in 1986-87, Martin Johnson had amended his famous initial assessment of the England party with: 'Right quote, wrong team.' Now he could just as easily have suggested: 'Right team, wrong tour.'

Duncan Fletcher demanded that any member of his side contributed in at least two of the three main disciplines of the game. In the case of some members of Gooch's team one would have been nice. The bowling relied so heavily on Angus Fraser that Gooch felt forced to bowl him into the ground. This precipitated the hip injury that removed the most gifted fast-medium bowler of his generation from the Test side for over two-and-a-half years.

If the bowlers at least had their moments, the lower order batting resembled a demented clone of Fred Karno and Heath Robinson. Jack Russell had negotiated an unusual sponsorship deal whereby he received a can of Heinz beans for each run he scored. Every one of his teammates could have come to the same arrangement and the world's haricot supplies would have remained undented. For once it isn't necessary to look any further than the bare statistics to get an impression of what it was like. In the three Tests that England lost, their innings concluded with the following collapses: at Brisbane 8-77 in the first innings and 9-72 in the second; at Melbourne 6-78 and 9-47 (including 6-3!) and at Perth 6-32 and 6-68. It seemed as if Craig McDermott, Bruce Reid and Merv Hughes didn't actually have to bowl at our tail, running up and shouting 'Boo!' was enough.

Hughes had come to an unusual financial arrangement of his own, in that he had insured his moustache for £200,000. The evil brainwashing process designed to turn me into a lawyer was almost complete and so this set me thinking about the circumstances in which you might be able to claim on such a policy. For example, was it voided if he went within a 50-yard radius of a razor or, if he got into financial difficulty, might it be possible for Merv to get former Australian middle-order batsman and legendary chimney, Dougie Walters, to arrange for it to have a little 'accident'?

The word 'accident' combined in the right sequence with 'happen', 'waiting' and 'to', comprises a well known saying that sums up England every time they went out to field on this tour. Several less than greyhound-like members of the party must have been grateful for the distracting presence alongside them of Phil Tufnell. That's Tufnell as in: 'Hey Tufnell! Lend us your brain. I'm trying to build an idiot.' England were generally pretty embarrassing in the field, but the unfortunate Phil came to embody the ineptitude of their effort, as a series of increasingly calamitous blunders made him Australia's number one figure of fun. His crowning glory in this respect must surely be the moment in a one-day international against Australia when, standing over the bowler's wicket with both batsmen apparently stranded at the striker's end, he managed to fluff a run out by first punching the ball away before hurling it past the stumps from a range of four yards. Greigy was left pissing himself, while poor Phil stared disbelievingly at his hands: 'Happy days!'

It wasn't as if everything else going on was a barrel of laughs. If I had thought the previous year was a rigorous examination of my academic stamina, I was now being disabused of this notion by a bunch of tutors for whom the joke 'What do you call 30 lawyers at the bottom of the sea?… A good start', might have been written. At least two of my friends ended up on beta-blockers. One still had a heart rate of 120 a day after our exams were over. Even so, it wasn't up there with being in the middle of Desert Storm.

This conflict was even shorter and more of a media event than the Falklands. American planes started the bombing of Baghdad four days before Gower and Morris did something loosely similar but much less threatening at the Carrara Oval and President Bush Snr declared victory less than a fortnight after England's final tour defeat to New Zealand at Auckland. At the time, many wondered why the Allies hadn't taken the chance to remove Saddam once and for all. Now we know. Stormin' Norman Schwarzkopf and Colin Powell (born in Jamaica and, according to Tony Cozier, therefore almost certainly distantly related to West Indian fast bowler Daren) had more sense than to risk escalating matters to the level where the global conflagration the doom-mongers had forecast became a possibility. The fact that World War III was no more likely than me living out my residual dreams of playing for England didn't make the realisation that I was of exactly the right age to be conscripted into such a conflict any less sobering. When such thoughts even enter your head you're dangerously close to being a grown up. The voice inside me shouting 'SADDO' at the mirror when I joined in an argument about international law was becoming ever more muffled.

Although I was very lucky to have made it this far into my life never having been one of those people 'just getting into their cars' for whom the Test Match Special team summed up the day's play at about 5.35, this didn't make me any less miserable at the prospect of becoming one. It wasn't as if the omens indicated a season of endless glory. We had just been a shambling embarrassment in Australia and our next opponents were, wouldn't you know it, the West Indies. What were they doing here a full year earlier than I would have expected?

But wait, who was this riding over the hill to our rescue? It was none other than the great Zim-Bradman, Graeme Hick. We were saved! He had made 405 not out at Taunton and now he was playing for us, so take that Curtly Ambrose!

Of course the reality was that Taunton was a flat track and Graeme

Hick was, in the words of John Bracewell, 'a flat track bully'. Ambrose took it, tore it up, ground it under his foot and stood at the end of his follow-through glaring as if to say 'What you gonna do about it?' To which the answer was usually 'Jab down late on a yorker and drag it onto my stumps or maybe poke it into the slips if that's alright with you Curtley?' It was a good job there was someone in the team who spelt Graham with an 'h'.

Gooch's 154 not out at Headingley is the best innings I've ever seen or, more accurately, listened to. I shouldn't even be able to say that given it coincided with two of my friends' wedding. The bride, Kate, is only still talking to me because I have sworn faithfully I didn't have my radio on during the service or the reception. However, while the photos were being taken, the combination of my then trendy trench coat and a small piece of electronic equipment apparently welded to my ear, led at least two other guests to ask if I was the hotel's security man. Also, a doctor sat at my table during the reception dinner, seeing how often I apparently needed the toilet, wondered if I had ever been tested for diabetes.

Gooch contributed more than 60 per cent of England's second-innings total and two brilliant catches as the tourists were bowled out on the last day. It was as if he was intent on proving single-handed that the team didn't need David Gower, who, along with Tufnell, had been made a scapegoat for the winter's failures. Gower's omission was a bit like capital punishment in that you could tell a lot about a person just by where they stood on the issue. I have a Corinthian-spirited friend whose opinion on the subject was the same as one-time Kent coach Gerry Weigell's view on the exclusion of another brilliant left-hander, Frank Woolley. Weigell described Woolley's non-selection for England as 'the greatest crime since the Crucifixion'. Even now, my friend can still barely bring himself to say Gooch's name, so strongly did he feel about it. Ironically, Gower was replaced in the team by another batsman who divided opinion almost as sharply throughout his career, Mark Ramprakash.

A murderous dasher in his youth, 'Ramps' is an excellent example of what trying to be too responsible can do to you. This is a man who has scored in excess of 25,000 first-class runs at just under 50, but fewer than 2500 of those were made for England and the two 27s he made on debut represent his Test average. He batted for hours against the West Indies that first year, but although he never failed in his nine innings to get into double figures he didn't once reach 30. His first-class figures and a Test average of 42 against Australia show he didn't lack talent, but if ever a man lost sight of why we start playing the game in the first place (i.e. it's fun) and tried far too hard, it was Ramprakash. The sight of him sat glowering on the pavilion balcony at Lord's became a reassuringly familiar sign of summer.

He had plenty of reasons to glower: a pair against the West Indies in 1995; 0 and two against the same opposition in 2000 and 12 and 0 against South Africa in 1998, the 12 coming courtesy of being given out caught behind off his elbow by Darrell Hair. Ramprakash's reaction to this last misfortune is indicative of the intensity that so undermined him. Following his dismissal he deliberately changed the route of his departure to inform the umpire that: 'You're messing with my career Darrell.' In the batsman's defence, Darrell Hair wasn't the only one doing that.

On England's tour to Australia in 1998-99 Ramprakash seemed finally to have established himself by topping the Test averages with 47.37 when the team were on the wrong end of another pasting. Even then he was accused of batting too mechanically with the tail and a mediocre series against New Zealand saw him dropped for the tour to South Africa to accommodate Darren Maddy and Chris Adams. I'm a Sussex fan, but Chris Adams? That can't have done wonders for Ramprakash's self-belief. The selectors then denied him Christmas at home by calling him up as cover for Vaughan, before sending him home again without facing a ball. When he got back into the side for real the following summer they tried to turn him into an opener with predictable results.

So then, Mark Ramprakash: temperamental lightweight or shabbily treated tortured genius? Either way he used to remind me of Cronauer's superior in *Good Morning Vietnam* in that he certainly needed something to help him lighten up a bit. Whether Robin Williams' suggested solution would have assisted is another matter.

I was still trying to convince my less than enthusiastic girlfriend, Fiona, that watching might be fun. Armed only with the attraction of the beautiful surroundings at Stoneleigh I succeeded in tempting her to come to another match. Fiona had by now submitted to an eye test and so had glasses that at least enabled her to recognise me and once more I struck lucky with the weather. Everything was in my favour, including the fact I bowled tidily, took two wickets and didn't drop a catch. However, the post-tea conversation was again a huge disappointment.

'Did you enjoy that?' 'It was alright until about halfway through. Up until then I was reading my book quite peacefully and then all of a sudden this massive screaming noise made me jump. I looked up and realised it was *you*. Do you have to? I didn't know where to put myself.'

It was clearly hopeless and I didn't even bother trying to persuade her to come to Edgbaston with me. This was a shame because, in contrast to the previous year, it was an incredibly exciting day.

By the time the teams reached Birmingham the series was level. The West Indies had come out on top at Trent Bridge courtesy of England's traditional one-two of a sub-par first-innings score followed by a second-innings collapse. As we arrived at Edgbaston on the Saturday morning things again did not look good. England had been bowled out for 188 and the tourists had closed on the Friday evening at 253-4.

I can never understand why people pay loads for Test tickets and then arrive more than half an hour after the start. Anybody who did that on this day would have missed quite a lot. It is one of my great cricketing regrets that I narrowly missed seeing David Gower's last Test innings, but at least I can say I saw Chris Lewis' best Test performance. Some regarded Lewis as lucky to be in the side after he had missed the first Test through 'feeling ill'. Nevertheless, Gooch entrusted him with the opening over of the third day. The first ball was a leg stump half-volley which was flicked for four by Gus Logie and the second a long hop outside off stump which the batsman obligingly slapped straight at Atherton in the gulley. Including Logie, Lewis took five for 12 as the West Indies lost their last six wickets for 35 runs.

My mate Pete, who had taken the ticket that might otherwise have been Fiona's, was watching his first Test. 'Is it always like this ?' he asked. When England collapsed to 5-3 before lunch I was able to tell him: 'No mate, it's usually like *this*.'

By the close we were 156-8. 'That was a great day,' said Pete. 'Yes' I said when what I was thinking was: 'I suppose so, if all you care about is being entertained.' I was still taking it all just a little bit too seriously. That evening we had arranged to meet some friends to try out something new called a Balti house and my day came to a perfect end when they informed us that, having completely overlooked the potential effects of eight hours in the open, we were both now suffering from a case of sunburn apparently visible from 150 yards.

Despite Lewis' 65 (a score he surpassed only three times in the remaining 27 Tests of his career) England still went to the Oval 2-1 down. This match has become more famous for a piece of summarizing than for Tufnell's triumphant 6-25 on his recall, or England's victory on Viv Richards' final appearance.

On the second afternoon Botham was out hit wicket as he overbalanced and just removed a bail in a failed attempt to hurdle the stumps. Everyone knows what happened to Jonathan Agnew and Brian Johnston when they reached this moment in their close-of-play summing up on Test Match Special. Fiona and I were in a traffic jam on the M1 and even she was crying with laughter, while on both sides I could see other drivers who were similarly affected.

It was like a massive fit of the giggles and even made the national news. Apparently Tony Cozier, sat in the back of the box, was deeply unimpressed and even Johnston himself was extremely annoyed afterwards at the lack of professionalism. He shouldn't have been, because he and Agnew had done us all a wonderful service by providing a moment of collective escape, an instant in which 'fat-cat' pay rises, international bank collapses (Mushtaq Mohammed apparently had his life savings invested in BCCI), looming war in the Balkans and even Brian Adams still being at number one, could all be forgotten and life could be a riotous joy. In this respect it was appropriate that it was Botham who couldn't get his 'leg over'.

As well as being able to laugh themselves senseless at any phrase that contains the merest hint of a reference to sex or flatulence, the British also have the gift of being able to make a serious point with gentle humour. We were now into the final decade of the 20th century, yet Rachael Heyhoe-Flint (someone whom I later met in a Citizens Advice Bureau in Wolverhampton incidentally) was rejected for membership of the MCC on the ground that she was female. As if to poke fun at their more illustrious colleagues, the committees of Mountaineers, Milton and Merrow cricket clubs all offered to let her to join them instead.

There is a thin line between upholding tradition and being hopelessly out of date. This is a fact appreciated by the seemingly more enlightened leaders of these other three MCCs and, more surprisingly, by those in charge at Yorkshire.

My father was cremated and so didn't have a grave to spin in at the announcement that the White Rose county was to abandon the policy of only using players born within its boundaries. Despite coming from Todmorden, whose cricket club played in the Lancashire League, my dad always claimed the village was on the border between the two counties and was fiercely proud of being born 'at the Yorkshire end'. He would have been appalled at the thought of any 'foreigner' getting into the county's side and there were many still among the living who shared his view. A Labour MP, Roland Boyes, even tabled a Commons motion deploring the decision. The fact that the rule had been invented by Lord Hawke, a man who led the county for 27 years despite the minor personal disadvantage of having been born in Lincolnshire, seemed to have passed both my father and Mr Boyes by.

Unfortunately for the traditionalists the hard facts were against them. Yorkshire had not won the county championship since 1968; Lancashire had Wasim Akram whereas they had Peter Hartley; membership had declined by 3,000 in the last four years and the club was looking at a £100,000 loss on the 1991 season. The committee and the membership did the sums, worked out that they needed more success on the field and offered Craig McDermott a three-year contract. In the end McDermott got injured and so Sachin Tendulkar became Yorkshire's first overseas professional. My dad would probably have preferred this to an Aussie but not by much.

Yorkshire weren't the only ones number crunching. The organizers of that winter's cricket World Cup had sold the television rights to the highest bidder, BSkyB, who had in turn refused to sell a highlights package to the BBC. The satellite broadcaster claimed that 2.6 million homes could now receive their service. On the other hand Refuge Assurance had just pulled out of sponsoring the Sunday league because only 47,000 people tuned in to BSkyB's coverage, whereas audiences of over a million watched when it was on BBC2. Clearly there is nothing new under the sun, or do I mean sky?

Given that the tournament was to be staged in Australia and New Zealand and no pubs were likely to open at 4 a.m. to accommodate the vast majority of cricket fans who didn't have a satellite dish, I wasn't going to see any of the World Cup. This was a shame because England were sending arguably the best all-round one-day team they have ever fielded and I could have done with the distraction.

Even once you have passed all of the exams you have to do two years of relevant work before you can call yourself a qualified solicitor. This is a perfectly sensible idea, I wouldn't have wanted to try and convince anyone I had the first clue what I was talking about straight out of college. However, this process also has the capacity to take you into work so dull that no sane person could emerge from any length of time doing it with their sense of humour still intact. Working in these areas on a permanent basis would be like spending your entire career bowling fast-medium at Lahore: repetitive, unrewarding and largely pointless. I appreciate that everything is relative and most normal people regard lawyers as a generally tedious breed. However, for your own self-esteem it's important to find someone duller than you. Lawyers make jokes about how boring accountants are and accountants do the same about actuaries.

Although I had a long-term plan to work somewhere worthy like a law centre giving free advice, I still had to go through legal purgatory in order to get into the position to do so. Two years of probate work: sorting out the affairs of dead people on behalf of relatives at each other's throats over who was to inherit grandma's Elvis Presley wall-carpet, filled me with horror. The team uniforms for the first cricket World Cup not played in whites would have provided some much needed colour in my life. Listening to coloured clothing didn't really help. At least the radio commentary provided the wonderful moment when Christopher Martin-Jenkins offered the opinion, when South Africa met Pakistan, that both sides playing in green might cause some confusion. Peter Baxter pointed out that cricket teams had both played in white for quite a long time without any problems.

England were in blue and unlike four years previously, an apparently rejuvenated Botham was joining them. However, he was excused the first part of the trip to New Zealand that preceded the tournament so he could fulfill 'television and pantomime commitments'. At least someone was going to be having fun that winter.

EIGHTEEN

England were clearly the best team in the 1992 World Cup but ended up being beaten by a side they had bowled out for 74 in the group stage. I used up one of my 15 days off a year to watch the final, couldn't find a pub showing it, and then they lost.

Probably because they have been so appalling ever since, England's defeat to Pakistan in 1992 still rankles slightly. We have reached the World Cup final three times and lost the lot. In 1979, against a rampant West Indies, we did well to come second but the 1987 and 1992 defeats were gut-wrenching. Gatting's side losing to Australia was more immediately painful because of who their opponents were and the narrowness of the margin of defeat. However, that side had exceeded all expectations by even making it through to meet the Aussies. Yes they should have won the final, but by rights they probably shouldn't even have made it that far and certainly hadn't built up my expectations.

On the other hand when, during the 1992 tournament, Ian Wooldridge, said that 'England, now, are the team every other country fears. It is some years since I have been able to write that about any sport.' He was right on both counts. Every member of the England side that played in the final had scored a first-class century, it was a team with six front-line bowlers and in Lewis, Fairbrother and DeFreitas, it possessed three of the best fielders in the competition. In the early matches they battered everyone in their path and only lost to New Zealand, on a pudding specially prepared for the home side's battery of dibbly-dobbly seamers, and to Zimbabwe, courtesy of complacency and an inspired spell from Eddo 'Biscuits' Brandes. Both defeats came after qualification for the semi-finals had been secured.

For years I wondered what it was like to support a successful side, when victory was an expectation rather than a vague hope. For a few short weeks in 1992 I found out. Then we ran out of steam at the vital moment and never looked like winning a game for which we started clear favourites. It was all such an anti-climax. When was it going to be my turn to support a winning side?

Neutrals remember this tournament for South Africa falling victim to the ludicrous rain rules. Because all the teams played each other once in the group stage, there was no time to schedule reserve days in case of rain. Hence England bowled out Pakistan for 74 but had no second day to come back and finish them off when it poured down with their reply at 24-1. The point Imran's men took for the 'no-result' meant the difference between elimination and qualification for the semis.

Any lawyer who has done matrimonial work will tell you that one person's fair outcome is another's glaring injustice. 'Why should he get the large Afghan adult toy (I don't know, I didn't dare ask)? If my Auntie Joan hadn't given us the money to have the guttering done we would never have afforded to go there on holiday in the first place.' So, what about the semi-final against South Africa when they ended up needing 21 off one ball because it rained for 12 minutes? What about it? I say.

There are two things South African supporters fail to mention whenever the subject of that match comes up. The first is that Kepler Wessels won the toss and even though rain was forecast, decided to field. The second is that they got through their overs so slowly that England only received 45 in the time allotted when they had started off expecting to get 50. England were deprived of potentially the five most productive overs of their innings and the South Africans ended up chasing 253 instead of something around 300.

Do I feel sorry for them? No I don't. They could have batted first but didn't; they could have bowled their overs at a reasonable rate but didn't; they could and should have beaten us in the group game when it was England who were on the wrong end of the rain rules and potentially ended up with a different semi-final opponent, but didn't. It was as much their own fault as Allan Donald's run out in 1999 or cocking up the Duckworth/Lewis calculation in 2003.

Some might say they were lucky to be in the tournament in the first place. Although Nelson Mandela had been released and the new multi-racial United Cricket Board of South Africa had been formed, the decision in July 1991 to admit this body to full membership of the ICC was taken before the official ending of the apartheid regime. South

Africa's participation in the World Cup was only confirmed after the Commonwealth Heads of Government, meeting in Harare, issued a statement urging inclusion and Mandela made it clear he was also in favour. The white majority didn't vote to accept President de Klerk's programme of constitutional reform until the last day of the tournament's group stage and full elections weren't held until 1994.

England then had every right to be in the World Cup final and given how the group game with Pakistan had gone, in a just world would have won. In fact they were utterly outplayed by the better team on the day/night. Two balls from Wasim Akram summed up his side's superiority and pointed the way to the next Anglo-Pakistani controversy that was to erupt when the teams met the following summer.

Chasing 250 to win, England reached 141-4 needing the remaining 109 at roughly seven an over. Imran brought back Akram and successive deliveries proved Geoff Boycott's old adage about adding two wickets to the score. Both were bowled left-arm around the wicket. The first, to Lamb, angled in with the arm before dipping away late in its flight and snaking past the outside edge to clip off stump. The second, to Lewis, started miles wide but boomed in at high pace to bowl the disbelieving batsman through the gate. How the hell did he do that!? This was a question that came up at regular intervals in the months that followed and not just with reference to John Major winning/Neil Kinnock losing the General Election.

England may have won the winter's Test series in New Zealand fairly easily but that was scant consolation. All I can remember about it now is that Dermot Reeve played his three Test matches and the unfortunate David Lawrence snapped his left knee-cap in half on a meaningless last afternoon at Wellington. The series was no more exciting than the Maastricht Treaty negotiations with which it coincided. The same couldn't be said about the summer's contest with Pakistan.

Sometimes sport is memorable for the high quality of the performances (Ashes 2005), sometimes for controversy (Maradona's 'Hand of God') and sometimes for both (England v Pakistan 1992).

Things started badly when England won the first two one-day internationals by impressive margins. Hammering Pakistan at home only rubbed salt into the wound of the World Cup final defeat. The tone for the summer was set in the second game when Miandad complained Botham had sworn at him. This was the equivalent of Robert Maxwell accusing one of his staff of 'borrowing' a pound from petty cash. You could hardly imagine the batsman had taken serious offence but in terms of deteriorating relations between the two sides it was only the start.

Both teams harboured simmering resentments and the tabloids were only too happy to stoke things up in pursuit of sales. The *Daily Mirror* started things off nicely with its headline referring to Miandad as 'CRICKET'S COLONEL GADAFFI' and then summed up the incident in the one-dayer with 'BEEFY TOLD ME TO ★ ! ϑ ★ OFF!' It went downhill from there.

The Pakistanis had their usual complaints about the Palmer family's umpiring. At Old Trafford, Roy gave a dubious caught behind decision against Ramiz Raja and then warned Aqib Javed for intimidation when he bowled a series of bouncers at Devon Malcolm. This was the first series in England overseen by a match referee and the unseemly altercation that followed the warning resulted in Aqib being fined 40% of his match fee and his captain, Miandad, receiving a severe reprimand from Conrad Hunte. If the tourists felt hard done by in Manchester, worse was to follow in Leeds.

England seemed to have a habit of picking journeymen county seamers for games at Headingley and this year it was Neil Mallender's turn. The selection proved a masterstroke as Mallender produced match figures of 8-122 and the home side were left chasing only 99 to win. As usual they threatened to make a horrible hash of things and were already two quick wickets down when Gooch appeared to be run out for 13. This time it was the elder Palmer, Ken, who intervened by turning down the appeal. Television replays showed England's captain was at least as far out as John Dyson had been all those years earlier. Gooch went on to make a vital 37 as England scraped home by six wickets.

Winning by six wickets may not sound like scraping home but that's what it felt like after England's last half-dozen batsmen (including Hick at number seven) had contributed two runs between them in the first innings. Knowing this, the Pakistanis realised how vital Gooch's removal could have been and under modern playing conditions England may well have lost. However, it wasn't until that winter's series between India and South Africa that television replays for line decisions were first experimented with.

Any indignation the visitors felt over how the series was being officiated was as nothing by comparison with the resentment harboured by both sides about how England's first innings collapse had been engineered. The home side had subsided from 270-1 to 320 all out thanks to a series of violently in-swinging yorkers from Waqar Younis. Wasim and Waqar had done something similar in both innings at Lord's and would repeat the dose at the Oval to bring a 2-1 series victory.

Wasim Akram and Waqar Younis were providing a first dramatic demonstration of an art that would help bring an Ashes victory to a future generation of England fans.

However, in 1992 no one had heard of reverse-swing and English bowlers certainly weren't capable of producing it. Taking these factors into account, and employing deductive reasoning of a sort that wouldn't have been out of place in *The Crucible,* some in the British press concluded the Pakistanis must be using the cricketing equivalent of witchcraft.

Once the ball got old, Wasim and Waqar were capable of producing alarmingly late high-pace swing of a kind no one had seen before. England's lower order and Graeme Hick were regularly blown away. In terms of knowing how to combat this sort of attack, our batsmen were like a platoon of Wellington's red-coated grenadiers suddenly confronted by tanks and were more than happy for the impression to be given that they were only losing because their opponents were cheating. However, since folding in an embarrassing heap is how England's lower order usually behaved, it's hard to see how you could conclude on this basis alone they were definitely the victims of sharp practice.

Whether the condition of the ball was being altered illegally was a subject of heated debate throughout the summer and there was some evidence for the prosecution. Most famously there was the close-up of Aqib Javed at the Oval seemingly indulging in a bit of gouging with his thumbnail to the accompaniment of Richie's 'Pfwoar! Steady on!' and the impounding of a ball Allan Lamb complained about in a one-day international at Lord's that followed the Test series.

For their part, the Pakistanis felt they were simply not being given credit for high skill levels. Whatever the state of the ball you still have to able to release it properly to get it to 'go' that much and that late. Even with an identical ball England's bowlers wouldn't have achieved the same results. Apart from anything else, with the exception of Malcolm (hardly renowned for his mastery of subtleties of swing and cut) they were nowhere near as fast as Wasim and Waqar. Even if Derek Pringle had been able to get the ball to swing round corners he wouldn't have been wanging it down at over 90mph. As Robin Smith has said: 'I'm the first one to say it was sour grapes because we were not good enough to cope and that was part of the reason why we were so angry…if we had been good enough to impart the reverse-swing with their pace, we wouldn't have said so much.'

In 2005, when it was England's bowlers who were flinging down the toe-crushers, the only time the condition of the ball came up was in Nathan Bracken's post-series comments about sticky mints. Ricky Ponting never moaned about it, but then he was more preoccupied with how often England's bowlers were apparently altering the condition of the toilets.

All of this raises interesting questions about what is a legitimate skill, what is cheating and, perhaps most importantly, who decides which is which? International teams often seem to have one player who is designated as the ball shiner. Sometimes that person is a bowler. Mike Gatting tells a story of Richard Hadlee in the 1987 MCC Bicentenary game telling him in no uncertain terms 'I shine the ball'. Presumably this is because there is a knack that not everyone possesses. After Wasim and Waqar had blown away England's lower order for the final time that summer, Derek Pringle asked to see the ball they had been using and described what he was shown as 'a work of art'. But when does skill become devilry?

The first thing to mention is there was a lot hypocrisy in the criticism levelled at the Pakistanis that year. As Angus Fraser said at the time: 'Virtually all bowlers would have to say they have tampered with the ball at some stage during their county career.' And it's not as if this was a modern phenomenon either. In the 1930s, Alf Gover was found to have been using hair oil, prompting umpire Harold Gimblett to offer the opinion that it was the most beautifully smelling ball he'd ever come across. The fact that 'everyone does it' can't justify breaking the rules, unless of course you regard yourself as an oppressed minority and refuse to recognize the legitimacy of the law-maker in the first place. As Nelson Mandela said of the ANC's struggle in South Africa: 'We were placed in a position in which we had either to accept a permanent state of inferiority, or to defy the government. We chose to defy the law.'

When Pringle commented recently that 'to paint ball-tampering in such a villainous garb is absurd and the work of batsmen', he was speaking for generations of bowlers around the world who have railed against the unfairness of a game constantly having its rules tweaked to promote the willow and subjugate the leather. Just as Richard III is generally regarded as a complete bastard because the only documentary evidence that survives about him was written during the reign of his arch enemy Henry VII, so, the argument runs, ball-tampering is only cheating because batsmen in high places say it is.

The origins of this 'conspiracy' must lie in the nature of society at the birth of first-class cricket in this country and the class distinctions that then existed between 'Gentlemen' and 'Players'. Most amateurs were batsmen of independent means, while most bowlers were professionals, represented by the stereotypical miner whistled up from down't pit. No prizes for guessing which of these groups moved more easily into cricket administration and therefore law-making, on retirement. Such distinctions no longer exist but by the time they started to blur – the Gentlemen v Players fixture carried on until the early sixties – it was too late and the notion that altering the condition of the ball was a sharp practice rather than a skill had become a given.

Thus, bowlers were forced to become a sort of cricketing resistance movement compelled to rely on whatever means possible to even up the contest. They may have been outside the rules on occasions but the rules were made by batsmen for batsmen so what the heck.

Adding something like Gover's hair oil, lip salve, sticky mint saliva or iron filings couldn't reasonably be deemed anything other than cheating. However, things become less clear-cut when you start talking about altering the condition of the ball by taking away from it in some way. For example I can't see the problem with wearing the ball by throwing it in on the bounce. I do this all the time but then that might have something to do with my appalling arm. There is a well known sexist phrase used to describe throwing ability like mine. However, at Stoneleigh we don't use it in that way. It's not because we are all 'new men', just that on one occasion we were so short, Larry Connor got his 13-year-old daughter to field and with the exception of her brother (strength by Mr Muscle, accuracy by Mr Magoo), she out-threw the lot of us. At our club 'you throw like a girl' is a compliment.

In terms of roughing up the ball the authorities would have to draw the line at anything requiring the use of safety goggles, but bowlers should be allowed some latitude. Richard Hadlee has suggested at least some ball-tampering should be legalized: 'As long as the bowlers or fielders use whatever means they have on their persons, I don't see anything wrong with it. I'm talking about the use of a finger nail to scratch the ball, not bottle tops or those sorts of things.' The run-soaked summer of 1990 had recently proved that enormous totals made for a boring spectacle. No one wanted to go and watch a game so slanted in favour of the batsman that Ian Greig was capable of making nearly 300 runs in anything less than a month, let alone a single innings. The game's legislators might do well to remember this, but given their current preoccupation seems to be maximizing revenue from matches that go the full distance, they probably won't.

However he achieved his results, Waqar Younis robbed me of seeing David Gower's last Test innings. I had tickets for the Sunday of the fifth Test and stayed overnight with a friend. As I drove down on Saturday evening Waqar began ripping through England's top order. Just as I was crossing Vauxhall Bridge, Gower shouldered arms and an in-swinger clipped his off stump. In that moment the ending of an era was completed. Earlier in the summer, Botham had also played his last Test.

Eight runs, five wicketless overs and two catches to equal Cowdrey's England record were as much as the great all-rounder contributed to his last Test match. Like Ali, Botham's sheer presence and magnetism extended his career beyond a time when his personality was matched by his physical powers and it was time to go. After Lord's he was dropped never to return. It seems unjust that a worthy but far less brilliant or significant cricketer like Alec Stewart was able to pick the moment of his passing and take his curtain-call on a sun lit Oval afternoon, while Botham was forced to slip silently away to see out his final days in the obscurity of Durham's first two seasons in the county championship.

However, if there was injustice in at least the manner of Botham's passing from the scene, it was nothing by comparison to what happened to David Gower. Recalled for Old Trafford, Gower had cover-driven past Geoff Boycott to become England's leading all-time run scorer during a typically sumptuous innings of 73 and at Headingley had contributed a vital second-innings 31 not out to secure victory for Gooch's side. Yet, after only three matches back, one misjudgment of Waqar's line proved to be his last.

Nelson Mandela was indirectly responsible. South Africa had begun their return to the Test fold with a symbolic first match against the West Indies in April and as from 1st October that year all of those excluded from international cricket for touring the Republic had their bans lifted. As a result, Mike Gatting became available again and was drafted straight back into the winter touring party at Gower's expense. The party line at the time was that Gower was omitted on grounds of age. Gooch was 39 and Gatting 35 and, so the story went, it wasn't a good idea to take three batsmen in their mid-to-late thirties. What that doesn't answer is why pick a man who had, less than three years earlier, effectively stuck two fingers up at the cricketing establishment and was only available because of political events which he had in no way helped to bring about by his actions? The answer was simple, Graham Gooch preferred him. When Gooch was subsequently not invited to Gower's wedding, the left-hander's explanation for the omission was a simple 'Too old'.

Gower had never toured South Africa, missed only one winter tour through choice in his entire Test career, averaged 56.90 in Tests on the sub-continent and had even been willing to step in and play when an injury crisis hit Gooch's team in the Caribbean despite the humiliation of being left out of the original party. By contrast, Gooch had lost three years of his career through touring the Republic, would have opted out of the 1988-89 tour to India if he hadn't been appointed captain, made it perfectly clear that he wanted to come home during Gower's tour to the West Indies in 1985-86 and had even negotiated being excused the Sri Lankan leg of the coming winter's excursion. Under Gooch's captaincy Gower scored 848 runs at an average of 53.00. When the roles were reversed Gooch managed 946 at 33.78.

Certainly 286 members of MCC knew what they thought of how Gower and, to a lesser extent, Jack Russell had been treated. They proposed a vote of no confidence in the Test selectors. The motion was defeated thanks to postal votes but those in the hall on the night who heard the debate voted 715 to 412 in favour.

In that winter's Tests, Mike Gatting averaged 33.25 and Richard Blakey, preferred to Russell on account of his allegedly superior batting, 1.75. As for Gooch and the team, let's just say that for once somebody got exactly what they deserved.

NINETEEN

The best horror movies are the ones that leave almost everything to the imagination. That's why England's tour to India and Sri Lanka in 1992-93 was even more awful to listen to on the radio than it would have been to watch on TV. Not to put too fine a point on it: England were dismembered losing all fours Tests that winter by large, sometimes huge, margins. At first it might seem that this was explained by the batsmen's ineptitude against spin and the bowlers' inability to dismiss anyone. However, Ted Dexter demonstrated that the TCCB were intent on looking beyond such a simplistic analysis and announced that: 'We will be looking at the whole question of people's facial hair.'

Apparently there was a view in the corridors of power that defeat might be a product of the England captain's failure to shave before a match. Gooch's appearance was not the only one criticised and the tour manager Bob Bennett came under fire for turning up to a press conference in a T-shirt and what were described as 'ill-fitting' shorts. While the image this description conjures up is another upon which it is probably not healthy to dwell, Bennett's choice of trousers had no bearing whatsoever on the team's performance, and this whole issue is just one of a number of bizarre distractions and excuses that appeared throughout the tour.

Mickey Stewart had just retired as England coach and been replaced by Fletcher. Unfortunately, the Fletcher in question was Keith. At the time he was seen as possessing a good tactical brain and his close Essex association with the captain made him a natural choice. With hindsight his tenure as national coach seems characterized by a series of off-the-wall statements and self-deluding excuses for bad performances.

Defeat in the first Test at Calcutta was put down to the smog. After

England's scorer collapsed during the match and had to be replaced by Dermot Reeve's mum, the effect of air pollution on cricketers was another thing Dexter committed himself to investigating.

Despite the smog, the last time England had toured India they had managed a perfectly respectable draw in Calcutta. When Fletcher was captain the time before that, the team had saved its best performance for the City of Joy and, under Greig, England had won. In Madras, prawns were apparently responsible. Subsequently, dodgy pork has been blamed for laying Gooch low just before the match. Picking Richard Blakey ahead of Mike Atherton and twice failing to make 300 on a pitch on which the opposition had racked up 560-6 had nothing to do with it. Finally, in Sri Lanka, Fletcher offered the opinion that, 'It's very nearly too hot here for Europeans to play cricket.' Obviously a process of 'global cooling' had improved matters by the time Nasser Hussain's team came from 1-0 down to win in 2000-01.

Unfortunately, a lot of thought, research and preparation were supposed to have gone into this tour. Fletcher was even flown out to South Africa to watch the Indians in the Johannesburg Test. At least the coach hadn't imagined he saw Anil Kumble bowl a leg-break: 'I didn't see him turn a single ball from leg to off.' However, as a result he had convinced himself that 'we won't have much problem with him'. In the three-match series against England Kumble took 21 wickets at 19.80.

In 2005, much of England's Ashes success was put down to their use of Merlyn the spin machine that helped them prepare for the threat of Shane Warne. Before this tour England had practised against their own spinners on 'spinmats', artificial surfaces specially designed to afford generous turn. This might seem like a good idea, but sadly as well as taking spin the mats were also quick and bouncy and therefore totally unlike the slow and low surfaces the team would encounter when they reached the sub-continent. As a result when they got to the first Test the team's response to India's spinners seemed as confused as Henry Blofeld's assertion that the minute's silence during the match was because 'Calcutta is celebrating the assassination of Mahatma Gandhi'.

As for England's own slow bowlers they had got themselves into a good rhythm, just for the wrong sort of pitch. Perhaps this explains why the tour selectors produced another confidence-building psychological masterstroke by not picking either Embury or Tufnell for the first Test? The Middlesex pair had been the originally selected first-choice spinners with Ian Salisbury taken along as a net bowler to gain experience before moving on to the A tour in Australia. For Calcutta the Indians revealed how they thought the pitch would behave by going in with three spinners and two seamers. Admittedly, England couldn't help being deprived of Atherton's services but as *Wisden* put it they 'added insanity to injury' by picking four seamers and Salisbury. It gets even better when you realise one of the seamers was the debutant Paul Taylor, a left-armer whose inclusion might have been designed to add rough outside the right-handers' off stump for the Indian spinners to exploit.

The implications of this went further than the almost inevitable eight-wicket defeat. At the time Sunil Gavaskar described Tufnell as 'to my mind the best left-arm spinner in the world'. Unfortunately the left-armer's own selectors disagreed and shattered his fragile confidence. Little wonder he ended up with his 'done the elephants, done the poverty' attitude towards India. I'm sure I picked which university I wanted to go to at least in part because it was a sunny day when I visited and I travelled home with a pretty girl. Maybe Tufnell would have had a much more positive view of the sub-continent if he had taken a lot of wickets there?

The selectors didn't need to shred Emburey's confidence: Navjot Singh Sidhu did it for them by frequently launching him into stands full of deafeningly delirious Indian supporters. When the Sikh was batting you didn't need the commentator to tell you how far the ball had gone, which was just as well because you didn't have a chance of hearing what was being said.

Now, Sidhu is a cricket broadcaster himself. Hearing him isn't the problem, it's understanding what on earth he's on about. When Paul Anka did a swing version of 'Smells like Teen Spirit', Dave Grohl was asked to comment and said something slightly ambiguous along the lines of never having heard anything quite like it before. In the same way, you might describe Navjot Singh Sidhu's broadcasting style as 'unique'. As with his batting, you could never accuse his commentary of lacking colour: 'I have seen many ladies displaying different styles and many styles displaying ladies'; 'Nothing ventured, nothing gained and venture belongs to the adventurous'; 'Third umpires should be changed as often as nappies and for the same reason'; 'He is like a one-legged man in a bum-kicking competition' and 'Eddie Nichols (the West Indian umpire) is a man who cannot find his own buttocks with his two hands'.

That's cleared that up then. All about as coherent as England's batting against spin. The previous autumn, when Britain crashed out of the ERM, Bill Cash stated that, 'We are in a state of political shambles.' By the end of a winter in which we had suffered our first ever defeat to Sri Lanka you could have replaced the word 'political' with 'cricketing' and you wouldn't have been far off the mark. The only saving grace seemed to be that the summer's tourists, Australia, didn't have spinners like the Indians or Sri Lankans. This turned out to be true. The Australian spinners were even better.

Fear is a powerful thing and contrary to how it may seem now, this wasn't something that only occurred to people after 11th September 2001. In fact 9/11 wasn't even the first time the Twin Towers had been attacked. While England had been in India a car bomb had gone off underneath the World Trade Centre and although it had failed to bring down the towers, the blast was still big enough to lead one eyewitness to comment with horrible irony that it 'felt like an airplane hit the building'. Do something dramatic enough and you can change the world simply by catching the imagination. In cricketing terms 4th June 1993 saw just such an intervention.

'If it had been a cheese roll it wouldn't even have landed.' That was how Graham Gooch summed up the ball with which Shane Warne broke the spirit of a cricketing nation. Unfortunately, the projectile Warne sent down to Gatting that afternoon was made of leather not cheddar and left the batsman looking, as Sidhu might have put it, 'as confused as a child in a topless bar'. The worst of it was Gatting was supposed to be England's best player of spin. In that respect it was like Achilles killing Hector.

Like every cricket lover, I have seen innumerable replays of that ball. The thing that strikes me every time is Gatting's face. He looks as if he's just seen something supernatural. He wasn't alone and in truth he had no more chance of knowing what was coming than he had of predicting black majority rule in South Africa when he signed up with Ali Bacher.

I didn't see the ball bowled but I remember where I was, standing next to Bath racecourse watching Webs field everything one-handed because the other was employed holding up his borrowed trousers. Martin had committed the basic cricket tour error of leaving a vital piece of equipment back at the hotel. As a result he was forced to play in the spare whites of a team-mate five inches shorter and four waist sizes bigger than himself. I used the word 'forced' advisedly because there were those of us of a similar stature who simply kept quiet about our extra strides. We could have lent them to him but it wouldn't have been half as funny. As any cricket club would confirm: 'all's fair in love and tour'. All he needed was a big hoop and some comedy braces.

That wasn't even the end of the saga. The following day Webs made the further mistake of leaving his bag unattended on the team bus. As any self-respecting team-mates would have done in the same circumstances, we checked he had remembered his whites this time and then hid them. I should point out the ringleaders of this plot were both over 60 years of age. Funny how a few collective nights on the beer can leave you convinced you're 15 again. Martin's reaction was that of someone even younger and teddy disappeared at a rate of knots in the direction of Taunton. Basically, he refused to play and spent our innings chuntering to himself on the sidelines. However, when one of his team-mates pulled a hamstring taking a quick single he recovered his equilibrium sufficiently to agree to field. By the end of the innings his mood had been brightened further by taking two brilliant catches. 'Oh well. I suppose I got something out of the day.' 'Yes Webs, well done mate. Of course you realise they'll go down in the book as 'caught sub'…'

Back at the racecourse our scorer had the radio on and as well as running the board for our match displayed a separate tally of the Test score to keep us updated. The most significant single moment in modern Anglo-Australian Test history was marked for me by the simple replacing of a one with a two in the wickets column. By the time I watched the highlights that night the accounts of those who had seen it would have had me believing Warne had produced a delivery that defied the laws of physics to a greater extent than JFK's 'magic bullet'.

Even though the reality was slightly (only slightly) less dramatic we all still sat there shaking our heads and wondering out loud 'How the hell do you play that?' One answer was 'by being left-handed'. The previous winter Warne had played four home Tests against West Indies and taken 10 wickets at 31.30. The top three in the tourists' batting averages were Brian Lara, Keith Arthurton and Jimmy Adams. Arthurton was the only one of this trio Warne dismissed in the series. Neil Fairbrother, according to Dexter one of the successes of the winter tour, never got a look in all summer and England didn't pick anybody who batted left-handed until they were already 2-0 down. That season David Gower made over 1,100 Championship runs in only 15 matches with four centuries. When Graham Thorpe was picked for his Test debut at Trent Bridge he made 114 not out.

Thorpe is naturally right-handed and only started batting the other way round as a child to annoy his brothers. Unfortunately it was too late for the rest of England's batsmen to do this.

Usually you only need to produce something dramatic once in order to get into people's heads. However, Warne dispelled any ideas that it might have been a fluke by producing equally vicious spin to dismiss Gooch at Trent Bridge and Edgbaston and an entire generation of English batsmen was out-psyched. Essentially we were back to Alfred Hitchcock and the 'anticipation of the bang'. It didn't matter that half of what Warne said was bullshit – I still don't know what a 'zooter' was supposed to be – after that for series after series he ran rings round our batsmen as much through their anxiety as his brilliance. That summer Shane Warne's best Test bowling analysis was 5-82 at Edgbaston. It was the only time he took five wickets in an innings in the six-match series. His bowling average was 25.79, which was good not superhuman, but, as with the 'Dread Pirate Roberts' in *The Princess Bride*, from now on 'the name was the thing that inspired the necessary fear'.

What England needed was a supremely confident superhero all-rounder not given to disabling bouts of introspection. Unfortunately Andrew Flintoff was 15 and despite making 234 not out in 20 overs in a club match, was a little young to be thrown into the fray. Ian Botham was 37 and on the point of retirement. Botham, along with my boyhood hero Derek 'Arkle' Randall, had announced that this was to be his last season in first-class cricket. Despite all of the great all-rounder's magnificent deeds, Randall remains my favourite cricketer. In some ways that feels like admitting you prefer the girl next door to Nicole Kidman.

It may be just be that there was something seemingly achievable about Randall's appeal. Whereas what Botham did was beyond most mortals, Arkle's idiosyncrasies and obvious technical flaws – one South Australian spectator once described his batting style as 'like an octopus with piles' – gave an impression of fallibility that was only added to by his apparent good nature and lack of sophistication. How could you not have a soft spot for a man who once took a dollop of caviar and then warned Tony Greig to steer clear of the blackcurrant jam because it tasted of fish? He even retained his air of innocence after his wife answered the front door wearing his pads. If it had been almost anyone other than Randall the proffered explanation that she did the dusting in them to speed the breaking-in process would have sounded like one of those stories in the Lancet that begin with 'I was hoovering in the nude when...'. With Randall you knew he was dotty enough for it to be true.

In their final seasons Randall made 280 runs at 28.00 and Botham managed 384 at 25.60 and 13 wickets at 34.61. This was hardly a blaze of glory for either of them but not as ignominious as the simultaneous exit of Ben Johnson who failed a second drugs test and was banned from athletics for life. In 2002, Johnson turned up as the personal trainer to Colonel Gaddafi's son (that's the real Colonel Gaddafi not Javed Miandad). By the same time, Botham was working for Rupert Murdoch as a commentator on *Sky*.

Unlike Flintoff and Botham, Chris Lewis, at 25, was the perfect age to be playing for England. Unfortunately this wasn't the only relevant criterion for selection. In the winter Lewis had made his one and only Test hundred as England crumbled in Madras. Impressive though this had been, it was generally recognised that the inevitability of defeat and the failure of all those around him had meant this was an innings played almost without pressure. It's amazing the confidence some people can draw from the failings of others.

On the final day of the Lord's Test, England were battling to play out time. I stopped for a moment outside a television shop to catch up with the score and saw the whole of Lewis' second innings. He was stumped seventh ball for 0 trying to block Tim May from three yards down the pitch. Earlier in the match a similar dismissal had seen Robin Smith become the first batsman to be sent on his way by the third umpire in a Test in England. Despite this, Smith escaped the cull that followed the innings defeat. The same could not be said of Lewis or the only other player to have taken a century off the Indians, Graeme Hick. Gatting, whose major contribution had been helping to run out Atherton for 99, also went. That was the closest Atherton ever got to a century in a Lord's Test and so like Warne's, his name does not appear on the honours board.

I once saw a lunchtime slot on Channel Four where Atherton took a film crew round Lord's. When he got to the honours board he limited himself to: 'Sadly I was never lucky enough to make a Test hundred here.' If it had been me, the temptation to add 'But that fat bastard Gatting did once run me out for 99' would have been overwhelming.

The wholesale changes made by the selectors for Trent Bridge stoked up one of the debates that raged through this summer and much of the 1990s. At the start of the season Chris Cowdrey had used a column in the *News of the World* to suggest Lord's should ban 'non-Englishmen' from playing for England. Apparently fed up with the number of 'foreigners' playing for our Test side, Cowdrey suggested the selectors should 'kick out' Smith and Hick and shut the door permanently on Allan Lamb. Presumably he would have approved of the removal of Hick and possibly Lewis but not of their replacement by the 'Australian' Martin McCague and the Madras-born Nasser Hussain.

Cowdrey's article raises two interesting questions. Firstly, how do you define a 'non-Englishman' and secondly what was the problem with these people playing for England anyway?

You could take a simplistic approach to the first question and restrict eligibility to those born in this country. Leaving aside the issues raised by the likes of Mike Denness (Scottish) and Steve Watkin (Welsh), a major problem with this definition is that it would have excluded Cowdrey's own father who was born in Putamala, India and the then chairman of selectors Ted Dexter who entered the world via Milan. I doubt if John Woodcock would have suggested either of them wasn't 'an Englishman through and through'.

Alternatively you could require English parentage, except that a combination of this and four years' residence is exactly how Lamb and Smith qualified to play for England in the first place.

You might try looking at where someone was raised, but then how would you define someone like Craig White who was born in Morley, went to Australia at the age of 10 when his parents emigrated and took years of abuse for being a 'Pom' before coming back to live here as a teenager?

Finally, how about using where someone has chosen to make their home? No, that doesn't work either because Hick qualified on residency grounds.

The complicated issue of how you define nationality wasn't restricted to England. Although he was born in Northern Ireland, Martin McCague had spent most of his life in Australia and even graduated from their national cricket academy. One Sydney newspaper went as far as to call him 'a rat joining a sinking ship', an attitude which completely ignored the presence for years in the Australian side of Kepler Wessels, a man who went straight back to play for South Africa on their readmission and the inclusion in Australia's football World Cup squad of Zamica, Bosnich, Zelic, Ivanovic, Durakovic, Glagovejic, Van Blerk, Lazaridis, Polak, Farina and Vidmar.

The question of what it means to be a particular nationality is only going to get more complicated. As travel becomes easier, cultures will mix ever more readily and the distinctions between them will become blurred and less of an issue. The England team has already had a Papua-New Guinean-Welsh-Australian wicket-keeper and the majority of the discussion about him revolved around whether he could catch. I always find it strange when people proudly claim to come from 'good old Anglo-Saxon stock' as if that proves they are 'proper English'. This overlooks the fact that neither the Angles nor the Saxons were indigenous to these islands and were every bit as much invaders as the Normans who overthrew them. The only difference is the Normans were nasty swarthy Frenchmen with helmets even sillier than Dennis Amiss'.

So what was Cowdrey's problem with the likes of Lamb and Smith playing for England? This is after all a country that has had kings who couldn't speak the language. I'm sure it wasn't that he felt having a 'pure English' national team was desirable in and of itself. Aside from being impossible to define, this sort of thinking has the potential to take you down a very dangerous road indeed. Much more likely is Cowdrey agreed with Ian Chappell's assessment of one of the reasons why the Australians won so easily that summer i.e. the inclusion of too many 'career cricketers' in the England side had diluted pride in playing for the national team.

Chappell's view was that, 'Lack of pride manifests itself in a number of ways and in England's case the most serious has been to capitulate in a Test when trouble loomed.' In this analysis the 'career cricketers' chose to play for England out of convenience rather than commitment so that when the chips were down their courage failed them. When England's football team lost a World Cup qualifier to Northern Ireland in 2005, Ian Wright suggested this was because a foreigner like Sven-Goran Eriksson couldn't rouse the national pride required to produce a performance of the necessary standard. Wright offered this opinion at exactly the same time as a Zimbabwean coach was masterminding the England cricket team's first series win for more than 18 years over the previously all-conquering Australians.

Perhaps the best examples of the sort of cricketers Chappell might have pointed the finger at are Lamb, Smith, Hick and from the modern era, Pietersen? I think Lamb's six centuries against the West Indies, the numerous physical batterings Smith took from the same bowlers and Pietersen's hundred at the Oval in 2005 make it hard to accuse the three

South African-born players on that list of lacking commitment to the cause.

Hick is another matter. His reputation of never scoring runs under pressure is not entirely deserved. His supporters can legitimately point to a battling 96 in the second innings at Jamaica in 1994, a vital counter-attacking 67 against the same opposition at Lord's in 1995 and a superb 141 against Donald, Pollock and Schultz at their fastest that rescued England from 64-3 on the first day of the series in South Africa in 1995/96. The potential significance of this last innings was lost when rain washed out the final three days of the match. Nevertheless, Hick was still clearly someone who never achieved for England at the level his talent demanded. But is that really to do with where he was born?

When he first played for England, Hick had lived here for seven years. By his retirement this had increased by 17. Judging by the number of runs he scored there, he regarded Worcester as his home. And that, it would seem, is the point. Hick's reputation is of never feeling comfortable at Test level, of being uncertain of his ability to dominate in the way he did in domestic cricket or, put another way, of whether he truly belonged in that company. In that respect he was no different to another young batsman selected by England that year, Mark Lathwell.

The only thing as big as Lathwell's obviously massive talent was the level of self-doubt about his ability and/or desire to perform in the Test arena: 'I'm the sort of person who would always prefer to be doing something in the background rather than the front.' When he was dropped after two Tests it seemed like a relief to him. Mark Lathwell was born in Bletchley.

It's interesting to muse on whether the apparently insecure Hick might have benefited from being a big fish in the smaller pond of the Zimbabwean Test team where his confidence might have been boosted by his pre-eminence in the side. Nevertheless the fact remains that some people thrive on the pressure of Test cricket – Gower could rarely rouse himself for anything less – and some people don't. That is a matter of personality not nationality. In 24 Tests for Australia, Kepler Wessels' batting average was 42.95; in 16 for South Africa it was 38.03.

The fact that Chris Lewis was born in Guyana, had nothing to do with his inability to lay a bat on Tim May's arm ball and to suggest that it did was to fall into the trap English cricketers fell into time and time again. That is to say, convincing themselves there was only one reason why the Test team lost so consistently. The attraction of this sort of thinking is that it's much easier to solve one problem than it is to solve many and the beauty of this particular explanation for failure was it wasn't even our fault. It was the bloody foreigners.

Ironically, given they went in with an attack led by McCague and the 'New Zealander' Caddick, England produced a much improved performance at Trent Bridge. Smith made 86 and 50, Hussain 71 and 47 not out, McCague took four wickets in the first innings and Caddick three in the second as England reduced the Australians to 115-6 at tea on the last day. The draw the home side achieved was bettered only by a win at the Oval. Indeed you could argue this effort was even more worthy coming as it did with the series still alive. Victory in the final match was only attained after Dexter, Gooch's hold on the captaincy and the Ashes had already gone.

I went to both of the Tests in between Nottingham and the Oval. At Headingley I saw the tourists put the finishing touches to their 653-4 declared before watching England subside to 195-7 on the Saturday. Warne took 1-106 in the match and England still lost by an innings and 148 runs.

At Edgbaston I picked the Friday on the basis you usually get to see both teams bat. At least I got that right. I saw England's number 11, Mark Ilott, caught behind off the fourth ball of the day from Paul Reiffel and Australia collapse to 80-4. For two balls it was possible to believe all we had needed was Atherton's vibrant new captaincy. Then Stewart missed stumping Steve Waugh on 0 (where was Jack Russell when you needed him?) and old flint-eyes spent most of the rest of the day putting on 153 for the fifth wicket with his brother.

It comes to something when losing by eight wickets is an improvement. Atherton became the eighth England captain in a row to lose his first match in charge. You had to go back to Bob Willis in 1982 to find someone who had started with a win. No one matched Willis until Nasser Hussain in 1999.

At least Atherton was in good company. I was starting my first season as captain at Stoneleigh with similar levels of success. Then, for one match at least, the recruitment of someone else who had been at Edgbaston provided us with an up-turn in fortunes.

Mushtaq Mohammed played one game for Stoneleigh. At the start of the season we had been joined by Masood, a Pakistani who possessed what looked like a genuine touring sweater and a fund of name-dropping stories about various internationals. He was constantly suggesting he could get 'Mushy' to play, so one day I called his bluff and said 'Go on then; Heckley at home next Sunday!' I couldn't believe it when he actually turned up.

At that time Heckley had what we regarded as a good bowling side and regularly skittled us for embarrassingly low scores. Therefore I had no qualms about fielding a former Test player against them. However, Webs thought it was ridiculous and unfair of us to spring such a thing on our unsuspecting opponents. The fact that he was the one who got dropped to accommodate our mate Mushy had nothing to do with it.

On the afternoon of the game, Webs turned up to pay his subs and have a quick moan. On his way home he briefly sat with me on the deep cover boundary to watch the great man in full flow. I was quite enjoying the easiest looking 89 I've ever seen but Martin thought it was 'just silly' and got up to go at the exact moment Mushtaq launched into a perfect lofted straight drive. The ball described an arc and disappeared behind some trees into the car park. An instant later there was a crashing noise. 'Now look! He's gone and broken some poor bastard's windscreen.'

He hadn't... it was Webs' sunroof.

England were 4-0 down and staring at only the second 5-0 defeat in Ashes history. Then my boiler blew up. It sounds like a bad thing, but actually a combination of this, Ernest a gas engineer who could only do 'this afternoon or Friday, mate', and an understanding boss, enabled me to watch the last afternoon of England's only victory of the summer.

This was the first series in which the BBC used stump cameras and Australia's first innings had already given me what is still my favourite view from one: an image of clear blue sky provided by Steve Waugh's off peg. Although the second innings produced no single moment quite as satisfying as this, while 'call me Ernie' returned my hot water supply, Fraser, Malcolm and Watkin restored at least some lost pride in my team. What a pity none of them had played before in the series.

In 1993, John Aggleton, a psychologist from Durham University, announced the results of a study of 10,000 first-class cricketers' careers. From his research he concluded that left-arm bowlers were likely to die two years earlier than right-armers. Phil Edmonds said he found the findings 'depressing'. He needed to find something more substantial to worry about. England's batsmen thought they already had. From now on it didn't matter where they went or what they achieved it was impossible to remove from the back of their minds the image of a blond Aussie beach-bum with a steel-sprung right wrist and no run-up. They couldn't always see him but they knew he was out there somewhere… waiting.

TWENTY

According to the Health and Safety Executive, in 1994 eight people were injured by placemats. Initially you would think anybody who got hurt in this way must have been a bit unlucky. However, the statistic does beg an important question: 'What were they doing with the placemat at the time?' It would seem even the most apparently innocent item can cause big problems if the wrong people are involved.

Take hair-clippers for example. Even if they had existed in his day they were unlikely to have been Sweeney Todd's weapon of choice. However, combine them with Devon Malcolm and Chris Lewis and you have a case of 'Just go through Mr Accident, Mr Lewis is ready for you now.'

At the start of England's tour to the West Indies in 1993-94, Chris Lewis asked Devon Malcolm to shave his head. Big Devon left Lewis with several bits of tissue paper stuck on nicks to his scalp but at least managed not to sever any part of his teammate's anatomy. Unfortunately, Lewis reasoned there was no point in having an impressive new look if you immediately hid it under a hat. As a result he got sunstroke and missed the opening match of the tour. The team's manager, Mike Smith, informed the press that: 'We shall be telling Chris to wear a hat and keep out of the sun in future.' A Test cricketer who stays out of the sun is an interesting concept and perhaps Smith's suggestion was one reason why, part way through the tour, it was announced that Ray Illingworth had been preferred as the new chairman of selectors.

Illingworth is regarded by many as England's best post-war captain, shading it over Brearley by virtue of having been worth his place in the side. He had been a summariser on the BBC for a number of years and had never been afraid to offer his opinions on what England were doing wrong. A professional Yorkshireman from the 'kick up the backside' school of management, he gave every impression the only reason why he might put an arm round a player's shoulder would be as a precursor to a head-lock. When he sacked the team's chaplain, the Rev. Andrew Wingfield-Digby, during his first Test in charge, his explanation was: 'If any of the players need a shoulder to cry on, they're not the men to go out and stuff the Aussies next winter.'

Also, not unreasonably, Illingworth wasn't interested in responsibility without control. In 1986 he had turned down the chance to be England's first team manager because the position carried too little power. Now it was widely rumoured that not content with securing the chairman's job Smith had coveted he was also after Keith Fletcher's.

Shortly after his appointment Illingworth completed a questionnaire for *The Cricketer*. In it he was asked which current players he admired, his response was 'None'. Apparently he had little regard for the likes of Lara, Tendulkar, Waugh and Warne and his reply could easily have been taken by his new charges as meaning 'as far as I'm concerned every last one of you is rubbish'. When this is combined with his desire to be a one-man management team, the timing of his appointment probably wasn't ideal from the point of view of building team morale.

If Illingworth, in contrast to recent Nobel Peace Prize-winners Yitzak Rabin and Yasser Arafat, may have been unlikely to win any diplomacy awards, he wasn't responsible for the make-up of the first England Test touring party since 1976-77 not to include at least one of Gatting, Gower or Gooch.

Having lost the captaincy, Gooch declined to make himself available for the tour and Gower and Gatting were considered too old to be part of the 25-year-old captain's brave new team. As Atherton himself said, it was time 'to identify young players with two things: talent and temperament and then show faith in them'. Gower's response to his omission was to retire from first-class cricket and take Illingworth's place on the BBC commentary team.

When I think of Gower's career, 'waste' is the word that comes to mind. This isn't because even a Test average as high as 44.25 does scant justice to his talent – the thrill of seeing him in full flow was only heightened by the fact there was nothing 'inevitable' about one of his hundreds – it's more that the whim of one man deprived England of potentially the best years of one of its rarest talents. David Gower was 32 when Gooch was appointed captain for the previous tour to the West

Indies in 1989-90. From that point until the left-hander's premature retirement at 36, England played 39 Test matches (40 if you include a washout in Georgetown). Gower featured in only 11 of these.

At least with a new captain in place the selectors' understandable decision to go with youth must have been easier to stomach than some of Gower's earlier omissions. As he himself said: 'The writing on the wall, as evinced by the direction England's selectors have taken both with their late-season and winter-tour choices, was enough to make me think now would be a good time to quit, with head held high...' The following winter England toured Australia and Gooch and Gatting were included in one of the most laughably immobile fielding sides of the modern era.

In the early part of 1994, American Olympic skating hopeful, Nancy Kerrigan was attacked by a mystery assailant who struck her across the knee with an iron bar. Investigations uncovered that the attacker was the wonderfully named Kevin Gilooly, ex-husband of Kerrigan's big rival Tonia Harding. Harding had hoped one of sporting history's least subtle attempts at nobbling the opposition would help gain her Olympic selection. The West Indies didn't need to stoop to anything so nefarious. As Lewis had already proved, if they wanted an Englishman to get crocked all they had to do was wait.

England's injury record in the Caribbean wasn't pretty. Since R.E.S. Wyatt had his jaw broken on the 1934-35 trip they had only twice managed to get through a West Indian tour without either their captain or vice-captain being invalided-out through illness or injury. It wasn't even as if they 'did it in singles'. In 1980/81 they lost two vice-captains when Willis had to go home with a knee injury and then his replacement, Geoff Miller, fell ill and in 1985-86 Gatting had his nose rearranged by Malcolm Marshall, bravely returned after corrective surgery, and promptly broke his thumb in his first match back. In this respect it was a minor miracle both Atherton and Stewart made it to the end of the trip unscathed. However, on this tour it was getting all the right bowlers on the field at the same time that was the problem.

When England had won at the Oval the previous summer, Fraser, Malcolm and Watkin had shared all 20 Australian wickets. In the Caribbean they didn't play a single Test together; in fact Watkin never played again. Fraser was injured for the opening match of the series and the Welshman wasn't selected. By the time the Middlesex man was available Malcolm had a knee problem that required a trip home for exploratory surgery.

England being unable to put out their best bowling attack wasn't an uncommon occurrence. For years I bemoaned how unlucky we were with injuries, particularly to key bowlers at vital times. Now I realise it had nothing to do with luck.

In 2005, England beat Australia and used only 12 men throughout the series. None of their four-pronged pace attack was required to exhaust themselves with seven-day-a-week county cricket and the only change the selectors made was forced on them by the bone-spur in Simon Jones' ankle. A few months previously, Andrew Flintoff had required surgery on a similar problem. The employment of a top surgeon and the implementation of a closely monitored rehabilitation programme, all under the auspices of the England set-up, enabled Flintoff to return to cricket ahead of schedule and fit enough to produce the series of stunning performances without which the Ashes would not have been secured. The system didn't guarantee victory over what was still a great Australian side, but at least we gave ourselves the best possible chance by being able to put out our best possible side.

During the 1990s, England's best four seam bowlers were Fraser, Gough, Caddick and Cork. In an era where Alec Stewart was the wicket-keeper and taking account of Cork's batting ability, there was no cricketing reason why these four (with a spinner like Croft or Giles) could not have formed England's bowling attack. From Cork's first Test in 1995 until Fraser's move into journalism at the start of 2002, England played 79 Test matches. In that period these four bowlers never played in the same Test team together and any three of them only combined on 19 occasions. Gough missed 37 Tests out of the 95 England played between his debut and retirement, Caddick sat out most of the 1995 season with career-threatening shin splints, Cork was ruled out of the 1997 Ashes series with a hernia and Fraser spent the early part of the '90s recovering from a hip injury caused by over-bowling and the latter part trying to convince the selectors (particularly Ray Illingworth) that the resultant loss of 'nip' in his bowling didn't mean he was a spent force at international level.

As Fraser's hip injury proved, in the Test arena this problem becomes self-perpetuating. If you only get one or two of your best bowlers onto the field then they do most of the bowling and can find themselves injured through over work by the time their team-mates are fit again. As England's team doctor for the 1996 World Cup put it when Cork was forced to carry a knee injury through the tournament: 'He doesn't need surgery or anything. He just needs a rest. But if you are England's best bowler it seems inevitable that you are bowled into the ground.' This was why for years it seemed England only had one, or possibly two bowlers to whom they could turn if they really needed a wicket.

The fact English cricketers were injury-prone didn't stop the West Indians 'going after' one or two of our players. Two in particular stand out for different reasons. The first, Mike Atherton, was an obvious target given he was the captain. Atherton had made his Test debut just before the previous trip to the Caribbean but had been sent on the A tour to Kenya and Zimbabwe instead because there seemed to be a perception that his fresh-faced appearance indicated he might be too delicate a flower to flourish in the West Indian hothouse. Appearances could not have been more deceptive. It turned out he was as hard as nails.

At the start of England's second innings in the first Test, Courtney Walsh bowled a two-hour spell during which he subjected Atherton to as searching a barrage of fast short-pitched deliveries as he can ever have experienced. Walsh did finally get his man but not before Atherton had stood up to the assault so well that nothing of its kind was attempted against him by the home side for the rest of the series. Derek Randall had just retired leaving a vacancy. If it's possible to have a hero younger than yourself then in the course of that spell Atherton became mine.

The captain wasn't the only England batsman Walsh targeted in that innings. The other was Devon Malcolm. England led by only 55 when their ninth second-innings wicket fell. Walsh tried yorking Malcolm but bowled a succession of half-volleys instead, which the batsman somehow spanked for four. The bowler responded by going around the wicket and aiming bouncer after bouncer at the body. Malcolm was hit three times in the same over. It was like watching a karate expert beat up a sheep, but Ian Robinson, the Zimbabwean umpire appointed for the match from the new international panel, did nothing.

It was as clear a case of intimidatory bowling as you could ever see but despite much huffing and puffing in the British press, nothing happened. Perhaps the advent of helmets and chest protectors made umpires less inclined to intervene because they concluded that 'at least he's not going to get killed'? Alternatively, maybe the problem went deeper? Ian Wooldridge wrote in the *Daily Mail* at the time: 'I am told that whenever the intimidation issue is raised at [ICC] conferences, the West Indies simply refuse to discuss it. Well they would, wouldn't they?

But what kind of an international governing body is that?' It's hard to blame an umpire for failing to tackle a difficult issue head-on if he thinks his masters lack the stomach to do the same thing.

Despite this, the West Indies didn't resort to those sort of tactics again. Indeed for the remainder of the series, England had more to worry about from Lara's intimidatory batting. Atherton made it onto the Georgetown honours board with 144 but was trumped by the left-hander's 167. The general feeling was that we had been lucky to get him for as few as that. After our defeat by an innings and 44 runs, Colin Croft commented that if he were in the England team he would 'resign from embarrassment' and, 'If this is the best young talent then the selectors need to go back to the drawing-board.' That was before we were bowled out for 46 in Trinidad.

To even the most ardent of West Indian fans England's utter humiliation at the hands of Curtley Ambrose must have come as a bit of surprise. For England fans 'shell-shock' better describes the experience. Unfortunately, I was now working at the Citizens Advice Bureau in Wolverhampton. Nothing particularly terrible about that in itself, except one of my colleagues was Mike, one of the most fanatical West Indies supporters in England. I thought he had 'given me loads' during the first two Tests, but as I slumped into work with England at 40-8 overnight I realised I was wrong.

You would have got very long odds on England dishing out a similar humiliation to the same opponents only ten years later. At 12/1 against in a two-horse race they weren't much shorter on what happened next.

In a strange way it was almost worse that England came out and won at Bridgetown. Supporting them was like a passionate love affair with the most mixed-up woman in the world, occasionally wonderful but constantly confusing. Even in victory I felt like screaming at them: 'If you can go out and defeat the most powerful side in the world on a ground that no one had beaten them on for nearly 60 years, why do you put me through 46 all out?'

This was a period in which England were involved in setting innumerable Test records; for the opposition, that is. Within five days of the win in Bridgetown the tourists conceded the highest ever individual Test score to Brian Lara. The Trinidadian was probably within a millimetre of falling at the last hurdle as photographs of the pull shot with which he reached 369 show his off bail out of its groove and perched precariously on top of the stump. 'Hit wicket bowled Lewis 365' would have been a bit of a sickener, but we all need something to aspire to and as Lara said: 'I will be aiming to beat my record and I think I can do it one day.'

When Gower's side had returned from the Caribbean, I had naively thought months of battling the fastest bowlers in the world would make facing India's battery of dibbly-dobbly medium pacers a cakewalk by comparison. They stuffed us 2-0 and Gower lost his job. In 1994, the first tourists of a split summer were New Zealand, so I feared the worst. Atherton's tenure of the England captaincy did come under threat but only when the Kiwis had gone home.

Illingworth's influence was immediately apparent. Of the 11 who played in the Antigua run-fest only five survived for the first Test at Nottingham and as Jessie from the newly arrived *Fast Show* might have put it: 'This week I shall mostly be picking Yorkshiremen.' Darren Gough had made a promising one-day international showing and would have been in the team if he hadn't started as he meant to go on and picked up a side-strain. At least he wasn't hanging by his balls from a hook in a sightscreen like the Mark Hubbard of Seaton CC. The *Sidmouth Midweek Herald* reported that his untimely slip during a repair job had resulted in seven stitches in his testicles. I only hope, for his sake, the reporter meant scrotum.

Despite Goughie's absence there were still another three Yorkies in the squad: Craig White, Steve Rhodes (who admittedly played for Worcestershire) and the left-arm spinner Richard Stemp. None of these established themselves in the side under Illingworth. Stemp became one of the 'nearly men', Rhodes' Test career was over by the following summer and White needed a Zimbabwean to bring the best out of him.

For years after his initial selection, Craig White seemed to be a prime example of one of the worst products of the English system, a mediocre bits-and-pieces all-rounder not worth his place in the side for one discipline alone. I had a running joke with a friend from Yorkshire who 'knowing' he was talking rubbish would constantly tout White as the solution to all England's ills. Illingworth had clearly spotted something in him that had passed Mike Atherton by and the captain's obvious lack of faith made it clear that here was a selection he resented having foisted upon him.

Duncan Fletcher saw the same potential as Illingworth, the big difference being the Zimbabwean, albeit only for a short time, managed to realise it. Illingworth's more than apparent absence of a touchy-feely side and Atherton's underwhelming assessment of his abilities must have fatally undermined White's notoriously fragile confidence. On the other hand, the all-rounder has spoken of coming out of his first meeting with Fletcher feeling '10 feet tall'.

The attitude of the most successful coach England has ever had is that any county all-rounder will, almost by definition, start off as a bits-and-pieces player at Test level. The secret is to improve their skills to a point where this is no longer the case. When Andrew Flintoff first made it into the England side he was the sort of player who might have taken two or three wickets in an innings and scored a quick 40. For a brief period Duncan Fletcher turned Craig White into an all-rounder capable of scoring a Test hundred and bowling in-swinging yorkers at 90 mph. The shame of it is that White was 30 before Fletcher got hold of him.

It was another all-rounder, possibly born in the wrong era, who dominated at Trent Bridge. Phil DeFreitas took nine wickets in the match and scored 51 not out as England crushed New Zealand. Even then Brian Lara managed to upstage this by finishing off his 501 not out on the same afternoon as victory was secured.

While this had been going on I had been in the process of nearly killing a green-keeper.

For as long as I had been a member of the club, Stoneleigh had always toured around Bath. We returned to the same place year after year mainly on the strength of our hotel's all-night bar and the close proximity of a snooker hall with the most liberal interpretation of the licensing laws I've ever seen. One further attraction for some members of the team was the nine-hole golf course. I'm a crap golfer but a similar lack of talent never stopped me playing cricket so I decided: why not have a go?

I played a four-ball with Webs, 'Sumo' and Brian. 'Sumo,' or Colin to use his real name, is the most talented cricketer I've played with. Numerous spells of accurate fast-medium outswing combined with an obviously 'comfortable' physique confirmed he was far more likely to eat a pie than bowl one. As for batting, only Gower made it look easier. Colin's feats were reported on by Brian, a talented leg-spinner and local sports journalist, who never missed an opportunity to refer to 'Stoneleigh's tubby all-rounder'.

We may have had divergent cricketing abilities but as a quartet of golfers we were evenly matched. On the final tee we stood all-square surveying a straight fairway. A solitary figure tending a bunker 100 yards away on the left was the only distraction. The green-keeper turned and watched us tee-off. All went well until I hooked in his direction. Had I been in his position, the collective shout of 'Fore!' would have been enough to find me on the deck. However, our man calmly turned his back on the ball and remained standing. There was just enough time for me to think he had seen it was clearing him and was helpfully checking the out-of-bounds, before it cannoned into the back of his head and ricocheted at a right angle. He dropped to his knees like a publicity poster for *Platoon.*

When we reached him he was mercifully still conscious and, incredibly, apologizing while reassuring me it wasn't my fault. Some of his colleagues quickly carried him off with blood pouring from the back of his head. The next time I saw him he was slumped against a wall mumbling at some paramedics. By now the story had spread to the rest of our party who, gathered to watch my discomfort, were making the sort of noises Boycott's England team-mates made when Botham deliberately ran him out in New Zealand. They nearly exploded when the man's boss tried to comfort me. 'Don't worry if he sounds a bit incoherent, son. He's been like that for a while anyway...ever since they had to put the plate in his head.'

Fortunately this story has a happy ending in that no lasting damage had been done to my victim. But I haven't played golf since.

If it hadn't been that green-keeper's year, 'What with his wife leaving him n'all', things seemed to be looking up for England. Draws at Lord's and Old Trafford had given us the series against the Kiwis. In the week leading up to the Manchester game DeFreitas had saved the life of an elderly neighbour by climbing in through a window and carrying him away from a kitchen fire. On the field his performances were heroic enough to earn him the man of the series award and when this was combined with Gough's 65 and 4-47 on debut the future was starting to look a lot brighter. Then, as Damon Albarn might have put it, we were 'rudely awakened by the dustman'.

South Africa were the second tourists of the summer. The series opened at Lord's almost 29 years to the day since the teams had last met there. Much had changed since, not least the fact the Republic now had a black president. There were many things for which the match could have been remembered: Wessels' hundred as captain, England being bowled out for 99 or even Archbishop Desmond Tutu being refused entry to the pavilion. I have a friend who claims his dog-collared, vicar cousin was once stopped in similar circumstances by a Lord's attendant who uttered in a single word 'sorrysiryoucantgointherewithoutatiebegginyourpardonreverend.'

However, this match will be forever recalled for the dusty contents of Atherton's pockets. On the Saturday afternoon, when England were already looking down the barrel of a big defeat, their captain was seen on television undertaking an 'unfamiliar action' with the ball. The match referee, Peter Burge, the man who had massacred England's bowlers the week before I was born, called Atherton in to see him and then announced he had accepted the player's explanation. Unfortunately, he neglected to tell anybody what that explanation was.

Then more TV pictures came out which looked even worse and Atherton was forced to admit he had lied to Burge about his pockets being empty. Illingworth issued a pre-emptive £2000 fine (apparently half for the dirt and half for lying about it) in an attempt to save the captain's neck. Despite resignation calls from many, including the BBC's cricket correspondent, he succeeded.

Atherton's explanation that he was using the dirt to dry his hands and his hands to dry the ball doesn't constitute a breach of Law 42 that governs unfair play. This does beg the questions: 'Why didn't he just say that in the first place?' and 'Why did he get fined for it?' The answer to both is probably, as a highly intelligent man like Atherton would have appreciated, that the appearance of things is sometimes more important than their substance. Cricket prides itself on an image of utmost probity – most sports have mere 'rules' rather than 'laws' – and the England captain is expected to be a paragon of gentlemanly virtue. Admitting to having dirt in the pocket would have been owning up to something that looked suspect, not an easy thing to do in context. Having said that, dissembling was probably crime enough in some people's eyes and although the umpires confirmed the condition of the ball had not been changed, both the image of the England captain and the game were damaged.

In a curious way, Illingworth was probably quite happy because now he had a captain who owed his job to the chairman of selectors. 'I think Craig deserves a place on the plane to Australia, don't you Mike?'

It wasn't just England's image that had taken a battering at Lord's. Not to put too fine a point on it, they had been murdered. However, after Trinidad and Barbados we knew this didn't necessarily mean anything. At Leeds, Atherton nearly answered his detractors with a century but fell one short (at least he wasn't run out this time) and Thorpe, Stewart and Rhodes took us to a total of 477 that was 198 runs more than we had managed in two innings at headquarters.

The point about what you can miss if you arrive late for Test matches was never better illustrated than on the Saturday. I sat smugly in my seat as the tourists went from 31-1 overnight to 31-3 in the first four balls of the day. We had them 105-5 and then Jonty Rhodes (annoying little bastard) put on 94 with Peter Kirsten and that was that: draw.

There is another way you can miss out on a lot of cricket. Buying tickets for the Sunday of an England Test match. Two years earlier I had witnessed only the last rites of a defeat by Pakistan. As I arrived at the Oval this time I knew again I was unlikely to see more than a morning's cricket. I didn't care, I was about to witness us square the series with a victory founded on brash, aggressive, uplifting, counter-attacking cricket.

With half an hour to go on the Friday evening, England had been 112 behind with only three first-innings wickets left. Then DeFreitas and Gough, proving Illingworth's stated belief in the value of having bowlers who could bat, smashed 59 before the close in a display of tail-end hitting, the like of which we usually received but never dished out. The pair were quickly separated the following morning and as the innings petered out, Fanie de Villiers thought it would be a good idea to bowl a first-ball bouncer to Devon Malcolm. Everyone knows it hit him between the eyes and the rest, as they say, is 'You guys are history.'

That afternoon 'Sumo' had a similar experience, except he was hit on the back of the head by a wayward throw while umpiring at square-leg. He didn't get up and take 9-57 but then, to be fair, he was unconscious.

The damage that results from some actions is apparent almost instantly and the recovery time for the injured party similarly speedy. From the moment it was released de Villiers' bouncer took well under a second to reach Malcolm's head. Thanks to the batsman's helmet the effects were momentary and the consequences for the South Africans almost immediate. However, other hurts are longer in the making and can't be shrugged off so easily. When John Major's government sold off Rover to BMW in February 1994, he commented that: 'The prospects for Rover in the future are excellent.' Try telling that to the staff who worked at Longbridge now.

On 1st October 1994, Fiona and I were married. I had made sure that this happened on the first Saturday outside of the cricket season, something about which she had seemed only jokily unimpressed. A month earlier, Illingworth and his colleagues, although they didn't mean to, selected a squad for Australia that ended up being an embarrassment.

However, a bit of thought can sometimes make even unintentional consequences seem obvious. If you put together a side that includes Gooch, Gatting, Tufnell, Malcolm and 'Fatty' Crawley you don't have to be Mystic Meg to know the fielding might be a bit of a problem. Similarly when you send the likes of McCague, Gough and White away for three and a half months Down Under, you might have an inkling that the odd injury is a possibility. As I was to find out, sometimes things can come back and bite you.

TWENTY-ONE

On 19th November 1994, the first National Lottery draw took place. I didn't buy a ticket because I reckoned the odds were shorter on me being called up to England's cricket team. I wasn't wrong.

Much to the relief of Phil Tufnell, the Durham University researchers had amended their conclusions and now believed left-arm bowlers didn't die younger than right-armers but, rather, were more prone to dying in warfare. They reached no conclusions about which group was more likely to get injured.

By the end of the tour to Australia in the winter of 1994-95, England had used 22 players. This was in the days before separate squads for the Tests and one-day tournaments so the turnover was entirely attributable to illness or injury. Six of the original squad were invalided out of the trip and one of the replacements, Neil Fairbrother, injured his shoulder and had to go home as well. In addition, at various times, the tourists lost Devon Malcolm (chickenpox), Joey Benjamin (chickenpox originally misdiagnosed as shingles), Atherton (bad back), Thorpe (strained adductor muscle), DeFreitas (groin *and* hamstring) and Crawley (strained calf). Two things occur to me looking at that list. What was Joey Benjamin doing there in the first place and how did John Crawley do anything strenuous enough to pull his calf?

The Australian press love ripping it out of the English. Sometimes this is done to try and destabilize a team they fear. In 1991, David Campese's widely reported comments about the England rugby team's 'boring' method of play succeeded in getting them to tear up their usual game-plan and blow the World Cup final as a result. In 2003, the Aussie media tried it again and the story was put about that Clive Woodward's side had abandoned a training session after a mystery 'white substance' had been found on the practice ground. Subsequent investigations showed this to be the try line.

On Atherton's tour, *The Age* took a similar approach by beginning its preview of the Melbourne Test with: 'England trained and grass grew at the MCG yesterday; two activities virtually indistinguishable from one another in tempo, but each with its own fascination.' Unfortunately, there was no fear involved in this assessment, it was merely an expression of contempt from a position of evident superiority. If the reporter had waited a bit he might have been able to mention the physio breaking his finger taking part in a fielding drill.

It wasn't just the press who were ragging the English. Before the tour had even started the home administrators had come up with the hilarious idea of scheduling the usually triangular Benson and Hedges World Series one-day tournament as a four-way affair between Australia, England, Zimbabwe and … Australia A. The potential for English embarrassment from such a line-up is obvious. The finals of the Benson and Hedges World Series that winter were played between Australia and Australia A.

In our defence, the top six in the second team's batting line-up were Blewett, Hayden, Martyn, Bevan, Langer and Ponting, but even so it comes to something when a 23-year-old (Crawley) is omitted from the one-day side because a 41-year-old (Gooch) is considered a better fielder.

Even as stern a critic as Mike Atherton would have struggled to blame chickenpox on the inadequacies of the English county game but he had plenty of other ammunition by the end of this tour. If a team is properly prepared by its domestic system and national set-up, it simply doesn't experience that many injuries. Excessive county cricket put inordinate physical strain on England's players. By the end of the Ashes-winning summer of 2005 the centrally-contracted Marcus Trescothick and Andrew Flintoff had respectively scored more runs and taken more wickets in Test cricket than they had in the County Championship. England won the Ashes because our batsmen made big enough totals to put the Aussies under pressure and because our four-pronged pace attack stayed together long enough to give us a lead in the series.

In 1994-95, it wasn't just a spate of physical injuries that made England look so disorganized and inept. There were also the panic attacks inspired by the spiky-blond-haired Bogeyman to contend with. Although Alec Stewart might have thought he had seen a long-hop that turned out to be a perfectly pitched flipper, there was nothing imaginary about the 8-71 Warne took at Brisbane. When he followed this up with 6-64 and a second-innings hat-trick at Melbourne, the phantom began to have some substance. By the time he slipped back into the mist – his seven wickets in the last three Tests cost 51.28 – and everyone stopped running around in different directions waving their arms about, the damage was already done.

Incidentally, Glenn McGrath made his Ashes debut in this series. He played two matches, scored no runs and took six wickets at 38.16. He bowled so untidily at Brisbane that Geoff Boycott, commentating on the radio, dismissed him as 'pretty ordinary'.

The previous year Nick Leeson had been suspended by Singapore Cricket Club for 'ungentlemanly conduct' after one of his guests was involved in an incident in the billiard-room. Now, as England were floundering their way through the first part of the tour, he was in the process of getting himself into some more trouble: £860 million's worth to be exact. Unfortunately, it seemed he wasn't the only one doing some gambling.

The footballing world had been rocked by allegations that Bruce Grobelaar, among others, had been paid by Far Eastern betting syndicates to throw matches. While I could see that if you wanted to chuck a game you would have to have the goalkeeper 'on board', I couldn't imagine he could lose all on his own. After all if your back four played so well the opposition never got a shot on target, how could you concede a goal? Alternatively, if your team includes the likes of Rush and Dalglish how do you guarantee they won't score more than you give away?

This suggested to me that there were three possible scenarios: 1) the allegations were false; 2) those involved were being paid to ensure that certain specific events took place within a match rather than actually fixing the result or 3) there were far more people involved and the problem was much bigger than the odd bent goalie.

The first of these was obviously the most palatable but unfortunately it seemed the least likely. The second was plausible if only because it had the potential to allow those involved to convince themselves they weren't doing anything wrong when the game wasn't being thrown as such. I'm sure this is exactly what Hansie Cronje managed to believe when he earned his leather jacket for the 'positive result' at Centurion Park in January 2000. The final possibility was too terrible to think about, so no-one thought about it.

Despite evidence of sharp practice in Yorkshire's Quaid-e-Azam league, cricket followers had congratulated themselves that theirs was a game with higher moral standards. Towards the end of the previous summer, Horton Print's captain, Mohammed Isaq, hadn't so much fixed a match as made one up. When a mix-up over pitches led to a cancellation of his team's league fixture, he submitted a fictitious win for the club that would have earned them promotion. I can't imagine how he thought the other team involved wouldn't notice when the results were published, but in any case the deception was quickly uncovered when several of those supposedly playing in the game were spotted watching other matches on the same afternoon. No one seriously thought anything so underhand would take place in the first-class game.

That was until two former Essex players, Don Topley and Guy Lovell, alleged that a Sunday League game in August 1991 had been fixed. At the time Essex were in contention for the County Championship title while Lancashire stood a chance of winning the Sunday League. The story ran that in exchange for losing the league match Essex received a generous declaration on the last day of the Championship fixture on the Monday that they in turn won. All of the captains involved: Derek Pringle (Sunday League), Neil Foster (Championship) and Neil Fairbrother (both), have always strongly denied the allegations and Pringle described Topley as 'a strange cove … who often gave the impression that he felt hard done by…' Nothing was proved but then how was it ever going to be? In the same way as one of the main points in Grobelaar's defence was that he was so eccentric it was impossible to tell what was going on with him, these were English cricketers we were talking about. Even Inspector Morse wouldn't have been able to prove they were doing it on purpose.

The story was placed alongside Sarfraz Nawaz's bizarre suggestion that Pakistan had thrown the 1987 World Cup semi-final and the issue of cricket match-fixing briefly forgotten. Then all hell broke loose with new allegations against the Pakistanis. More precisely, Shane Warne and Tim May claimed Salim Malik had offered them large wads of cash to throw the Karachi Test match the previous October and Mark Waugh stated he had been offered $US100,000 to get out cheaply in a one-day match at Rawalpindi. Waugh was at pains to stress he had made 121 not out in the match in question.

The timing of the allegations couldn't have been worse for Malik. Less than a fortnight earlier his Pakistan team had lost a Test to

Zimbabwe. The African nation, though not as pathetic a sight as they were to become, still had never beaten anybody in a Test previously and weren't even deemed worthy of the attention of England, Australia or the West Indies. One Indian bookmaker had offered odds of 40-1 against them. Zimbabwe made 544-4 declared and won by an innings and 64 runs. In the next two games they produced totals of 174, 146, 243 and 139, and Pakistan became only the third side in Test history to come back to win from 1-0 down in a three-match series.

Then the plot didn't so much thicken as curdle. Mushtaq Mohammed admitted he had suggested to Allan Border that £500,000 might be on offer if Australia lost the 1993 Edgbaston Test but insisted he had only been joking. He hadn't offered me a penny for us to lose our game to Heckley.

Pakistan's tour manager in Zimbabwe, Intikhab Alam, revealed that, before leaving for Africa, he had required all the players to swear on the Koran they would not accept bribes to 'throw matches or perform poorly'. This was supposed to quell the 'ugly rumours' about the tour but had the opposite effect prompting as it did the obvious question: 'Why did you think that was necessary?'

Aamer Sohail, a Pakistani opening batsman on the tour in Zimbabwe, was quoted in *The Australian* as saying that 'several' players should be dropped because of their involvement in betting and that he knew 'many' who had accepted bribes. The same day as these statements appeared, Malik claimed Sohail now denied ever having said any such thing. Then two other tourists, Rashid Latif (26) and Basit Ali (24), announced they were retiring from Test cricket and took the next flight home.

Inevitably, Sarfraz, by then a 'special advisor' to Benazir Bhutto, got involved, claiming there was widespread corruption in Pakistani cricket and illegal betting involved 'millions of rupees'. Clearly from the moderate wing of Benazir's party, he then threw in for good measure that in his opinion Imran Khan was 'cunning, selfish and money-minded' and also a 'cheat' and an 'adulterer' who should be stoned to death. Imran himself appeared to hold equally strident views as he was reported as saying he believed that anyone found guilty of match-fixing should be 'hanged'. It later transpired what he had actually said was 'banned'. Nevertheless he stuck by his view that, 'Sarfraz is the biggest gambler there is. In England you always find him in Ladbrokes.'

Faced with a situation that threatened the integrity of the sport it purported to govern, the ICC did what it does best and passed the buck. This time it landed in the lap of the Pakistani cricket authorities. The Pakistan Cricket Board (PCB) commissioned an independent inquiry by Fakhruddin G. Ebrahim, a former Pakistani Supreme Court judge. Unfortunately, Warne, Waugh and May refused to go to Pakistan to be cross-examined, preferring to offer themselves to a hypothetical ICC enquiry in London that the sport's governing body had no intention of holding.

Therefore, Ebrahim was left with sworn written statements from the Australians and oral evidence under oath from Salim Malik. In the judge's defence any lawyer will tell you that a witness who refuses to submit to cross-examination runs an enormous risk of having their evidence taken with a large brown envelope of salt. This is exactly what happened, and when his investigation ended in October 1995, Judge Ebrahim's conclusion was that, 'The allegations against Salim Malik are not worthy of any credence and must be rejected as unfounded.'

However, while it's understandable from a legal perspective that the judge might have taken a cautious view of the Australians' evidence, some of his reasoning for acquitting Malik is a little worrying. Warne and May alleged the Pakistani captain had offered them $200,000. The leg-spinner thought it was proposed that this be split between them, while May believed they would both receive this sum. Either way it was a lot, but Judge Ebrahim stated he couldn't believe '…that Malik should offer a large sum of money not for direct personal gain, but for the sake of the nation's pride.' It seemed what his enquiry had needed was a prosecution barrister with a loud, slow voice summing up along the lines of: 'What the Antipodeans are insinuating, Your Honour, is that Mr Malik was, at the relevant time, in the employ of a bookmaker with a sizeable financial interest in the result of the match in question.'

Malik was deemed by many to have got off simply because his Australian accusers had not felt safe enough to go to Pakistan to give evidence against him. In fact had they gone, and told the whole truth, the result of the enquiry might well have been the same.

In the lead-up to the second Gulf War, a joke went around that Donald Rumsfeld knew Saddam Hussein possessed weapons of mass destruction because he had kept all of his receipts. The little detail Warne and Waugh had omitted from their story was that they knew for certain that parties interested in cricket might be willing to hand over substantial sums of cash because they had received some.

The same autumn that they claimed to have been approached by Malik, Warne and Waugh were playing in a one-day tournament in Sri Lanka. During the course of this competition they were approached by an Indian bookmaker known only to them as 'John' who offered cash for apparently innocent information about the toss and weather conditions. For this intelligence Waugh received $A6000 and Warne $A5000. At best this was incredibly naïve. 'Look mate this fella John's just given me five grand for telling him it's sunny but humid in Colombo. What a nice bloke!'

After Malik's approach, the players, perhaps twigging that 'John' might want something slightly more than next-to-nothing for his money, informed the Australian Cricket Board of the payments. The ACB fined Warne and Waugh more than they had received and informed the ICC's chairman and chief executive. Unfortunately none of them saw fit to mention this to anyone else. In other words they covered it up. The story stayed covered for nearly four years. Then, in December 1998, David Hookes, speaking on a Melbourne radio programme, happened to mention two Aussie cricketers had passed information to an Indian bookmaker. It was only at this point, after Waugh and Mark Taylor (speaking on Warne's behalf) had given evidence to a further Pakistani enquiry without mentioning their indiscretion, that the ACB were forced to come clean.

However, for now it was still possible to convince yourself that if there was a problem with corruption, it was restricted to a few nasty bandit types from the wrong part of the sub-continent. Even so, like a cuckolded husband just getting the first inkling something might be up, cricket followers couldn't help but start to have tiny doubts about anything even slightly unexpected. All of a sudden delight at our victory in Adelaide seemed slightly tarnished. After all, the win featured a cobbled-together England side with Steve Rhodes batting at six, Phil DeFreitas smashing Craig McDermott all over the place on the final morning and the powerful Aussie batting line-up being shot out for 156 between lunch and the close on the last day. It was almost a relief that they had massacred us at Perth.

No one has ever seriously alleged anything on that tour – other than England's preparation and performance of course – was suspect in any way. To this day it has never been credibly suggested any Ashes contest wasn't genuine. Nevertheless, Malik's 'acquittal' didn't represent an ending; rather, it was the start of a period in which suspicion and innuendo eroded the reputation of a sport whose name was supposedly synonymous with honesty and fair play.

The ICC knew as early as the start of 1995 that at least two leading cricketers had received cash payments from a bookmaker and those same players alleged an international captain had offered them a huge bribe to throw a Test. The failure of the governing body (if such it can be called) to take any meaningful action at that time to investigate corruption in the sport, beggars belief. It's not just your sporting heroes that can let you down.

Salim Malik was banned from all meaningful cricket until a Pakistani High Court ruling in 2008. Nevertheless his last international was as late as the World Cup in 1999. I've tried to block out that tournament because England were so woeful but I remember one thing: Bangladesh beat Pakistan.

Even if the ICC or the Conservative Party didn't think it was particularly important, the English cricketing authorities decided that strong leadership was what they needed. Within a month of the team's return from Australia, Keith Fletcher was sacked and Ray Illingworth given his duties.

Fletcher's departure hardly provoked the outpourings of emotion demonstrated by fans when Robbie Williams left Take That at around the same time. The feelings about Fletcher were more akin to the apathetic reaction to John Major's attempt to tackle the 'bastards' by resigning and putting himself up for re-election as Tory leader. Illingworth represented a much more viable alternative to the previous coach than John Redwood did to Major and his appointment was welcomed with much more enthusiasm than the victory the Prime Minister achieved during the Edgbaston Test match. Now we were getting somewhere, a 'Supremo', that was the answer.

Just before the new season started, Tim Rice accepted an Oscar for Best Original Song in *The Lion King* and thanked, among others, Denis Compton. A slightly confused spokesman on behalf of the Academy revealed that: 'We don't know who Denis Compton is. He doesn't appear to be at Disney Studios or have anything to do with *The Lion King*.' Some of England's cricketers could have been forgiven for at least having to reacquaint themselves with some of their team-mates as the side for the first Test showed six changes from the one that had played out the last match of the previous winter. Now where have I heard that before?

Not that the sweeping changes made any difference. The West Indies were supposedly in disarray. They arrived for the traditional tour opener against Lavinia, Duchess of Norfolk's XI without their scorebook and left without their flag. More pertinently, less than two weeks earlier they had lost the final Test against Australia to suffer their first series defeat for 15 years. They hadn't been beaten at home since 1973. The captain, Richie Richardson, had only just returned to the side after several months out with 'acute fatigue syndrome' and was blamed by many for the loss. There was talk of divisions in the camp, with Lara openly coveting Richardson's job and allegedly trying to undermine him at every opportunity. In short they were there for the taking.

In the first Test at Headingley the West Indies battered us by nine wickets. I went to the Saturday of that match and all I remember is that it was bloody freezing and Graeme Hick hooked one down Walsh's throat straight after Atherton got out.

Then it was England's turn to appear divided. At Headingley, Smith had opened while Stewart kept wicket and batted in the middle order. For Lord's the selectors picked Steve Rhodes so the Surrey man could resume his successful opening partnership with Atherton without the additional pressures of keeping, while Smith dropped into a more natural position. Then, the day before the match, Illingworth unilaterally decided to send Rhodes away, persuaded Stewart to fulfil two major roles and put Smith on standby to go in first if England had a long stint in the field. This high-handed action, born of the Supremo's near obsession with the need for five front-line bowlers, had the disadvantages of overloading Stewart, disrupting Smith's preparation and aggravating the captain who ended up leading a side he didn't want.

On the other hand there were two big advantages. The first was a debut for Dominic Cork, teaming him for the first time with Gough and Fraser. The second was England won. Stewart made 34 and 36 and took a brilliant low left-handed catch to dismiss Lara on the final morning, Smith contributed 61 and 90 batting at five and the latest 'next you-know-who' produced the best figures by an England debutant with 7-43 to bowl out the tourists on the last afternoon. That was just after I had told anybody who would listen how ordinary he had looked in the first innings.

I remembered my colleague Mike's attitude to the 46 all out

debacle when West Indies lost their last eight wickets for 99. Then again there was enough excitement in the office that afternoon to distract anyone from crowing too much about a cricket match.

The Citizens Advice Bureau I worked in had, among its volunteers, a large number of public spirited, middle-class, retired people, many of whom had lived quite sheltered lives. The most sheltered of these was June.

On the afternoon of England's victory she began what appeared to be a run-of-the-mill enquiry with a man complaining that a recent purchase was not fit for purpose. On a Monday it was my job to support the volunteers and as June came to find the relevant information she reported in to me that, 'He says it's no good and he'll show me what he means when I go back in.' She looked up the consumer advice file and set off expecting to find nothing more racy than a dodgy toaster. Within a minute she was back, flustered almost to the point of panic, to relate that what she had actually been confronted with was a gently hissing inflatable woman and a client asking: 'What am I supposed to do with this?'

After that it was hopeless, I couldn't keep anybody's mind on what they were supposed to be doing, they all just wanted to go and have a look. The only one who seemed unperturbed was our receptionist Phil. But then he had seen it all before in his previous career with West Midlands Travel when somebody had left one on a bus. It turned out Phil hadn't actually seen the item in question. When he had visited the lost property office a couple of days after the discovery he was told it had been disposed of 'because the flies had started to gather'.

If there appeared to be no flies on Ray Illingworth after his authoritarian gamble had paid off so spectacularly at Lord's, there was the odd vulture circling over Richie Richardson. In between the second and third Tests, the West Indies lost by an innings against Sussex, Winston Benjamin was sent home for disciplinary reasons and it was rumoured, Lara went AWOL. A win at Edgbaston, it was reckoned, would shatter their morale for good.

The Great Dictator's powers even extended to instructing the Test groundsmen as to what sort of pitches to prepare. Steve Rouse was told to produce something of even bounce with the grass taken off on a spinner's length at both ends. What England actually got was green and uneven in the middle where the West Indians pitched it and shorn of grass and more predictable on the fuller length we bowled. In other words it was even more suited to our opponents than the Jamaican minefield that had greeted Gower's Caribbean tourists in 1986. From the moment that Ambrose's first ball of the match disappeared from short of a length four feet over the wicket-keeper's head, we were doomed.

Having been stung in previous seasons by buying tickets for the fourth day, I played it safe this time and went for the Saturday. I saw less than two hours of action. I use the word 'action' advisedly because what I witnessed was too brutally one-sided to be called cricket and there was more than one occasion when I thought Robin Smith might get killed. That morning Smith made the bravest 41 I've ever seen. Time after time he was hit on the body but kept trying to counter-punch with the cut shot every chance he got. Over the course of the whole match, Smith batted for a total of exactly five hours on a pitch on which no other home batsman managed even two. Just think what he might have managed if he hadn't been a 'non-Englishman'.

When Illingworth had turned down the England manager's job in the 1980s it was because he didn't want responsibility without power. Hearing him talk after this fiasco it seemed what he really desired was the exact opposite. Having placed his order with the Warwickshire ground authorities, Illingworth took no action to supervise the pitch's preparation and only saw it for the first time 48 hours before the match started. By then it was far too late to do anything other than work out who else to blame. Steve Rouse copped most of the flak but it was his first Test as Edgbaston's head groundsman and a proper pitch is what he should have been asked for. It was indicative of Illingworth's lack of faith in our ability to compete on equal terms that he tried, and spectacularly failed, to skew the conditions in our favour.

There's nothing wrong in making use of home advantage. What Illingworth wanted was no different to Indian groundsmen using scrubbing brushes to rough up their pitches to assist the home side's spinners. What's more he was probably right about our bowlers needing a bit of help and certainly wasn't alone in his attitude. Two years later, those then in charge of English cricket tried to ensure the touring Australians played on a series of surfaces offering encouragement to our seamers. Ultimately though, this is a futile policy. In 1997, the England management got pretty much the pitches they wanted and the Aussies still beat us. In the whole of the 1990s, India and their scrubbing brushes won nine home series and only one away, in Sri Lanka. Fixing the pitches wasn't the answer.

Various broken bones inflicted at Birmingham meant another six changes to the England team for Old Trafford. This was bad news for Michael Holding. The great West Indian fast bowler was commentating for Sky and staying in the same hotel in Copthorne as the home team. Despite the fact he had played for Lancashire in the early 80s he wasn't entirely sure of his way to the ground from there. When he spotted an England player's sponsored car he followed it. It was only when he was half way down the M63 he realised he was behind the released Graeme Hick on his way to home to Worcester.

When Holding finally made it to Old Trafford he found the sort of playing surface Rouse should have been asked to produce and saw a combination of the West Indies' cocky batting and profligate bowling mixed with Dominic Cork to produce an England win. The tourists tossed wickets away on the first day and gifted their hosts 64 extras. Cork took eight wickets in the match, including his famous hat-trick, and made 56 not out.

However happy Cork might have been, his was not the first televised hat-trick of the summer. That honour had gone to Bill Wyman.

Bowling slow, loopy leg-breaks for the Bunburys against the Imperial War Museum in a VE-Day match at the Oval, Wyman dismissed Trevor McDonald, Charles Colvile and Gary Lineker with successive deliveries live on *Sky*. Quite how this trio came to be representing the Imperial War Museum is unclear, but it didn't really matter as by the time Wyman was interviewed about the feat in 2003 they had become 'some former England players'. You can't blame the bloke for embellishing, but he was stretching it a little as although Lineker undeniably played for England and Colvile is international class at fluffing things live on television, I suspect, given the identity of that year's tourists, Sir Trevor would have failed Mr Tebbit's 'cricket test' that summer.

Alternatively, perhaps Wyman wasn't embellishing, just mixing up two of his great cricketing moments? Dominic Cork wasn't the only man the Stones' bassist had eclipsed on the field, he had also out-cooled 'Simmo'.

In one respect, and one respect alone, Ed Simpson is like Kylie Minogue: they both only need one name. Just as there is only one Kylie so anyone who has ever met him knows who 'Simmo' is. This is a man who won a Jaguar XJS in a Friday night game of spoof, drove to his mate's wedding in Basingstoke the next day and then deliberately refused to use his hotel room just so he could say 'I slept in the Jag'. A talented all-round sportsman good enough to lead the line for Stratford's hockey team, he also played cricket for Stoneleigh. His finest moment for us came in the unlikely setting of deep midwicket at Ilmington.

Untroubled by the ball for eight or nine overs, Simmo concluded he was safe to light up. As luck would have it, the next delivery was drilled aerially but flat in his direction. A lesser man would have panicked. Simmo merely popped the fag in his mouth, pouched the catch in front of his face and hurled the ball back before taking a long, satisfied drag and blowing three smoke rings. Even as captain I had to admire his style. What Dougie Walters might have given for similar latitude from Ian Chappell?

The previous year, again playing for the Bunburys, this time against Norma Major's XI, Wyman took a one-handed catch in the gully to dismiss Brian Close while never at any point relinquishing the cigarette in his other hand. There is a hierarchy of 'cool', which explains why Simmo is a hockey player and Bill Wyman is a rock star.

England's victory at Manchester left the series 2-2 with both sides having won when they were expected to lose and vice versa. Four positive results in as many matches surely meant the series was heading for a thrilling finale. The last two matches were drawn. Ironically, England's best chance of winning the series disappeared when Mike Watkinson (remember him, the two-bowlers-in-one man?) was dropped on the last afternoon at Nottingham. If Sherwin Campbell had caught him the tourists would have had to go for 215 in 42 overs, the sort of target they could easily have made a mess of under Test conditions. As it was, Watkinson made 82 not out and ensured the draw.

As for the Oval, all I remember it for is poor old Alan Wells' one and only Test. As a Sussex fan I can't help contrasting my county captain's first ball in Test cricket with David Gower's. Like the left-hander's 17 years earlier, Wells' opening delivery landed half way down. Unfortunately that's where the similarities end as the bowler was Curtley Ambrose rather than Liaquat Ali and instead of sitting up nicely to be spanked to the boundary the ball arrowed in at the heart and Wells could only prod it to short-leg. Alan Wells was 33 and his first-class average in 1995 was 54.42. He had spent years scoring thousands for Sussex waiting for a chance to play for England and then what happens? 3 not out in the second innings must have been scant consolation. David Gower was 21 when he first got picked on the back of a first-class average in the mid-twenties, he ended up with 8,228 more Test runs than Alan Wells.

For Wells, the difference between success and failure must have felt more than a bit random but then that's what happens when no one appears to be in charge. This was a familiar feeling in the early 1990s. At least we had narrowly escaped having John Redwood as our prime minister. The only less suitable incumbent for a major position you could have come up with at the time would have been Liam Gallagher as Archbishop of Canterbury. Redwood was after all the Secretary of State for Wales whose toe-curling attempt to mumble his way through the Welsh national anthem seemed to sum up the arrogant ineptitude of the government. Obviously it was asking for trouble appointing a 'non-Welshman' to a post like that, but the man who had given him the job was at least nominally running the country.

We certainly knew who was running the English cricket team and we all tried to have faith that his 'no nonsense', pragmatic style would revive our fortunes. There was even evidence Illingworth was improving the support systems. Well, the side were taking a doctor with them to the World Cup. Despite even this stunningly forward-thinking development the feeling still persisted that the manager's methods, like Gooch's, would prove too one-dimensional to bring out the best in all the players and by extension the team.

Illingworth's vision of leadership contrasted greatly with that of a newly appointed international captain who preferred a more inclusive approach: 'I'm a democratic leader. I like to get input from the rest of the team and make them feel important. We all share responsibility – we must all have a share in our destiny.' The winter ahead provided a victory for this more enlightened approach over English autocracy.

However, the notions of inclusivity and shared accountability have more sinister connotations in the context of the match-fixing allegations that had emerged in this year. The sort of connotations that none of us, least of all the cricketing authorities, have ever wanted to confront openly. Put simply, just as a goalkeeper alone can't throw a football match, so a cricket captain can't engineer defeat without help.

The author of the rallying call for collective responsibility was Hansie Cronje.

TWENTY-TWO

One thing you could deduce from England's tour to South Africa in 1995-96 is that jelly babies are better than garibaldi biscuits. Before the Test series the home side's coach, Bob Woolmer, offered the opinion that the sweets 'deliver much more controlled and long-lasting beneficial effects' than chocolate. As a result he had instructed his team to consume them at a rate of 12 an hour. On the other hand England's new doctor, Phil Bell, while conceding jelly babies were 'not on the banned drugs list', had advised our men to munch garibaldis. When you consider the Proteas beat us 1-0 in the Tests before handing out a 6-1 drubbing in the one-day series, the conclusion is obvious.

Perhaps the mixture of dried fruit and biscuit, combined with the impounding of 1,500 cans of the team's Tetley bitter by the South African health ministry, left the players too parched to perform? If so, Dr Bell's advice wasn't the last self-inflicted wound of the winter.

The last time these two teams had met, Devon Malcolm had taken 9-57 and on his introduction to the president, even Nelson Mandela recognised him as 'The Destroyer'. However, the only thing Ray Illingworth seemed intent on destroying was his main strike bowler's confidence.

At the start of the tour, Illingworth and his bowling coach, Peter Lever, tried to re-model Malcolm's action. At the time, both members of the management team took a lot of criticism for trying this with an established Test cricketer. However, much of England's success in the couple of years leading up to and including the Ashes triumph of 2005 was attributable to Troy Cooley's work with Flintoff, Harmison, Hoggard and Jones. With Harmison in particular, technical changes in his delivery turned him from pacey-but-inaccurate like Malcolm, into the nearest thing England have had to Curtley Ambrose.

Closer examination of his ideas show Illingworth's thinking wasn't a million miles away from Duncan Fletcher's. Rightly, neither saw anything wrong in seeking greater accuracy from their quick men and both possess a similar belief in the desirability of having five front-line bowlers all of whom are capable of contributing at least something with the bat. Furthermore, while Fletcher had the benefit of central contracts, Illingworth also asked for the right to withdraw England players from county matches if he saw fit. This is where differences begin to appear.

On 13th December, shortly after Atherton's heroic 185 not out to draw the Johannesburg Test, the TCCB announced Illingworth had been denied the power to remove players from championship and domestic one-day matches. The chief executive A.C. Smith suggested that, 'If he really wanted to do something he could talk to the county chairmen involved, who would be sympathetic.' Given that what had brought the issue to a head was Yorkshire's inclusion of Darren Gough in their team for the Natwest Trophy semi-final when he was supposed to be recovering from injury, this had to be nonsense. Realistically, no county was going to withdraw their player from any match just because the England manager asked them to, especially not when a domestic trophy was at stake. The inevitable response to any such request would have been 'who pays his wages?' The same thinking underpinned the rugby union Premiership clubs' defiance of the RFU's instruction to rest players who had been involved in the 2005 Lions tour at the start of the 2005/06 domestic season.

All this goes to show that simply getting a man with a lot of sensible ideas in the England coach's job wasn't enough on its own. The success Fletcher enjoyed was as much about the system the ECB were willing to put in place to support him as his own coaching. Similarly, the failings of the Illingworth era were as much those of the TCCB as the man himself. Not that the Yorkshireman was completely blameless; the handling of Malcolm is a perfect example of where his methods diverged from Fletcher's.

A few weeks into the tour, Peter Johnson in the *Daily Mail* reported that Illingworth said they had given up on trying to change Malcolm and told the press: 'We hoped Devon would be the leading strike bowler, but at the moment he wouldn't frighten you, never mind the South African batsmen.' Worst of all, the manager also allowed Lever to make public his infamous opinion of The Destroyer that, 'Apart from his pace he's a nonentity in cricketing terms.'

When my younger daughter was six her standard reply to any insult was: 'I know you are but what am I?' While this is hardly in the Oscar Wilde class of witty rejoinders, it seems to me it would have been Malcolm's perfect response. Peter Lever took 41 wickets in 17 Tests; he never got 10 in a match and only managed five in an innings twice. In his 40 outings for England, Malcolm took 128 wickets with two 10-wicket matches and five 'five-fors'.

Malcolm later described this tour as 'the worst time in my life' and ended up loathing Illingworth: 'His management skills were crap...I've never seen him again and I don't want to.' The manager probably didn't care if his players liked him as long as they performed to the best of their ability. The problem was: they didn't, and they didn't.

Ironically for a Yorkshire professional, Illingworth seemed to embody one of the worst failings of the English gentleman cricket administrator. This was a failure that infected the way cricket was run in this country and undermined the efforts of the national team for most of the time I've been supporting them. Put simply, Illingworth demanded respect but showed none in return. Exactly this attitude, shown by those running the game in the 1970s, made England's best cricketers willing to throw in their lot with Packer. In the 1980s, a similar lack of trust in their bosses led Gooch and his men to South Africa. Now, in the 1990s, here was Illingworth showing the lesson still hadn't been learned. Malcolm wasn't the only one he publicly criticised. During the early part of the previous tour to Australia the then merely chairman of selectors summed up Atherton with: 'He's been to Cambridge. He's never really gone out to work and earned a living in his life. It's pretty hard-going for him.' No mention of having lumbered the captain with the wrong players. As for Keith Fletcher and Mike Smith, they had apparently let things drift. 'When the players need to be geed up. It's up to management to do that.'

Illingworth had done a great job in geeing up Devon Malcolm but of course that wasn't his fault, it was the player's for not responding to his methods. It never seemed to occur to the manager that the methods might be wrong. In the end he developed a reputation for taking credit for success and blaming anyone but himself for failure. But then he isn't alone in that.

When football managers leave their jobs there is often talk of them having 'lost the dressing room'. In Paul Gascoigne's case you would probably have to take this literally, but the phrase's more normal meaning describes perfectly why Illingworth's days as Supremo and John Major's as prime minister were numbered.

Our premier's attempts to return to Victorian values had been scuppered by his colleagues' inability to keep the members of parliament in their trousers and the noses out of the trough. Major failed to appreciate that leading Victorians got away with preaching to the masses because, in the main, there was neither a will nor ability on the part of the fourth estate to highlight their hypocrisies. The modern press had no such qualms or restrictions. Therefore the 'sleazy' antics of the likes of Jonathan Aitken, David Mellor and Neil Hamilton served to ensure that the prime minister had 'lost' not just a cabinet but an entire country. Even Major himself, had we but known it, was involved in a dalliance with Edwina Currie that demonstrates a lack of judgment operating on so many levels that I don't know where to begin.

Illingworth too had tried to go 'back to basics' by using methods that had succeeded in regaining the Ashes in the early 1970s. The problem was the players he had been working with then were born in the 1930s and 1940s. This was a generation brought up on war and National Service, for whom time wasted questioning orders could literally mean the difference between life and death. In other words most of them expected to do what they were told. Even the ones who didn't, like Geoff Boycott and John Snow, knew their regard for the captain's cricketing ability was mutual.

The players Illingworth was trying to manage in South Africa were born in the 1960s and 1970s, a period in which rebelling against authority was the norm. Atherton and his men had been raised to know their own minds and weren't about to respond positively to being told to 'do it my way' unless they were given a compelling reason why they should. From the manager's point of view these lads 'didn't know they were born' and crucially, he didn't trust their ability. He expected his charges to listen to him because 'I've won the Ashes and you haven't', while simultaneously undermining them with public pronouncements about how rubbish they were.

Duncan Fletcher appreciated you can't just trade on what you might have achieved in the past. He may never have played Test cricket and could be hard about rejecting players who he thought weren't up to the job, just ask Usman Afzaal, Jimmy Ormond and Jason Brown, but, until he made an unfortunate exception in the case of Chris Read, he didn't go around making his feelings public.

If Craig White was left feeling '10-feet tall' by his first meeting with Fletcher, Illingworth cut Devon Malcolm down to about a quarter of that. In the vital last Test, the fast bowler was given the task of knocking over Paul Adams. If Adams bowled like a frog in a blender he had a reputation for being as much use with the bat as what was left at the end of the process. To this point the young South African had faced 16 deliveries in first-class cricket, but in an hour against Malcolm and the others with the new ball he and Dave Richardson put on 70 and the Test and series was lost: nice one Ray.

If a 1-0 defeat in South Africa was a disappointment, it hardly came as a surprise. Our Test form had never been anything better than patchy for the previous 20 years. In one-day cricket however, we had always been a force to be reckoned with. England had been the beaten finalists in two of the four World Cups and had never yet failed to make the semis. No one, not even the West Indies, could afford to take us lightly in the shortened version of the game. Unfortunately all that was about to change.

In Australia in 1992, England had regularly used Botham at the top of the order, the New Zealanders gave Mark Greatbatch a similar role and, against Zimbabwe, the Indians used Kris Srikkanth and Kapil Dev, which was like opening with two helicopters. However, in 1996 Sanath Jayasuriya and Romesh Kaluwitharana gave a whole new meaning to the concept of pinch-hitting.

England had a pinch-hitter, they just didn't know who it would be from one match to the next. In the one-day series in South Africa the tourists had used Phil DeFreitas and Craig White alongside Mike Atherton. These choices made sense, but the England management only gave both men two matches to try and make a fist of it before changing things again.

In the World Cup they returned to Alec Stewart and Mike Atherton for one game, before trying Neil Smith for three. Smith opened twice with Stewart and once with Atherton before another change, to the captain and Robin Smith, for the last group game and the quarter-final. In other words: they went into the tournament with not a clue as to what their best batting line-up was.

It wasn't just the pin-in-the-team-sheet batting order that was problematic. Practice left a bit to be desired too. This description from Robert Winder's excellent book on the tournament, *Hell for Leather*, sums it up:

> 'Fairbrother came in for a bat, but who was he facing? Thorpe, the physio Wayne Morton, and the tour manager, John Barclay, an Old Etonian former Sussex off-spinner. "Bye-bye! Bye-bye! You nicked that," called Morton. No-one wondered why he had nicked it, or suggested a way not to nick it – there wasn't a coach in sight… The English idea of nets seemed to be that you could acquire, by catching a few in the middle of the bat, a feel good factor that you could take into a proper match… '

The thing that strikes me most about this passage is that in terms of attitude towards practice, it paints a picture remarkably reminiscent of the approach for which David Gower was so castigated when he had captained England in the Caribbean ten years earlier. If our methods really had stood still for an entire decade it was no wonder the only teams we beat in this tournament were Holland and the United Arab Emirates. When they were 195-4 in pursuit of our 279 it looked as if we might even lose to the Dutch and as for the UAE, they had a captain who went out to bat against South Africa in a sunhat and got carried off after his first ball (from Allan Donald) hit him on the head.

When the most memorable image of an England cricketer from the world's premier one-day competition is of Neil Smith losing the previous evening's dinner next to the pitch – 'He had pizza last night and now it's out there' (Illingworth) – it's no wonder the 'Islamabad, Faisalabad, England-are-bad' joke started doing the rounds.

Even though we had the pleasure of the Sri Lankans thrashing Australia in the final this was generally a fairly crap tournament. The Calcutta semi-final between Ranatunga's men and India ended in a riot when it became apparent that the home team were going to lose. Even the sight of the tubby wicket-keeper catching Brian Lara between his thighs as the West Indies were bowled out for 93 in losing to Kenya, was accompanied by the slight uneasiness that Salim Malik and ICC inertia had ensured would accompany any such result from now on. It says it all that my favourite moment from this World Cup is one I only think I heard.

The M.C. for the presentations after the final was Ian Chappell. As is the way with such occasions, anyone with even the remotest justification for being there was clogging up the podium and Chappell found himself trapped behind an Asian woman. As he tried to force his way to the front I swear I heard the former Aussie skipper utter a slightly irritated 'Excuse me, love'. Nothing too comical in that, except the woman in question was Benazir Bhutto.

After England returned from the World Cup Illingworth resigned as team manager shortly before the TCCB announced that the post would no longer exist. It was no more than a year since he had been given the job. Not long to bring about a fundamental change in England's fortunes, but a damn sight longer than he gave most of his players to prove themselves. In Illingworth's place David Lloyd was appointed coach for an initial period of six months.

It's hard to imagine someone more different to Illingworth. For a start Lloyd was a Lancastrian. Both men's first-class careers had ended in 1983 but that was only because Illingworth had returned to the Yorkshire team in his fifties. Lloyd was nearly 15 years younger and his previous TCCB job of promoting Kwik Cricket was not the only reason why his new bosses might have seen him as better able to connect with young players. Without a doubt, Lloyd had a very different outlook to his predecessor: 'I'm looking to instill enthusiasm, rebuild confidence and get some enjoyment back.'

Graeme Fowler, who had played with Lloyd at Lancashire, thought he was an eccentric genius who would make you 'laugh first and then realise there is seriousness underneath.' Fowler tells a story of a team meeting on the eve of the fixture against Somerset in 1981. Lloyd asked the overseas pro, Michael Holding, how to dismiss Viv Richards. 'He likes to hit his first ball, so pitch it up a foot wide of off stump. With luck he'll swipe at it and nick it to the slips.' The next morning Holding was bowling when Richards came in. Lancashire put in four slips and the fast-man duly delivered a wide, swinging half-volley.

Richards left it. There was a brief stunned silence before Lloyd, at square-leg, piped up with, 'Well, we're knackered now.' When they all stopped laughing they realised the serious point he was making. They didn't have a Plan B.

In addition to a sense of humour, Lloyd also had boundless enthusiasm, a tracksuit, a baseball mitt, a video camera and some unusual motivational techniques. As well as a big sign with a TCCB lion and the word 'WIN' on it, inspiring quotations from the likes of George

Bernard Shaw and Jim Steinman were pasted all over the dressing room walls. This invited a good deal of ridicule from more traditional quarters, but Justin Langer had similar things stuck all over his house and he got more than 7,000 Test runs.

The new coach also gave every player a video of themselves taking wickets or making runs cut to their favourite music and a five-minute cassette containing M People's 'Search for the Hero' and an extract from Churchill's 'We shall fight them on the beaches' speech. According to Alan Mullally the video made you 'feel a million feet tall'. In other words: 100,000 times better than Duncan Fletcher managed with Craig White.

Despite losing the manager's job, Illingworth had retained his role as chairman of selectors. Have a guess how many changes England's team for the first Test showed from the one that had contested South Africa's series-winning victory in Cape Town. Yes, you've got it: six.

Perhaps concluding that three 'new Bothams' might add up to one old one, England picked debutant Ronnie Irani to bat at six, with Dominic Cork and Chris Lewis opening the bowling. Lewis made his third Test duck in a row, the sequence being spread over the nearly three years that had elapsed since his pair at Lord's in 1993. David Lloyd had told a 23-year-old Graeme Fowler that: 'You can't be promising forever, it's time to produce the goods.' Chris Lewis was 28 and as far as England was concerned it was now or never. I know I wasn't alone in praying the new coach would finally get the best out of him.

It all started so well. On the Saturday, Lewis contributed 5-72 to a day of Test cricket so perfect I might have ordered it when I bought my tickets. Tendulkar scored a brilliant hundred but India were bowled out, and then England cruised to within 50 of their target with nine wickets left. Victory was achieved before lunch on Sunday and Lloyd demonstrated another difference from his predecessor by giving the credit to his players. He might also have thanked Darrell Hair who reprieved the returning Nasser Hussain when he appeared to be caught down the leg side on 14. Hussain went on to make 128, putting on 98 for the last two first-innings wickets with two debutants, Min Patel (yes, he played for England) and Alan Mullally.

Sometimes umpires can 'mess' with people's careers in a positive way. Having been on the periphery of the side since 1990, Hussain made the most of his escape and although his breadstick fingers saw him miss a few games through injury, he was never dropped again by the selectors. Despite the fact Hair's mistake arguably changed the course of the match, the Indians didn't make a fuss about it and Hussain certainly didn't receive any criticism for not walking. This provides a neat example of a difference in attitude between Test and village players.

Test cricketers don't always bear such injustices with equanimity, Allan Donald's reaction to Mike Atherton's escape at Trent Bridge in 1998 is an obvious example of the opposite happening, but generally it seems internationals adhere to the view that the umpires are paid to make decisions and the dodgy ones even out over the period of a career. This evening-out process can't apply to 'walkers' as the only 'bad 'uns' they get will be those that go against them. In an environment where you are competing with others hungry for your place in the side, striding off every time you know you've nicked it must place you at a disadvantage. Therefore the temptation to stand your ground and wait for the umpire must be almost overwhelming.

In the modern game the only two cricketers who made great public play of the fact they always walked were Brian Lara and Adam Gilchrist. What these two had in common is they played the game at a level that made them practically 'fireproof'. When cricket is your livelihood and the financial rewards of playing at the top level are so much greater than those available in the domestic game, I can understand why mere mortal Test cricketers don't walk. However, at village level, when the umpire is a smoking, bare-footed teammate of the batsman, wearing nothing but shorts and a white coat left open because it won't stretch over his gut, the argument is different.

Two days after Hussain had his lucky escape I was keeping wicket and took a regulation edge from the opposition's opener. We all went up but the bloke with the fag and the sunburnt belly shook his head. I knew he had hit it, the umpire knew he had hit it and worst of all for the batsman, the bowler, Ben, knew it too.

Off the field Ben is one of the most unassuming men you could ever wish to meet; on it however, he is a total red mist merchant. Alone, this wouldn't have been a major problem for the batsman. But Ben had, in the not too distant past, opened the bowling for Warwickshire U19s. Despite the fact he possessed an action not dissimilar to Derek Randall's eight-legged batting style and would have only counted as medium pace in the first-class game, at our level he was 'shit off a shovel'.

After the appeal was turned down we followed our usual procedure.

This involved Ben adding ten yards to his run-up before charging in sounding like a steam train and me taking five steps back towards the boundary. It took two balls. The first gave the striker just enough time to turn white before it flashed past his nose and thudded into the gloves above my head. The second presented me with another catch, except this time it was the off stump that landed in my lap. As Tennessee Williams put it: 'Sometimes there's God so quickly.'

Unfortunately retribution is not always so swift. When the umpires aren't paid, the game depends on the honesty of the players. At club level the arguments about leaving it to the officials don't stand up.

Having said that, perhaps appealing against yourself and then walking when you're given not out is taking things a bit far? Batting for Langlebury against Northwood in a cup-tie in Hertfordshire, Chris Spinks made it to 31 before deciding he had had enough and throwing his bat onto the stumps. The umpires turned down the fielding side's appeal because Spinks hadn't been playing the ball or taking a run. The batsman then made an appeal of his own and when that was turned down, walked off anyway. His weary explanation was: 'I've been playing too much cricket.'

Someone who might have had good reason to feel similarly about umpiring was Dickie Bird. By the time he got to Lord's for his sixty-sixth and final match in charge he had been a Test official for 23 years. Goodness knows how many games he would have done if the international panel had existed throughout his career. By the end of the 2005 season Steve Bucknor had officiated in over 100 Tests in only 16 years.

Quite a fuss was made of Dickie. The players formed a guard of honour for him on the first morning and there was a lot of eye-dabbing with his hankie going on throughout the match. However, not everyone bought in to the idea that we were witnessing the passing of a sporting institution. At the end of the match Jonathan Agnew was doing his closing summary with Trevor Bailey: 'And what about Dickie's last match? Seeing him coming off at the end was an emotional moment wasn't it Trevor?'

'He's only an umpire,' came the dark reply.

If Bailey's view of Dickie was controversial it didn't cause as much argument as England's recall of Alec Stewart in place of the injured Nick Knight. At 33, the age at which Atherton ultimately retired, Stewart was seen as close to 'over the hill' and it was felt by many that his selection was typical of the short-termism that had plagued English cricket for so long. Alec Stewart played for England for another seven years and became their most capped player.

At the other end of the scale, India selected Sourav Ganguly and Rahul Dravid for their debuts. When he first played for Glamorgan, Ganguly nearly left his kit on the team bus because he expected someone to carry it for him. It's been suggested he was under the impression the lower caste Dravid was partly there to fulfill this role at Lord's. The potential for friction this attitude carried with it didn't stop them from sharing a big partnership. Lord Snooty made a hundred and they fell only five runs short of being the first pair of debutants to compile centuries. However, Dravid's dismissal for 95 meant the most remarkable thing that happened during the match was England winning a penalty shoot-out.

It didn't matter what the cricketers did in the early part of that summer, no one really noticed because, like a brother who had emigrated, football had come home.

On the Saturday of the Lord's Test Chris Lewis bowled the ball of his career. Delivered from the Pavilion End, it shaped in, pitched on a line of middle-and-off, cut away against the slope, flashed past the outside edge of Tendulkar's bat and clipped the top of off stump. It was a ball worthy of a motivational video all to itself. But no one will remember it. The sporting image of that day will forever be of an even more psychotic than usual Stuart Pearce screaming out his penalty demons at the Wembley crowd.

In sporting terms, Pearce taking that penalty is one of the bravest things I've ever seen. It still pricks the back of my eyes now to think of it. The cheers that followed after he had rammed it home stopped the Test match for several minutes.

If the Spanish, having lost a penalty shoot-out to England, could regard themselves as the unluckiest country in the footballing world, spare a thought for the Indians. Draws at Lord's and Nottingham, where they made 521 and saw England bat past them, meant they lost a Test series to our cricketers.

By the end of July that year there were several things I wanted, really, really wanted. These were, in no particular order: The Spice Girls to just piss off now please, Paul Gascoigne to have had longer studs on his boots and England's batsmen to have had the first idea how to play leg-spin.

The first Test against Pakistan is the only occasion I can remember England's cricketers having the excuse that their preparations were disrupted by the coach and captain being called away on the eve of the match to give evidence in a libel trial.

Ian Botham and Allan Lamb had sued Imran Khan following an interview for *India Today* in which the former Pakistani captain was quoted as describing the two Englishmen as racist and attributing their strong stance against ball-tampering to a lack of education, upbringing and class. Botham also brought an individual action against Imran arising out of an article in *The Sun* in which he had claimed that all leading English cricketers had tampered with the ball. As a result two of the all-time greats lined up against one another in the High Court: Charles Grey QC for the plaintiffs and George Carman QC for the defendant.

Lloyd and Atherton were called on behalf of the defence and, in the course of his evidence, England's captain suggested that, 'The laws should be changed to allow current actions which the players tacitly accept as part of the game.' Grey, presumably a batsman, submitted on behalf of the plaintiffs that ball-tampering was 'cheating according to anybody's right-thinking definition of that word'. Unfortunately for Grey and his clients the jury disagreed and found for Imran by a majority of 10-2. Botham and Lamb ended up looking at a costs award in the region of £500,000.

Despite the pre-match distractions, England's defeat at Lord's had more to do with Mushtaq Ahmed than George Carman. Funnily enough Chris Lewis was injured and so England went in with Simon Brown of Durham opening the bowling and Mark Ealham batting at six. This and the fact they had 'Mushy' and we had Ian Salisbury, might help explain a 164-run defeat.

At lunch on the last day England had only one wicket down. By tea we were all out. On a pitch on which Salisbury managed 1-105 in the match, Mushtaq took 5-57 in 38 overs. Once he had removed Atherton the only thing more predictable than the collapse that ensued was Waqar Younis yorking Hick for the second time in the match. At the time I couldn't stand the little leg-spinner. Now I think he's wonderful. I'm a Sussex supporter, remember.

As well as an end to the Spice Girls, another thing I wanted was a new job. I had spent over two years commuting between Coventry and Wolverhampton and Michael Palin wasn't going to be doing any documentaries about that train journey in a hurry. Whenever I saw county cricketers complaining about how much travelling they have to do I thought: 'At least you don't have to go to the same place day after day.'

By the end of the summer Ray Illingworth was also looking for new employment. It wasn't the journey to work that was the problem but rather the path England were now taking. By contrast with the previous incumbent of the post, England's new coach was like that year's new action hero, Buzz Lightyear: he had an imagination that stretched to infinity and beyond.

Lloyd, it seemed, had something his predecessors had lacked: an open mind. He was bursting with ideas about how the England team could be better and wasn't so much a breath of fresh air as a bracing gust of Blackpool breeze. Many traditionalists laughed at his theories but some, such as the belief that a ball thrown in on the bounce arrives quicker than one sent on the full, are now generally in use. Others seemed more hair-brained. I thought David Lloyd was great, but even I wasn't convinced by his suggestion that batsmen could complete two runs faster if they sprinted all the way into the crease rather than running their bat in before turning. Having said that, Lloyd admitted this sounded wrong but claimed to have tested the theory and had found, to his own surprise, that it worked on the basis that batsmen slowed down less in putting one foot over the crease than they did in stopping short of it and using the bat to make their ground.

The fact this latter idea hasn't become generally accepted isn't the point. What's important is Lloyd was prepared to test an idea even if, at first sight, it seemed unlikely to work. Duncan Fletcher's England employed the theory that throws should be taken in front of the stumps when trying to effect run-outs. This flies in the face of traditional thinking, but probably works on the basis that any throw from the outfield is decelerating rapidly by the time it reaches the stumps and pulling it onto the wicket speeds it up. Whatever the reason, you can guarantee the technique is used because it has been tested and shown to make a difference. Similarly, the use of wide slip fielders sends the like of Ian Botham and Michael Holding into 'why-oh-why-oh-why' mode but is based on statistical analysis of where an edge offered by a particular batsman, from a given bowler, is most likely to fly in certain conditions.

I've heard commentators offering opinions along the lines of: 'England were lucky with that dismissal because the catch flew straight to Trescothick standing in the solitary wide slip position.' No, they weren't lucky, they played the percentages and won. There will be times when you do the same thing and lose, but why is it better for the ball to fly at catchable height into a big gap to a fielder's right than it is for it to go through a smaller one to his left?

If Lloyd might have been ahead of his time, Illingworth had had his. The new coach, popular with the players and, for the time being, the press and cricketing public, had left him looking like an irrelevant relic from a bygone age. By mid-season, the so recently all-powerful figure in English cricket was sat on the periphery waiting to 'clear off to his house in Spain and put his feet up'.

Pakistan produced a second victory at the Oval (Salim Malik 100 not out) and the series was lost 2-0. Nevertheless, Lloyd had already been appointed for the winter tours to Zimbabwe and New Zealand. This seemed to represent about as easy an introduction to coaching England abroad as he could have asked for. Although the record shows he hardly covered himself in glory, it's impossible to do a comparison with how any other England coach has handled a Test tour to Zimbabwe. Despite the fact the southern Africans played their first Test match in October 1992, Lloyd's is the only full tour England have ever undertaken to the Republic. What was the point in going there? We would only flippin' murder them.

TWENTY-THREE

At the end of 1996, *Newsweek* declared London to be the coolest capital city in the world. It seems more than a little odd that the concept of 'Cool Britannia' came into being during John Major's premiership, about as likely in fact as England's cricketers bestowing their title for coolest capital on Harare.

The players and management behaved as if they were doing Zimbabwe a huge favour by even deigning to be there in the winter of 1996/97 and spent most of their time moping about in hotels. Given they only had to play in two centres, Bulawayo and Harare, this must have got pretty boring. You could argue that wandering around downtown in either city might have necessitated following Imran Khan's recently revealed example of carrying a gun everywhere. Admittedly Imran only did this when he was in Pakistan rather than Hove, but you never know. Graeme Hick and his wife had cut short their holiday because the couple next door had been gunned down in a gangland murder, and they were in Spain.

Nevertheless, off the field, England's tour to Zimbabwe was a PR disaster. Before the side had even arrived the selectors had shown scant regard for the opposition by only picking 15 players and then not bothering with a replacement when Cork withdrew because of personal problems. Once they got there, things got worse and worse. 'We were not happy with the way the England team presented themselves. Their demeanour was fairly negative and not particularly attractive.' Tim Lamb the chief executive of the newly formed England and Wales Cricket Board said that. The language the Zimbabweans used about us was a little more colourful.

It might not have been quite so bad if we had had anything to be so superior and stuck-up about. Zimbabwe stood eighth out of nine in *Wisden Cricket Monthly's* new world ranking system and had just two first-class teams. However, England were only seventh and lost to one of the two, Mashonaland, by seven wickets in their opening three-day fixture.

If you played for one of only two first-class teams you might think there was a fair chance of making the Test side. The previous season, Matabeleland's wicket-keeper, Wayne James, had produced the sort of performance that in normal circumstances might have given the selectors a nudge. Playing, unsurprisingly, against Mashonaland in the final of the country's domestic first-class competition, the Lonrho Logan Cup, James broke the world record for wicket-keeping dismissals with 13 in the match. Not content with this, he made 99 in his side's first innings and finished on 99 not out in the second when the opposition's keeper, perhaps in a fit of jealous pique, conceded four byes.

James' batting performance was certainly unlucky. However, in terms of his Test prospects he had the even greater misfortune of competing for selection with Andy Flower. If Heath Streak's 202 wickets at 27.58 leave him in the 'very good' category, Flower's record makes him the only Test cricketer his country has produced who even approaches greatness.

Rightly, much is made of the fact that George Headley averaged over 60 while batting in an extremely weak West Indian side. Although Headley is undeniably one of the giants of the game and has a significance that exceeds mere statistics, his record was maintained over only 22 matches. Flower played 63 Tests for his country, kept wicket in all but eight of these, and scored 4,794 runs at 51.54. Of Zimbabweans who have scored more than 2,500 Test runs, the next highest average is his brother Grant's 29.54. The undeniably great Viv Richards, who played in one of the strongest West Indian batting sides of all time, averaged 50.23.

Andy Flower was in the Zimbabwean side taking on Atherton's England and we still thought we were going to destroy them. Drawing the Test series 0-0 and losing the one-dayers 3-0 doesn't count as destruction. Unless of course you're David Lloyd.

The autumn before the tour, John Crawley had appeared as a panelist on *Call My Bluff*. If he had lined up against his coach it would have been interesting to see what definition of 'murder' Lloyd might have come up with.

Generally the coach's passion and his loyalty to the players were positive qualities but Lloyd's infamous rant at the end of the drawn first Test was the cricketing equivalent of Kevin Keegan's 'I'd love it if we beat them' from the previous Premiership season.

After he was appointed to the England job, Keegan famously commented that, 'If it's a 0-0 draw in the Ukraine you want, then I'm probably not your man.' Lloyd obviously was the man for a 0-0 draw in Zimbabwe, but this wasn't what anyone wanted. After such a result all you could do was hope Tony Blair was right when he said: 'Things can only get better'.

In the immediate future, England were visiting New Zealand, the only country in the world rated lower than Zimbabwe. For the longer term, a number of things happened all at once. From 1st January 1997 the ECB, with Lord MacLaurin at its head, replaced the TCCB as the body in charge of English cricket. Then, shortly afterwards, David Graveney was made chairman of selectors and Duncan Fletcher became coach of Glamorgan. None of these things seemed particularly significant at the time, least of all what appeared to be little more than a name change for the governing body of the sport in this country and the appointment of the head of a supermarket as its leader.

Ian MacLaurin played football for Corinthian Casuals and second XI cricket for Kent. When he left the county in 1959, Colin Cowdrey commented that he was leaving a decent cricket club for 'a lousy grocer'. By December 1996, MacLaurin had led Tesco to a position where a poll of leading business figures voted it the most admired company in Britain. Encouragingly for me, his instinct for commercial reality had led him to the conclusion that the national team had to be the main priority if the game was to thrive in this country.

The persuasive powers that had enabled him to convince the Tesco board, against the advice of Jack Cohen, to drop Green Shield stamps, would be tested to the full in trying to get county chairmen to prioritize 'Team England'. Nevertheless, the period of success leading up to and including the Ashes summer of 2005 had its origins on page 20 of the 1997 *Wisden*. There, on a single side, MacLaurin set out his vision for the game under the heading 'English Cricket: A Manifesto'. It was the first time in my memory anyone in charge of the national summer game had had one of those.

In his manifesto, MacLaurin calls Tetley's withdrawal as the England's team sponsor 'depressing', while at the same time making the point that, not unreasonably, 'People want to be associated with winners.' No real mystery about Tetley's decision then. The 'amber lights flashing over our game' to which the chairman refers, had been there for some time. The relief was that someone had noticed and knew that 'we had to respond'. Not that the coming into being of the ECB had an immediate galvanizing effect.

The first Test of the series with New Zealand was in Auckland. The tourists took the home side's ninth second-innings wicket 37 minutes after lunch on the final day. At that stage the Kiwis led by 11 and striding to the crease was the then world record holder for the most ducks in Test history, Danny Morrison. For England to fail to win from this position would be like Wakefield Trinity's Don Fox infamously missing his conversion from right in front of the posts with the last kick of the 1968 Rugby League Challenge Cup final. Fox still got the Man of the Match award that day. England's bowlers won no such prizes. Alan Mullally employed his usual method of achieving impressively economical figures, i.e. bowling so wide that hitting the ball became optional, and Morrison batted through 166 undefeated minutes. His unbroken partnership of 106 with Nathan Astle was a record for New Zealand's tenth wicket against England.

Drawing this Test was a potentially crippling psychological blow. Fortunately the selectors managed to minimize the effects. Both sets of selectors that is.

Morrison's reward for his efforts was to be dropped, never to play Test cricket again. This was an unpopular decision, not least with the merchandising men who were left with boxes of redundant 'Danny the Duck' whistles that they might otherwise have flogged off at $5 a time.

If New Zealand's selectors made a mistake by dropping a Kiwi fast bowler for the Wellington Test, England's got it right by picking one. Andy Caddick had made his debut for England in 1993. Now, nearly four years later, he played for the first time in the same Test team as Darren Gough. The pair took England to victory with 15 wickets in the match and began a partnership that became the third most prolific fast bowling combination in English Test history. In 30 Tests together the pair took 233 wickets. By the time their careers ended, only Willis and Botham with 476 in 60 Tests and Trueman and Statham (284 in 35) stood ahead of them. In the period from Wellington until Caddick and Gough's last Test together in August 2001, England won 13 out of 30 when they combined and six out of 23 when one or both was absent.

As well as a fast bowling combination worthy of the name, England also seemed suddenly to unearth a new pair of spin twins. Croft was a major cultural icon at this time. Although the Croft in question was Lara rather than Robert, it was the Glamorgan off-spinner who, with Phil Tufnell, spun out the Kiwis at Christchurch. England won two successive overseas Tests for the first time since their previous visit to New Zealand four years earlier. Prior to that, they hadn't managed the feat since Brearley's side had defeated a Packer-weakened Australia at Adelaide and Sydney in February 1979.

The reality of this last statistic had prepared me well for the birth of my first child.

However much you adore them, very young babies don't seem much more than helpless blobs who do little but keep you awake at night and shower you in shit. Therefore having a child wasn't as much of a culture shock as it might have been for someone who hadn't spent the previous 20 years supporting England's cricket team.

When I first held my daughter I remembered a changing room in Whitchurch near Bristol and a conversation with Pricey (the ingrown toenails and piles man). I had just scored my first 100, I smiled across and told him I could die a happy man. It was only now I realised I had been talking nonsense.

My first daughter had been due on 25th March but arrived exactly a week late. This isn't as bad as being born on the 29th February or 25th December, but having April Fool's Day for a birthday is still not ideal. Where else would I look for comfort but the Births and Deaths section of *Wisden*? Bhupinder Singh (Punjab), Essex's old wicket-keeper, Neil Smith, and even Stephen Fleming, were of little comfort. However, consolation lay in the Gs: Gower, D.I. (Leics & Hants; CY 1979) b April 1, 1957. 'That'll do', I thought, 'that'll do.'

However much it might have pleased me, my daughter sharing her birthday with a left-handed batsman that none of her contemporaries would have heard of wasn't going to help make things any better in the future. Neither, it turned out, was Lord MacLaurin's first stab at revitalizing English cricket.

While it was refreshing that MacLaurin seemed to have a vision of what he was trying to achieve, not everything he did inspired confidence he was going to succeed. In early 1997 the ECB published a document called 'Raising the Standard' which contained, among other things, an incredibly complicated, hair-brained proposal to split the 18 counties into three 'conferences', with the county champions being decided by a series of play-offs in September.

'Raising the Standard' now smacks of the political technique that works on the basis of proposing something outrageous, waiting for the incandescent reaction and then apparently backing down to settle for the merely radical idea you had always intended in the first place. Nevertheless, the changes put into to place at first, were half-baked and short-lived. The idea that the top eight in the Championship would contest a one-day Super Cup the following year, while the bottom four had to pre-qualify for the Natwest Trophy, lasted one season. The County Championship wasn't divided into two divisions until 2000.

After the start of May we could thank Tony Blair for MacLaurin having extra time to devote to rethinking his proposals. Prior to the general election, the openly Conservative ECB chairman had also been the head of the UK Sports Council. After it, the new Minister for Sport, Tony Banks, suggested his relationship with MacLaurin was likely to be 'interesting' but 'short'. He was right. MacLaurin resigned as sports council chairman before he could be sacked.

Labour's victory also set up a slightly macabre new ashes contest.

Keith Narey had been the umpire of The Brewery Tap pub in Idle, Yorkshire. Unfortunately, cricket was not Mr Narey's only passion and his celebration of Labour's win was of such alcoholic intensity it killed him. The pub's regulars felt he deserved a permanent commemoration and challenged the Bradford Campaign for Real Ale to an annual cricket match in his memory. The prize for the winners of this contest was Mr Narey's cremated remains.

As for the real Ashes, they were coming home. At least that's what the crowd at Edgbaston was singing at the end of the opening Test.

On the first day, Australia collapsed to 54-8 before finally mustering a still paltry 118. On the second, Hussain and Thorpe added 288 for the fourth wicket at nearly a run a minute and on the fourth, Atherton and Stewart launched an adrenalin-soaked charge to victory. In between, on the Saturday, I saw England lose three wickets adding 29 in 40 minutes and Australia make 256-1. The first time in over 10 years England had beaten the Aussies while the urn was still at stake, and I had tickets for the crap day.

Nevertheless, we were 1-0 up. Then someone showed Glenn McGrath the right length to bowl in England. As a result he produced figures of 8-38 at Lord's and came up with the idea of holding the ball aloft to the crowd in the manner of a batsman raising his bat. England, 77 all out, were saved from defeat because the fifth day was the only one not affected by substantial amounts of rain.

At Edgbaston in 2005, England came within three runs of going 2-0 down with three to play, a position from which they would never have recovered. Had we won at Old Trafford in 1997, it's hard to see how even Mark Taylor's great side could have come back. Everybody knew the series hinged on what happened at Manchester. And where was I when this pivotal match was taking place? In France, enjoying, if that's the right word, my first 'family holiday'.

Fortunately it's possible to pick up Radio Four long wave in Brittany. Fiona thinks beaches are for lying on and she was more than happy to let me wander off with a daughter and a radio while she got on with staying completely still for three hours at a time.

On one of these excursions I stopped to watch an obviously English tourist put up a set of stumps to play cricket with his eight-year-old son. At least that's what I thought he was doing. I was wrong, as it quickly became clear he was preparing to play cricket *against* his eight-year-old son. The first time I realised something was amiss was when Dad won the toss! Unsurprisingly he grabbed the bat and threw the tennis ball to his lad.

Dad took up his two-eyed stance, resplendent in his knee-length khaki shorts, deck shoes, black socks and (I promise you) a knotted hanky on his head. I noticed his hands were too far apart on the handle and his pick up was towards second slip. Maybe this explained why he was reduced to taking on eight-year-olds? Son, it seemed, had some talent for the game and given his lack of height he could be forgiven for the fact that his first offering, while respectable enough, was a little loopy. However, Dad was clearly not in a forgiving mood and laced it back, striking him full in the left eye. Instead of the outpouring of remorse and concern I expected, the first words out of his mouth were: 'That was it! That was your chance!' His, by now mildly concussed, offspring was shown no sympathy and merely directed to get back and bowl.

Understandably, the next delivery lacked the accuracy of its predecessor and was smashed, cross batted, 40 yards back over the young bowler's head. Son looked pleadingly at his six-year-old brother who I now noticed stationed at mid-off, but he simply stared back and motioned that he wasn't going anywhere as the ball had been hit fractionally to the on-side. The first-born was forced to set off in pursuit. By the time he returned, Dad had run 19, all of which were marked off in a box drawn in the sand for the purpose. I scrolled through my vocabulary looking for a word to describe this man. I didn't stop until I got to W... If all of this had happened on a Brighton beach I would have known where *The Fast Show* got the idea for 'Competitive Dad'.

I couldn't watch anymore and wandered away thinking two things: 'No wonder the French think we're a bunch of tossers' and 'Maybe my Dad wasn't so bad after all?'

At Manchester, three members of England's team had fathers who had also played Test cricket. Two of them, Alan Butcher and Mickey Stewart, had even played for England. The third, Ron Headley, had turned out twice for the West Indies in 1973. In each case it was the son who had easily the longer international career, and for poor Ron, not only did his boy outshine him, but his own father also happened to be the greatest batsman the Caribbean has ever produced. With this in mind, Dean Headley had sensibly a) elected to play for England and b) become a bowler. However good he was – and he bowled England to victory in Melbourne less than two years later – I couldn't escape the thought that if he had ever turned out against his grandfather in his prime, the results might have been very similar to those I had just witnessed on a French beach.

There were many things my father had been that I didn't want to be. Dead at 42, leaving my own child one parent short, was chief among them. Then there were talents I didn't have a hope of possessing: the ability to bowl fast for example.

I have only the vaguest childhood memory of my father on a cricket field, but I know even this may have been created by my desire to have seen him play rather than because I really did. The image I have fits the Barcombe legend that he was erratic but pacey and bowled, Tyson-like, with a billowingly half-unbuttoned shirt. I now know that the 'pacey' part means he must have had good 'twitch fibres'. I didn't inherit these. Far from being twitchy, my fibres never seem to get beyond mildly concerned. Condemned to have every short delivery I ever bowl categorised as a long-hop rather than a bouncer, I ended up a wicket-keeper. Perhaps this explains how I came to see the 1997 Ashes series as having turned on a stumping?

Throughout that year the received wisdom was we had to play Australia on pitches offering help to the seamers. England's constant problem since I had been following them was their inability to bowl out decent batting sides on good surfaces. The tourists' top seven consisted of Mark Taylor, Matthew Elliott, Greg Blewett, Mark Waugh, Steve Waugh, Michael Bevan/Ricky Ponting and Ian Healey. They also, of course, had Shane Warne in their ranks and so, despite the success Tufnell and Croft had enjoyed in the winter, raging turners were out of the question.

The pitch at Manchester started damp. Mark Taylor won the toss and decided to bat. In the aftermath of victory this was seen as tactical genius. Put another way, it was a massive gamble that came off. Things weren't looking too clever at 160-7, but you could guarantee if anyone was going to spoil things it was Steve Waugh. Even so, Waugh's 108 still only got them to 235 and on a bright second day with the pitch seemingly drier and easier, England cruised to 94-2. Then Michael Bevan bowled a leg-side full toss to Mark Butcher.

He may have been Alan's son, but spiritually Butcher was a successor to Gower, a silky left-hander who made batting look incredibly simple before finding a teeth-grindingly infuriating way of getting out. On this day he glided to 51 before Bevan or, more accurately, Ian Healey, intervened. If the ball Shane Warne had delivered to Gatting on the same ground four years earlier was from 'Hell', this one was from 'Help yourself'. A clip through square leg for two was the minimum it should have yielded. Unfortunately, in trying to do just that, Butcher missed and overbalanced.

Batsmen generally love full tosses but wicket-keepers hate them, because, if you're standing up, by the time it reaches you the delivery has usually become a yorker. This is exactly what happened to Healey but there are few keepers I can think of who could have made what he did next look any easier.

Most stumpers in the history of the game could have been forgiven for conceding four byes. Not only did Healey field the ball by his toes, he had to do so having lost sight of it behind the batsman as he moved from off to leg. At best, Geraint Jones or Matt Prior might have padded it back down the pitch. In one movement, Healey gloved it cleanly with the ease of a man intercepting a beach ball lobbed from two feet and swept off the bails with Butcher stranded. The match and the series turned on that moment as 94-2 swiftly became 123-8.

England ended up trailing by 73. In the previous 16 years we had beaten the Australians only once after conceding a first-innings lead.

History was against us and more pertinently, so was Steve Waugh. Seemingly going on and on even longer than Celine Dion in the theme to *Titanic*, Waugh made another hundred in the second innings before McGrath, Gillespie and Warne mopped us up by 12.30 on the last day. David Lloyd's assertion that 'It's 1-1 at the halfway stage' was even more unconvincing than Michael Portillo's smile after he had lost Enfield to Stephen Twigg in May.

Despite their successes in the winter, the Old Trafford Test was the last Caddick and Gough played together for two-and-a-half years. It was the 'New Zealander' who was dropped for Headingley. His replacement was Gloucestershire's Mike Smith.

In England's first innings, Jason Gillespie, tall, right-arm, fastish and bouncy (remind you of anyone whose name begins with C?), took 7-37. When Australia batted, Smith (short, left-arm, fast-medium and skiddy), managed 0-89. Mike Smith never played for England again and could thank Graham Thorpe's fumbling of a dolly off the shoulder of Matthew Elliott's bat for the fact he ended his Test career without a wicket to his name. Elliott, 29 at the time, made 199 and Ricky Ponting, on his Ashes debut, 127. Australia won by an innings and 61 runs. When the teams met on the same ground four years later, Ponting made another century. Perhaps leaving Headingley off the rota for the 2005 Ashes series wasn't such a bad idea after all?

If Old Trafford had been the match for sons, Trent Bridge was the one for brothers. The siblings in question were the Hollioakes. Younger brother Ben, at 19, had literally swept into the cricketing public's consciousness by dropping on one knee to dump Warne into the stands during a gloriously uninhibited 48-ball 63 in the third one-day international at Lord's earlier in the summer. Now, with his captain from the previous winter, Andrew Flintoff, still 'eating Kit-Kats and drinking coke' in the corner of the England U19 dressing room, he became the second youngest man, after Brian Close, to make the Test team.

The tennis-playing David Lloyd once said if he had been able to combine his brother John's talent with his own battling attitude, he would have been Wimbledon champion. You got a similar impression about the Hollioakes. If Adam was all 'first-over-the-top', bristling aggression, squeezing every last drop from the ability God had given him, Ben combined obvious flair with a demeanour that made him seem cooler than the comic creation of the year, Austin Powers. The thought of him playing in the same U19 side as Flintoff and the other young all-round talent of the time, Alex Tudor, should give any England cricket follower a moment's pause to lament what might have been. That Tudor fell victim to a fragile body might have been a waste of talent, but it wasn't 'tragic'. That word should be reserved for the accuracy of Hollioake's own prediction that he was too cool to get old. A breezy 28 with five boundaries should have represented a promising start, it turned out to be Ben Hollioake's highest Test score.

Within a month of Hollioake's debut, the 'People's Princess' was killed in the Paris car crash. The death of Mother Teresa less than a week later went almost unnoticed. When the MCC played the Rest of the World in a match in the princess' memory the following summer, only Steve Waugh turned down his invitation because he had a prior engagement doing something similar in Calcutta.

Perhaps the death of the young seems more tragic because our imaginations can create a future fuller and happier than any reality might ever have been? It's possible to look at what Ben Hollioake achieved in his two Tests (44 runs at 11.00 and four wickets at 49.75) and think it's an exaggeration to say that when he died in a car crash less than five years later, English cricket lost one the greatest talents of his generation. Hollioake's Test career was over before he reached 21. When a 20-year-old Andrew Flintoff made his debut against South Africa the following year, his two Tests yielded 17 runs at 5.66 and one wicket at 112.00. He didn't make it past 50 in a Test match until he was 25 and first took five wickets in an innings a year after that. Ben Hollioake was 24 when he died.

Remembering the ease with which Hollioake dismantled an Australian attack containing Warne and McGrath in the late spring of 1997 meant when Christopher Martin-Jenkins interrupted commentary on a Test in New Zealand to announce his death, it pulled me up short every bit as much as Peter Allen on Radio Five reporting the passing of Princess Diana.

Ben Hollioake did have time to create one piece of Test history. Perhaps, given the true tragedy was for his family and not for English cricket, it's fitting this was made by bowling in tandem with his brother to the Waugh twins?

There are no prizes for guessing that, in the first direct contest between brothers and brothers at Test level, it was the batting pair who came out on top. Mark made 68, Steve 75, Australia won by 264 runs to retain the Ashes and Shane Warne did his wiggly jig with a stump above his head to taunt the crowd from the pavilion balcony.

Perhaps Warne over exerted himself? At the Oval it was clear he had a groin strain that restricted him so much Phil Tufnell, selected for his only Test of the summer, out-bowled him on a sand pit of the sort the English cricketing authorities had been trying to avoid all series. Warne managed 4-89 in the match but Tufnell, like his namesake Nigel in *This is Spinal Tap*, went all the way up to 11. The Australians, chasing only 124 to win, imploded for 104 on the third afternoon.

The image of Graham Thorpe losing his sunglasses as he plunged forward at mid-off to catch Glenn McGrath lifted the spirits and made it feel like we were finally closing the gap on the Aussies. Nevertheless, despite the fact a 3-2 defeat was the best result we had managed in five Ashes series, the win at the Oval had put a hardly deserved gloss on another summer in which we had been thoroughly outplayed.

However, there was a glimmer of hope. The year had started with the announcement of the successful cloning of Dolly the sheep. Now, with his real son having opted for a career in rugby, all the scientists had to do was apply this technology to Ian Botham as soon as possible.

TWENTY-FOUR

I can say in all honesty that I've watched an entire Test match without ever leaving the pub.

This was the time during which the first shoots of the David Beckham phenomenon began to appear. Newly betrothed to 'Posh Spice' (the least appropriate nickname since someone dubbed Geoff Boycott 'Fiery'), Beckham began to attract attention on all pages of the newspapers, partly by getting sent off during the World Cup for a petulant little back-heel kick at Diego Simeone, but more for being photographed poncing about in a sarong. I was 34 and obviously out of touch because no man I know has ever worn one. Similarly, a dubious boast about pubs and whole Test matches shouldn't be taken to indicate I was an outrider for the binge drinking culture that so concerned politicians and health professionals in the new millennium. It was just a very short Test.

By the time England embarked on their tour to the West Indies in 1997-98, I had my new job. More than that, I had my dream job. Working in a law centre giving free legal advice counts as an ambition if you're a leftie lawyer. There were the major disadvantages of having a wife for a supervisor and a majority of colleagues with an 'anyone but England' attitude to cricket but these were counter-balanced by flexi-time and the presence of Mark, the ironic Craig White supporter.

On the opening day of the series, Mark and I knocked off early to troop into the Slug and Lettuce in time for the first over. My boast was very nearly that I missed an entire Test match without ever leaving the pub, as we immediately encountered a major problem in persuading the barman to turn over from Aerobics Oz Style. He took some convincing that the sight of Mike Atherton and Alec Stewart playing dodgeball with Courtney Walsh and Curtley Ambrose was preferable to Aussie models in bikinis getting sweaty on a beach. Only the most reconstructed of men wouldn't have been forced to admit he at least had a point, but we were there for the cricket and not to be denied.

What Mark and I had anticipated were the tentative first salvoes of a closely fought series. What we got was the cricketing equivalent of the opening sequence of the newly released *Saving Private Ryan*. The match lasted 56 minutes. It was only that long because England's physio came onto the field six times to attend to batsmen who had taken blows from Walsh or Ambrose. The pitch started ridged and the third ball flew straight past Atherton's nose off a length. The fourth, pitched in roughly the same place, went practically straight along the ground. Alec Stewart, generally credited with the bravest nine not out in Test history, greeted Nasser Hussain to the crease with: 'It's Saturday; it's eight o'clock; it's the lottery.'

It wasn't just Stewart's batting that was brave. Venkat and Steve Bucknor's decision to call the game off on a ground that had known riots in the past required courage too. There was no riot this time because anyone who knew anything about cricket understood it was the right decision. Even the groundsman, Charles Joseph, escaped censure by pointing the finger at the senior Jamaican cricket officials who had instructed him to relay the square at only six months' notice. Atherton, who had been on the receiving end of Ambrose's first offering at Edgbaston in 1995, must have been sick of administrators sticking their noses into pitch preparation. Having said that, Joseph's decision to dig up the whole square without leaving any of the previous surfaces intact as a contingency plan and his use of a heavy roller that turned out to be concave in places, can't have helped.

Even if Atherton and Stewart had good reason to curse more than one of the locals, the four men I feel sorriest for are, in ascending order: Nixon McLean, whose Test debut this was; Mark Butcher, whose first ball in the middle since the previous September was a head-high, off-a-length screamer from Walsh that he did well to fend to third slip; the man I met four years later who told me he had spent half his pension lump sum on the trip of a lifetime to see a Test in Jamaica and the bloke in the pub who made the mistake of asking me 'What's happening?'

Admittedly this was a dangerously open question to direct at a complete stranger, but he could be forgiven for assuming I was a normal person. Sadly, I had got a bit overexcited by what I was witnessing. Instead of the single sentence he was clearly expecting, my interrogator got a ten-minute forensic analysis of why the pitch was such a disgrace and a further ten on why this was a moment of Test history. I think he only wanted to know who was batting, it was either that or where the Aussie models had gone. I still cringe when Mark reminds me of the glazed and slightly frightened look he had on his face by the time I had finished.

Still, even my reaction wasn't as extreme as the match referee, Barry Jarman, who claimed: 'I am crying tears of blood.' Such a phrase might have been better saved for a more personally humiliating situation such as, taking an example completely at random, being President of the United States and getting caught with your pants down in the Oval Office.

As my friend who had spent half his retirement fund on a trip to Jamaica had discovered, not all opportunities of a lifetime turn out as you might have planned. Monica Lewinsky was 24 and had gone to work in the White House for experience. Ashley Cowan (remember him?) was 22 and in the Caribbean for similar reasons. However, if Monica succeeded in her aim – albeit not in the way she might have intended – Ashley didn't. He sent down 72 first-class overs in the whole tour and the young fast bowler's place in the Test team that had previously been handed to the likes of Graham Stevenson, Greg Thomas and Devon Malcolm, went instead to the 32-year-old Angus Fraser.

Not that you could quibble with the selectors' decision. In a hastily arranged extra Test in Trinidad, Fraser produced figures of 8-53 to become the only Englishman to take eight wickets in an innings twice against the West Indies. Supposedly only on the tour as a fill-in /bowling coach, the Middlesex man equalled John Snow's England record of 27 wickets in a Caribbean series and provided a poke in the eye for those who had written him off.

One detractor in particular obviously stuck in the bowler's mind. During the course of his heroics in Trinidad, Fraser removed Lara courtesy of a skied catch to Atherton at mid-off. His ecstatic celebration was out of proportion even with the dismissal of a batsman as great as the West Indian captain. When his own skipper asked him why he was making such a fuss, the telling response was: 'That wicket's just taken me past Illingworth.' He didn't mean Richard.

England still lost that game when they should have won it.

Fortunately, in a second Trinidad Test they then did what they had done at Barbados on the previous tour and won a game they should have lost. Then El Nino and Brian Lara's luck with the toss took a hand.

El Nino was the Pacific Ocean water temperature phenomenon about which we all became extremely knowledgeable and very frightened, for around a fortnight. Linked to global warming in a way only meteorologists could hope to understand, El Nino (warm) and its sister La Nina (cold) were apparently responsible for every extreme weather occurrence in the Americas and were just another example of why we're all going to hell in a bucket. This, in the short term, was roughly what was about to happen to England's cricket team.

El Nino was accused of causing the longest drought in Guyana anyone could remember. Four years earlier, the Bourda ground had disappeared under water and not a ball was bowled in the Test match. Now, Karachi would have looked verdant by comparison. Lara won the toss and batted on the only day the pitch didn't look like one of the Maldives and that was that.

Men accuse women of being fickle. El Nino was catagorised as male, but it rained in Barbados just as England were getting themselves into a winning position.

The Jamiacans had a groundsman whose roller wasn't round, the Barbadians had one who claimed he couldn't find his motorized super-sopper. With the West Indies 2-1 up, I suspected this was only true in the same sense as President Clinton 'did not have sexual relations with that woman'. Nevertheless, a draw left the home side with the Wisden Trophy. The only pleasing memory from the match was of Mark Ramprakash's outstretched arms and beaming face on reaching his first Test hundred. He couldn't have looked any more exultant if he had just lost his virginity to Hollywood's latest It girl, Cameron Diaz.

There was still time for further humiliation in Antigua. Bowled out for 127 in their first innings, England rounded off Atherton's tenure as captain with a super-special collapse of 6-26 in their second effort on the final afternoon.

Immediately following this defeat, Atherton resigned. When he had passed Peter May's England record for most Tests in charge the previous summer, Fred Titmus said it was 'a travesty'. Certainly a record of 13 wins out of 52 Tests wasn't earth shattering and smacked of his keeping the job on the basis many club captains rely on – the absence of suitable alternatives. However, this may be harsh on Atherton as he was hardly helped by his selectors. Their preference for captain may have been consistent, but their choice of players wasn't.

During Atherton's reign, 50 men played for England and of these only the captain himself was an ever-present. No bowler made more appearances than Fraser's 27. It can't be easy to develop team spirit, or indeed a consistent strategy, when half the team changes from one match to the next. This must be doubly difficult when someone else is leading the one-day side.

Atherton had a strangely mixed record as one-day captain. At home he could boast of six Texaco Trophy victories but abroad he had lost 3-0 to Zimbabwe and his best result was a 2-2 draw with New Zealand. Before the Caribbean tour, Adam Hollioake had been preferred to lead England in a quadrangular tournament in Sharjah. The Surrey man's victory in the Middle East seemed to support the idea that splitting the captaincy was the way to go. As a policy this represented yet another short-lived miracle cure for the ills of the national team.

Unfortunately, Hollioake's achievement is now devalued by the possibility that not all of England's opponents were trying quite as hard as they might have been and when he followed it up with a 4-1 defeat in the Caribbean and a 2-1 loss to South Africa the next summer, the experiment was quickly shelved.

England returned from the Caribbean with no Wisden Trophy, no captain and no series victory over a major Test-playing nation since Gatting's Ashes win in 1986/87. In other words, England hadn't won a five-Test series since before Atherton started playing first-class cricket. Yet in all that time it had never occurred to me to stop watching them. The only explanation I can give for this is that, like the football fan who swears 'never again' every Saturday but is back again the next week, they were my team and I couldn't shake them off.

The tourists that summer were the second best side in the world, South Africa. Not for the first time, prospects weren't good.

The captaincy issue was resolved by the appointment of Alec Stewart. Not a bad result for a bloke who two years previously had supposedly been too old to even be in the team.

Stewart was preferred to the nominated vice-captain in the West Indies, Nasser Hussain, on the basis that the Essex man might be too intense and volatile to be an effective captain. Surrey's wicket-keeper, on the other hand, was as straight-backed, crease-in-the-underpants safe a choice as you could imagine. The most embarrassing thing the press could dig up about him was that he had once played in the same school second XI as *The Sun*'s cricket correspondent, John Etheridge.

However, the England selectors were nothing if not inventive and managed in the course of their deliberations to employ thinking that was simultaneously safe and muddled. Stewart may have been made Test captain, but Adam Hollioake was retained to lead the one-day side. The main reason Hollioake had been given this job in the first place was because it had been felt Atherton might no longer be worthy of his place in the shortened version of the game. By contrast, Stewart's ability to multi-task made him the lynch-pin of the side. How else do you explain the fact he played in the 2003 World Cup when only weeks away from his fortieth birthday?

The inconsistency of their position slowly dawned on the selectors over the course of the summer. By the time the final one-day international of the season came around, Stewart was captain, Atherton was opening and Hollioake wasn't even in the team.

Four days after Stewart was appointed, the transsexual Dana International won the Eurovision Song Contest for Israel. Yes, I know Israel's not in Europe, it's to do with them being a member of the European Broadcasting Union. Despite being at least two kinds of everything, this Dana was slightly different from the Irish version who had won the 1970 contest and she wasn't the last person that year to prove appearances can be deceptive in Birmingham.

The song contest was held at the National Indoor Arena; the first Test was at Edgbaston. The pitch started green; the opposition's opening attack consisted of Allan Donald and Shaun Pollock; Atherton had made one fifty in his previous 19 Test innings and his opening partner, Butcher, two in his whole career. I clamped my eyes shut and waited for the clatter of wickets. England closed the first day on 249-1.

The last time I had seen such a collectively appalling bowling attack was when England failed to dislodge Danny Morrison in Auckland. Alan Mullally was gun-barrel-straight by comparison. The only wicket came when Butcher slogged frog-in-a-blender Adams into the deep. Donald and co. must have wanted to slink out of the ground in a trench coat and false beard. It was a public humiliation matched only by the men trying out Viagra live on Richard and Judy.

From England's point of view, Mullally was otherwise engaged bowling 18 inches outside off stump for Leicestershire at Headingley (0-53 in 21 overs), and the selectors had put Gough, Fraser and Cork together in the same Test XI for the first time since December 1996. Stewart informed us that these three had dubbed themselves 'The Dream Team', which smacked of asking for trouble almost as much as Paul Ince styling himself 'The Guv'nor'. Sure enough, as England dawdled past 400, Donald found one straight enough to break Gough's right index finger.

My day at the Saturday of the Edgbaston Test should have been spent watching England's penetrative three-pronged seam attack flying in at the South Africans. Instead I had to make do with a proto-Gary Pratt called Ben Spendlove taking two short-leg catches to help reduce the tourists to 125-4. Then, just as he had done four years earlier, Jonty Rhodes spoiled my day. At least the irritating little sod had gone by the time they toured here in 2003.

South Africa avoided the follow-on, England slogged on the fourth afternoon and Stewart, safe in the knowledge that it was going to piss down all day, made a nominally attacking declaration on the final morning.

At Edgbaston the red faces had predominantly been South African. At Lord's they were, with one notable exception, all English. It's fair to say England don't have a great record against these opponents at headquarters. To say the South Africans won in 1994, 1998 and 2003 doesn't quite cover it. The margins of victory were 356 runs, 10 wickets and an innings and 92 runs. Although England's batsmen didn't cover themselves in glory on any of these occasions, their effort in 1998 was particularly special as the biggest individual contribution to their first innings came from extras. To put this in some kind of context, England had been playing Test cricket for more than 120 years and on all but three previous occasions the top-scorer had been someone with a bat.

The only man to buck the trend of English discomfort, was the South African Cricket Board's chief executive, Ali Bacher. Due to make a speech in the President's box, he was unable to do so because he was trapped in the ladies' toilet. He claimed to have wandered in there by mistake while going through his notes. Sounds more like another of those hoovering stories from the Lancet to me, but the interesting thing is that there was a ladies for him to wander into.

Women were obviously allowed to go to the toilet in the pavilion but they still weren't allowed to be members of the MCC. Less than three months earlier, more than 55 per cent of the club's members had voted in favour of admitting women, but had failed to win the day because a two-thirds majority was required to change the rules. This result inevitably provoked strong views on both sides of the debate.

Public condemnation came from the prime minister, the heritage secretary and the sports minister. This wasn't something you could have imagined happening under the previous administration and one contributor to *The Cricketer* summed up the level of much of the debate by suggesting if these three were against them, then the MCC must have got it spot-on.

Whatever the rights and wrongs of the argument, it seemed the ECB's efforts to maintain cricket's popularity in what MacLaurin had referred to in his manifesto as 'an increasingly competitive market place' were hardly assisted by the game's most famous club continuing to treat half the population as second-class citizens. This is a point the MCC appeared to accept when another vote in September, pushed through by the president Colin Ingleby-Mackenzie, produced the necessary support for women's membership. Helpful though this may have been, the board itself wasn't doing much for the game's image in this respect.

In March, the ECB had been involved in an extremely damaging industrial tribunal case, in which one of their female former staff, Theresa Harrild, successfully sued for sex discrimination. The nature of the substantive allegations: that senior staff had pressed her into an abortion when she became pregnant by a colleague and then sacked her when she suffered from depression afterwards, were bad enough. However, worse still were the claims of a generally demeaning atmosphere in the workplace and more specifically, that the chief executive, Tim Lamb, had made derogatory comments about England's women cricketers. 'We want our good dykes on board so that we can get more lottery money' is what he was supposed to have said.

Then, despite losing in the tribunal, members of the board made public comments about Ms Harrild, including that she was 'a liar'. This brought a threat of further legal action and forced a public apology from Lord MacLaurin. In an age of spin, it's hard to imagine something being handled worse from a public relations point of view. Even the Australians, not usually noted for their reconstructed views, managed to show us up. The first issue of *Wisden Australia* was in production. When it was published the following January, the Cricketer of the Year was Belinda Clark, captain of the Aussie women's World Cup-winning side and scorer of the first one-day international double hundred by anyone, male or female.

At least the ECB appeared to have learned some lessons by the time England's women shared the open-top bus ride through London during the Ashes celebrations of 2005.

One magazine of the time headlined the Harrild story with 'Lord's 0 Ladies 1'. The score was now the same in the Test series as the teams reached Old Trafford.

The third Test of this series was when I realised just how brave you must have been to face Jeff Thomson in the 1970s.

Gough was back for England and Allan Donald, as he did all summer, continued to charge in for the tourists. Whatever he says, Gough was catagorised as at the quick end of fast-medium, whereas Donald was universally regarded as just plain fast. For the first time, grounds made regular use of a speed gun during this series. Although Gough occasionally had cause to puff out his chest when he touched 90 mph, he was more representatively clocked at 88. Donald regularly beat 90 and his standard figure was more like 92. This said to me that either Gough was quicker than he was given credit for or the difference between quick fast-medium and just plain quick, was about 4 mph. In the 1970s, Jeff Thomson was timed at 99.7mph, i.e. nearly eight mph quicker than Donald's standard delivery. Thommo himself reckons this was measured at the batsman's end rather than, as now, at the point of release by the bowler. In other words, in modern terms he thinks he was bowling at about 112 mph. Even allowing for Thomson's ego and the limited technology of the time, he had to be at least as fast as Brett Lee or Shoaib Akhtar. The most a 1970s batsman would have had on his head when facing Thomson at his fastest, was a cap. No wonder most of the English batsmen who went on the 1974-75 tour to Australia never got over the experience.

David Lloyd had been one of those on the receiving end from Lillee and Thomson. At Manchester, the team he now coached delivered a blow to the tourists from which they never fully recovered. It's unusual to sap an opponent's morale by scraping a draw, but England managed it when Robert Croft blocked his way through three hours on the last afternoon and Angus Fraser survived a huge appeal for lbw in Donald's final over of the match. The end came with scores level and one wicket remaining. I can still see Stewart jumping to his feet and punching the air with both fists as the draw was assured. I remembered this game when the Australians indulged in similar celebrations on the same ground in 2005. And I remembered what happened next.

In 2005, Vaughan tried to lift his frustrated men by inviting them to look at how enthusiastically the Aussies were celebrating a draw. However, as Stewart so inspiringly put it at after Old Trafford 1998: 'I'd rather be one down than two down.' While this was hardly in the Mike Brearley class of incisive analysis, it did at least mean their captain had spotted England could still win the series. Not that anyone seriously expected them to given how one-sided the series had been up until now.

However, just as England seemed incapable of being anything other than abject at Lord's, so the South Africans have a habit of making substantial first-innings scores and still losing. At the Oval in 1994 they totalled 332 (not enormous, but more than England usually managed in the period) and lost by eight wickets. In 2003, on the same ground, they racked up 484 and still went down by nine wickets. At Trent Bridge in 1998, South Africa batted first and made 374.

The last time the Proteas had toured here I had gone to the fourth day at the Oval and seen less than half a day's cricket. By plumping for the Saturday of this Test I got to see Mark Ramprakash take four and a half hours over 67 not out and missed one of the most compelling one-on-one cricketing duels in Test history.

Ramprakash's effort had nursed the tail (i.e. Hick, the debutant Flintoff and the Dream Team) to within 38 of the tourists. When 'the Team' worked their way through the South African second innings the victory target was 247. England hadn't made that many to win a home Test since 1902. If they were going to get there this time, it seemed vital that Atherton made a major contribution.

When you are chasing nearly 250, 27 doesn't count as a major contribution. But that's how many Atherton had when he gloved Allan Donald to Boucher. Spare a thought for the South African wicket-keeper, because it was a fantastic catch, diving forwards and sideways to secure a ball that was dying on him inches above the turf. If the appeal had been upheld, Boucher would in all likelihood have joined Healey in turning a series with one moment of keeping brilliance. However, what were now termed 'third-country umpires', had, as Gideon Haigh put it, 'simply brought about impartial incompetence'. The New Zealander Steve Dunne who, grey-haired and mustachioed, reminded me of the fishmonger in Camberwick Green, detected arm-guard rather than glove and Atherton stood his ground.

Calm, cold-blooded fury carries far more menace than frenzied rage. To describe the stare Donald gave Atherton as icy would be like saying Siberia is 'a bit nippy'. The batsman couldn't have been in any less doubt that retribution was about to be sought, if he had just fouled Vinnie Jones. What followed was described by Donald himself as 'the most intense 60 minutes I have experienced in a Test'.

When I first listened to commentary from Australia my radio crackled. Listening to this passage of play on the boundary at Stoneleigh I had a similar experience, except this time the signal was perfect. Figures of 8-3-11-0 tell nothing of the unremitting nature of the assault Donald launched at Atherton from round the wicket. A spoilsport umpire might have stepped in and invoked Law 42 on intimidation. This was a series littered with mistakes by the officials, but Dunne and Mervyn Kitchen's inaction in this respect was absolutely right: partly because, as David Hopps wrote in *The Guardian*, 'great sport transcends the normal rules of engagement' but more than anything because Atherton absolutely refused to be intimidated.

When Courtney Walsh had torn into the England opener in a similar way in Jamaica four years earlier 'Iron Mike' had been dismissed close to what must have been the end of the bowler's spell. At Trent Bridge he survived, and in doing so ensured England would win. The 16 runs he made between his reprieve and the close that evening were every bit as magnificent as the 185 he had chiselled out in Johannesburg.

If the Trent Bridge Test had been 'the Atherton and Donald show', the series decider at Headingley belonged to someone else. Surprisingly, the man in question was neither English nor South African, but rather a Pakistani by the name of Javed Akhtar.

Anyone who wasn't following English cricket at this time could be forgiven for never having heard of Mr Akhtar. Based on his performance at Leeds, he was an umpire of such mind-boggling incompetence that you could only conclude he had ended up on the international panel by virtue of a series of bizarre misunderstandings. He couldn't have been any worse if he had been the individual who, on one occasion at Stoneleigh, was forced to turn down a run out appeal because he was in the process of composing a text message when the wicket was broken.

To be fair to Javed Akhtar, another masterstroke from the ICC had pitched him into the middle of a vital Test match on the back of one second XI game in three months. Umpires need match practice every bit as much as players and the more forgiving commentators reasoned his performance was probably more a product of rustiness than ineptitude. Whatever the reason, England benefited from eight of the ten lbw decisions in the match and appropriately it was Akhtar who fired out Ntini on the last morning to spark Stewart's air-punching, stump-clutching gallop from the field.

It's worth remembering that this emotional victory came only a year before the nadir of being unofficially rated the worst Test team in the world. The momentum that could have been gained from the first major Test series victory in over a decade was halted alarmingly quickly. Firstly, the Oval groundsman produced another dust bowl for the touring afterthoughts that were Sri Lanka. The visitors responded to the dismissive way in which they had once again been treated, by giving us a good hiding. Muralitharan's 16 wickets in the match included 9-65 in 54.2 overs in the second innings. He didn't so much spin us to defeat as corkscrew us into the ground. Secondly, the winter tour was to Australia.

The fact the BBC had never provided full live coverage of England's winter tours was something I lived with. I couldn't miss something I had never had. However, the prospect of being unable to watch in the summer was too awful to contemplate. The decision of Labour's culture secretary, Chris Smith, to remove home Tests from the list of sporting 'Crown Jewels' reserved for terrestrial broadcasters, made this a real possibility. There was a genuine fear Test cricket would be lost to satellite television.

In the midst of the furore that blew up in 2005 over the deal the ECB struck with Sky, Smith made it clear Test cricket had been removed from the 'Crown Jewels' in 1998 on the basis of a gentleman's agreement (a nod and a wink) with Lord MacLaurin. The gist of this understanding was while the declassification would be used to negotiate a 'fairer' (higher) price for the television rights, ultimately the matches would be sold to a terrestrial broadcaster, assumed by everybody, including the Corporation's Head of Television Sport, to be the BBC.

As MacLaurin said at the time: 'The ECB have a duty to try to improve the game's financial position, but that does not necessarily mean accepting the highest bid for television rights…I would be pretty certain that at the end of the day, if we are able to negotiate a reasonable price, the BBC would still show Test matches.' Oops! The following summer, Channel Four introduced us to Mark Nicholas' 'Hello ladies' style of fronting the cricket.

TWENTY-FIVE

At the start of 1999 my second daughter was born; head first down the toilet. Actually that's not completely true, because I caught her. Alright, that's not quite true either, but I did get my hand on her head. Whether, if I had dropped her into the bowl, I would have incurred more than the standard 25p fine for such indiscretions I will fortunately never know, because I was rescued by the midwife. Not that she didn't have a bit of making up to do having told Fiona 30 seconds earlier she had 'bags of time' to go to the loo before the baby arrived.

We had always intended she would be born at home, just not within 45 minutes of going into labour and certainly not down the bog. Nevertheless it provided one of those family stories that endures and is endured by those who have heard it over and over again. That's why so many stories become wildly embellished over time: you have to do something to try and hold the interest of those who have heard them before. Anyway, not many people have one of Armitage Shanks' finest as the first picture in their baby album. If I had a more entrepreneurial spirit, a few months later I might have been able to sell that photo to the cricket magazines for their end of season front covers. As the New Zealanders departed in the early autumn, down the pan is precisely where our team seemed to be going.

At the start of England's tour to Australia, Ian Healey was asked if he thought the tourists were resilient enough. His diplomatic, if less than erudite reply was: 'I would never call England the opposite of resilient. Whatever that is.' By the end of the first month it appeared that resilience was something the tourists were going to need in abundance. Atherton's back gave almost immediate cause for concern and Graeme Hick was called up as cover; John Crawley was mugged after being mistaken for an Irishman; Peter Such cracked his nose open running into Mark Butcher during practice and Butcher himself was hit over the right eye batting against Western Australia. The Surrey man may have won a trouser press for being the best turned out player in the tour's traditional opener at Lilac Hill, but he went into the first Test with more stitches than first-class runs on the tour. I was sure I had seen a similar scenario somewhere before. As the Warwickshire man who owned a house on a right-angled bend immediately after a hump-backed bridge said to my friend when he landed his car on the garden wall: 'Oh no, not again!'

At least England didn't lose the first Test, but that was only because a massive tropical storm flooded the ground at tea on the fifth day when defeat looked inevitable. Even this mini-triumph was marred by the subsequent loss of Graham Thorpe (tour average 87.60) when his back gave out before Atherton's. Brisbane also marked the end of the 'Dream Team'. Fraser was immediately dropped and by the time he returned for our traditional consolation victory, Cork and the Ashes were gone. Less than a year after his triumphs in Trinidad, the Middlesex warhorse ended his Test career forlornly sending down four wicketless overs as Headley, Gough and Mullally stole the Melbourne Test from under Australia's nose with 12 runs to spare.

This was supposed to be the series in which England finally had a chance to wrest back the Ashes. Warne, despite all his pre-tour psycho-bullshit about aiming to play, had no chance of recovering from a shoulder operation in time. Unfortunately, as was often true of Australia at this time, they had a second-string who would have walked into most other Tests sides in the world. Up stepped Stuart MacGill.

MacGill had played club cricket in England with little success and *Wisden* commented euphemistically that 'his temperament had betrayed him'. What this meant was: he had received a life ban from the Lancashire League for swearing, which presumably meant he possessed one of the foulest mouths in world cricket. He also had a better-disguised googly and arguably more variations than Warne. He was less accurate than the great, tubby bottle-blond, but Mark Taylor managed to deal with this by the simple expedient of putting a fielder on the point boundary. It would have been interesting to hear what the Australian press would have said if an England bowler had started his spells with a man back, probably something about typical English negativity.

Mark Taylor was a great captain but his use of this field placing irritated me. Not because he wasn't right to employ it, but because he was. When Brian Lara had come to England with the 1995 West Indians, he had sought to establish his dominance over our bowlers with early boundaries, particularly square on the off side. I had suggested to my teammates that one way to counter this would be to set a man back square on the line, cutting down his run flow, getting him off strike and building pressure by making him work harder to establish himself. You feel a lot less settled if you're five not out than if you've raced to 20. My colleagues shouted me down, saying what I was advocating amounted to setting the field for bad bowling. Now, here was the best captain in the world apparently doing exactly that. When Michael Vaughan employed the idea against Langer and Hayden in 2005, he was a hailed as a tactical genius. MacGill took 27 wickets in the series and with Glenn McGrath, naggingly accurate rather than striving for wicket-taking 'magic' balls all the time, proved that defence isn't always negative.

A defence of any kind was something England's lower order could have done with developing. Time and again the paper-thin tail took up origami and folded itself into a shape usually recognizable as a duck. The collapses were, in order: six for 60 in the one completed innings at Brisbane; 10 for 110 and five for 33 at Perth; seven for 40 and five for 16 at Adelaide; seven for 70 in the first innings at Melbourne and seven for 83 and eight for 78 in Sydney. The only time there was even a hint of a wag, in the second innings at Melbourne, England won. Again there was something depressingly familiar about those statistics.

My first experience of following England in Australia had been Brearley's 5-1 rout of the home side in 1978-79. More recent successive defeats by margins of 3-0, 3-1 and 3-1 again, showed things had certainly changed.

So completely had they dominated us in the previous decade we had begun to worship Australians as representing the ultimate in cricketing manhood. No fewer than 12 of the 18 counties employed an Aussie as their overseas professional for the 1999 season. Of these players only three, Slater, Langer and, for one match, Kasprowicz, had played any part in the previous winter's Ashes series. 'Look!' we marvelled, 'Even their second-teamers are gods!'

The Australians wanted us to believe they were unbeatable. The moment we were convinced was when it became true. Sadly, it wasn't just the Aussies we had trouble with.

A few years back *The Observer* magazine ran a series of articles along the lines of 'the cricketers' cricketer' or 'the footballers' footballer'. When it got to the level of running 'the makeover show presenters' makeover show presenter' or something like it, they spotted the formula might have become a little tired and the series ended. Had they continued with it, England's 1999 World Cup would have strolled home in 'the sodding disasters' sodding disaster' category.

The previous autumn the team's new kit was unveiled. It was modelled by Alec Stewart, Adam Hollioake and that well known cricket(er) lover, Caprice. The only reason I can think of for her presence was someone at the ECB was indulging their own variation of a David Mellor-style fantasy. Things went downhill from there.

Most major sporting events, particularly if they are staged in Europe, have opening ceremonies that feature thousands of extras from New Order videos. Even if Barry Davies' 'Look, I'm just telling you what it says here' commentary leaves you none the wiser as to what's going on, at least some time, thought and money appear to have been invested.

The ECB's effort at opening the World Cup consisted of some big flags on the Lord's outfield, a small group of freezing cold school children, five fireworks Tim Lamb had left over from Bonfire night and a speech from Tony Blair in the 'Ich Bin Ein Berliner' class of unintentional toe-curling comedy.

Blair wasn't the last politician who might have had cause to regret opening his mouth in public during this tournament. The Mayor of Taunton welcomed the Kenyan squad to Somerset's ground by informing them that, 'Great names have played here, such as Bill Alley, Ian Botham and Cliff Richards.' Still, given the game was against Zimbabwe, at least there wouldn't have been many people there to hear him.

Then there was England's team; it was a quizmaster's dream. Who were the two members of England's 1999 cricket World Cup squad who didn't play a single match in the tournament?

The first was Nick Knight, who ended his career with 100 ODIs and a batting average over 40. The second was Vince Wells. No, you do remember Vince Wells… played for Leicestershire… that Vince Wells… you know! They might as well have picked Caprice. In fact an entire XI made up of supermodels wouldn't have gone out of the competition at an earlier stage than England did.

Of those picked who did get a game, our cult-hero-in-waiting and secret weapon was Ian Austin. The Pakistanis had Shoaib Akhtar and Wasim Akram, the Australians Glenn McGrath and Shane Warne and the South Africans Allan Donald and Lance Klusener. We had 'Bully'.

What we didn't have was a grasp of the importance of net run-rate.

Despite a heavy defeat by South Africa in the group stages, England were confident of progressing after disposing of Sri Lanka, Kenya and Zimbabwe. The only way we might not go through was if Alistair Campbell and his men did a job on the South Africans. That's the captain of Zimbabwe's cricket team not the Labour Party's knee-capper.

Until this point the South Africans had mangled everyone in their path and the most controversial thing they had been involved in was Hansie Cronje's use of an ear piece to communicate with the dressing room while in the field. This was the year before Cronje's fall from grace and it was assumed he was receiving tactical suggestions rather than information about what the odds were on when the next wide would be bowled. Nevertheless, he was deemed to be gaining an unfair advantage and told he couldn't carry on using it. Despite this, England had every confidence the South Africans would roll over their neighbours and render academic their final group match, with India.

So confident was Stewart, that he won the toss and chose to bowl in what, if you believed the weather forecast, would be the best batting conditions of the match. India won and so, incredibly, did Zimbabwe. England ended up in a three-way tie with the pair of them.

It's not unusual for a World Cup to have at least one rule nobody understands. In 1992 it was Richie Benaud's system for deciding rain-effected matches and in 2003 Messrs Duckworth and Lewis' for the same circumstances. In 1999 it was the rule for deciding who went through if sides ended on the same number of points at the group stage. In the event of a tie, progression to the next round was decided by most wins, results of head-to-head matches and net run-rate in that order. The last of these was very unlikely to apply. Unless, that is, you ended up in a three-way tie.

When England lost to South Africa they appeared to give up the ghost rather than trying to get as close to their opponents' score as possible and in their victory over Zimbabwe left Flintoff cooling his heels in the pavilion while they took 38.3 overs to knock off 168 to win. In so doing they had effectively ignored their net run-rate. In terms of lack of attention to a potentially important detail it was the equivalent of not practising penalties during a major football tournament. They paid the same price as our footballers have done so many times.

Flintoff was left to be described by *Wisden* as 'one of the disappointments of the tournament' and David Lloyd, who had long since signalled his departure as coach at its conclusion, had his emotional farewell to his players constantly interrupted by counties enquiring if the national team's early exit meant they could have their best players back.

Dave Stewart's World Cup song, which incidentally contained no reference to cricket, was released the day after England were eliminated. The following week, two major high street retailers reported zero sales. The only way things could get any worse was if Australia ended up winning the thing.

Within a month Herschelle Gibbs had spilled 'that catch' and Waugh had seen his side to the semis almost on his own; a batless Allan Donald had been run out to leave the Aussies in the final and Pakistan had then mustered even fewer than they had managed against Bangladesh. All of these were things I wanted to see even less than *The Blair Witch Project*. It was so awful you just wanted to pull the covers over your head and wait for it to go away. A bit like the teas at Stoke Canon Cricket Club.

At the start of the 1999 season the Devon village was forced to disband its cricket team because nobody would play them. Their teas were too atrocious. Until 1993 they had a regular tea lady called Vi. However, when she retired they were forced to introduce a rota of the players. I'm not sure how it's possible to make an inedible cheese roll, but these boys managed it. As the captain, Tim Keehner, put it: 'some of the lads made really terrible sandwiches'. Obviously some cricket-related skills are more important than others in terms of retaining fixtures. No one wanted to stop playing England because they couldn't bat.

During the course of the World Cup Jonathan Aitken, slain by the sword of truth, had been sent down for 18 months for perverting the course of justice, and England's rugby captain, Lawrence Dallaglio, had been forced to resign over allegations he had taken and dealt in hard drugs. If there was justice in Aitken's fate, Alec Stewart saw a lack of it in his. Sacked as England's captain, he said, 'Some might use the word "scapegoat".' The word 'some' meant what 'sources close to' means in journalistic circles and Stewart clearly felt hard done by, particularly as he gave the impression of never having handed out anything harder than a cherry brandy at Christmas.

It was a moot point whether it was better to lose your captain before or after a World Cup. The following autumn, the England rugby players did at least make it to the quarter-final stage before Janie de Beer drop-kicked them out of the tournament. In each case the change of leader was to have a profound effect on the fortunes of the national team. To replace Dallaglio the RFU appointed Martin Johnson, while the ECB chose Nasser Hussain.

Some doubted Hussain could be the right man for the job because of his ethnic origin. This was an attitude that fundamentally misunderstood the man and was based on the same outdated and simplistic notions of 'Britishness' as Chris Cowdrey displayed when questioning the commitment of the likes of Robin Smith and Allan Lamb. Hussain finished his career with 96 England Test caps. To the end of the 2005 season, the next highest for a player of Asian origin remained Ranjitsinhji's 15, and he made his debut in 1896 when India was still part of the British Empire.

These statistics demonstrate one of the fundamental flaws in Norman Tebbit's 'cricket test', namely it demanded support before acceptance rather than the other way round. Some have accused Yorkshire Asians of ghettoizing themselves by playing in their own separate leagues. On the other hand, only recently have British Asians started to have significant representation in the county side.

As Nasser Hussain was growing up in Essex, one of the most popular comedy programmes on British television was *It Ain't Half Hot Mum*. This featured a blacked-up Michael Bates as the turbaned Rangi Ram. Although Bates was born in Janshi, India, and spoke Hindustani before he learned English, he was nevertheless white and one of the running gags of the show was his character's constant references to 'We British'. The enormous joke was of course you only had to look at him to know he couldn't be anything of the kind. Which comes first: the chicken or the egg? Feeling British or being accepted as such? As Owais Shah put it when given grief by Pakistan supporters for playing for England in a one-dayer in 2001: 'They don't realise what sort of life I've led. I've lived in England since I was 15, England's my home country.' Note, he sees England as his home because, 'I've lived here since I was 15', not because 'I was born here'. Nasser Hussain was born in India but his captaincy of England certainly didn't lack passion or commitment.

Even more controversial than Hussain's selection as captain was the appointment of Duncan Fletcher to succeed Lloyd as coach from the end of the season. We had started the summer with as fervently English a coach and as British bulldog a captain as you could hope to imagine. Now we had a Zimbabwean and an Indian in charge of resurrecting the fortunes of the national team. Like that was ever going to work.

England's opponents for the Tests that summer represented a two-edged sword. On paper New Zealand seemed like weak enough opponents to give Hussain a relatively easy introduction to the captaincy. On the other hand, lose to them and we would end up bottom of the unofficial Test rankings.

For Edgbaston, Hussain was joined by two debutants, Aftab Habib and Chris Read. Habib (born in Reading) lasted only one more Test match, not because he was Asian but because he didn't bring his bat down straight. Read became the youngest England wicket-keeper of the twentieth century and at 20 years 325 days was only one day older than the all-time record holder, the wonderfully named Gregor MacGregor.

Despite sounding like a character from *Blackadder*, MacGregor was described by his obituarist in the 1920 *Wisden,* the equally magnificently monikered Digby Loder Armroid Jephson, as 'one of the finest wicket-keepers who ever lived'. Judging by one comment on his technique, he was arguably the father of modern wicket-keeping. In the course of the obituary Jephson reports that, in contrast to many of his contemporaries, MacGregors' fingers were 'untouched – unmarked'. The reason for this was that, in his youth, MacGregor had learned to 'bend his wrists backwards… so that he took the ball with his fingers pointing down'. Jephson reports, with the air of a man revealing the mystery of a googly, that, 'In other words: the front of his hand faced the ball – *not* his finger tips.' Can you imagine what would have happened to Rod Marsh's fingers if he had tried to take the ball with his fingers pointing straight at Jeff Thomson?

MacGregor ended his Test career with a highest score of 31 and an average of 12.00. He wasn't the last brilliant keeper to be let down by less accomplished batting and at Birmingham, the latest in a long line of such players contributed one run as England subsided to 45-7 in reply to the tourists' 226. From this position England somehow contrived to win, with much improved second-innings bowling and batting efforts marred only by Graham Thorpe's 'cold-eyed professionalism' in denying Alex Tudor his one and only chance of a Test century. Just as Atherton now admits that, with hindsight, he shouldn't have declared on Graeme Hick at Sydney in 1995, so I'm sure Thorpe, on reflection, wishes he had let Tudor score at least one more as the team cruised home. This victory proved to be the home side's only success of the summer and, under the new television deal, it was on Sky.

The BBC had ended its coverage of live cricket with the World Cup. Now, Sky covered one Test a season and Channel Four got the rest. In the first summer of this arrangement the satellite company got the win while the terrestrial broadcaster got the unmitigated disaster.

The traditional heavy defeat at Lord's was memorable mainly for Read's dismissal, ducking a yorker from Chris Cairns. 'Where's that nasty hard ball gone? Oh, there it is shattering my stumps.' This was followed by much the worse of a rain-ruined draw, under Mark Butcher's captaincy, at Old Trafford. Yes, you've guessed it, Hussain had a broken finger.

The teams came to the Oval for the deciding Test with England teetering on the brink of becoming unofficially worse than the visitors and Zimbabwe. So what did they do in such circumstances? They selected Darren Maddy and three number 11s.

England had Andy Caddick at eight followed by Alan Mullally, Phil Tufnell and Ed Giddins. Usually it is said sides have to take 20 wickets to win a Test match. England were effectively challenging New Zealand to take 14. At the Oval England lost their last three wickets for nought in the first innings and two in the second. They might as well have had three Swan Vestas at the bottom of the order.

When defeat was confirmed by a collapse of 8-39, the crowd booed and Hussain cried. Which only went to prove we had a captain who, regardless of where he was born, cared enough to want to improve things.

TWENTY-SIX

Ed Giddins spent the winter of 1999-2000 selling Christmas trees with Nadeem Shahid of Surrey. He wasn't otherwise engaged in South Africa because David Graveney promised that England would 'never again' go into a Test match with three number 11s. Once Phil Tufnell and Alan Mullally had been selected, Giddins had no chance. He wasn't the only one left out.

Following England's humiliation at the hands of New Zealand, the press indulged in its usual demands for blood letting and the inclusion of younger players. Graham Thorpe, much to Duncan Fletcher's annoyance, made himself unavailable for the tour for personal reasons at short notice and Graeme Hick and Mark Ramprakash were dropped again. Many, myself included, felt Ramprakash was a little hard done by. However, had he been picked or Thorpe been available, the future of English cricket might have been very different.

The omission of the old stagers left three batting places up for grabs. Darren Maddy was the man in possession and had a work ethic that would have appealed to the new coach. Chris Adams, a man never afraid to let his mouth do the talking, had been pushing his own claims for years. Both at least deserved a chance and their inclusion took few by surprise. The third place, however, went to someone hardly any of the TV, radio or newspaper pundits had considered. This was the selection that was to prove the value of picking a foreigner to coach the national team.

Being Zimbabwean, Duncan Fletcher was not hidebound by the English attitude that you had to have years of big runs in county cricket behind you before you could be considered for the Test team. Hick was living proof that an imposing county record was no guarantee of international success. The new coach, more interested in trusting his own judgement of talent and temperament than statistics, went for a man who had averaged only 27.12 in the previous championship season, Michael Vaughan.

Before the tour started, both Fletcher and Hussain indulged in a bit of expectation management by repeating that what they were hoping to do was 'compete' with South Africa. In a curious way both men benefited from the nation's cricketing stock being at rock bottom. This was what allowed them to get away with publicly stating such limited aspirations.

It wasn't just the management and much of the team that were new. For the first time the radio coverage of a winter tour was in the hands of someone other than the BBC. Talk Sport, or 'Radio Sky' as I prefer to call it, had snatched the rights from under Peter Baxter's nose by using an underhand tactic that had proved successful in the world of television – offering lots of money. Despite having love-him-or-hate-him Geoff Boycott, the coverage was awful. Constantly interrupted by adverts, the presenters were also forced to plug the sponsors (from memory a company offering temporary office space for itinerant businessmen) at the end of every other over. Worse even than this, however, was Mark Nicholas. He may have proved suave and smoother than a three-blade razor on television, but he clearly needed some coaching on the principles of radio. His commentary on the dismissal of Mark Butcher during England's collapse to 2-4 on the first morning of the series consisted of 'Oooooooooooooooooo!'. 'Mark, the listeners, they can't see what's happening mate. They need you describe it rather than just having an orgasm on air.'

Not that Arlott at his most poetic could have made 2-4 sound good. It was, after all, the worst start to a team's first innings in Test history. In better times that collapse might have been the abiding memory of the tour. However, in the end even this, Klusener's brutal hundred at Port Elizabeth, Hussain's 635-minute blockathon at Durban and even Gary Kirsten's 275 in the same match, were forgotten in the wake of what happened at Centurion Park on 18th January 2000.

By the time England and South Africa reached Centurion for the fifth Test we had supposedly entered a new millennium. Gregson CC and Pressbox's XI of Lancaster claimed to have played the last UK cricket match of the old one by carrying on under floodlights until 4.55 pm on 31st December. A pedant might have suggested they were a year early, but the leaders who arranged the world-wide celebrations said otherwise and we were more than happy to take them at their word.

Within three months of the 'River of Fire', Jonathan Aitken had been released having served less than half his sentence, Harold Shipman had been jailed for life and Augusto Pinochet, after a protracted legal battle, was free to return to Chile. It's hard to imagine three better men to foreshadow a massive breach of trust.

In the 1999 *Wisden,* Tim de Lisle, summarising the previous summer's tour by South Africa, unwittingly put his finger on one of the root causes of what was to come: 'The South African board, so enlightened in many ways, seems incapable of turning down an invitation. Rare is the triangular or quadrangular tournament that does not include South Africa. Probably the only person who has done more touring than Cronje in the past few years is Bob Dylan. How many roads must a man walk down, before you give him a break?'

What Cronje proposed to Hussain on the final day at Centurion, that a run chase be set up by England forfeiting their first innings and the South Africans their second, was technically outside the laws of the game. It was not until later in the year that first-innings forfeitures were permitted in Tests. Nevertheless, the South African captain's suggestion seemed a triumph of ingenuity and common sense over the kind of pedantry that would have sought to discredit the lads of Gregson CC. The match referee, Barry Jarman, squared things by instructing the scorers to record England's first innings as 0-0 declared even though they had never taken the field. He really might have cried 'tears of blood' if he had known what he was unwittingly assisting.

In the aftermath of England's victory on the back of a brilliant 69 by Vaughan, Hussain paid tribute to Cronje: 'It was a very special thing that Hansie did and I hope he gets the credit he deserves.' What he had done was special all right.

On 7th April 2000 I was, appropriately, off sick when the story broke that Indian police were charging Cronje, Pieter Strydom (who?), Nicky Boje and Herschelle Gibbs with 'cheating, fraud and criminal conspiracy relating to match-fixing and betting'. I followed the emerging story on the radio with complacent disbelief. Salim Malik, well he was the sort who would call 'Heilds' at the toss in a Test match, but Hansie Cronje? It was just too ridiculous.

Ali Bacher spoke for the cricketing world when he referred to Cronje's 'unquestionable integrity and honesty'. In other words, all

Hansie had to do was say it ain't so and that would be good enough.

For a while, like a batsman who knows he's nicked it but stands and trades on his reputation as a walker, Cronje did say it wasn't so. On 9th April he held a press conference with Gibbs and Boje during which he denied receiving any money 'during the one-day series in India' and speaking to any member of his team about throwing a game. In the same way as Bill Clinton had denied 'sexual relations' with Monica Lewinsky on the basis of one judge's very specific definition of the term, so Cronje, it seems, was indulging in similar sophistry.

When the truth, or at least part of it, came to light, it transpired Cronje had received $US 30,000 from a bookmaker called MK Gupta during the Kanpur Test match and the offer of in the region of $US 250,000 made by Gupta to throw a one-day international in Mumbai was discussed with the whole team rather than any individual member. Cronje might also have pointed out that the Mumbai match wasn't originally designated as a full one-day international. Intended as a benefit game for Mohinder Amarnath, it only received its elevated status at the last minute from the ICC. In so doing the game's governing body rendered the match Cronje's 100th ODI, a milestone none of the match's organizers saw fit to acknowledge and which the player himself had wanted to reach at home.

Even when the Indian authorities revealed they had Cronje on tape discussing money with a bookmaker, I clung to the belief that this must be a fake. A journalist from the *Pretoria Star* claimed to have heard the tape and said the voice that was supposedly Cronje's had an Indian accent. It transpired what he was listening to was a transcript voiced by actors and Cronje knew the game was up. Within two days of his press conference, he was on the phone to Ali Bacher tearfully confessing 'dishonesty'.

Bacher called a conference of his own and revealed Cronje had denied match-fixing but had been sacked as national captain after admitting accepting $US10,000-15,000 during a triangular one-day series with England and Zimbabwe. Almost simultaneously the South African sports minister, Ngconde Balfour, was releasing a statement on Cronje's behalf to the effect that 'the allegations were devoid of all truth', that he had never spoken to other players about match-fixing and he had received 'no financial rewards'. These contrasting accounts were indicative of the months and years to come, as cricket followers were forced to try and sift through an impenetrable mixture of the truth, the half-truth and anything but the truth.

Although the findings had not yet been made public, Pakistan had already undertaken a further enquiry into match-fixing under Mr Justice Malik Mohammed Qayyum, when the Cronje story broke. On 4th May, Judge Edwin King was appointed by the government to investigate the South African end of the affair.

Some of what emerged from these enquiries was almost comical. Herschelle Gibbs and Henry Williams admitted to Justice King that as recently as March 2000 they had been offered $US15,000 each to perform badly in a one-day international against India in Nagpur. Gibbs, described during the enquiry as 'not the sharpest knife in the drawer', was supposed to make fewer than 20. He 'batted like a train' in making 74. Williams had to go off injured before he had completed two overs. So embarrassed was Cronje by these failures that he apparently promised to make up Gupta's losses with poor performances in the return series at home. However, he failed, as the Indians' abject efforts raised the terrible possibility that some were involved in a contest of sorts, deliberately playing badly on behalf of different bookmakers.

Then there was Mushtaq Ahmed's evidence to the Qayyum enquiry that he 'was ok in *that* match' when questioned about a particular ODI. Funniest of all was Ray Illingworth admitting that during the 1996 World Cup he had been offered money by a Pakistani bookmaker, who presumably hadn't been watching the tournament, for England to throw one of their matches.

What you could unravel of the rest wasn't funny at all. Most disturbing was Gupta's claim that, through the agency of former Indian Test player Ajay Sharma, he had managed to get the pitch doctored for a one-off Test between India and Australia at Delhi's Feroz Shah Kotla ground. You wanted to believe this wasn't true but how the hell did you know? All we had for evidence was the word of men who were, by their own admission, dishonest and a series of 'they would say that wouldn't they' denials by international cricketers keen not to lose their livelihood. All of this was conducted in the context of domestic cricket authorities desperately trying to deflect attention from their country.

When Cronje sought to blame that well known claimer of dodgy catches, Satan, he wasn't alone in trying to abdicate responsibility. Bacher had taken the tack of alleging two 1999 World Cup matches had been fixed and that an umpire on the international panel had been paid to ensure a particular result in a recent Test involving South Africa in England. I think everyone knew which one he meant, but curiously he waited until ten days after Cronje's admission to make these allegations.

Meanwhile, the chairman of Sporting Index was offering the opinion that the Centurion Test was 'the least likely game ever played' to have been manipulated, because there wasn't enough time for collusion with bookmakers. At the same time the English cricketing authorities were busy denying Chris Lewis' suggestion that an Asian sports promoter had told him three senior England cricketers were involved in match-fixing. Lewis also claimed when he had offered the relevant names to the ECB the previous summer they were 'not interested'. Here is the nub of the Cronje case.

In the wake of the South African captain's admissions a senior ICC official confirmed that, 'We have known for years match-fixing goes on, helped by the fact betting is illegal and in the hands of criminals there (the sub-continent). But in the past, whenever the matter has been raised, they have said we are cricket administrators not cops. Then a clean-cut white South African, Hansie Cronje, was caught in the net, the game changed and everyone has had to come clean.'

Those running the game had known for years that it was corrupt but had done nothing about it. This has the potential to be self-perpetuating if you think about it, because what do many senior players do when they retire? They go into cricket administration. Leave a problem long enough and it becomes endemic. What I'm not satisfied about is that anybody truly 'came clean'.

Professor Bruce Murray, the author of a study into race and politics in South African cricket, uses this phrase about the reasons why many South Africans are willing to rehabilitate Cronje. They believe, Murray says, that he 'owned up and came clean'. There are enough of his countrymen who share this view for Cronje to have come 11th in the South African Broadcasting Corporation's survey to find the 100 Greatest South Africans. The only selection of this kind more amazing to me is the Americans' choice in their equivalent vote of Jesus at number one.

I don't believe for a second that Cronje told everything he knew or that the cricketing public have found out even a tiny fraction of what went on in international cricket in the 1990s. The fines recommended for Wasim Akram, Waqar Younis, Mushtaq Ahmed, Inzamam-ul-Haq,

Akram Raza and Saeed Anwar were for what Qayyum called their 'partial amnesia' and perceived non-cooperation. Cronje's demeanour before the King enquiry was that of a man who was still, from a misguided sense of loyalty, protecting others. More than anything else, it also seemed he hadn't got his head around the scale of what he had done and could not admit it, even to himself.

His basic defence was he had taken money under false pretences with no intention of doing what he had been paid for. In other words he had fraudulently obtained large sums of money from a known criminal. Not a very sensible thing for an intelligent man to do. Cronje claimed all he had done at Centurion Park was ensure the game wasn't drawn. He went to his death denying he had ever fixed a match. Even if this is true, and no-one has ever proved that it isn't, he must have known those who had. His evidence before Justice King about the involvement of others was pretty much limited to what he knew the Indians could already prove.

We know match-fixing was widespread, the ICC admitted it, but only a tiny handful of international players have ever been banned, even temporarily, for their involvement. In this respect I keep coming back to the Chicago White Socks' throwing of the 1919 baseball World Series. The film about that case is called *Eight Men Out* because of the number of players involved in the scam. There are nine men in a baseball team on the field at any one time. When Arnold Rothstein offered his infamous bribe he knew that he had to have almost the entire side on board in order for his plan to work. There are eleven in a cricket team, you don't have to be a genius to do the maths.

The ICC created a situation in which corruption could thrive by promoting more and more meaningless games the players didn't care about. This doesn't mean those paying to watch didn't care. The result matters and the spectators want to believe in the integrity of what is before them. Which brings us to the worse thing about what Hansie Cronje did: it was Hansie Cronje that did it.

In his own country Cronje was nothing less than an icon. To everyone else in the cricketing world he may have appeared a little dull, prissy even, but he seemed integrity personified. Many may have felt that most of those at the ICC were an arrogant, incompetent shower more interested in selling the game than promoting it, but as long as teams were led by men like Cronje its soul was safe.

Ravi Shastri said the affair made him 'feel like a fool' in his job as a commentator. How did he think the rest of us felt? I had loved and watched cricket since I was 11 years old. Now, in one stroke, Cronje was forcing me to question every game I had ever seen. When Alec Stewart denied allegations by one bookmaker that he had accepted money for information (he was never accused of fixing anything), everything cried out that I must take someone as apparently ramrod straight at his word. But that was the point; if Cronje could do it then nobody's word counted for anything anymore. One woman in South Africa who blamed her mother's death on the way Cronje's actions had undermined her parent's belief system, may have been overstating things slightly, but I knew what she meant.

This is what I feel Cronje never fully grasped: that he had played a major part in undermining the faith of an entire generation of cricket followers. He may have been rehabilitated in the eyes of many South Africans but he missed his chance of redemption by failing to tell King and the rest of us, all he knew. How do you forgive a man who won't acknowledge what he's done?

I still want to believe that what I'm watching is a proper and pure contest. It would be soul destroying to think for one second the 2005 Ashes series was anything other than sport played at a level the like of which I'd never seen before. But because Hansie Cronje was party to bribery and corruption I can never again 'know' that what I see is what I get.

Cronje and any number of unidentified international cricketers were not the only ones who made less quick money than they might have done that year. Peter Lee, a 65-year-old retired sailor rather than the former Lancashire medium pacer, missed the chance to become the first to win £1 million on *Who Wants To Be A Millionaire*. I dreamed of getting a cricket question at the final stage of that programme, but Mr Lee 'didn't follow cricket' and bailed out at £500,000 because he was unaware that Chester-le-Street was the home of Durham County Cricket Club. At least he had earned himself considerably more than the Zimbabwean tourists were going to.

Over the course of the winter Zimbabwe had lifted England off the bottom of the Test rankings by losing to Sri Lanka and West Indies. In the latter case this had involved being bowled out for 63 after being set 99 to win. What were the odds on that I wonder?

Despite this, we could drop to the basement again if we lost our first ever home series to Andy Flower's men. Always assuming they ever arrived that is. Since 2000, not a single England v Zimbabwe series has been arranged without there being some doubt about it going ahead. In this case we had the unusual scenario of a tour *to* England being threatened by Robert Mugabe's attitude to human rights. The Zimbabwean president was in the process of implementing his policy of 'redistribution' (forced seizure) of land from his country's white farmers, many of whom were close family or friends of the touring cricketers. Fears for loved ones and doubts about who they were representing can only have been compounded by discovering their coach driver was earning more than they were.

If the tourists were distracted, then England seemed buoyed by the introduction of the first set of central contracts. Not all of the initial recipients played a part in the resurgence that was to come. Dean Headley, ultimately forced out of the game by the back injury he was carrying when he was awarded his contract, never played for England again. Chris Schofield, fast-tracked more in hope than expectation and way before he was ready, was discarded after two wicketless Tests. Many doubted the value of the new system and foresaw the devaluing of the county game that has, to some extent, taken place. Nevertheless, England wouldn't have won the Ashes back under Michael Vaughan without central contracts.

In the circumstances it came as no surprise that England bowled the Zimbabweans out for 83 and 123 at Lord's. Neither the winners nor the losers gain anything from mismatches like this.

That year Stoneleigh played a tour game at Trowbridge, then probably the most powerful club side in Wiltshire and a team boasting several Minor Counties players. I faced one over from their opening bowler during which I was so consistently beaten for pace, the only thing I laid on the ball was my inner thigh. Twice. When he played for Wiltshire this lad was a batsman who bowled occasional off-spin. It was no better in the field. Stoneleigh legend has it that one of the sixes we conceded went so far the RAF had to be scrambled to shoot down the ball.

By contrast, later in the same tour we played one of the local village sides. Their square is the only one I've ever seen with cow hoof prints across it and the 'pavilion' was a caravan on bricks. The differences didn't end there. Whereas Trowbridge's captain was suave and drove a sports car, my latest opposite number, Barry, was a psychotic with a tractor. Later that evening he explained to me, in increasingly eye-bulging detail, how we had to drink two miles away because he had 'kicked the shit' out of the landlord of the pub next to the ground for failing to prevent his 15-year-old son's amorous advances towards Barry's 13-year-old daughter. 'I did warn 'im Paul!' 'More than fair Barry, more than fair.'

The match itself was surprisingly uneventful but did contain my favourite ever piece of 'anti-sledging'. Thanks in part to the absence of the home side's leading all-rounder, still in the cells for assaulting three police officers the previous evening, Stoneleigh mustered 120. This was worth 250 on a pitch unaffected by bovine intervention and, after the first delivery of their innings, clearly more than enough.

The opposition's opening bat was a spotty, skinny 18-year-old, roped in at the last minute to cover for his absent friend and sent out by 'Mad Baz', possibly at knifepoint, because no one else fancied it. The first delivery, from our quickest bowler, lifted off a length and thudded into the poor lad's twig-like chest before he even twitched. He turned to me at first slip and coughed up in his best Somerset accent: 'Jesus! I never played this game afore…I didn't think the idea was I shit Iself!'

Victory over this lad's team and defeat at Trowbridge were two of the emptiest cricketing experiences I've ever had. When the ICC next consider Zimbabwe's Test and one-day international status perhaps they should think about whether the development of the game in that country is best served by sending young club batsmen out to shit themselves in the face of the likes of Brett Lee?

The state of mind that our young opponent had described to me was one whole generations of English batsmen must have shared at the prospect of facing the West Indies' pace battery. However, now, like the last remnants of a once glorious army, only Walsh and Ambrose remained. At the end of the previous summer England had found themselves in the gutter. Under Fletcher they were at least looking at the stars and the West Indian one appeared to be on the wane. The home side, it was said, had their best chance in a generation of regaining the Wisden Trophy.

It didn't seem that way to begin with. The crushing defeat of Zimbabwe at Lord's was followed by an embarrassing draw at Trent Bridge. This match contained Schofield's entire Test match bowling career (18-2-73-0) and a big hundred from Murray Goodwin that had me cursing. Three years later, Goodwin pulled Phil DeFreitas for four to seal Sussex's first ever County Championship title.

The stalemate at Nottingham felt like a defeat and the real thing followed at Edgbaston in the first match of the series with the West

Indies. In 2005, after England were crushed by the Aussies at Lord's, I clung to the scrap of comfort given by the fact the next match was in Birmingham, on the ground described by Vaughan as his team's 'spiritual home'. In 2000 it was the other way round and the teams headed for Lord's on the back of the tourists' innings-and-93-run victory at the home side's supposed stronghold.

'Stronghold' is not a word you would apply to Lord's. England beat Australia there only once in the whole of the twentieth century and in the last three years had been taken apart by New Zealand, South Africa and Pakistan at HQ. When they conceded a first-innings lead of 133, the fact their last victory over a major Test nation at St John's Wood was against their present opponents seemed irrelevant.

Even when Caddick bowled the tourists out for 54, a target of 188 on a bouncy seaming pitch against Walsh and Ambrose seemed more like 400. The second day had been the first in Test history during which a part of all four innings had taken place. On the third morning it appeared for a time that the cricketing gods had decided such an occurrence was unnatural and had begun to rewind the match. Atherton took 27 balls getting off the mark and Vaughan 29. Ambrose stood cursing at the end of his follow through when he allowed the former captain off strike with a pushed single to mid-on.

The only time I've been more tense watching a cricket match was on the fourth morning at Edgbaston in 2005. Oh, and the fourth afternoon at Trent Bridge as well. Even so, those days would not have been possible without the events of that Saturday evening in July 2000. During the day there was just the merest sense that more than a match or even a series hung on the success or otherwise of a single run chase.

Atherton and Vaughan eked out 92 for the second wicket but Ambrose and Walsh refused to tire and at 160-8, England had only Hoggard left in the hutch. He may have cover-driven Brett Lee for four and helped see England home at Nottingham five years later, but this Hoggard was on his debut and, in the days before Fletcher got to work on him, had a batting reputation on a par with Tufnell's.

It is generally accepted that Alex Ferguson's job as Manchester United's manager was saved by a single goal scored by Mark Robins against Nottingham Forest in the third round of the 1990 FA Cup. United went on to win the Cup that year, Ferguson avoided his P45 and the rest, as they say, is Cantona and Schmeichel. What it wasn't was Robins. The young striker played only 70 games for United's first team and in 1992 transferred to Norwich. Without him the Red Devils' period of dominance through the 1990s would probably never have happened, but he didn't share in it.

At Lord's in 2000, Dominic Cork walked out to bat at 140-6. Unfazed even by the loss of Knight and Caddick, he lofted Walsh for four over mid-on and then gloriously pulled Franklyn Rose for six into the grandstand. Then, in company with Darren Gough, he engineered a motley collection of scrambled singles and leg-byes that brought the scores level, before securing victory with a back-foot drive to the cover boundary.

In all likelihood that one innings saved Duncan Fletcher's job. Coming from 2-0 down would almost certainly have proved impossible and an embarrassing defeat could easily have seen the idea of a foreign coach quickly ditched as an embarrassing experiment gone wrong. Dominic Cork saw out the rest of that series, but thereafter was little more than a bit-part player in Fletcher's brave new England. That's not a criticism of the coach, it's just a fact. Cork may not have been one of the men capable of taking England where they needed to go, his record against Australia in particular is poor and Geoff Boycott once dismissed him as a 'show-pony'. But, love him or loathe him, English cricket owes Dominic Cork a lot.

Potentially the most exciting home series in more than a decade stood at 1-1 and following the victory at Lord's, all the momentum was with England. So what happened next? A three-week triangular one-day tournament, that's what. Whoever came up with that idea needed one of Mad Baz's warnings.

At least the Natwest series enabled Duncan Fletcher to indulge in another of his inspired punts on a talented young English player. Fletcher had never forgotten a brilliant hundred Marcus Trescothick had scored against his Glamorgan team. Now, with Knight injured, he threw the Somerset left-hander in against the West Indies and Zimbabwe. His first four innings produced 244 runs at an average of 81.33 and were good enough to get him into the team for the third Test at Old Trafford.

The Manchester game was memorable for the Queen Mother and Alec Stewart making it to 100 (Tests and runs in the Surrey man's case) and for Thorpe 'doing a Read' by ducking a slower ball from Walsh to be as plumb lbw as a man can ever have been. Rain on the last day saved England from a Lara-inspired West Indian fightback and the teams reached Headingley still level.

When the names to be awarded central contracts had been announced, all except one had been uncontentious. If Schofield's selection ultimately proved to have owed too much to optimism, at the time a promising young leg-spinner seemed worth the risk. Similarly, while it was not yet matched by achievement, Flintoff's potential was obvious. Craig White, however, was another matter.

When Fletcher had called him up, seemingly from nowhere, to act as reinforcement to England's one-day squad in South Africa the previous winter, White had been out of Test cricket for three years. His last game had been as part of the bowling attack that had failed to dislodge Danny Morrison on the last day at Auckland in January 1996, and an eight-match career had yielded a highest score of 51 and a best bowling analysis of 3-18. In short, he was the embodiment of the sort of bits-and-pieces player clogging up county cricket at the expense of talented specialists with the potential to make a significant impact at international level. At least that's what I thought. Duncan Fletcher saw something different, which is why he was the national coach.

Flintoff's latest run of failures had seen him replaced by White for the Lord's Test. For two games the Yorkshireman's contributions were moderate and then, with England on the brink of the series victory over the West Indies they hadn't achieved for 31 years, he repaid Fletcher's faith. That Headingley Test is now mainly remembered for Andy Caddick's four-wicket over to bowl out the tourists for 61 on the second afternoon. However, White set up the victory with a first-innings 5-47 that included Lara, rushed into fatally leaving a late inswinger. Then, at the Oval, with England having posted a moderate 281, he produced 5-32, including Lara again, bowled behind his legs first ball, to skittle the West Indies for 125.

On the final afternoon of the series, with victory now assured, the home side formed guards of honour for Walsh and Ambrose as they came out to bat for the final time in a Test in England. That 18,500 were jammed in to see it and thousands more left locked outside speaks volumes for how much the success of the national cricket team mattered to English sports fans. And you only had to look at the way Nasser Hussain sank, head in hands, to his haunches when the final appeal for lbw was upheld, to realise how much the achievement of winning back the Wisden Trophy meant to him.

At Centurion Park Hansie Cronje may have directly duped Hussain, but his betrayal of all of those 18,500 and indeed of the millions across the globe who cared about cricket, was just as real. He wasn't alone.

The ICC betrayed us all as well. Not just by creating the conditions in which corruption could flourish and by turning a blind eye, but also by how they handled matters once the issue was out in the open. They spoke of stricter security and of programmes to 'educate' international players about match-fixing. As Gideon Haigh has pointed out, cricketers don't need 'educating' to know taking money to deliberately perform badly is wrong. What they need is naming and shaming and rooting out. If the ICC had been more open and honest about what had gone on and more people had been held to account, I could have known that the game had been dirty but was now clean again and the *News of the World* wouldn't still have been conducting sting operations ten years later.

TWENTY-SEVEN

I am a lucky man. This is true because the year I now had ahead of me was the worst I've ever experienced. All I can hope is it stays that way. In so many ways it was a period that changed the world forever. But, for now, on a personal level, let's just say this was a year I ended with half as many CDs as I had started it.

The previous autumn had been mixed. Dietmar Hamann's long-rang free kick had slithered past David Seaman to condemn England's footballers to a 1-0 defeat in the last game at the old Wembley and immediately afterwards they also mislaid their manager, who decided 0-0 draws in Ukraine weren't the only thing he wasn't the man for. On the plus side, Steve Redgrave secured his fifth Olympic gold medal and, in a development that was obviously key to England's recovery of the Ashes in 2005, Bangladesh played their inaugural Test match.

By defeating the West Indies, Hussain and his men had hauled England up to sixth in the world rankings. The Banglas' elevation meant this position now represented mid-table respectability. However, if there was one thing English batsmen couldn't do it was play spin, and the winter tours were to Pakistan and Sri Lanka. A draw in either series would be a triumph, but realistically a drop into the 'relegation places' beckoned.

However, while half of the country's footballing public, and especially Ian Wright, were beside themselves at the FA's heretical appointment of a foreign coach to succeed Kevin Keegan, English cricket's equivalent of Sven Goran Eriksson quietly proved his worth on the sub-continent.

England's success that winter introduced a new phrase into the cricketing vocabulary, 'the forward press'. Fletcher's method for blunting the threat posed by the likes of Saqlain Mushtaq and Murali wasn't very pretty, but it proved mighty effective. Australian carping about negativity was like Manchester United criticizing Derby for not playing three up front. We didn't have the confidence boost of 16 consecutive Test wins in our recent history. Fletcher and Hussain were only doing what any sensible manager inheriting a struggling side would do. They were building from the back.

My first experience of an England tour to Pakistan, Mike Brearley's expedition in 1977-78, had contained some of the most mind-numbingly dull cricket in the history of the game. Hussain was rapidly developing a reputation as England's best captain since Brearley and it came as no surprise when his tour went much the same way. Like Gower before him, Hussain took the method acting approach to his impersonation and contributed only 92 runs at 23.00.

Fortunately, both men had an all-rounder at their disposal capable of making a telling contribution.

In Brearley's case this was Geoff Miller and in Hussain's, Craig White.

Ian Botham didn't play a Test against Pakistan in 1977-78 and Andrew Flintoff suffered a similar fate in 2000-01. Flintoff had a bizarre tour. First he contributed a murderous 84 to help win the opening one-day international. Then he was sent home after the ODIs because his dodgy back prevented him from bowling, only to be recalled as specialist batting cover for the injured Hussain and Vaughan. On his return to Pakistan he discovered there was no room available for him at the team hotel, had his nose broken at first practice and was out first ball in his only first-class innings of the tour. What was it Ian Botham said about Pakistan? 'The country and its people have absolutely blown me away. All I would say is: Mothers-in-law of the world unite and go to Pakistan! Because you'll love it.' Oh no, my mistake; it was his mother-in-law who said that.

The cricket on that tour wasn't going to blow anybody away, not unless you count boring people to death. In the first Test Graham Thorpe reached three figures having hit only one boundary and in the third, Mike Atherton made 125 in nine hours and 38 minutes, during which time he played 350 dot balls. The most memorable image of the series came on the last evening, as a barely visible Moin Khan stood with his arms outstretched staring at Steve Bucknor. The umpire merely tapped his watch and shrugged, which is sign language for 'You shouldn't have been time-wasting earlier on you cheating little bastard.'

In a curious way I was glad the Pakistanis were slowing things down on that final afternoon. At least it meant they were trying not to lose. The only thing I was happier about was that they did.

England's victory in Pakistan was the equivalent of kicking lumps out of a superior opponent for 89 minutes before grabbing a last-gasp winner. This was worthy in its own way, but hardly a recipe for long-term success. The team would need to produce far more against Muralitharan on his own pitches. It says all you need to know about Murali that he was in a different class from a bowler as good as Saqlain Mushtaq.

Fortunately, before the side departed, England's premier fast bowler received a timely confidence-building endorsement – from Anna Kournikova. Despite the fact he now worked for the ECB, Darren Gough had been granted a benefit by Yorkshire for 2001. The brochure to accompany the season contained this glowing testimonial from the Russian famous for looking good in Lycra: 'From the moment Darren made his breakthrough as a Test player, his character, personality and performances have made an impact on every game he has played in. You can't ignore Darren!' Reading that off a piece of paper by any chance were you, Anna? As far as Anna was concerned cricket was obviously a bit like tennis i.e. a sport she was 'not too familiar with'. Anna Kournikova: singles titles 0, money made from being pretty – loads.

At Galle, neither Anna nor the forward press seemed to be much help. Marcus Trescothick made 122 and 57, but the next highest score for England was Mike Atherton's 44. In Pakistan, Atherton had begun to morph into Geoff Boycott. Now he completed the process by becoming the bunny of a left-arm seamer. Chaminda Vaas dismissed Atherton five times out of six and that 44 ended up as the opener's highest contribution of the series. It was just as well we had a good coach and the Sri Lankans had a crap umpire.

As well as ideas about technique for playing spin, Duncan Fletcher had ground-breaking views about how to get the best out of his charges. 'I prefer to talk to the players one-to-one. I find I get a much better response that way because the individual feels comfortable expressing himself...Simple, clear ideas work the best, with each and every man knowing precisely what he has to do. This also helps a player to think for himself and take some responsibility.' Cor, who would have thought it? Ray Illingworth must have been sitting at home smacking his forehead with his palm saying, 'Now why didn't I think of that?' Fletcher also had an eye for potentially important details and had spotted that despite the gulf in class between the two, Saqlain Mushtaq had something Murali didn't: a doosra. This, the coach reasoned, meant if you played him correctly it was practically impossible for the little man to get an lbw decision.

In this respect Murali was a victim of his own ability to extract prodigious turn from any pitch. He turned the ball so far that in order to be hitting he had to pitch outside the line of wicket and wicket. This placed left-handers at a particular advantage as if Murali landed it outside leg stump they could kick it away and if he pitched on line it was almost certainly missing. Two of England's three centuries in the series were made by Trescothick and Thorpe, and the third, from Hussain, owed much to the generosity of the Sri Lankan umpire BC Cooray.

The system for officiating in Test matches was, at this time, a half-way house between the old and the new. One home umpire still stood but was accompanied by another from the international panel. The previous winter, BC Cooray had been the 'neutral' umpire on duty when England played South Africa at Cape Town. Seemingly reasoning that if he didn't give a decision he couldn't make a mistake, for three-and-a-half days Cooray had stood like a waxwork denying the bowlers anything. Then, out of nowhere, he suddenly fired out Nasser Hussain, lbw to one he had middled for four.

In the first innings at Kandy, Hussain's luck evened itself out. Twice he bat-padded to silly point only for the Sri Lankan to reprieve him. England's captain at least made the most of his good fortune to make a vital hundred. Cooray also gave Graeme Hick two lives and he still made 0.

For years England had railed against the injustices meted out by sub-continental umpires. Now, it seemed, Cooray was intent on repaying all of these in one go. One of Hick's let-offs had been a blatant caught and bowled that the umpire had wrongly seen as a bump-ball and at the start of the Sri Lankan second innings Jayasuriya was given out caught by a flying Thorpe when he had jammed the ball into the ground. There were errors the other way, but the vast majority favoured England and a combination of this and the self-belief Fletcher was giving his men saw them scramble back to 1-1. Despite having received more than the rub of the green from the officials, you couldn't help thinking previous

England sides would still have made a mess of a target of 161 on a turning pitch against Muralitharan.

Prior to the Lord's Test against Zimbabwe the previous summer, England hadn't bowled a side out for fewer than 100 in more than 20 years. At Colombo they did it for the fourth time in 10 months and a first-innings lead of eight proved potentially decisive, as six wickets were lost chasing down 74 to win. Coming back from 1-0 behind in this series was Duncan Fletcher's second greatest achievement with England. This was a side he had largely inherited rather than shaped and almost all of the players had been part of losing teams for the majority of their careers. Yet, in under a year, he had taken those same cricketers and turned them into a side capable of wresting back the Wisden Trophy and winning two series in the most alien conditions an Englishman could encounter.

England's victory in Sri Lanka was all the sweeter as it coincided with the Australians having the opposite experience in India. Steve Waugh had been robbed of the one achievement that always eluded him, leading his team to a win on the sub-continent, and now, we thought, England finally had a side capable of challenging the Aussies.

Shortly before the 2005 Ashes series, Graham Thorpe gave a magazine interview printed under the heading 'Last chance, basically, last chance.' Little did he know that his final opportunity had passed him by in 2001. He wasn't alone in this respect. The niggling worry about Fletcher's resurgent England team was its age. The side that took the field at Kandy had a total of 542 caps, which made it the most experienced in English Test history. The suspicion was that the England cricket team, like its rugby counterparts under Clive Woodward, was growing old together and the dramatic improvement in results would be short-lived. After all, the key player who balanced the side was Alec Stewart. He was 38 and there was no obvious replacement. In his nine matches to this point, Andrew Flintoff had a highest Test score of 42 and a best bowling analysis of 2-31. England, with a bunch of old-stagers clinging onto their places at the expense of the younger brigade, were in just the sort of position you would never catch the Aussies getting themselves into.

Except, the Australian team for the Chennai Test match in March had boasted 628 caps and their 17-man touring party to England contained only two players under 25. Peter Roebuck described them as 'an ageing and conservative team'. Of those 17 men, 10 returned to

England in 2005 as part of a squad that had only two players under 30.

By 2005 it was England who were easily the younger team. John Buchanan's assertion that McGrath and Warne had no immediate plans to retire was designed to undermine English optimism about the imminent demise of his side. In other words it was meant to sound like a threat. However, in reality, it had the ring of very un-Australian desperation. What he was really saying was, 'We can't let them go yet, because we haven't got anyone coming through to replace them.' The Australian press had berated the English for carrying Gooch and Gatting through a tour Down Under, now their head coach was trying to convince us we should remain 'Oh so scared' because a 35-year-old and a 36-year-old weren't hanging up their boots yet. Woodward managed to keep some of the greats of English rugby union going just long enough to win a World Cup. Similarly, a taped-together Aussie cricket team had a humiliating Ashes massacre left in them, but look what happened to English rugby after 2003.

Unfortunately, in 2001, all those Test caps merely meant the Australians were very experienced rather than decrepit. In particular they were more than familiar with doing one thing the English were not: thrashing the opposition in Ashes Test matches. I had got very excited about our prospects and bought tickets for the first two days of the series at Edgbaston. This is exactly how long it took to realise we were going to get another hammering.

England came into the series on the back of a drawn two-match series with Pakistan. Having murdered the tourists at Lord's, the home side managed to lose eight wickets in the final session of the second Test. Much was made of the fact that four English batsmen fell to uncalled no-balls, but there was no disguising the panic that seized the middle and lower order. Michael Vaughan had made a superb maiden Test hundred in the first innings but then picked up a knee injury. Now where have I heard that before? Vaughan missed the entire Ashes series. His replacement at Birmingham was Usman Afzaal.

In 2005, Mark Nicholas and his colleagues went into raptures when England launched the Edgbaston Test by blasting 407 in 79.2 overs. The first day on the same ground in 2001 saw 427 runs, 236 of which came after tea. Unfortunately, these weren't all scored by England and although I didn't lack for entertainment, not inappropriately as it turned out, I ended up riding an emotional roller-coaster. England were 2-1, then 106-1 and 191-9, before finally reaching 294 thanks to a riotous last-wicket stand by Caddick and Stewart. During the course of this partnership the Australians, and Jason Gillespie in particular, lost the plot, proving even they could be rattled if put under pressure.

After England's abject defeat on the 1994/95 tour to Australia, folklore had it that Michael Slater had delivered a decisive psychological blow by slapping Phil De Freitas' opening ball of the series for four. As with most folklore, sporting or otherwise, this was nonsense inspired by a large helping of hindsight. Slater's shot may have ended up being symbolic of the Australian dominance that followed, but it no more determined the destiny of the series than if he had edged the ball through to Steve Rhodes.

Nevertheless, such legends only become truer in their constant retelling and English cricket fans were nothing if not fatalistic, particularly when it came to our prospects of beating Australia. Finally getting the better of the West Indies was one thing but these blokes, well they're superhuman aren't they? I sat nervously in the press box stand 'knowing' the fate of the Ashes hinged on how Slater dealt with Gough's opening over. He smashed it for 18.

At the time, everything that followed seemed as inevitable as the manner of Afzaal's first-innings dismissal, bowled through the gate aiming a flowery drive at Shane Warne. Subsequent events, i.e. those that came after England's crushing defeat at Lord's in 2005, proved there was nothing inevitable about any of it. One bad over didn't mean the next 14 had to go for 80, any more than Peter Mandelson 'had' to involve himself with the Hinduja brothers' passport application or Sven 'had' to incur the wrath of the tabloid press by shagging Ulrika Jonsson and, later, Faria Alam. The ECB had a Lamb as well, but Duncan always managed to resist Tim's charms. However, once something gets into your head it's not always easy to get rid of.

In the case of the recently resigned former Northern Ireland Secretary the thought was along the lines of 'I'm Peter Mandelson and I can do whatever the hell I want' and in Sven's 'What's it to you who I'm sleeping with?' For England's cricketers it was more like 'Here comes Gilchrist…hide!'

Mike Atherton tells a story that Duncan Fletcher had a chart with the name of every opposition batsman written on it. Against each one was a short plan of how to bowl to the man in question. When he looked over the coach's shoulder, the entry by Gilchrist was no more than a question mark. It's a good job he had four years to work on that one, because during the course of the Aussie keeper's brutal 152 from 143 balls, England appeared totally psyched-out.

As a child I had no concept of the extent to which sport is played in the mind. Missing a game because of a pulled hamstring I could understand, but 'personal problems', what effect could they have? As an adult I was about to find out.

You know you're in trouble when your nearest and dearest gives you a pair of oven gloves as a present. This is the last gift I ever received from Fiona. It wasn't even as if I could keep-wicket in them. For a start they broke all the rules about not having webbing between thumb and forefinger. Looking back I think there might have been a hidden message. Perhaps it was merely 'You're going to be needing these son'. Or, more pointedly, it could have been 'Stop watching the cricket and do some sodding cooking.' Either way, the fact Fiona and I were in the process of splitting up had some sporting consequences I didn't expect.

In the same way as that spring's foot and mouth outbreak wouldn't immediately make you think of the abandonment of the Cheltenham Festival or the ending of England's chances of a Grand Slam in the Six Nations, so I didn't think the break-up of my marriage would make watching Wimbledon a painful experience or destroy my batting average.

Nevertheless, the risk of the infection spreading to Ireland caused the cancellation of the Festival and the postponement of England's match at Landsdowne Road until the autumn, by which time the team had lost all its momentum and crashed to defeat. Similarly, the BBC's obsession with Henman and Rusedski's supportive wives meant the progress to the final of another Australian, Pat Rafter, wasn't the only reason why the tennis stayed off in my house. As for the cricket, let's put it this way: I've never played a forward defensive and then stood vacantly out of my ground waiting for short-leg to run me out before. Afterwards I just went and sat on a stile and stayed staring across the ground, alone with my one thought: 'What the bloody hell is happening to me?' I couldn't score a run and I couldn't hold a catch. I think the phrase sportsmen usually employ in such circumstances is 'mentally shot to pieces'.

Still, on the other hand, if Fiona and I hadn't been splitting up I would never have got to meet Daley Thompson and Sebastian Coe.

I went to London for a weekend to escape and tell one of my best friends what was happening. He told me he went 'training' on a Saturday morning, but afterwards he undid some of his good work in a greasy spoon café on the Ebury Road. We arranged to meet there. It was only when I arrived that I realised 'training' was a group affair run by a two-time Olympic gold medal-winning decathlete. I had about half-an-hour of slightly surreal, dream-sequence conversation about sport with D. Thompson C.B.E. Then Sebastian Coe arrived and ordered his fry-up. I considered telling him I always preferred Ovett but was put off by the memory of a story a friend of Fiona's had told me about an American girlfriend.

The woman was waiting for someone in a diner. She went to put some music on the juke box and was immediately engaged in conversation by a heavily–bearded man sat at the end of the bar: 'You like music huh?' 'Yeah'. 'Who do you like?' 'Bruce Springsteen and Billy Joel.' 'Really? And if you had to choose between them who would you go for?' The woman thought for a moment and then said 'Billy Joel'. The man began to laugh uproariously. It was only then that she realised she was talking to Bruce Springsteen.

I decided that as this was likely to be the one and only time I was going to meet Sebastian Coe it was probably better not to wind him up. I had already upset an Australian woman – who was probably only a Commonwealth Games medallist or something – by daring to mention C.L.R. James' tentative theory that George Headley might have been fractionally better than Bradman on wet pitches. This, it turned out, was a heresy that, had I repeated it in Adelaide, might have seen me pelted to death with cricket balls.

Sadly, both Coe and Thompson were great individual sportsmen. They could offer me no insight into what the England cricket team needed to do to bring an end to Australia's dominance of the game.

Leadership was obviously important but England couldn't even find a captain. Hussain was out injured (finger broken by Jason Gillespie, need you ask) and the only man seemingly keen on taking on the task was Goughie. However, he had effectively ruled himself out by admitting in his recently published autobiography that he was either hungover or still drunk when he hit the winning runs in England's Cronje-inspired victory at Centurion Park. An assumption that the game was going nowhere and an encounter with Ian Woosnam on the fourth evening had combined to leave the Yorkshireman in a 'disgraceful, self-induced state of disrepair'. For 30 years this would have been a good way of describing England's middle order.

With Stewart and Butcher ruling themselves out and Trescothick considered too inexperienced, Mike Atherton was prevailed upon to extend his record number of matches in charge. The fact that all the other candidates seemed to be staring at their shoes when the selectors were looking for a stand-in gave little hope that inspired leadership would spark a fightback. Steve Waugh had another reason to slag off the English.

To this point Atherton's captaincy record against Australia was four wins out of 13 matches. He didn't improve it in 2001. Defeats by eight wickets at Lord's (Gilchrist dropped four times making 90) and seven wickets at Trent Bridge (115-2 to 162 all out) left Waugh licking his lips at the prospect of a 'Greenwash' to match that being simultaneously handed out by Australia's women.

The fourth Test was at Leeds. Every time Australia visited Headingley the big screen showed scenes from 1981. The intervening years had not been kind and I had wiled away almost as many hours with the yellowing heroics of I T Botham as I now spent with my pre-school children following the exploits of B T Builder. The latter had produced an updated version of 'Mambo No.5' just as successful as the original. Mark Butcher was about to do the same thing with his own reworking of the miracle of Headingley.

There is no doubt England were helped by a number of things, including the tourists' belief in their own invincibility and the bad weather that limited their second innings to manageable proportions. Nevertheless, nothing should diminish what Butcher achieved. England had been stuffed out of sight in each of the three previous matches and were now challenged to make 315 to win on a fifth day pitch at Headingley against McGrath, Gillespie, Lee and Warne. Faced with this and a start of 33-2, some men might have bowed to the seemingly inevitable.

Instead, having survived McGrath's menacing opening, Butcher went into overdrive. Every other ball, it seemed, was either crashed square, sent skimming through the covers or clipped off his legs for perfectly timed boundaries. By the end, England were scoring at a rate that would have seen them match Bradman's 1948 Invincibles in chasing down 404 in a day.

David Baddiel has said that what he wants in a sportsman is 'not someone to start me thinking but someone to stop me'. This is exactly what I needed. The best thing I can say about his innings is that for one afternoon Mark Butcher helped me forget everything that was happening to me.

As for the rest of the summer, let's just draw a veil over that. England's defeat by an innings and 25 runs at the Oval about sums it up. At least Tom and Nicole were splitting up as well. But then I didn't get the compensation of a Christmas number one. Unfortunately, work, if that's what you call duetting with Robbie Williams, isn't something I could throw myself into. A canal was more likely. Fiona and I worked in the same place.

David Frith has written a great deal about the high number of suicides among retired cricketers. Professional cricket, and the county game in particular, must be so completely all-consuming that for many it must literally be their life. As I had grown up, my plan, such as it was, had consisted of: meet the right woman, get married, have children, find good job and try to be happy. By the end of 2001, I was asking myself the question countless cricketers must have asked themselves when their careers came to an end. What do I do now that everything I planned for my life is behind me?

TWENTY-EIGHT

Robert Eaton was a Brighton fan. His support was far more avid, genuine and committed than my following from afar has ever been. I have no excuses; Robert still managed to carry on making regular contributions to the Brighton website even after he moved to New York. I mention him because he was another cricketing team-mate from school I hadn't kept in contact with and because he was on the 105th floor of the north tower of the World Trade Centre on 11th September 2001.

When I heard that Robert had been caught up in the horrors of the Twin Towers, a lot of long overlooked memories returned. I remembered his embarrassment at being chosen to sing a solo as a choirboy, something about which he received far less ribbing than he anticipated, but then one of our teachers did describe his voice as 'breathtakingly beautiful'. I remembered a conversation in the biology lab on a wet February afternoon about how you never got 0-0 draws in rugby. I remembered his vigorous bowling action, a Botham-like bounding approach with all the pace generated by the shoulders. But most of all I remembered what it was like to feel sorry for someone other than myself.

Robert worked for Cantor Fitzgerald. Until September 11th all I knew about them was that they sponsored one of the most over-hyped heavyweight boxers in history, Audley Harrison. Then nearly two thirds of their 1000-strong workforce was wiped out in a single stroke.

You wouldn't immediately associate a terrorist atrocity committed on American soil with giving a man in Coventry a more positive view of life after matrimonial breakdown, nor would you think it would have a significant impact on cricket. However, September 11th was one of those moments in history that leaves hardly any part of life untouched.

The ending of Robert Croft's Test career may not have been one of Al-Qaida's stated aims but, when combined with President Bush's need not to seem powerless, it was one of the side effects of their actions.

Not that anybody was certain at the time what Al-Qaida's aims were or indeed even what it was. Al-Qaida became the embodiment of the terror against which the West is 'at war'. Prior to September 2001, it was merely the collective name given by western security organisations to a disparate collection of at most loosely connected terrorist groups with varying agendas. To describe Osama Bin Laden as its leader was like saying Nasser Hussain was the captain of Test cricket. Nevertheless, the desire on the part of President Bush to have an identifiable enemy against whom to extract revenge caused him to identify Bin Laden in this way and, on equally spurious grounds, to go wading into Afghanistan.

At the same time as US-led forces began bombing the Taliban, the Afghan cricket team was playing in Grade II of Pakistan's Quaid-e-Azam Trophy. Their captain, Allahdad Noori, described his side as 'ambassadors for peace' and hoped that 'people across the world may respond to our message positively'. It wasn't to be.

Pakistan was the Test nation hardest hit by the fall-out from September 11th. The West Indies, New Zealand, Sri Lanka and even their own South African-based coach, Richard Pybus, refused to go there. Pybus was replaced by Mudassar Nazar, he of the nine hours and 17 minutes Test century in 1977. The New Zealanders did eventually arrive, but the West Indian series was played somewhat bizarrely in Sharjah and the Kiwis' visit, postponed until April, was cut short when a car bomb exploded outside the team's hotel in Karachi.

England's trip to India was further complicated by deteriorating relations between their hosts and the Pakistanis. The tourists also had a potential equipment problem in that cricket balls and 'similar round objects' had been banned on internal Indian flights because they were considered offensive weapons. Nevertheless, the players' main concerns related to the 'proximity' of the war in Afghanistan. The fact that most Indian cities are further from Kabul than London is from Sarajevo didn't appear to reassure them greatly. Even before September, Gough (Indian pitches) and Stewart (elbow operations and distracting questions about bookmakers) had decided to give the sub-continent a miss. Afterwards, Caddick and Croft opted out as well. Caddick's Test career survived this decision, Croft's didn't.

Shortly before the emergence of the pack of fast bowlers that swept all before them in 2004 and wrested back the Ashes in 2005, Gough and Caddick represented England's firepower and so knew they were almost certain to get back into the side. Croft on the other hand was just one in a long line of spinners selected to 'do a job'. The job in question was usually to take 2-65 while the fast bowlers had a rest and score 35 at number eight. Scaring the opposition in reasonable batting conditions wasn't something English spinners did. Fred Trueman frequently bemoaned the paucity of spin bowling talent in this country and I'm sorry to say he had a point. Croft's replacement in the touring party to India was Martyn Ball of Gloucestershire, a man who, since his debut in 1988, had never managed more than 38 wickets in a County Championship season. Now, it seemed, he was England's fourth best spinner. The men ahead of him were Croft, Ashley Giles and Richard Dawson.

Former cricketers of a particular generation, i.e. those who were summarizing when I first started watching the game, believed the decline of English spin bowling was attributable to covered pitches. When I watched Test cricket in the late 1970s I could never understand why Peter West always informed the viewers after a rain break that 'it's not the pitch that's the problem but the surrounds'. 'Of course the pitch isn't the problem,' I thought, 'it's been covered up.' It took me a while to appreciate that West came from a time when pitches stayed open to the elements from the start of the day and he was used to the game being held up by the state of the playing surface. The likes of Ray Illingworth had honed their skills on drying wickets of a sort Martyn Ball could only dream about.

Nevertheless, I've never completely bought this argument. Partly because just as the prominently seamed ball in use at the end of the 1980s allowed journeymen fast-medium bowlers to produce misleadingly impressive figures, so unduly helpful pitch conditions could presumably do the same thing for spinners. Certainly there is value in learning your craft, but being able to bowl in the wet is of limited help in Test cricket where pitches will always be covered because of the financial need for games to go the distance. Also, it's possible to argue that, notwithstanding the existence of uncovered pitches during most of the period, post-war England have produced only two great spinners, Jim Laker and Derek Underwood.

Laker took 193 Test wickets at 21.24. That's nearly two runs better than Muralitharan and more than four better than Warne. Although

Tony Lock's figures bear comparison with Underwood's in terms of average and strike rate, the Surrey man never had the same reputation of being able to destroy a Test batting line-up on his own. Of the others you could mention, Illingworth, Titmus, Emburey or Edmonds, none has a Test bowling average lower than 31. Looking at those figures, the notion that the period leading up to the permanent covering of pitches was a golden age of English spin bowling starts to seem like a myth.

Indeed, if you look at the Test figures up to the start of the 2009 Ashes series, you come to the staggering realisation that in the whole history of the game only four English spinners: Underwood, Laker, Lock and Titmus, have taken 150 or more wickets. You could argue that this is partly a product of the smaller number of Test matches played in the past when spinners were better, but even Wilfred Rhodes, whose Test career stretched from 1899 until 1930, still only managed 127 wickets at a strike rate significantly inferior to Underwood's. England may have produced spinners who dismissed thousands in the domestic game, but few of these, it seems, made an impact at international level.

Incidentally, in quoting those figures I've excluded Sydney Barnes. This is because although he undoubtedly spun the ball, to catagorise him as a mere 'spinner' would be misleading. Indeed, to describe Barnes as a great Test bowler seems insultingly inadequate. The legend has it that such was his mastery of swing, seam, cut and spin, he could bowl every type of delivery ever invented with the exception of the googly and even that omission was because, as he said himself, he didn't need it.

Sydney Barnes still holds the record for the most wickets in a Test series, 49 against South Africa in 1913-14. This record was set in only four matches, Barnes having declined to play in the final game because the South Africans didn't represent a challenge worthy of his skills. In 27 Tests he took 189 wickets. Ian Botham holds the record for the most Test wickets by an Englishman with 383 in 102 appearances. If Barnes had played 102 times and carried on at the same strike rate, the English record would be 714. Shane Warne took his 708 wickets in 145 matches.

When Don Bradman died Garry Sobers said: 'You can't call Bradman great...If Lara and Gower were great, then you simply have to invent a different word for Bradman.' The same can be said of Sydney Barnes by comparison with any other English bowler who ever lived.

What Nasser Hussain might have given to have had Barnes to call on? Barnes never played against India and, in the absence of Gough and

Caddick, Hussain was left with a senior bowler who is the only man in Test history to have been confused with a wheelie bin and the monarch of a major European country. Ashley Giles took 43 fewer wickets in the series with India than Barnes had managed against South Africa but nevertheless made an important contribution to a spirited performance. A 1-0 defeat may not sound like a triumph but this series marked the beginning of the side's transformation into the best I've ever seen represent England.

Hussain had obviously tired of comparisons with Brearley and began trying to perfect an impersonation of Jardine. In 1933, the Aussie-hater in the harlequin cap had developed Bodyline because he needed a tactic to deal with Bradman. In 2001, Hussain had a similar problem with Tendulkar. If the Essex man's answer was marginally less brutal than his predecessor's, it was certainly no less ugly and he no more apologetic.

In some ways Hussain was ahead of Jardine. True, Flintoff, called away from the Academy in Australia specifically for the purpose, bowled short at the ribs from round the wicket, but this modern variation on an old theme wasn't the only plan. In addition, Hoggard aimed wide of off stump to a 7-2 or even 8-1 field and Giles shamelessly fired ball after ball into the foot marks with the wicket-keeper, James Foster, taking up his stance outside leg stump.

Before the tour, England's cricketers might have wondered how on earth they could follow the Foreign Office's advice to Europeans in India to 'keep a low profile'. Hussain found a way. No one was going to stick around to watch this. Nevertheless, the way Hoggard and Flintoff rose to the challenge pointed the way to the future and the former 'fat lad' triumphantly rounded off the tour by tearing off his shirt to give his newly slimmed down torso an airing after he had bowled Javagal Srinath to tie the one-day series at 3-3.

The previous summer, one of the factors in England's thrashing by the Australians had been the lack of high quality support for Gough and Caddick. Now it seemed Hoggard and Flintoff might be the ones to provide it. In fact, had we but known it, Gough and Caddick had played their last match together. Having opted out of the Indian leg of the tour, the Yorkshireman returned for the one-day series in New Zealand and aggravated a knee injury so badly that he missed the whole of the 2002 international summer and the tour to Australia that followed it. By the time Gough returned briefly, against South Africa in 2003, Caddick was injured. Much as they may not have wanted to, England were going to have to move on.

They weren't alone. Graham Thorpe left India after the first Test in an ultimately doomed attempt to save his marriage. This created a place in the side for Vaughan. Thorpe meanwhile was to learn, as I was, how quickly things can deteriorate. At the time of his departure he commented that, 'Nicky has been enormously supportive to me.' Shortly before his triumphant return to the England side at the Oval in 2003 she sent him a text message along the lines of 'I hope the South Africans break your head'.

Although the circumstances were different, the fact that Thorpe's troubles ran pretty much parallel to mine left me with a curious emotional affinity with a man I've never met. The following season was a cathartic experience for me. Cricket was where I went to escape, it was my refuge and my ever present help in a time of trouble. The game and the friends I played it with, got me through. Batting in the sunshine was certainly far more helpful than dressing as Batman and shouting at people from high buildings would have been. I had the best season of my life.

When I made a hundred in the first innings of the summer, I experienced a surge of emotion from within and from my team-mates, individual joy mingled with the collective in a connection that only someone who has played team sport can hope to understand. It is just this experience that Michael Vaughan's captaincy brought to the England team. You could see it when Thorpe reached his hundred at the Oval and I'm not ashamed to admit the echo of my own experience in that moment brought a tear to my eye.

By contrast, unlike Nasser Hussain, I've never had any kind of strong emotional reaction to anything involving New Zealand cricket. Rugby, yes, because the All Blacks have always been the team to beat. Even though I didn't watch the game at the time, 'Gareth Edwards! A dramatic start! What a score!' still gets me every time. However, even the defeat at the Oval in 1999 that triggered Hussain's tears provoked no more in me than a resigned sigh. Perhaps all the years of failure had finally started to take their toll? Alternatively, it could be that beating the Kiwis is no more than you would expect and, if they win, it will have been with professional, efficient and functional-but-unexciting cricket.

Alright, I know I'm being unfair to the New Zealanders. They have had some exciting cricketers: Richard Hadlee, Martin Crowe, Chris

Cairns and Brendon McCullum spring to mind. Stephen Fleming was the best captain in international cricket and, when he moved his feet and didn't, in modern parlance, 'nick off' to slip, Nathan Astle was capable of belligerent brilliance. Incidentally, where did 'nick off' come from? When I was at school it meant playing truant. 'Sir, sir! Astle's nicked off again, who are we going to get to bat at five?'

It's fair to say that Nathan Astle got his feet moving at Christchurch that winter. England went from India to New Zealand and because their reasons for absence from the sub-continent were deemed acceptable, Caddick and Thorpe returned. Both made a significant impact. Caddick took nine wickets in the match and Thorpe made what was, for about 24 hours, the third fastest double hundred in Test history.

Flintoff's bowling might have made an impact in India but he left with a batting average of 5.20. However, in company with Thorpe, he finally came good in England's second innings. Starting with a burst of 26 in his first 13 balls, the Lancashire all-rounder smashed 137 out of a stand of 281 to beat his previous highest score by 95. Thorpe meanwhile went to 200 not out in 231 balls. Only Gilchrist, three weeks earlier, and Botham had managed the feat any quicker. England set the Kiwis 550 to win, but Thorpe and Flintoff were about to be jaw-droppingly upstaged.

Five years earlier, Nathan Astle had, alongside Danny Morrison, famously thwarted us in Auckland. In the process he and Morrison had broken New Zealand's tenth wicket partnership record against England. Then, he had taken 214 balls to score 102 not out. Now, in company with an injured Chris Cairns, he broke the record again. Only this time he made 120 more runs in 46 fewer balls.

New Zealand were 333-9 when Cairns limped out at number 11. Astle had already begun to attack the second new ball in company with Ian Butler, but when the all-rounder arrived he went berserk.

Stoneleigh have a bowler called Stuart Waite who once produced the wonderfully lop-sided figures of 2-1-28-0. However, this represented economy in the Derek Underwood class by comparison with Hoggard and Caddick's efforts against Astle that afternoon.

Four overs with the second new ball, including a wicket maiden from Caddick, disappeared for 61. Hoggard conceded 41 in two overs and at one point had the incredible field of three slips and everyone else on the boundary. Seven successive deliveries from Caddick – kept on longer than his partner – were battered for 38. When he swept Giles for a single, Astle had taken 153 deliveries in reaching 200. Going from century to double century had used up only 39 of these. Viv Richards took 56 balls when he butchered Botham and co. at Antigua in 1986 to record the fastest hundred in Test history.

Astle's innings was one of the most magnificent displays of sustained hitting Test cricket has ever seen. In isolation it was far superior to Botham's 149 not out at Headingley, an innings which mixed brilliant strokeplay with wild slogging. Astle didn't slog, he just cleanly drove, pulled and hooked perfectly decent deliveries out of the ground over and over again. However, Botham's innings is the one with iconic status because his side won the match. Astle was finally caught behind off a more than relieved Hoggard with his side still 98 behind. The day after the majority of his batting heroics had been completed, Botham plunged to his left to hold a brilliant low catch offered by Kim Hughes off Bob Willis. The day before his innings, Nathan Astle had dropped Graham Thorpe on four.

Despite his mauling by Astle, Andy Caddick still took six wickets in New Zealand's second innings at Christchurch. He did the same thing in the first innings at Wellington. It was the first time an England bowler had taken six wickets or more in successive Test innings since Ian Botham had managed it in the Jubilee Test match in Bombay in February 1980. We still didn't win.

Flintoff scored 75 from 44 balls and, in contrast, Stephen Fleming made 11 from 108. Meanwhile, Steve Dunne, perhaps repaying England for reprieving Atherton at Trent Bridge in 1998, twice missed inside edges from New Zealand's opener, Lou Vincent, and England's wicket-keeper grassed three catches diving to his left. Now I know I've heard that somewhere recently.

However, all of this was irrelevant. On the third morning of the Test the news came through that Ben Hollioake had been killed. Less than a month earlier he had been in the squad contesting the one-day international series. The impact on the team is conveyed by the banalities in Hussain's description of how the loss would affect his men: 'It won't be easy for a while, he was very close to this team. He wasn't just some cricketer, somewhere, that we once played with. This was a lad the coach coached. The physio rubbed his Achilles four weeks ago. I left him out four weeks ago...'

There was irony in where England were playing at the time. Perhaps the most heartrending story in the history of Test cricket concerns a fast bowler from Wellington.

In 1953-54 New Zealand toured South Africa. The Kiwi team had a 22-year-old fast-medium bowler called Bob Blair. Hopelessly out gunned, the New Zealanders lost the first Test by an innings but, on Christmas Eve, they put in a much better showing to reduce their hosts to 259-8 on the first day of the second match. The next morning the news came through of a terrible train crash at Tangiwai between Wellington and Auckland. Bob Blair's fiancée was one of 151 killed. In the face of this and an assault from the South African fast bowler, Neil Adcock, the Kiwis collapsed on Boxing Day to 81-6. With Blair back at the team hotel they were effectively seven down and, in a four-day game, still 41 short of saving the follow-on.

In addition to taking three early wickets, Adcock had put two New Zealanders in hospital. One of these, Bert Sutcliffe, returned with his head swathed in bandages to make a brilliant 80 not out. This required one type of courage. What followed required another.

Sutcliffe had enabled his team to save the follow-on and at the fall of the ninth wicket the players started to leave the field. What happened next is described by Ray Robinson.

'Then there was a sudden, almost chilling silence, as Blair came out to bat, giving a dramatic day its most poignant moment. He had heard at the hotel that his team was in trouble, and somehow had summoned the courage to come to the ground. It was distressing to see how much trouble he had trying to get his gloves on, how he tried to brush them over his eyes as Sutcliffe came to meet him in the sunshine, and to put an arm round him'.

Sutcliffe hit the South African off-spinner, Hugh Tayfield, for three sixes in an over before taking a single from the penultimate ball to leave Blair only one to face. Robinson again: 'He hit the last ball far into a half-demented crowd. They were together only ten minutes but added 33 before Blair was stumped. So they went off together, arms about each others' shoulders into the tunnel.'

Despite Blair and Sutcliffe's bravery, New Zealand still lost that match. England showed great character in having the better of a draw at Wellington, before losing at Auckland despite having the home side 19-4 on the first day. The death of the Queen Mother at the age of 101 had considerably less effect on the tourists than Hollioake's, and, not for the first time, a Test match involving England hinged on a controversial decision about the light.

On the fourth evening the home side were chasing quick runs to try and set up a declaration. But it was getting dark and the floodlights were turned on at 5.50 p.m. The day didn't finish until nearly eight o'clock. Hussain complained that his fielders couldn't see a red ball against the night sky and, as if on cue, the substitute Usman Afzaal curled up 'like an armadillo' (*Wisden*) when he lost sight of a skyer at deep square leg. However, the presence in the sky of the moon inspired the umpires to follow the spirit of Arthur Jepson's famous 'Well how far do you want to be able to see?' retort to Jack Bond at Old Trafford in 1971. The extra two hours of play that the lights bought New Zealand enabled them to declare overnight and bowl England out on the final afternoon. Hussain had been more than happy to play on in palpably unfit conditions at Karachi the previous winter and made no complaint when the boot was on the other foot.

When England toured South Africa under Michael Vaughan two and a half years later, Steve Bucknor was one of the umpires who took the players off at Johannesburg after Graeme Smith complained his fielders couldn't see the ball under floodlights. This illustrates a number of things: how difficult it is to get consistency of decision-making when judgements are being made by as many as six different umpires during the course of a series; how the laws on bad light are widely misunderstood and how changing attitudes in society effect the way the issue is dealt with.

The umpires at Auckland, Venkat and Doug Cowie, reasoned that they had never seen a fielding captain successfully appeal against the light and they were not going to be the first to allow one to do so. Nevertheless, as we have just seen, less than three years later, that is exactly what Bucknor and Aleem Dar allowed Graeme Smith to do. Partly this is a product of different men making different decisions on different days. While the laws are, to some extent, open to interpretation, inconsistency can cost a side a series. You could argue there is little validity in comparing judgments made on separate continents two and a half years apart. However, even within the 2004-05 series questions were raised about the contrasting approaches taken by Darrell Hair and Simon Taufel at Durban and Bucknor and Dar at Johannesburg. Ian Botham suggested on Sky that the problem could be solved if the same two umpires were appointed for an entire series. This would be a good idea but for back-to-back Test matches.

Simon Taufel is arguably the best umpire in the world. In 2004 he was required to officiate in the second and third Tests between England

and New Zealand with no more than a two-day break in between. It was generally accepted that his decision-making in the second of these matches fell below his usually impeccable standards. Much is made of player burn-out in the modern game, but spare a thought for the umpires who spend the whole match on the field. This is just another reason why the ICC and the home boards need to rethink playing schedules.

Having said all of that, it's not just an issue of *how* the umpires interpret the laws but also *which* laws they seek to interpret. Most spectators and, it seems, commentators seem to think that umpires' powers are limited to 'offering' bad light to the batting side and then only if there is a risk of physical danger to the batsmen. However, and this is where the lawyer in me bubbles to the surface, under the laws, umpires are given a general responsibility to judge whether conditions, including light, are fit. They can also (under Law 3.9) suspend play if conditions of 'ground, weather or light' present an 'obvious and foreseeable risk to the safety of any player or umpire'.

In the 1970s, the main worry about a fielder missing the ball in the dark related to the possibility of Brian Close seriously altering its condition with his forehead. Jepson was able to get away with his wonderfully facetious response to a captain complaining he couldn't see because the players accepted the spirit of a decision designed to ensure a full house saw an exciting finish. The same would not be true now. In the increasingly litigious society of the new millennium the concern is more likely to be whose insurance company is going to pick up the tab for the fractured skull suffered by the fielder who fails to pick up the flight of a skimming drive. As a result, umpires now feel the need to bend over backwards to protect the players from injury and themselves from being sued.

The preamble to the Laws of Cricket states that it is against the spirit of the game to 'dispute an umpire's decision by word, action or gesture'. This can involve more than merely staring in disbelief or indeed jabbing your finger in his face when he calls you a cheat. Arjuna Ranatunga led his players off the field during a one-day international against England at Adelaide in 1999 because umpire Ross Emerson no-balled Murali for throwing. This certainly wasn't the first show of public dissent by a Test captain. At Melbourne in 1981, Sunil Gavaskar disagreed so strongly with the lbw decision he had just received that led his batting partner, Chetan Chauhan, to the gates of the pavilion.

However, the difference comes in what happened after these incidents. In 1981, the Indian team manager intercepted the players at the gate and ordered Chauhan back into the middle. When the ICC charged Ranatunga with bringing the game into disrepute, his board supplied him with, as Gideon Haigh put it, 'more lawyers than O.J. Simpson'.

While these sort of developments are worrying enough at international level, what does it mean for clubs using our old friend the fat fag-smoker as a match official? How long is it going to be before an insurance company tries to weasel out of a club's public liability policy because the match in which a player was seriously injured wasn't being officiated properly? A badly injured club rugby player has already successfully sued a referee for failing to protect him from persistently collapsing scrums. Perhaps we are all balanced more precariously on the head of a pin made entirely of goodwill than we realise?

Goodwill is not something England had ever shown much of towards Sri Lanka. Keith Fletcher's team had played in the island nation's inaugural Test match more than 20 years earlier, but over the whole of the intervening period the English cricketing authorities had never once granted them more than a one-Test tour to this country. Zimbabwe were given a two-match series before the Sri Lankans.

Nevertheless, although the three-match series that they had been given was long overdue, the reality was that, from a sporting profile point of view, Sanath Jayasuriya's men didn't represent much competition for Beckham and co. in the World Cup. Despite our cricketers' successes, the enduring image of that early summer is the England football captain's badge-kissing, shirt-tugging celebration of his penalty winner against Argentina. The whole Stoneleigh team watched that match in the bar of our tour hotel. Webs, the side's biggest football fan, had placed a £50 hedge bet on our opponents. He announced, several times, that this was the best bundle he had ever lost and was last seen drunkenly shouting 'Eva Peron, General Galtieri…er…Tim Rice! Your boys took one hell of a beating!'

Back in the parallel universe in which cricket was being played, England had the small scare of being forced to follow on by a Murali-less attack at Lord's, but racked up more than 500 second time round before pummelling the tourists in the next two matches.

The Fletcher effect was evident when Hoggard, whose batting had previously been regarded as like Tufnell's but without the air of permanence, dominated the strike in putting on 91 for the last wicket with Thorpe at Edgbaston. When Vaughan and Trescothick successfully chased down 50 to win at Manchester with one of their allotted six overs to spare, the future began to look brighter than it had ever done for my cricketing generation. After all, the win at Old Trafford came after Andy Caddick had broken down inside six overs. England's remaining seam bowlers, Hoggard, Flintoff and man-of-the-match Alex Tudor, flogged themselves on a flat pitch to see England home. It was the first time since 1996 that we had won a Test without a wicket from either Caddick or Gough. Less than a year earlier this pair had appeared indispensable. Now, it seemed, we had a trio of young pacemen capable of leading our attack for years to come.

Well, as David Lloyd's favourite inspirational rock composer, Jim Steinman, might have put it, two out of three ain't bad. By the time the Indians arrived for the second half of the summer, Tudor was injured. His place in the side for the first Test at Lord's went to Simon Jones, which I think it's safe to say counts as a like-for-like replacement.

Jones followed two great English fast bowling traditions in this match. First, he made what remains his highest Test score in his debut innings (cf. John Lever, Paul Allott and Darren Gough). Second, he got injured and didn't play another Test for the rest of the season. More long-term injuries were to follow. I hope his first innings 41 doesn't end up being Jones' highest Test score because England wouldn't have won the Ashes in 2005 without his 18 wickets. You only have to look at how toothless our attack appeared at times in the second innings at Trent Bridge and the first at the Oval, to realise what a vital component of the team he was. But that, as the great Australian radio commentator Alan McGilvray might have said, was for the future.

Jones' muscular fast bowling helped England win at Lord's. However, by the time the teams got to Nottingham both he and Graham Thorpe, as 'mentally shot to pieces' by his personal problems as I had been the previous season, were gone.

Fiona and I never got to the stage where she expressed the wish that Long Itchington – yes that is a real village name – would break my head. Nevertheless, the previous season had been topped off by their Warwickshire U17 opening bowler sending me to hospital. The ball in question was quick, bowled from left-arm round the wicket and got big off a length. I top-edged it into my helmetless head and was caught at cover 20 yards away.

The worst and most embarrassing thing about this was that he was a junior and four balls into his sixth over. Two more deliveries and ECB regulations would have forced the captain to take him off. These were the rules relating to juniors designed to prevent the undetected stress fractures that had so hampered Flintoff's development as a bowler. The principle had to be right, but nevertheless, any system has the capacity to produce comical anomalies. From where I was lying crumpled it didn't feel like it had been the bowler whose physical well-being had needed protection. At Nottingham, similar rules compelling anyone under 18 to wear a helmet unless a parent gave written authority for them to do otherwise, gave us the delicious situation of India's 17-year-old debutant wicket-keeper, Parthiv Patil, technically requiring a note from his mum before he could stand up to the stumps without protective headgear.

Despite Patil's 19 in 84 minutes on the final afternoon, a high-scoring draw at Trent Bridge might nevertheless have finished with a positive result (probably an England win) if rain and 'bad' light had not carved six hours playing time out of the first four days. Every time a cloud appeared the umpires had their light meters out and on the Saturday evening the players left the field in what seemed, to the untrained eye, to be sunshine. Even so, England didn't have to accept the offer and Stewart and Flintoff's caution, coming as it did at 341-5, was shown up by Ganguly's decision to stay out in similar circumstances in the next match at Headingley.

At Nottingham, England's batsmen had scurried for the pavilion and in so doing surrendered much of the initiative that a brilliant 197 from Vaughan had seized for them. At Leeds, Ganguly and Tendulkar stayed out in much murkier conditions and plundered 96 runs from the first 11 overs with a new ball. India won by an innings and 46 runs to level the series. England's cricket team was no longer a national joke but they were still a long way from possessing the innate belief in their own ability that would almost certainly have seen, for example, Martyn and Gilchrist stay in the middle at Trent Bridge. That Langer and Hayden took the light at the Oval in 2005 is a measure of how far England had succeeded in undermining the Australians mentally by that stage.

At the Oval in 2002, it wasn't the light, or indeed Kevin Pietersen, that ensured a draw. It was just a flat pitch. Vaughan, this time falling five runs short of a double century, gave another glimpse of what he was going to achieve the following winter and Dravid seemed to eliminate any possibility of a bowler taking his wicket before finally being run out for 217. That the 1-1 draw with India was seen as a disappointment showed how far England had come in the three years since Hussain and Fletcher had taken over. They may not yet have fully believed in themselves but at least they were going in the right direction rather than just treading water like Beckham and his ludicrously overpaid colleagues. Whether the same could be said for the game itself is another matter.

That autumn the ground authorities at the Adelaide Oval felt compelled to ban impromptu ball games from the outfield during intervals because of rising insurance costs. The previous January a female spectator had suffered permanent eye damage after being hit by a ball from such a game. On the face of it this appears to be a decision triggered by financial considerations and could be seen as another example of how a modern obsession with money was picking away at what remained of the game's innocence.

The ICC may have started to become obsessed with generating revenue from increasingly large numbers of one-day tournaments but in so far as it was about money at all, the culture that was shaping the behaviour of umpires and even spectators wasn't about earned income. Rather it was about the ability to profit from being able to blame someone else for your misfortunes, combined with an almost psychopathic absence of shame. Arjuna Ranatunga appeared not to care whether, on reflection, his behaviour had been reprehensible or whether he had brought the game into disrepute. All that mattered was that his battery of lawyers could get him out of having to suffer any consequences of his actions. In the 1950s the House of Lords had given Bessie Stone fairly short shrift in her claim for damages when she was struck by the ball outside a cricket ground.

Here are a few examples of more modern legal decisions. Kathleen Robertson of Austin, Texas, awarded $80,000 by a jury after she broke her ankle tripping over her own toddler son running around a furniture store. Amber Carlson of Lancaster, Pennsylvania, awarded $113,500 from a Philadelphia restaurant after she broke her coccyx slipping on a soft drink she had thrown at her boyfriend 30 seconds earlier during an argument. Terrence Dickinson of Bristol, again Pennsylvania, awarded $500,000 for undue mental anguish after he accidentally locked himself in the garage of the house he was trying to burgle and was forced to live on a case of Pepsi and a bag of dried dog food for eight days. All of these come from the 2005 Stella Awards. The awards, named after 81-year-old

Stella Liebeck, the woman who successfully sued MacDonald's when she spilled hot coffee on herself, are for the year's most ridiculous successful lawsuits in the U.S.. None of the above examples won the award.

The winner of the 2005 award was Mrs Merv Grazinski of Oklahoma City. Mrs Grazinski bought a brand new Winnebago motor home. On her first trip she set the cruise control to 70mph and left the driver's seat to go and make a sandwich. To her surprise, she crashed. Mrs Grazinski successfully sued Winnebago on the basis their owner's manual didn't make it clear this isn't the way the cruise control worked. She was awarded $1,750,000 and a new motor home. The company were forced to change their manuals.

Admittedly these cases come from the American legal system. Nevertheless, they illustrate the total lack of shame that characterises the behaviour of many in modern western society. On the day that Matthew Hoggard and Graham Thorpe put together their last-wicket stand at Edgbaston, Hansie Cronje was killed in a plane crash.

Arthur Jepson began his first-class career before the second World War and was the last Nottinghamshire cricketer to be dismissed by Hedley Verity (stumped at Bramhall Lane in 1939, since you ask). The Yorkshire left-armer was a far greater cricketer, and man, than Hansie Cronje. He lies, alongside his comrades, in a war grave at Caserta in Italy. If you want to go and pay your respects, as post-war Yorkshire cricketers did, it won't cost you anything. When Hansie Cronje died, a South African called Leon Dorfling recovered the wreckage of the air freighter in which the former captain was travelling, displayed it at a place called Mossel Bay and charged people 20 rand (about £1.50) to come and have a gawp.

In the 1970s Arthur Jepson could still see the moon. In 2002 all Leon Dorfling could see was an opportunity.

TWENTY-NINE

At Edgbaston in 1975, England's captain, Mike Denness, won the toss and put Australia in to bat. As a result of this decision Tony Greig was in charge of the national cricket team by the time my father took me to Lord's. Presuming the ball would swing on an overcast morning, Denness put his faith in Chris Old, Geoff Arnold and John Snow to make early inroads into the tourists' batting. The Australians lunched at 77-0 and racked up a total of 359. A thunderstorm on the second afternoon, one over into England's first innings, saw the home side batting on a rain-affected pitch. England lost by an innings and 85 runs, Denness resigned as captain and never played for his country again.

Despite the depressing number of hapless performances we had turned in over the intervening 27 years, no England captain – not even Willis at Adelaide in 1982-83 or Gower at Headingley in '89 – had made a more calamitous decision to field first. Then Nasser Hussain won the toss at Brisbane in November 2002.

England would probably have lost the series even if Hussain hadn't put Australia in. To stand a chance we needed our strongest 11 on the field and Gough, Thorpe and Flintoff didn't play a Test between them. Nevertheless, every commentator or correspondent I listened to or read in the lead-up to the series thought England must bat first if they won the toss. A substantial first-innings score creates pressure on even the most formidable of batting sides and, perhaps more significantly, handing Shane Warne the use of a fourth-innings pitch probably wasn't a good idea.

At least Denness had the defence that a cloudy morning had prompted him to gamble on the ball swinging enough for his opponents to be bundled out cheaply on the first day. Hussain's reasoning that he thought he might have Australia 300-6 by the close, made no more sense to me than the commentary that accompanied the soon-to-be-installed Birmingham Eye would make to the majority of Brummies. The only soundtrack delivered with the Midlands' newest tourist attraction was in French.

Even if England's captain had achieved his stated aim, with Gilchrist in the opposition's line-up, 300-6 could still have been turned into 500. As it happened, the Aussie keeper didn't even get in on the first day and the home side closed on 364-2.

In many ways this match represented a microcosm of the previous 13 years of Ashes contests Down Under: England started with prominent players missing and lost another (Simon Jones to his horrible knee injury) during the opening match; a creditable fight back from a horrendous start saw England dismiss Australia for 'only' 492; in reply, four of our top six made fifties but the highest score was Trescothick's 72 and, facing a fanciful victory target, we subsided to Warne and McGrath with embarrassing haste second time around.

In previous years, England's chances in Australia had been hampered by the selectors' tendency towards blind optimism. If they had been honest with themselves, Ray Illingworth and his colleagues couldn't seriously have hoped that Graham Gooch and Mike Gatting, at 41 and 37 respectively, would be able to last the pace when they were selected for the 1994-95 Ashes tour. This time England chose to try and carry players who were too damaged rather than too old. David Graveney and co. ought to have known Thorpe's personal difficulties and Gough's knee were never going to allow them to play any part Down Under. Gough, at least, was arguably a justifiable risk given that none of the other selected bowlers had ever taken a Test wicket in Australia. To take one calculated risk that doesn't come off might be regarded as unfortunate... England took a minimum of four.

Graham Thorpe was in no fit state to tour anywhere but was picked only to drop out before the team even left home. If Thorpe's situation was beyond the control of anyone in the England camp, the other 'risks' only go to illustrate the point that injuries to key players at vital times are not always a matter of ill luck. Before the tour, Gough, Flintoff and Vaughan all had operations. The Yorkshire fast bowler was never expected to be fit by the start of the trip but was hoped to become so during it, much as Wayne Rooney did in the course of the 2006 World Cup. Vaughan and Flintoff on the other hand were supposed to be raring to go from the off.

Andrew Flintoff had a double hernia operation after the Headingley Test against India at the end of August. At the time, Hussain admitted selecting the all-rounder for that match had been 'almost unprofessional'. Flintoff bowled 27 overs while patently unfit, made a pair and England still lost. By the time he arrived in Australia, he still couldn't run. Lord MacLaurin publicly suggested Freddie might have been 'doing things he shouldn't' during his rehabilitation. Even then this was seen as an attempt to deflect criticism from the system and brought a defence from the physio working with the player who described his charge's attitude as 'exemplary'. Darren Gough, who was undertaking his own recovery programme alongside the Lancashire all-rounder, called the ECB chairman's comments 'disgusting' and escaped any punishment.

Michael Vaughan had a 'minor' operation on his right knee in September. He didn't play until the fourth match of the tour against Queensland, when he admittedly made 127. However, injuries to others forced Vaughan's participation in the second Test in Adelaide despite him having tweaked his knee in fielding practice and he required an injection to get onto the field at Perth. Four years later, Vaughan never made it onto any Test arena in Australia because of the state of his right knee. England's first full-time medical officer, Dr Peter Gregory, wasn't appointed until after this tour had started.

By the time the teams arrived at Adelaide for the second Test, England were without Thorpe, Gough, Flintoff, Jones and Giles. The last of these was measured for a new, longer armguard just before going into the nets. Before his new equipment could arrive Steve Harmison broke the slow left-armer's wrist.

Phil Tufnell unexpectedly ended up in Australia. Sadly, this wasn't for another six months and far from turning out at the Sydney Cricket Ground, he was sat in a jungle proving that saying 'happy days' at regular intervals was enough to win *I'm a Celebrity, Get Me Out of Here*. His former team-mate, Angus Fraser, who described Tufnell as 'a pain in the arse at times', presumably wasn't one of those who voted for him.

England weren't the only ones who lost their main spinner. On 10th December, Shane Warne dislocated his right shoulder in a one-dayer at Melbourne and was ruled out for the last two Tests. Unfortunately, England were already 3-0 down by this stage, having surrendered the Ashes in a mere 11 playing days. How were we ever going to beat this lot?

Warne had a more pressing concern: whether he would be fit for the World Cup in February. He made a literally incredible recovery in time for the start of the VB Series finals on January 23rd. Shortly afterwards it was announced that the great leg-spinner had tested positive for banned diuretics. While not performance-enhancing in themselves, such drugs were known as masking agents for other illegal substances. Protesting his innocence, Warne used the Philip Larkin defence and claimed he had innocently taken pills given to him by his mum to help him look slim when he announced his retirement from one-day international cricket. The ACB said 'Hmm, really?' and banned him from all cricket for 12 months.

Warne was the first cricketer I could remember who had been banned for drug taking of this kind. Even then, it was more a case of an improbably speedy recovery from a major injury, combined with a lame explanation for the presence of masking agents in his bloodstream, amounting to guilt by high suspicion. Perversely, the conviction of such a prominent player only served to highlight how minor the drugs issue was in cricket and how diverse sports will always have different major problems for their leaders to wrestle with.

Throughout the 1970s and 1980s the main issue those running cricket had to deal with was that of apartheid South Africa. This was a political problem born of cricket's history and the importance of certain sports to the Republic's white population. ICC originally stood for Imperial Cricket Conference and the founder members who met at Lord's for the first time in 1909 were England, Australia and South Africa. As far as the Republic's white population was concerned, arguably only rugby union was more important than cricket. Therefore, in the 20 years leading up to Nelson Mandela's release, hardly a series went by without the South African issue raising its head in some form or another. However, in the whole of that period, the only time I can remember South Africa being mentioned in the context of athletics was in relation to the fast-tracking of Zola Budd's British passport application. In the summer of 1982, the sponsors of Boycott's rebel cricket tour, South African Breweries, persuaded Jimmy Hill to put together a football team to tour the Republic on the spurious pretext of encouraging inter-racial contact through sport. The venture was criticized by FIFA and the FA, but hardly threatened to destroy the fabric of the international game.

Curiously for sports that are both much more global in appeal than cricket, in the 1970s and 1980s athletics and football had major concerns that were much more domestic in nature. Of course athletics was not unaffected by politics, the Moscow and Los Angeles Olympics were badly devalued by tit-for-tat boycotts by the Americans and Russians over Afghanistan. Similarly, the hooligan problem that plagued football in the 1980s can't be completely divorced from its political context. Nevertheless, whereas the issue that threatened the existence of international cricket in the period was directly political, the difficulties preoccupying the governors of athletics and football were more sociological in nature: drugs and violence. The only cricket fixture in this country where opposing supporters were habitually segregated was the annual meeting at Lord's of Eton and Harrow. Similarly, in the same period as athletics had to deal with the disgrace of an Olympic 100 metres champion, David Boon gloried in setting a new record by consuming 58 tins of lager on the journey from Australia to England.

Cricket is less about explosive power and more about skill and stamina. Some drugs might help you build up the latter but no amount of pseudo-ephedrine in your system will help you tell the difference between a googly and a flipper. Even Warne was effectively only convicted of taking something to try and speed up his recovery from an injury rather than enhance his performance. In so far as cricket has a problem in this area at all, it is to do with players consuming substances of a recreational nature. Usually the substance in question is alcohol and countless stories of performance-damaging excess in this regard are retold with amusement and affection rather than disapproval. Cricket followers generally love tales about the likes of Frank Ryan.

Ryan was an American-born Hampshire and Glamorgan left-arm spinner of the 1920s and a drinker of such legendary proportions that he was once found asleep under the covers after he got too drunk to remember which hotel his team were staying in. Even the more modern revelations that Warwickshire players have taken recreational drugs provide the wonderful irony of Ed Giddins joining the county straight after completing his 18-month ban for testing positive for cocaine.

As far as violence is concerned, those who care enough about county cricket to get into a fight over it are too few and far between to represent a major sociological problem. Also, cricket followers tend to be better at mickey-taking banter than aggressive taunting. Shouting, even drunkenly, 'I'd rather be a bear than a pear' is unlikely to trigger running battles between Warwickshire and Worcestershire fans through the streets of Droitwich. Judging by the way cricket's leaders dealt with the issue of South Africa, it's lucky this is the case.

The ICC took 20 years to agree a policy for dealing with individuals playing and coaching in South Africa. This agreement was never tested because within a year of its formulation Mandela's release rendered it meaningless. Cricket's authorities now have a similar difficulty with Zimbabwe and are taking just as long to deal with it.

Because of scientific advances, athletics will probably always have to deal with the issue of drugs. However, football's leaders can congratulate themselves on having successfully dealt with hooliganism to such an extent that a World Cup in potentially the most explosive of venues, Germany, passed off without a major incident. However, the sociological nature of the problem has enabled the FA to work with the government to find a solution. But what if football's problem had been a political one? Would that have brought the footballing authorities in this country into conflict with the government?

Far more countries with dodgy human rights records are potential and even actual opponents for England's football team than will ever be the case for our cricketers. Yet in all my time following sport I can't think of a single instance where it has been suggested an England football fixture shouldn't go ahead because our opponent's country was run by a politically unacceptable regime and certainly neither our government, nor the FA, nor FIFA have ever publicly sought to prevent an individual from playing or coaching anywhere on this basis. Turkey's treatment of its Kurdish population leaves a little bit to be desired, but no one seriously suggested England shouldn't play their Euro 2004 qualifier in Istanbul or Les Ferdinand should be banned from international football because he had a loan spell at Beşiktas. Not only do governments pick and chose which countries to lean on – wade into Iraq, don't wade into North Korea – they do the same thing with sports.

Ignore for a moment the infrastructure issues that would render the scenario impossible and imagine the South African organizers of the 2010 football World Cup agreed that some of the matches could be staged by their neighbours Zimbabwe. Then consider that one of England's group games gets scheduled for Harare. Is it likely that the British government would lean heavily on the FA to boycott the fixture, thus risking the country's qualification for the second phase or, worse, a total exclusion from all international competition? And would they leave the footballing authorities with little or no political backing in their attempts to get FIFA to move the fixture? Such is the place of football in our society, no government in its right mind would behave in this way. However, that is exactly what the British government did to the ECB over the scheduling of the 2003 cricket World Cup.

At the end of the Ashes tour, England produced their usual winning performance in a dead match. Andy Caddick took ten wickets in a Test for the first time to bowl us to victory at Sydney. The Australians had been deprived of the services of both Warne and McGrath and the win hinted to the most optimistic among us that there might be better times ahead at some point in our lifetime. The presence of the Aussies in our World Cup group might no longer have to go down as a banker for two points dropped. Unfortunately, the same could not be said of our fixture with Zimbabwe.

Ever since the draw for the World Cup had been made, England had known they were due to play the co-hosts in Harare during the group stages. As Heath Streak pointed out, 'hundreds of British companies were trading in Zimbabwe', but relations between Tony Blair's government and Robert Mugabe's despotic, oppressive and violent regime were practically non-existent. Opinions on whether England should fulfil the fixture ranged, in the usual way, between: 'There has to be a very serious dilemma about representing your country on the cricket field in a land where people are suffering so much at the hands of their government' (Mike Gatting!) and 'There are political issues in many ICC countries but they are issues for politicians, not for cricket administrators' (ICC Chief Executive Malcolm Speed).

Both of these statements are stunning in their hypocrisy, but Speed's ignores not only recent cricket history but also the fact that in Zimbabwe cricket administrators and politicians were one and the same thing. The men running the game in that country were political cronies of Robert Mugabe, put in place for the specific purpose of ensuring government control of the sport. Even FIFA, not an organisation with a squeaky-clean reputation for always holding the moral high ground, has rules about such things. In 2006, Greece was suspended from international footballing competition because of excessive government involvement in how the sport was run.

Political interference in Zimbabwean cricket was blatant and the parallels between how Mugabe and John Vorster ran their respective countries, obvious. Nevertheless, the only excuses the ICC would accept for cricket teams refusing to play in Zimbabwe were their government had forbidden them to so or the security of the players would be compromised. As a result, the ECB found itself sandwiched between the British government and the ICC.

On the one hand, cricket's ruling body threatened that if England didn't go to Harare the game would be awarded to their opponents, they would forfeit about £1 million in revenue and face a fine of a similar amount. In addition, there was the possibility of the Zimbabweans pulling out of the proposed tour to England the following summer. The total losses that might flow from a decision not to play the World Cup fixture were estimated to be in the region of £10 million. This may have been roughly the equivalent of Chelsea's weekly wage bill, but it was potentially enough to bankrupt an organisation the size of the ECB. What would happen to England's participation in international cricket if their governing body ceased to exist? In Tony Blair's case the answer to that question was 'Don't care.'

During Prime Minister's Questions, Blair stated 'We have made it quite clear to the cricket authorities that we believe it is wrong that they should go and I hope they take account of that advice. Whether they go or not is a matter for them.' He went on to make a comparison with the situation that arose over the 1980 Olympics and suggested it was not within the government's power to order the ECB not to go. As Lord MacLaurin pointed out, Mr Blair's opinion couldn't easily be ignored. Apart from anything else, the ECB had received around £13 million in lottery money over the previous four years. Nevertheless, the government could have got the ECB off the hook.

At face value, Blair's assertion that he didn't have the right to order the ECB to keep England's cricketers out of Harare has some validity. As we have seen, overt political involvement in the running of the national cricket team is one of the many objectionable things about Mugabe's regime. However, in making reference to the Moscow Olympics, our prime minister was being as disingenuous as Malcolm Speed. In 1980, the British Olympic Association wanted to send a team to the Games clearly against the wishes of the government of the day. In 2003, the ECB was practically begging Tony Blair to forbid them to go to Zimbabwe. He didn't have a right to invade Iraq but that didn't stop him doing it. All Blair had to do was cooperate with Tim Lamb. That he didn't obviously had quite a lot to do with all those businesses Heath Streak was on about.

Even if you accept that political reality dictated that British business interests were more important than the future of English cricket, Tony Blair might have helped the ECB in another way.

What the government was effectively asking the English cricket authorities to do on their behalf was make a political stand against Robert Mugabe's regime. Potentially there were disastrous financial consequences in doing so. Nevertheless, the government offered the ECB no financial backing whatsoever. The Foreign Office junior minister, Mike O'Brien, said that: 'It would be very odd for the British taxpayer to be asked to foot the bill for a decision taken by an independent sporting organisation.' So, if I understand you correctly Mr O'Brien, you want to try and bully English cricket into delivering one in the eye to Robert Mugabe, but then scarper when it comes to cleaning up the consequences. True, £10 million is a lot of money, but British public opinion was far more solid in its condemnation of Robert Mugabe's regime than it ever was in its support for a legally dubious invasion of Iraq, and how much has that cost so far?

The British government was treating the English cricketing authorities with the same contempt that it was simultaneously showing for international law. Blair hung the ECB out to dry. Yet, when England won the Ashes two years later, he had the team round Downing Street like a shot. What was it Matthew Hoggard called Tony Blair? 'A knob'.

Not that the ECB came out of this saga with a great deal of credit. Beset by bullies on both sides, it stood up to neither and effectively left the situation in the hands of a man who, as he himself said, a few years ago was a lad playing cricket for Ilford second XI.

Nasser Hussain was the one leader in this whole sorry affair who came out of it with his reputation enhanced. He may not have been able to identify a batting pitch at Brisbane, but he knew a situation that required a bit of backbone when he saw it. Exasperated by a lack of action, Hussain and the players issued their own statement asking for the match to be moved on 'moral, political and contractual grounds'. The ECB were forced to back their men and when the 'Sons and Daughters of Zimbabwe' issued a statement threatening to send English cricketers 'back to Britain in wooden coffins', they had their excuse to pull out. Even then, the head of the World Cup security directorate tried to dismiss the threat as a hoax, despite the fact that an official from the ICC's own risk-assessment company took it seriously.

Little wonder that Hussain told Speed face-to-face exactly what he thought of him at a meeting in Cape Town shortly afterwards. He was the one major figure in English cricket who had the balls to do it.

Surrendering the points from the Zimbabwe game left England needing to beat at least two of Pakistan, India and Australia to make it through to the second stage of the tournament. England's new pin-up boy, James Anderson, took 4-29 to see off Shoaib Akhtar and his mates, but a heavy defeat to India left us needing to beat Australia in our final match. Unfortunately, Nasser Hussain had one more regrettable cricketing decision left in his winter locker.

With Andy Bichel taking 7-20, England totalled only 204-8 batting first. However, on a slow pitch, this was, unlike Derek Pringle batting at seven, better than it sounded. We had the Australians 135-8 before Bichel and Michael Bevan got the target down to 14 off the last two overs. Flintoff had gone for 21 in his first nine and was nailed on to bowl the last of the innings. But who should deliver the penultimate over, Caddick (4-35 at the time) or Anderson (0-54)? Hussain threw the ball to the lad from Burnley, Bichel hit his second ball into the scoreboard and the over went for 12. The Aussies squeaked home by two wickets with two balls to spare.

When people reel off 2003 in a list of abject England World Cup performances, they forget two things: no one else in the competition got anywhere near as close to beating Australia as we did and we would almost certainly have qualified for the second round were it not for the fact that our captain was a better leader and a better man than those supposedly above him.

Despite the fact England had refused to play in Harare, one potential consequence, the cancellation of Zimbabwe's tour to England, didn't materialise. The financial costs of calling off the visit would have been far more significant for the visitors' board than the home side's. Nevertheless, the ECB gave away 6000 tickets for the first day of the Lord's Test to schoolchildren in order to swell the crowd. Peter Tatchell's promised demonstration might at least have had meant there were some grown-ups queuing outside the Grace Gates on the first morning.

In the end, Tatchell only proved that Mugabe was much better at 'chaos and mayhem' than he was, and the protest was limited to 100 people with a placard suggesting that: 'Tim Lamb is Mugabe's Lord Haw-Haw'. This was inaccurate in a number of ways. For a start, The Honourable Tim Lamb, to give him his full title, is the son of a real Lord, whereas William Joyce was described in the introduction to Rebecca

West's biography as 'a queer little Irish peasant who had gone to some pains to make the worst of himself'. 'Northamptonshire Calling' doesn't sound the same at all and Lamb, despite his recent run-in with Tony Blair, was unlikely to supplant Joyce as the last man to be hanged for High Treason by the British Crown.

The match itself was predictably one-sided. In the absence of, among others, Andy Flower and Henry Olonga, the Zimbabwean team resembled your average village side: half a dozen first choice players accompanied by almost as many making up the numbers. Flower and Olonga had almost certainly ensured the end of their international careers by wearing black arm-bands during the World Cup to mourn the 'death of democracy' in their country. Both could have given lessons in bravery to any number of people in the upper echelons of the sport. Their absence left the national team well on the way to becoming the complete joke it is now.

Tatenda Taibu, Test class in the sense of being a good wicket-keeper and a useful number seven, batted at five and Travis Friend, now performing with reasonable but hardly earth-shattering results in the Birmingham Premier League, was one of the side's all-rounders. Even these cricketing luminaries are now lost to the Zimbabwean team. Taibu, forced during the humiliation at the hands of Sri Lanka a year later to take off the pads and bowl, retired from Test cricket at the age of 22, citing death threats as one of his reasons. Is that an issue for a politician or a cricket administrator Mr Speed? Despite being a Test nation only in the same sense that *Little Britain*'s transvestite, Emily Howard, is 'a lady', Zimbabwe remains a full member of the ICC.

For England, Jimmy Anderson made his Test debut and, courtesy of Paul Collingwood's ill-timed dislocated shoulder, so did Anthony McGrath. That Anderson took five wickets while bowling like a drain and McGrath made 69 and took 3-16, tells you all you need to know about the quality of the opposition. Still, after the hammering they had taken at the hands of the Australians in the winter, two innings victories represented the equivalent of a rest cure in the country. Unfortunately, reality soon arrived in the form of the South Africans.

At the end of the Ashes summer of 2005, Darren Gough blotted his copybook by opting out of the winter's one-day international cricket and then appearing on *Strictly Come Dancing*. In the spring of 2003, his extra-curricular public appearances were no more time consuming than featuring in *The Beano*. Turning up in the Billy Whizz cartoon alongside

Paula Radcliffe, his contribution was limited to one word: 'Chortle'.

For the start of the South African series, Gough made a much-trumpeted (by him) return to the England Test side. He had made a successful comeback in the one-day internationals that had marked Michael Vaughan's accession to the limited overs captaincy. A string of efficient performances had been capped off by a spell of 7-2-9-2 as South Africa were crushed in the Natwest series final.

If Gough's return was a testament to the courage and determination he had shown in recovering from such a bad injury, his figures on his return to Test cricket told the story of its effect. Contributions of 1-88 at Edgbaston and 0-127 at Lord's were as insubstantial as his effort in *The Beano* and told him it was time to go. Gough now believes he came back too soon and might have prolonged his Test career if he had waited until he was fitter. The alternative view, shared by most outside of Darren Gough's house, is he retired two matches too late.

Blessed with a Trueman-like belief that he was even better than he actually was, there is still no doubt Gough was a magnificent cricketer, capable of brilliance, who never seemed to be bowling within himself. That was probably the problem. In order to achieve his best results he had to push his body to the absolute limit. Injuries and a stop-start career were inevitable. There was sadness and a touch of injustice in the end of Gough's Test career. Sadness because he was humiliated by Graeme Smith, a man who, in his prime, he would probably have fancied dismissing lbw for fun with 90-mph inswingers and injustice because his final figures are so much worse than those of his old partner.

On his return from the World Cup, ankle and back injuries had ended Andy Caddick's season. By the time he was fit again, England's pace attack had handed a drubbing to the West Indies and there was no way back. Caddick's final Test match figures were the 10-215 he produced at Sydney. Who was the more whole-hearted cricketer, Andy Caddick or Darren Gough?

Someone else who had decided it was time to go was Nasser Hussain. At the start of the series, Hussain tried to intimidate the tourists' young captain by deliberately calling him 'Greg' and suggesting his team were 'there for the taking'. As it transpired, the 'there' to which the South Africans were taken was an all-you-can-eat buffet serving a never ending supply of long-hops and half-volleys. Smith and Herschelle Gibbs tucked in to such effect that the Proteas ended the first day of the series on 398-1. It was a good job Vaughan's right knee had not yet gone the way of Gough's, as he provided the only wicket when Gibbs obligingly smacked a half-tracker straight down Mark Butcher's throat.

Perhaps the winter's controversies had taken a greater mental toll than he knew, but Hussain seemed lost for an answer. At the time he suggested that he realised the team now responded better to Vaughan's more inclusive style of leadership and English cricket would be best served if he moved aside. Interestingly, Vaughan said he worried that Freddie Flintoff was 'not aloof enough' to make a good captain. This suggests that the Yorkshireman's own approach to leadership is not as different to Hussain's as it first appeared.

Some criticised Hussain for the timing of his departure, leaving his successor with only two clear days between back-to-back Tests to settle into the job. Vaughan, with 156, had enabled his predecessor to at least bow out with a draw. At Lord's, Nasser Hussain was unable to return the compliment, dropping Smith when he had made only eight of his eventual 259 and top-edging a rash pull to end an obdurate second-innings 61. Nevertheless, Hussain finished his England captaincy career with the ledger substantially in credit.

Soon after the Essex man inherited the England cricket team it became unofficially the worst international side in the world. A long four years later, we were in the top three, with only the promised land of an Ashes victory seemingly beyond us. As it turned out, Hussain was Moses to Michael Vaughan's Joshua. An innings-and-92-run defeat in his first match in charge seemed to suggest that Vaughan had landed the England job in an undue rush. Now it seems like perfect timing. Two years later he was marching his side seven times around the previously impregnable Australians.

Vaughan's triumph in 2005 represented only the second time in 30 years that cricket had dominated the country's sporting consciousness. However, in 2003, the most watched leader in Britain cited the dominant figure from the first occasion as one of his greatest influences. David Brent described his leadership style as that of a 'chilled-out entertainer' and revealed Ian Botham as his role model. 'Beefy will happily say *that's* what I think of your selection policy. Yes, I've hit the odd copper. Yes, I've enjoyed the odd dooby. Now will you piss off and leave me alone. I'm walking to John O'Groats…' You can't, as they say, argue with that.

England's resurgence in 1981 owed a great deal to Botham's heroics but was also assisted by the fact that the Headingley pitch was atrocious. Over the years England had on many occasions clawed their way back into contention against superior opposition by playing on inferior surfaces. Indeed, in 2001 it had been their unspoken policy to do so at every possible opportunity. It was a tactic that stood them in good stead in 2003.

If the pitch at Trent Bridge for the third Test looked like crazy-paving at the start, it ended resembling something totally psychotic. On the second evening Smith described it as the 'worst Test wicket' he had ever seen. But then, at 22, he wasn't old enough to get insurance for a hire car to drive around in Britain. Old-timer Alec Stewart could have told him he had seen one in Jamaica that might have been a bit worse. You couldn't imagine Butcher and Hussain making centuries on old-concave-roller Charles Joseph's Kingston minefield.

Hussain benefited from the new captain's ability to win the toss and listen to the voices screaming 'BAT!'. That the English cricketing public appreciated all that they owed the former leader was reflected in the sustained ovation he received on reaching his hundred. Thinking he was safe to continue, Jaques Kallis was forced to abort his run in to bowl as the applause swelled again. Hussain sheepishly backed away and raised his bat for a third time.

First innings totals of 445 and 362 wouldn't lead you to think that the match had been played on a terror track, but Channel Four's pictures of the rolling of the pitch on the final morning told a different story. In close-up, large chunks of the surface visibly moved as the roller passed over them. South Africa were already 63-5 in pursuit of 202 to win by this stage. To face Harmison and Flintoff on such a pitch required courage of the Brian Close variety and England's newest bowling recruit, James Kirtley, benefited from being at the other end to the tune of 6-34. My only reservation about Kirtley's performance was that it meant his absence from Sussex's push for their first ever championship title. When football supporters moan about players going away on England duty, they should remember that at least the clubs aren't forced to play important league fixtures in their absence.

Another thing fans of the over-hyped winter sport rarely have to put up with is their heroes turning up only just in time or, worse still, late for the start of matches. Premiership football clubs run a coach for their players. County cricketers sometimes still car share. In this respect, at least, the pros remain touchingly close to their club counterparts. After an away fixture against Lancashire, Frank Ryan once stayed behind with friends in Manchester before taking a taxi to the following day's fixture in Cardiff. He bounded at the last minute into the home dressing room with a cheerful 'Ryan never let's you down', before handing the taxi bill to the club treasurer. 2003 was the year in which Stoneleigh Cricket Club was joined by their equivalent of Frank Ryan.

David Gallagher was part of a wave of new players who joined the club at once. All of them were called David. Adding these to an already high proportion with this Christian name meant it would have been possible to field a team containing nine of them. The last thing you called whenever a high catch went up was 'Dave's'. Among all of his namesakes, Gallagher was clearly a special talent. A wonderfully gentle, caring and hospitable man, Dave's contribution to the club had only one down side: his 'pre-match preparation'. He remains the only Stoneleigh cricketer to have required a shower *before* the game in order to get himself into anything resembling a fit state to take the field. However, his effort for our away match in Milton Keynes was his crowning glory.

Having arranged to give a lift to one of his team-mates, Gallagher allowed 60 minutes for a journey that required a minimum of an hour and a half and then compounded this by going to the wrong house. He got lost on the way, tried to call for directions after the start time when we were all in the field and then made it onto the ground two overs after his passenger because he was throwing up in the car park. Such was his state of 'confusion' that he dropped two catches, threw the ball over his own head and, with two runs required from the final ball of the match, failed to run the bye that would at least have levelled the scores. It wasn't funny at the time; 10 points for a tie would have won us the league title. Flintoff's had the right idea in 2005: get pissed up after you've won, not before you start playing.

Freddie's drunken ramblings the day after the Ashes had been secured was just one of scores of memorable cricketing images of 2005. England's efforts against South Africa in 2003 were less stirring and provided nothing more iconic than the sight of the mighty all-rounder holding aloft a spectacularly split bat during his consolation century at Lord's. That hundred may not have staved off defeat but it marked a key staging post in Flintoff's development as a true Test match player. In 2000, a giant 22-year-old reacted as if he had answered all of his critics by making a beefy 42 not out in a one-day international against Zimbabwe: 'Not bad for a fat lad'. When he reached his hundred at headquarters three years later there was little more than the most cursory wave of the bat to the applauding spectators. However brilliant his own effort had been, the team was still losing, something a mature 25-year-old realised was more important. The maturity showed in the greater consistency with which Flintoff now began to produce substantial contributions.

Tied at 1-1, the teams moved to Headingley. The England all-rounder's previous performances at Leeds had been consistent, it was the substance that had been missing. In four Test innings at Yorkshire's headquarters, Flintoff had made the same score every time: 0. As if to highlight the change that was coming over him, the big man now made a brace of 50s. However, the transformation of the team was not yet complete and some familiar failings remained.

Reducing South Africa to 142-7 on the first day, England allowed a debutant with no batting pretensions, Monde Zondeki (or 'All hand' as the home side dubbed him), to make 59 batting at nine. In their second dig, the tourists' number eight, Andrew Hall, made 99 not out. The Proteas' last three wickets added 200 in the first innings and 133 in the second. England lost by 191 runs.

We were now 2-1 down. The only victory had come with the assistance of a crumbling Trent Bridge pitch. Throughout the period I had been watching them, England had always needed this sort of help to win Test matches and had never been a major international force as a result. The Oval 2003 was when that began to change. The South Africans made 484 in their first innings and lost, as Flintoff produced his first truly match-turning performance.

When the all-rounder made his first Test hundred he was out scored by Graham Thorpe and upstaged by Nathan Astle. His second, at Lord's earlier in the summer, had done no more than soften a humbling defeat. A first five-wicket haul in a Test was nearly six months away. At the Oval, Trescothick's brilliant 219 and Thorpe's emotional century had all but eliminated the possibility of defeat. However, England needed to win. When the eighth wicket fell they led by only 18 and Freddie had Harmy for company. When Paul Adams bowled Flintoff for 95, Harmison had made three, but the pair had added 99, of which the all-rounder had contributed 85 from his last 72 balls. Graeme Smith looked as helpless as Nasser Hussain had done at Edgbaston.

Flintoff had led a charge and now Harmison, for the first time, truly led the attack. The Durham pace-man took 4-33 from 19.2 overs including Kirsten and Kallis and the tourists ended the fourth day doomed at an effective 65-6. Trescothick blasted England to an eventual target of 110 at nearly five an over. For once, a stirring victory at the Oval represented the start of something rather than a one-off consolation prize.

The quality Napoleon most desired in his generals was that they should be lucky. Michael Vaughan was a superb captain, but he was fortunate to inherit the England job at a time when the team enjoyed unprecedented levels of support. The success of the national side had become a priority even for county chairmen. The likes of Gower and Botham must have looked on from the commentary box with just a hint of envy at the central contracts and extensive back-room staff that gave Vaughan the opportunity to bring on his team in a way they could never have hoped to have done. As a result of these developments, under Vaughan, for a short time at least, things were about to go gloriously right for the England cricket team.

Despite the fact that the Vaughan era was about to bring success of a kind I had never witnessed for the national side, at least his predecessors had won the occasional Test series. By contrast, all of those who had gone before Chris Adams in the job of Sussex captain had never secured the County Championship title. This isn't surprising when you consider that those who had led my county in the past included a co-founder of the Hollywood Cricket Club in Aubrey Smith; a candidate for the throne of Albania, C.B. Fry; England's very own astronomer and facial hair detective, Ted Dexter, and…Ian Gould. Adams had been in charge since 1998, hauled the side from bottom up to seventh in his first season and secured the second division title in 2001. Nevertheless, the county only retained its first division status by the skin of its teeth in 2002 and were many commentators' favourite for relegation the following season. Then, with timing as fortuitous as the arrival of the Prussians at Waterloo, those responsible for selecting a second overseas professional in 2003 hit upon Mushtaq Ahmed.

The first Sussex bowler since 1966 to take 100 Championship wickets, the 'villain' of Lord's in 1996 became the hero of Hove and a small corner of Coventry. Sussex winning the County Championship was about as likely as England winning the Ashes. After years of having to listen to Warwickshire supporters telling me how great their team was, I finally had the bragging rights. At every opportunity I tried to go through the details of the triumph with my team-mates. Strangely, they didn't want to stay and discuss them.

THIRTY

In the autumn of 2003 England's rugby union players did something the cricketers have never done. They won the World Cup. Jonny Wilkinson may have become a national hero with one sweep of his right boot but, like generations of back garden cricketers, he didn't get his ball back.

The one Mike Catt managed to find touch with to end the final is a fairly rare commodity but the ball Wilkinson launched so gloriously between the uprights was estimated to be worth in the region of £500,000. Unsurprisingly, the RFU wanted it. But, like the curmudgeonly old bloke next door who likes nothing better than spoiling other people's fun, the Australians claimed they had lost it. An unseemly argument resulted, with *The Sun* urging its readers to badger the Australian High Commission in London for the ball's return and the *Sydney Daily Telegraph* responding with: 'Want the ball? Then give us the Ashes.'

If the Australians' outgoing captain, Steve Waugh, was to be believed, it was hard to know why they wanted the urn so badly. While England's cricketers were watching Martin Johnson and his men's triumph between washed out one-day internationals in Sri Lanka, the Australians were preparing for a home rubber with India. Waugh, who had turned the series into his valedictory procession by announcing it would be his last, had publicly stated on more than one occasion that he now regarded his side's contests with the Indians as more meaningful than those with England. Expressing this opinion didn't prevent the Aussie captain from predictably adhering to the idea that although the Ashes remained physically in England, morally they belonged in Australia. This is a stance that overlooks the view of the descendants of the Hon. Ivo

Bligh; namely that the urn represents not a sporting trophy but rather a family heirloom lent to the MCC. Nevertheless, it wasn't the last moral argument the Aussies got involved in that year.

During the World Cup, Adam Gilchrist had surprised many people, not least his own captain, by walking in the semi-final against Sri Lanka despite the fact Rudi Koertzen had given him not out. Ricky Ponting's surprise, not to say shock, at Gilchrist's actions didn't seem to seem to sit easily with one of his stated ambitions for the side. When he took over as Aussie skipper, Ponting continued to express his predecessor's view that the team should play in a way that always upheld the spirit of the game. A cynic might suggest this was a slightly cocky aspiration, born of the knowledge Australia didn't need to indulge in sharp practice to hand out a thrashing to any other side on the planet. Not only did the Australians want to be the best cricket team in the world, they also wanted to be seen as the most virtuous. It was as if Chelsea, to make things interesting for themselves, had set out not just to win the Premiership but also the fair play league.

Cricket has a perhaps slightly mythical reputation as the embodiment of fair play. Everybody knows what 'it's not cricket' means. But let's not forget that the game emerged in its organised form as a means of enabling the landed gentry to indulge their love of gambling, or that no lesser figure than W.G. Grace was well known for his gamesmanship. It would be naïve in the extreme to assume that there was some glorious moral past in which everybody walked.

Nevertheless, when I first started playing and watching cricket in the 1970s, my teacher taught me to walk, and non-walkers were the ones disapproved of in the county game. I know of at least one boy at another school who was caned for not walking in a first XI match. Implicit in the stories about Grace is that his stature enabled him to get away with behaviour utterly unacceptable in any lesser figure. It was more a case of 'one rule for you' rather than 'everybody's doing it'. Even in July 2006, the outgoing president of the ICC, Ehsan Mani, offered the opinion that walking represented 'one of the unique spirits of our game'. Yet, when a new player in his early twenties joined Stoneleigh in 2002, he told me his teacher had made clear that under no circumstances should he walk in a school match. By 2003, the captain of the most successful side in the world could boast of his pride in the way his team upheld the spirit of cricket while being one of the most confirmed non-walkers in the game. Did that mean the spirit of the cricket had changed, or just that Ricky Ponting and Ehsan Mani have different views about what it means to adhere to it?

In the autumn of 2004, Australia played a two-Test home series with New Zealand. Towards the end of the first match, as the Kiwis were subsiding to a heavy defeat, Craig McMillan appeared to inside-edge Jason Gillespie through to Gilchrist. The Australians' confident appeal was turned down by Steve Bucknor. A full and frank exchange of Antipodean views ensued. The gist of this was, minus the Anglo-Saxon: 'You know you hit that; what are you still doing here?' to which the batsman's response was to the effect of 'Why do you think you've got the right to shove your morality down the throats of the rest of us?' As a reflection of the society in which cricket was now being played, this incident and the comments made in its aftermath are, as Stephen Fry might have put it, quite interesting.

When he was interviewed after the match, Craig McMillan offered the opinion that, 'Just because one or two guys are on a crusade doesn't mean it changes the way of 95 per cent of other cricketers.' The use of the word 'crusade' is interesting, as it appears to be an attempt to paint Gilchrist as the bad guy for having the temerity to suggest that McMillan might be a bit more honest in how he plays the game. At the risk of sounding like Tony Blair, such an attitude seems indicative of a society in which the rights of the individual have reached a level of importance far higher than their responsibilities. This is an impression supported by the attitude of the Kiwi captain, Stephen Fleming: 'An individual's right to decide [whether or not to walk] should be respected.' What he was in effect saying was any individual cricketer has an absolute right to put one over his opponents if he so chooses and can get away with it, and everyone else must respect his inalienable right to do so. Or, as someone once put it to me: 'Human beings have an absolute right to pursue their own personal happiness.' Such a notion has a superficially attractive ring to a modern ear, until you scratch the surface and find the sub-text, which is 'at the expense of everybody else's if necessary'. Take that reasoning to its logical conclusion and you can justify almost anything.

Given that he chooses not to walk, Ricky Ponting presumably agrees with Stephen Fleming. So what does he mean when he says he wants his side to uphold the spirit of the game? The apparent disagreement between Ponting and Mani could lead you to the conclusion that this is largely a matter of interpretation. However, to some extent at least, what constitutes the spirit of cricket is written down as a preamble to the Laws. That preamble states, among other things, that it is against the spirit of the game to 'direct abusive language towards an opponent or umpire' and 'to indulge in cheating or sharp practice, for instance: to appeal knowing that a batsman is not out'. Although walking is not specifically mentioned, what is the moral difference between standing when you know it's out and appealing when you know it isn't? By these standards Australia would never sledge anyone or appeal for a short-leg 'catch' straight off the pad.

The problem is that standards have a habit of changing. Charles Wentworth Dilke, a radical Liberal MP of the nineteenth century, had his political career ended in 1885 by no more than being named as a co-respondent in a divorce case. In the 1960s, John Profumo resigned not because he had involved himself in extra-marital activities with Mandy Rice-Davies and Christine Keeler, but rather by reason of having lied to Parliament about doing so. By the 1990s, William Waldegrave was able to say publicly that there were circumstances when even this was legitimate. If anything, John Major's standing in the eyes of the male population improved when news of his affair with Edwina Currie became public. It made him interesting rather than dishonourable. In 2004, at around the time Gilchrist and McMillan were standing toe-to-toe, David Blunkett had to resign from the cabinet, not because he was sleeping with a married woman, but rather because he got caught allegedly speeding up her nanny's visa application.

The spirit of cricket that Ehsan Mani identifies dates from the Victorian age in which the game began to become more structured. This was a period of great hypocrisy, many of those who hung Dilke out to dry were guilty of the same offence but didn't get caught. Nevertheless, it was also a time when certain sections of society – i.e. those from whom the 'gentlemen' who played cricket were drawn – prized honesty, honour and integrity above all other human virtues. For many Victorians, living a good and godly life amounted to an aspiration. Being a 'good person' was something admirable. Any game adopted by such men was bound to have a deeply moral streak.

Despite her wholesome reputation, it's very unlikely that any of this would immediately make you think of Doris Day.

However, about the time Craig McMillan and Adam Gilchrist were having their little set-to, I was channel surfing and came across a documentary on the 1950s Hollywood star. A man I had never seen before was sat in a cinema offering the opinion that if Ms Day were starting her career now, she would still be a great actress. It was his qualification of this assertion that caught my attention: 'Of course, she would have to have a different image, because modern society despises goodness.' This idea is at the heart of the argument between Gilchrist and McMillan.

The question of whether or not a batsman should walk is a moral one. Deep down every cricketer knows what he should do if he nicks it and is caught. Whether or not he can come up with a well-reasoned rationalisation of why he doesn't is just a question how good he is at shouting down his own conscience. Some have always been better at doing this than others. Gilchrist explained his actions in the World Cup semi-final by saying that, 'Something inside me said "Go!".' Many cannot derive any pleasure from sport unless they play absolutely honestly. For others it appears as if the opposite is true. Witness the antics of footballers, not all of them from Portugal, diving to try and get not only free kicks or penalties, but also their opponents sent off.

At first it's hard to see how you could object to a cricketer deciding to be honest in his dealings with opponents and umpires. The problem, as Craig McMillan identifies, is that such a stand has the capacity to show up everybody else. By way of a defence, McMillan relies on accusing Gilchrist of a sin even greater to modern eyes than adultery was to the Victorians; that of being moralistic. Also, by suggesting Gilchrist's attitude is at odds with that of 95 per cent of other cricketers', the Kiwi is implying his own attitude is more in keeping with the spirit of the time.

Whether Gilchrist or McMillan is upholding 'the spirit of cricket', comes down to whether morality can ever be absolute or whether it must always be relative. Is the spirit of the game immovable and inviolate, or is it open to reinvention through the prism of modern attitudes? Ironically, snooker, a game with the most bar-room of images, has one of the strictest codes of ethics of any modern sport. Any professional who gets caught failing to call a foul against himself runs a very real risk of ostracism by his fellow players. You might think honesty, honour and integrity are constants, but modern society appears to have redefined, if not the qualities themselves, at least how you establish whether or not an individual possesses them or how valuable they are. The Victorians believed in absolute morality and ended Charles Dilke's career, regardless of his abilities as a politician, for no other reason than he was an adulterer. David Blunkett would have survived the same revelation had he not abused his ministerial position on behalf of his married lover.

The first known version of the Laws of Cricket dates from 1744. The MCC made its initial revision in 1788. The preamble that attempts to define the spirit of cricket wasn't added by the ICC until 2000. Perhaps this is because it was felt no one needed telling before? However, as we have already seen, there are elements in this document that seem at variance with how the Australian team, and indeed every international side, play the game. Is the new preamble an assertion of the true spirit of cricket or merely an attempt to impose Victorian standards on post-modern cricketers? However you answer that question determines whether you think Ricky Ponting and his men are adhering to the spirit of the game or merely its zeitgeist.

As well as adding a preamble to the Laws, the ICC also felt the need to publish a mission statement. As I was growing up with cricket in the 1970s and 1980s, the game's governing body having such a thing was about as likely as the chairman of the TCCB having a manifesto. This is hardly surprising, given that at the time the administrative resources of the ICC consisted of little more than a filing cabinet in the corner of the one of the offices of the MCC. The unwritten understanding was that the president and secretary of the Marylebone Cricket Club also held the respective offices of chairman and secretary of the ICC. This wasn't a huge problem in a world where only six countries played Test cricket and the activities of all the associate members of the game's governing body put together merited less than seven pages in the 1977 *Wisden* (three on Ireland and Scotland, one on Sri Lanka and two-and-a-half on Canada). The Public Schools got 57 pages. In the 1975 World Cup the numbers were made up by the emerging Sri Lankans and a team representing 'East Africa' that included Derek Pringle's dad.

By 2004, the ICC, long since expanded beyond a couple of meetings a year on the MCC president's itinerary, was committing itself not only to protecting the spirit of cricket but also to 'promoting the game as a global sport...and optimising commercial opportunities for the benefit of the game'. This pledge goes some way to explaining England's first touring destination in the winter of 2003/04.

The idea of 'promoting the game as a global sport' doesn't sit well with only six sides playing the game at the highest international level. The elevation to Test status of Bangladesh was a logical part of the programme of expansion and obviously had nothing to do with a desire on the part of Indian cricketing power broker and sometime ICC chairman, Jagmohan Dalmiya, to have another sympathetic sub-continental representative with full voting rights sitting at world cricket's negotiating table. As East Pakistan, the country had already hosted Test matches in the 1950s – Fazal Mahmood's 12-100 at Dacca in 1959 remains the best match analysis by any bowler in Tests between the West Indies and Pakistan – and the country remains as passionate about cricket as its neighbours. The 'commercial opportunities' available in a cricket-mad land of more than 140 million people are obvious. The question was not whether Bangladesh should become a Test nation, but rather when.

That the Banglas were elevated too early is beyond doubt. They played their first Test match in November 2000. By the end of 2009, they had three Test wins, one against a Mugabe's XI weaker than Derbyshire and two against the West Indies' 3rd XI. Bangladesh possesses no bowler with more than Mohammed Rafique's 100 Test wickets and only one batsman, Habibul Bashar, with more than 3000 runs. The fact that Bashar's average is hovering in the low 30s means this is roughly equivalent to England having Graeme Hick as their all-time best Test batsman.

Think of the potential for embarrassment, then, when the Tigers entered the final day of their first ever Test against England with a lead of 153, four wickets in hand and a turning pitch to bowl last on. A similar situation had faced England when they had been the opponents in Sri Lanka's inaugural Test match more than 20 years earlier. Then, Underwood and Emburey had pulled our nuts out of the fire with the ball and Tavare had knocked off 85 of the 171 required to bring a seven-wicket victory. This time it was Hoggard and Harmison who came up with the bowling heroics and Vaughan whose 81 not out secured an identical result. The home side's failure to convert a good position in the first Test and what happened in the second, illustrated why they weren't ready for international cricket.

Notwithstanding the efforts of 2001, England are often accused of not making enough of home advantage in the way Test pitches are prepared. However, few English venues can ever have produced a surface so spectacularly in favour of the visitors as the one the groundsman at Chittagong rolled out for Vaughan and his men. *Wisden* described the surface as 'all green and tufty, like a Martian's chest hair'. It probably tells you all you need to know about the pitch, and how the

Bangladeshis play the short ball, that they were twice bombed out by Richard Johnson, a man whose usual method involves pitching it up and aiming for the stumps and pads. Quite what carnage might have ensued had Harmison and Flintoff been fit to play doesn't bear thinking about.

In the course of charting the England cricket team's various travails over a period of 30 years, I know that whenever I've been in need of a contrast to whichever failing applied at a given time, I always have to come back to what you might term the 'Vaughan era'. The Oval fightback against Graeme Smith's men; the massacre of the Banglas; destroying the Windies twice in six months; panning the New Zealanders; winning in South Africa for the first time in 40 years and the exultation of the Ashes victory, all create the impression of a seamless, triumphant progression of improved management and performance.

In reaching this conclusion, many, myself included, overlook the series with Sri Lanka that fell between the tours to Bangladesh and the West Indies. Ironically, before the period of unprecedented success that was about to follow, England's 2-1 victory on the island three years earlier had been arguably the greatest achievement of the previous 30 years. Now, however, facing Murali armed for the first time with a doosra, the highlight of this visit was the rugby players' World Cup win.

In the first two Tests, Ashley Giles and Gareth Batty proved that having spinners who can make 35 batting at number eight has some value, and England scraped draws with one and three wickets respectively remaining. If Vaughan's men had the excuse of having been forced to bat second in these matches, for the third Test the captain won the toss. Confusion reigned all round.

Outside, the local police were involved in a struggle with a crack unit of Buddhist monks attempting to storm the ground. In 1975, there may have been some uncertainty about whether George Davis was really innocent, but as far as these monks were concerned there was no doubt the Venerable Gangodavila Soma Thera was dead, and his recent demise made it disrespectful to be playing cricket. Inside the ground, the only confusion was how England, on a pitch that should have seen 610-4 play 634-6, had found themselves 139-5. Flintoff produced his one and only fifty against Sri Lanka (his first nine matches against these opponents saw him with a batting average of 19.33) and the side ended up with 265, a total with a net value of 93 on a surface offering any assistance to the bowlers.

In response, the Sri Lankans produced a mediocre batting display and lost eight wickets in making 628. The third worst defeat in England's Test history, by an innings and 215 runs, followed shortly afterwards. The idea of England being about to sweep across the cricketing world like the Huns across Asia, seemed as likely as an injury-plagued Kelly Holmes becoming a double Olympic champion.

Ok, so Michael Vaughan as Attila the Hun might be a slight exaggeration, but what was to follow was the most sustained period of success at Test level I have ever seen or, it seems, am likely to see from my team. From the start of the tour to the Caribbean in March 2004 until the end of the Ashes in August 2005, England won six successive series. In that time they played 23 Test matches, winning 16 and losing only two. To put that into some kind of context, discounting one-off matches against Sri Lanka, England only won seven series in the whole of the 1980s. That entire decade only produced 19 Test victories.

When England had visited the West Indies under Botham, their best bowler had supposedly been an off-spinner who finished the series with an average fractionally under 60. However, when the England side returned home after the rout of 85/86, the great all-rounder's 2-0 defeat looked like a triumph.

Gower's attack was led by a Welsh fast bowler doing his best to fight fire with fire. When Vaughan arrived, he too had a Glamorgan pace-man at his disposal. However, whereas Greg Thomas had been hopelessly outnumbered, Simon Jones had Harmison, Flintoff and Hoggard for company. It's no coincidence that the run of success began with the first Test these four played together.

Collapsing from 281-5 to 311 all-out, gifting the opposition 60 extras in an innings where no batsman made more than 58 and then, having conceded a first-innings lead of 28, setting the opposition only 20 to win; who does that sound like? Throughout the two series we played against the West Indies in 2004, the side our opponents most resembled was the England of the 1980s and '90s. A team containing some talented individuals was capable of creating promising positions, but never of nailing the opposition when the opportunity arose. Vaughan's England on the other hand, suddenly seemed to develop the ability to recognise the pivotal moment in a match and to seize it ruthlessly.

No better image sums up the way the balance of power had shifted than the sight of the umbrella field Vaughan set for Harmison as the

West Indies' second innings disintegrated for 47 at Jamaica. Only Hussain, at short-leg, was not stationed in the slip/gully region and as Trescothick, as opposed to Clive Lloyd, snapped up the number 11 at first slip, the home side had only the forlorn crumb of comfort represented by making one more than 46 to cling to. We'll draw a veil over what happened on the same ground four years later.

Even then the West Indies still had their chances. At Trinidad, 100-0 on the first morning became 208 all-out and in Barbados, England trailed by 69 when their eighth first-innings wicket fell, only for Thorpe's remarkable 119 not out to take them into a tiny but psychologically devastating lead. The next highest score by a batsman was 17. Matthew Hoggard was the only one of England's new pace battery not to record a five-for in this series, but he had the consolation of following up Thorpe's effort with a Test hat-trick as we dismissed the West Indies for under 100 for the fourth time in seven Tests. The Yorkshireman's exultant, arms-in-the-air, tears-in-the-eyes charge towards the catcher, Flintoff, as Ryan Hinds became his final victim, summed up the emotions this tour provoked in the team's supporters. At last, it seemed, we had the firepower to stick it to anyone and it was wonderful.

Our sense of inferiority left us with the feeling that 'anyone' still didn't include Australia, but we should have had more faith. By the middle of the following summer, Justin Langer was offering the opinion that batting against this new England was just like facing up to the West Indian pace battery against whom he had made his debut. High praise when you consider Langer started his career taking on Ambrose, Walsh and Bishop.

Interestingly, with a shift in the balance of power came a change in attitude. When Flintoff landed one on the chin of Pedro Collins at Manchester, the incident passed with hardly a comment. Indeed, despite the fact Collins was only batting a nine because Corey Colleymore and Fidel Edwards would have been second favourites in a double-wicket contest with Malcolm and Tufnell, the only controversy concerned whether or not Lara had declared, or Collins had retired hurt at lunch. In more ways than one, England had come a long way since Bob Willis had smacked Iqbal Qasim in the mouth at Lord's in 1978 and Clive Lloyd had unleashed his "Bouncing Billies" in 1984.

By the end of the series in the Caribbean, the West Indies were in the same position England habitually found themselves against Australia: looking for some sort of consolation in the final match of a dead rubber. The pitch at the Antigua Recreation Ground is weighted to an immoral degree in favour of the batsman and an Oval-style victory seemed unlikely. Instead, the Windies had to be content with a feat of individual brilliance from one of their batsmen.

It was only six months since Matthew Hayden had passed Brian Lara's record Test score by making 380 against Zimbabwe at Perth. The fact that 'Zimbabwe' was one of three words (the other two being 'and Bangladesh') that help explain why a number of leading batsmen had Test averages in excess of 50, to some extent devalued the Australian's achievement. No doubt Steve Waugh thought taking 375 off the England attack of the mid-90s was no more difficult. However, Lara had a record to reclaim and this time, although it might have been a toss-up between Gareth Batty and Ray Price in the spin department, no one could argue Harmison, Flintoff, Jones and Hoggard compared unfavourably with Streak, Blignaut and Ervine.

One of cricket's most often quoted facts is that the only two men who were on the field for both Lara's 375 and his 400 not out were Graham Thorpe and Darrell Hair. Funny how the Aussie umpire always seems to have been around when something big happened. If Lara was lucky that he didn't fully dislodge the bail when he trod on his stumps in pulling Lewis for four to break Sobers' record, he could thank Hair for turning down a concerted caught-behind appeal on 0 at the start of his assault on Hayden's.

As *The Sun* put it, 400 might be 'A LARA LARA RUNS', but the man himself was right when he said that the feat was 'dampened by the result of the series'. At least he didn't say, as Vaughan did after the victory in Barbados, that 'The achievement that we have achieved is a fantastic achievement.' However, a whitewash by England was postponed by only four months.

On their return from the Caribbean, Christopher Martin-Jenkins identified the England side's remaining shortcomings as the absence of an 'established spinner other than Ashley Giles, a reliable bowler but seemingly limited on pitches outside the sub-continent and no young batsmen thrusting from below with unanswerable claims to oust the established top five'. Leaving aside whether or not the ability to thrust from below was a vital talent for an England Test batsman, few would have disagreed with him. Yet, by the time the Australians arrived little more than a year later, the entire middle order of Butcher, Hussain and Thorpe had been supplanted by Strauss, Bell and Pietersen. The following winter, Monty Panesar emerged.

Most England cricket supporters will never have heard of Zac Taylor. However, the 19-year-old left-arm spinner played a small but vital part in changing the face of English cricket. What is even more surprising is that young Mr Taylor's contribution consisted of a single mediocre ball.

Three days before the Lord's Test against New Zealand at the start of the 2004 international summer, Zac Taylor was acting as a net bowler for the England team. A significantly less than devastating delivery to Michael Vaughan produced a routine sweep, a yelp of pain and an England captain lying in a heap with a twisted right knee. 'Thanks for coming Zac.'

In fact, Zac Taylor should have been on the open-top bus ride through London the following summer. Vaughan's absence from the team created a place for Andrew Strauss, previously no more than a player on the periphery of the one-day side and surprisingly preferred to Robert Key who had made a century in each innings against the tourists the week before. Despite Key's claims, you don't need Sue Barker to tell you what happened next.

That's right, a Dane fielded for England at Lord's. Frederik Klokker, then an MCC Young Cricketer, now playing for Berkswell near Coventry, acted as a substitute for Nasser Hussain. Oh yes, and Andrew Strauss scored a hundred on debut.

Strauss was only robbed of twin centuries by Hussain 'doing a Boycott' in running him out for 83 on the last afternoon. If his batting showed the Middlesex captain's class, Hussain's response, both to the run out and the younger man's contributions, demonstrated he possessed an abundance of the same quality.

I can still see the two extra-cover drives with which the former captain first drew England level and then brought up his own glorious final Test century. His initial preference may have been for the glow of a late-summer farewell at the Oval, but, sensing the needs of the team now demanded otherwise, Hussain decided a sunlit spring evening at Lord's would do just as well: not bad for a bloke thought too intense and self-absorbed to ever make a decent captain.

The New Zealanders, we were told, would represent a true test of how far England had come. They were a strong, well-led side who batted a long way down. Despite having to get past totals of 386, 409 and 384, England brushed them aside 3-0. In fact, although much was made of our developing pace attack, in the seven Tests played that summer, England's bowlers only once dismissed their opponents for a first-innings total smaller than 336. After years of collapses, it was the batsmen who never failed. Three times they successfully chased down more than 230 in the fourth innings (twice in excess of 280) and made more than 440 in five out of seven first innings.

At last I knew what it had felt like to support the West Indian team of the 1970s and 1980s. Even when we were 40-3 in reply to the Windies' 395 at Old Trafford I still expected us to win. My father's last summer had ended with Tony Greig forced to reflect on a 'me and my big mouth' 3-0 trouncing by Clive Lloyd and his men. Never since had England threatened a performance of such dominance in reply, until now. Even Hussain's victory in 2000 had to be prised from the fingers of Walsh and Ambrose and was no more than a few leg-byes and a couple of Dominic Cork's lusty blows from failure. This though was different; the possibility of losing seemed non-existent. Beating West Indies 4-0 was an experience for which I had waited a long time.

Something else that had been a long time coming was the Dredge family's revenge. In 1978, Colin and his Somerset team-mates, the champion one-day side of their generation, had lost to Sussex in the Gillette Cup final. Twenty-six years later, Stoneleigh pitched up at Frome.

The 'Demon' Dredge still played for the first team but didn't turn out against us, contenting himself instead with what should have been a quiet net beside the pavilion. Unfortunately for us, selected in the Frome XI to face Stoneleigh, were the great man's son, Neil, and a shambling youth by the name of Liam Chrisp.

The latter's appearance was not unlike that of the teenager in a previous West Country encounter who hadn't anticipated faecal incontinence as one of the side effects of opening the batting. However, spots and a shuffling gait were where the similarities ended. Once Liam got going, it was the fielders who were shitting themselves. It was only after the match they told us he had just returned from the U19 World Cup where he had been opening the batting for New Zealand. His only 'failure' for Frome that season had been an innings of 58. Liam Chrisp, remember the name, firstly because he is very good and secondly because I got him out.

I have to admit that of all the wickets I've ever taken, this is the one for which I deserve least credit. So complete was his dominance, it was he who formed the opinion we must be a rugby team in disguise. Every other bowler had been dismissed from his presence and, goaded by a team-mate suggesting I normally liked bowling at people under 20, I was forced to show willing and put myself on.

At first, I tried firing in what I regarded as quick darts at his toes. However, Liam was now batting like a man who had more time to see the ball than Neo from *The Matrix* and he merely skipped outside leg stump, waited and then smashed each one back over my head. As the third successive such delivery landed on Colin's net 80 yards away, I reasoned I might as well try tossing the ball up. Even if it went still further, it couldn't cost me any more than 6. I sent down a loopy off-break that possessed the single merit of being straight.

In 1948, it was claimed, despite Jack Crapp's assertion to the contrary, that Bradman had missed Hollies' googly because he had a tear in his eye. I can only think something similar, this time prompted by laughter, accounts for what happened next. Well, it was either that or Liam was fooled by his own inability to believe a fully-grown human being was capable of delivering a cricket ball so slowly. Either way, he charged down the pitch, aimed in the direction of Mars and missed. It was at this point that the delivery's solitary merit came into play and he trudged off with what he clearly regarded as an embarrassingly paltry 146 to his name. Shortly afterwards it was our turn to bat.

Fortunately, I scraped a few runs together against an opening attack of two 15-year-olds who were both quicker than anything in our side. Then Neil came on. Bowling, out of pity, well within himself and off what was clearly a shortened run, he spent a couple of overs toying with me before delivering his knockout blow. My final ball of the match started on the line of leg stump, swung away late, nipped slightly further off the pitch past my groping outside edge and sent off stump careering towards the wicket-keeper. At least, that's how I saw it. My batting partner, who clearly should have gone to Specsavers, claimed it was merely straight and I missed it.

Without even realising it, Colin Dredge's son had extracted a miniscule measure of revenge for a shock cup final defeat 26 years earlier. As Craig McMillan would no doubt tell you, these things have a habit of evening out in the end. Even as my off stump was being knocked from the ground, a member of the victorious 1978 Sussex side, Imran Khan, was being arrested for a second time at Dulles Airport Washington, because his name was similar to that of someone on a list of terrorist suspects. It was a good job he didn't have his gun with him or he would have ended up in Guantanamo Bay. On the other hand, if he had, at least somebody might have noticed.

The idea that you can protect freedom, or indeed truth and justice, by locking up thousands of people for years with neither charge nor trial, is an interesting one. At least as interesting as whether you uphold the spirit of cricket by respecting an individual's absolute right to be dishonest.

THIRTY-ONE

The summer of 2004 had ended in failure. Alright, the summer of 2004 had ended in *a* failure. The final cricketing image of the season was not of a huddle of English fielders bouncing up and down in celebration, but rather of the West Indian left-arm seamer, Ian Bradshaw, barely visible in the late-September Oval gloaming, down on one knee punching the air as his team secured the Champions Trophy. Despite the fact that four days earlier they had beaten Australia in a one-day international for the first time since 17th January 1999, England managed to maintain their record of never having won a major tournament. All the other seven leading Test playing countries have won either the World Cup or the Champions Trophy at least once.

For all of his successes with the Test side, Duncan Fletcher never seemed to take the one-day team any further forward. True, England's performance in the 2003 World Cup had been better than that of 1999, but Kevin Pietersen's brief dalliance and her mates couldn't have done any worse. Even making the final of the Champions Trophy only required winning two matches of any significance in conditions alien to anyone used to playing cricket in the summer.

It's hard to understand why the limited overs side didn't improve in the same way as the Test team. More recent failures could be attributed to the disruption caused by injuries to key players, but Fletcher was in charge from 1999. It shouldn't even occur to me, as it did the other day, to get all nostalgic about Nick Knight's ability to hit over the top in the first 15 overs.

One idea that is traditionally trotted out as an explanation for our one-day failures is that the English are too sniffy about limited overs cricket, seeing it as somehow not the 'real thing'. This is an interesting analysis to apply to a country that so absolutely embraced the experiment with Twenty20. You could argue the very frivolity of this format, that it's just a bit of 'hit and giggle', accounts for its popularity. However, the likes of Paul Nixon always look and sound as if they are taking it quite seriously and finals day is a date in the domestic calendar to rival, or even outrank, the climax of the 50-over competition. Also, one of the criticisms that have been levelled against England is their apparent fear of taking the initiative in the early, 'powerplay', overs of a match. If something doesn't matter to you, surely fear of failure doesn't enter the equation?

Interestingly, Duncan Fletcher continually bemoaned a lack of experience in his one-day charges, while in another context warning of the dangers of player burn out. This is perhaps where the real problem lies.

When challenged in early 2006 on the problem of burn out, Malcolm Speed pointed to the ICC's Future Tours Programme (FTP) as providing an ideal upper limit of 15 Tests and 30 ODIs for every Test playing nation in any 12-month period. The FTP, he believed, should adequately protect players from the risks posed by too much cricket. Warming to his theme, Mr Speed noted that from the end of the second Test against Bangladesh on 20th April 2006 until the conclusion of the 2007 World Cup, Australia would play only five Tests. In the same period, both India and the West Indies would be involved in seven and New Zealand three. Significantly, no mention was made of England's programme. From the start of the first home Test against Sri Lanka on 11th May 2006 until the end of the World Cup, England were scheduled to play 12 Tests and, assuming admittedly unlikely levels of success, a maximum of 37 ODIs and three Twenty20 internationals. Even if the Australians won everything in which they took part they would still play fewer than 30 ODIs in the same period.

Even this doesn't tell the whole story. The previous winter, England had gone from the epic Ashes encounter almost straight into the tour to Pakistan, had a brief break over Christmas and then embarked on arguably the hardest tour of all, to India, an excursion that ended less than a month before the start of the next domestic season. After the 2007 World Cup, England were due to move almost immediately into home series against the West Indies and India.

Despite the fact the international calendar has begun to encroach on the months of May to August in a way never thought possible in the

1970s, England remains the only country whose domestic season comes at this time. As a result, our top cricketers play nearly all year round. Having, with the introduction of central contracts, solved the problem of their best men being ground down by the county circuit, within five years English cricket's leaders now face the problem of the international programme doing similar damage. It's not even just the number of games played that is the problem, but the unremitting nature of the calendar. For England's top cricketing stars life has become one long fixture list. This was a significant problem even before the IPL came along to provide another money-spinning distraction.

In these circumstances it is little wonder some types of cricket are prioritized over others. It is not that one-day internationals are seen as unimportant, it's just they are *less* important, and, given the euphoric reaction to the Ashes victory, understandably so. It's hard to imagine England's cricketers would have had a triumphant parade through London if they had won the 2007 World Cup. Some commentators are of the opinion England's one-day side should be practically identical to the Test team. The relentless strain this would place on a small set of individuals makes this a practical impossibility. Although part of me wants to scream 'Try being a miner!', I can't help but have sympathy with Marcus Trescothick's 'stress-related' difficulties.

England's progress through their Test programme in 2004 had not appeared from the outside to be overly stressful. With the exception of the aftermath of the Champions Trophy final, Michael Vaughan had worn an almost permanent smile. However, as Stephen Fay put it: 'His skill and resilience remained to be proved at the highest level of Test cricket.'

Despite the wishes of a media already slavering at the prospect of the Ashes, the ultimate test would have to wait. In the short term, Vaughan first had to prove himself at the higher level represented by South Africa. This was good preparation for dealing with a country coached by an eccentric.

Australia's John Buchanan has a degree in 'human movements' from the University of Queensland and a penchant for quoting from Sun Tzu's *The Art of War*. This might explain why he never hit it off with Mike Gatting during his unsuccessful season with Middlesex. Opportunities may 'multiply as they are seized' but cheese rolls don't. In the summer that followed, I came to realise Buchanan was frequently given to utterances in which it was possible to understand each individual word without gaining the sense of what they were meant to mean in combination. In short, he over-complicated matters to such a degree that half the time you had no idea what he was on about.

Over-complicating is not something of which you could accuse South Africa's Ray Jennings but he was no more normal than Buchanan. Before his brief stint with the national team, Jennings was coach of the South African domestic side Easterns. One of his charges was the shy retiring opening bowler, Andre Nel. During one match against Free State, Nel became visibly upset when he felled his hero, Allan Donald, with a bouncer. Jennings' reaction is instructive: 'I was really pissed off. His hero ducks into a short one so what does he do? He goes and sobs over him like a girl guide. I told him to pin him with the next ball and pin him again until he didn't get up.' Subsequently, Jennings was accused of offering his bowlers money to hit Donald and was forced to admit that he had made a joke that 'was perhaps taken seriously by a certain few of the younger fellows'. When he took over as South Africa's coach, he used to hit up high catches to players standing in the middle of the team's kit scattered on the outfield and employed tennis pros serving balls at well over 100mph to the batsmen in the nets. During the fourth Test he managed to concuss his own captain by accidentally whacking a 'catch' into the side of his head from five yards. It was as if Mad Baz from Bath had gone into coaching.

When England lost their only warm-up match against South Africa A, Duncan Fletcher was the one the media portrayed as mad for insisting the players were not 'undercooked'. However, the loss of the five-day matches on the Zimbabwe leg of the tour that had preceded the team's arrival in South Africa had robbed England of two practice games and the scheduling of five Tests in a 40-day period in South Africa made the coach understandably reluctant to take too much out of his men before the serious business began. The demands of modern international itineraries leave touring coaches with the choice between being under prepared at the start or totally wrung-out before the end. Fletcher preferred to take his chances with the former and was proved right when England nailed South Africa by seven wickets at Port Elizabeth.

England were undoubtedly helped in securing this victory by South Africa's political history. This was not just because Andrew Strauss (126 and 94 not out) and his family moved away to England when he was six. Strauss may, at Newlands, have become the fastest man in terms of days

(228) to 1,000 Test runs, but the home country's desire to select a side with which every part of the 'Rainbow Nation' could identify, assisted their opponents almost as much as the Middlesex man's ability to play the cut shot.

For the first Test South Africa's wicket-keeper was Thami Tsolekile, a worthy selection but self-evidently inferior to the absent Boucher or even De Villiers. An embarrassing second-innings dismissal, bowled for nought by a Simon Jones off-spinner, saw him immediately dropped. Even Hashim Amla, picked on the basis of weight of runs in domestic cricket, employed a technique involving a pick-up towards gully that made him look like the proverbial 'walking wicket'. Amla made 36 runs at an average of nine and was gone by the fourth Test.

This selection policy saw Kevin Pietersen representing England rather than South Africa in the one-day internationals that followed the Test series. Put simply, Pietersen had felt forced to leave his home country because he perceived himself the victim of post-apartheid positive discrimination. Therefore, it was more than a little ironic when he scored 158 against Australia at the Oval and in so doing exactly emulated Basil D'Oliveira, whose identical effort and subsequent selection for the tour to South Africa in 1968 had led indirectly to the Republic's sporting isolation.

However, given that at the Downing Street reception that followed the Ashes victory Pietersen was rumoured to have cornered Cherie Blair in conversation for half an hour before asking his team-mates 'Who was that then?', I doubt this is an irony that would have preoccupied him over much.

For years England had been hamstrung, literally on occasions, by having only one Test-class bowler fit at a time. Their success in 2004 had been built on having a bowling unit capable of dismissing sides twice with some degree of regularity. There was further irony then in England's series-winning fourth-Test victory coming courtesy of one man carrying his team in the manner of Angus Fraser.

Of England's pack of fast bowlers, Matthew Hoggard was the slowest and apparently the most expendable. His effectiveness seemingly halved when the ball didn't swing, Hoggard looked the most likely to make way if England ever managed to get Simon Jones and James Anderson fit and in form simultaneously. Fortunately for the Yorkshireman, this never happened.

For the fourth Test at Johannesburg, the Glamorgan man and the

Lancastrian were both fit. However, Anderson, the embodiment of one major fault with the central contracts system, hadn't played a first-class match for more than four months and had difficulty locating the pitch, let alone the stumps. Jones had been dropped to accommodate the Lancashire man on what now, given the Welshman's ability to reverse the ball both ways at 90mph, seems the ludicrous pretext that the ground suited swing bowlers. Meanwhile, Flintoff was both injured and knackered and Harmison soon developed a calf strain and a burning desire to go home. In short, Michael Vaughan had only one fully fit seamer to call on and spent most of the match whistling him up for another spell.

Bowled into the ground to the tune of 5-144 in the first innings, Hoggard ripped through the South Africans' second effort with 7-61, including Jacques Kallis first ball, neatly taken at first slip by Trescothick behind Geraint Jones' trademark unavailing dive.

England's win in South Africa ensured the Ashes hype-train not only stayed on track but built up speed. Glenn 'I'd have to say 5-0' McGrath and his mates were up to their usual tricks and *Sky* courted controversy with adverts for their coverage depicting Shane Warne as a transported 18th century convict threatening to be back. Despite their recent successes it was generally agreed that England would have to be at their very best to beat Australia and couldn't afford to make a single mistake.

A man who is unafraid to offer his opinions, albeit unknowingly, to President Blair's first lady, is unlikely to be backward in coming forward in his dealings with the selectors. Kevin Pietersen had been firmly and publicly of the belief that he should have been included in the Test squad for South Africa. In the arguments that raged before the Ashes as to whether Thorpe or Pietersen should play against Australia, Paul Allott plumped for the South African on the basis that in 10 innings he might play two that were match-turning. In the winter, Thorpe had contributed 118 not out at Durban to help save a game in which his team had mustered only 139 on the opening day and at Centurion, his 86 ensured a first-innings lead and the series victory.

The debate about the choice between these two was just one of a number of mistakes England made in the lead up to the Ashes. Even Thorpe himself thought Pietersen should play; it was Ian Bell's place the Surrey left-hander felt he should have taken.

Although he eventually ended up in South Africa as cover for the injured Mark Butcher, Bell had not been in the original touring squad. He was then selected ahead of Pietersen, but not Thorpe, for the meaningless contest against a hopelessly out classed Bangladesh. In a two-match series shorter in terms of playing time than a single Test is supposed to be, Bell made bigger runs than Thorpe by virtue of being one place higher in the order and held his place when Pietersen's claims became unanswerable. Although Bell contributed to the Ashes victory, not least with his sharp reactions at short-leg, it's hard to believe the older man would not have produced more than two half-centuries for the cause. It's at least arguable England played the whole of the Ashes series without putting out their strongest side.

Before the season, the doubts still remained whether even England's best team could be a match for the all-conquering Australians. We had been here before in 2001, when we thought we had a team of worthy challengers only for a thumping defeat at Edgbaston to trigger the usual mental disintegration. Apart from anything else, how were we going to get over the psychological hold they had on us; our own belief that they were unbeatable superhumans? Then they captured Hussein: Saddam that is, not Nasser.

Within a short time of his imprisonment, the British press published pictures of Saddam in nothing but his big, baggy Y-fronts. Here was a man whose pre-eminence in his own country had, until recently, been unquestionable. Now, he was, if not humanized, then humiliated; no more than a man, robbed, like the Wizard of Oz, of his power to inspire fear. It was in considering this parallel with the inhabitant of the Emerald City that it struck me how England could win the Ashes.

Any good sports psychologist will tell you that it's all about 'visualisation'. What Michael Vaughan and his men had to do was imagine Ricky Ponting and as many of his team-mates as they cared to, in ludicrous kegs. One of the assistant accountants on the film of *Harry Potter and the Prisoner of Azkaban* was called Geraint Jones. Considering Ponting in his pants was the cricketing equivalent of England's wicket-keeper pointing his bat at the Australians and shouting 'Riddikulus!' Instant de-mystification would be guaranteed.

Before anybody at the ECB could pick up on this admittedly none too original idea, the Bangladeshis did the job for them.

One of the other mistakes the English made in the summer of 2005 was scheduling the one-day internationals before the Test series. In so doing, they allowed the Australians a substantial period of acclimatization in which to shake off any ring-rustiness before the main business began. At least, that's what the received wisdom was at the time. In fact, the events of 18th June, when England weren't even involved, had a major impact on the fate of the Ashes.

The moment the Australians lost to Bangladesh is when they became merely a very good cricket team, as opposed to gods. Two days earlier England had thrashed the Banglas by 10 wickets. After the defeat at Cardiff, all the 'mental disintegration' became just so much big talk. In other words, what it had always been: bullshit, but now no longer designed to undermine the opposition, but rather an increasingly desperate attempt to recover an aura of invincibility that had already evaporated. From then on, every time Ponting tried to come over all Steve Waugh in his public pronouncements about the forthcoming Test series, I just felt like shouting 'Ricky, your pants are showing mate … and they're on fire!'

Then, a passing cold shower in the form of the first Test match extinguished Ricky's underwear and drenched English spirits.

Whose idea was it to schedule the opening encounter of the series at Lord's? Don't these people read *Wisden*? 'Right, so it's 71 years since we've won at headquarters and four since we've won at Leeds… OK, that's agreed then gentlemen, first Test at Lord's and Headingley gets an ODI.'

It was all so depressingly familiar. For all Langer's swollen elbow, Hayden's ringing helmet and Ponting's bleeding cheek of the first morning, by the end there was no denying it had been another capitulation. It was particularly galling to see the Aussie captain at the post-match press conference, fully justified in his relieved gloating about the 'gulf between the sides'.

In the lead-up to the most hyped series in history there was general agreement that the one thing England must not do is let the Australians get in front. Now, they had done exactly that and it seemed, to take a parallel completely at random, the equivalent of trailing AC Milan 3-0 at half time in the Champions League final.

If Steven Gerrard had been the obvious candidate to spark Liverpool's revival earlier in the summer, you would have got rather longer odds on the identity of the man who kick-started England's fightback. From an English perspective it was delicious that it was the supposedly uber-professional John Buchanan.

'Glenn, I think that I should counsel you to take great care in choosing where to place your feet in relation to the small red spheroid situated in your vicinity.' 'What? Ow! Hang on mate, I've just trodden on this bloody ball some idiot left lying around. I think I've broken my ankle!'

'Ricky Ponting has won the toss. What you gonna do Ricky?' 'Ah, we're gonna have a bowl this morning mate.' It wasn't Nasser Hussain at Brisbane, but it was, at last, arrogance shading into complacency.

By mid-afternoon Mark Nicholas and Mike Atherton were pointing out a score of 240-4. This, they reminisced, was the total their coach on the first England A tour, Keith Fletcher, had told them they should expect to see at the end of a typical opening day of a Test match. As Nicholas was leading England's second string round Kenya and Zimbabwe I was doing my first set of legal work experience. The firm had just acquired its first fax machine and was by no means the last to do so. It was a world in which Test batsmen still scored at 2.25 runs per over and lawyers could buy themselves time by requiring their opponent to put something in writing. Now, they can have an e-mail on your computer in 10 minutes and 2.25 is when the 250 comes up.

In this respect at least, cricket is reflective of the breakneck speed of life around it. However, in other ways it remains reassuringly anachronistic. In a society in which eating in the street is now acceptable, cricket remains charmingly wedded to the regularity of at least one of its mealtimes. Professional cricketers must be one of the last classes of employees left in this country who still stop work to have a regular lunch break.

Those present on the Sunday at Edgbaston had reason to be grateful for the pace of the modern game. Australia had started the day needing 107 more runs to win, a target that in Nicholas' day would have taken just over a session to attain. Imagine what it would have been like if, with the tourists requiring six to win with one wicket left, the umpires had been compelled to take the players off for lunch. As it was, the agonies of that morning were compressed into less than two hours.

Five yards: that was the difference between the greatest series ever played and another humiliation. The moment Harmison bowled a full-toss at Brett Lee I thought that was it. Five yards either side of deep cover and the 'sporting theatre at its most intense' (Mark Nicholas) represented by Flintoff's Saturday afternoon sixes; 'that over' to Langer and Ponting; Harmison's slower ball and Warne treading on his own stumps would have counted for nothing. Instead, Lee hit it straight at the man on the boundary. I think it was Simon Jones, I can't tell for sure even if I pause the DVD, but, in the words of Barry Davies, 'frankly who cares'. The only thing that mattered was moments later Richie was shouting 'Jones!…Bowden!' and cricket fans all over the country were cheering at their mates down their mobiles.

That was when it started. The enduring sporting image of the year was Flintoff with his arm round Brett Lee. The all-rounder had since been quoted as saying that he was telling him 'It's 1-1 now you Aussie bastard.' I hope he was joking because it spoils the story more than a little.

Everything that followed – the tens of thousands locked out of the last ball finish at Old Trafford; Hoggy's cover drive in the suffocating tension of Nottingham; Flintoff shouting his own nickname as he ran through the Aussies at the Oval; Pietersen's century and an English crowd singing 'there's only one Shane Warne' as the Ashes came home – made me proud.

Two friends of mine, Matt and James, lifelong football fans, went to the Sunday at Trent Bridge. I saw them a few days later: 'Mate, what a sport, it was like watching a whole day of penalties. But the way they play it too…what a sport! We went to watch City the next day. Halfway through I said to him: "This game's played by tossers".' With the likes of 'Cashley' Cole whining about the 'slave wages' Arsenal were offering him, it was hard to disagree. I told my friends following England's cricketers hadn't always been like this.

Hardly anyone's life comes to a crescendo. Almost all of us go on way beyond the point when we were at our best or happiest. That's why I don't want to go beyond 2005, because that was when my team was everything I wanted it to be: skilful, fearless and magnificently capable of standing toe-to-toe with the best, never taking a backward step and coming out on top. It was a time that made all of the heartaches of the previous 30 years worthwhile.

But even then it was hard to escape the fear of it all being 'blink of light between two eternities'. The ticker-tape parade through London was just one outward sign of the ECB taking their eye off the ball. The five-year plan in 2002 had been to make England the best Test side in the world by 2007. Despite their defeat, Australia retained that title but this Ashes win felt like a culmination; an ending not a beginning.

Much of what followed was a process of regression, of falling back into old ways, or, perhaps more accurately, finding new ways of creating the same old mediocrity. Even the Ashes win of 2009 owed as much to Australian decline as English progress. The security provided by central contracts and consistency of selection shaded into cosiness and complacency. The benefits of more organised and business-minded men running the game was replaced by the lack of shame and the refusal to take responsibility that characterises the worst excesses of modern capitalism. Andy Flower and Andrew Strauss might be turning it round again, but I may, nevertheless, have seen the best the England cricket team will ever offer me. Even if I have, maybe the moment when the kids on Hearsall Common were playing cricket on the afternoon before a football World Cup qualifier made the future worthwhile too.

On the final afternoon at the Oval, as Pietersen reached 150, I sat at home with my girls and told them to watch the cricket with me: 'Just for a minute or two, because this is important.' At six and eight they were never going to feel what I felt, but I wanted them to have a sense that even though what they were watching was only a sport, it was nevertheless, in a tiny way, important. I don't know if watching that had any impact on them, but then I'm certain my father had no idea what he had set in train with a simple trip to Lord's. If I succeed in giving them as much as my dad unwittingly gave, I wonder if they'll thank me.